Testifyin'

Contemporary African Canadian Drama
Volume I

edited by
Djanet Sears

Playwrights Canada Press
Toronto • Canada

Testifyin': Contemporary African Canadian Drama, Vol. 1 © Copyright 2000 Djanet Sears
Each play in this collection is copyrighted in the name of the author
whose name appears on the appropriate play.
Introduction to Testifyin' © Copyright 2000 Djanet Sears
Introduction to each play is the property of the author/editor of the piece.

Playwrights Canada Press
54 Wolseley St., 2nd fl. Toronto, Ontario CANADA M5T 1A5
Tel: (416) 703-0201   Fax: (416) 703-0059
cdplays@interlog.com   http://www.puc.ca

Playwrights Canada Press publishes with the generous assistance of The Canada
Council for the Arts – Writing and Publishing Section and the Ontario Arts Council.

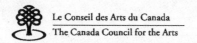

Le Conseil des Arts du Canada
The Canada Council for the Arts

ONTARIO ARTS COUNCIL
CONSEIL DES ARTS DE L'ONTARIO

Cover Design: Allen Booth
Cover Illustration: Lloyd Pollard
Production Editor: Jodi Armstrong

Canadian Cataloguing in Publication Data

Main entry under title:
Testifyin': contemporary African Canadian drama

ISBN 0-88754-597-1 (v.1)

I. Canadian drama (English) – Black Canadian authors.* 2. Canadian drama (English)
– 20th century.* 3. Black Canadians – Drama.* I. Sears, Djanet.

PS8307.T47 2000   C812'.54080896071   C00-930559-9

First edition: April 2000
Printed and bound by Hignell Printing at Winnipeg, Manitoba, Canada.

ACKNOWLEDGEMENTS:

The AfriCanadian Playwrights' Festival; American Library Association; Jodi Armstrong; b current; Norval Balch; David Baile; maxine bailey; Mercedes Baines; Joël Benard; Ardon Bess; Ayanna Black; Blizzard Publishing; Allen Booth; Laura Bennett; Denise Bukowski; Candice Burley; Cahoots Theatre Projects; CAN:BAIA; Michael Cooper; Crow's Theatre; George Elliott Clarke; Afua Cooper; Andrea Davis; Eastern Front Theatre; Ramabai Espinet; Factory Theatre; Maureen FitzGerald; Harold Ober Associates; Jeff Henry; Sonia Hind; Sarah Hood; Patricia Keeney; David Kinsman; Pia Kleeber; Jacoba Knaapen; Angela Lee; Leslie Lester; Kate Lushington; Jim Millan; Shadi Mogadime; Andy Moro; Maureen Moynagh; Nightwood Theatre; Donna Nurse; Obsidian Theatre Company; Modupe Olaogun; Paul Perron; Lloyd Pollard; Random House; Diane Roberts; Kim Roberts; Angela Rebeiro; Don Rubin; Leslie Sanders; Schomburg Center for Research in Black Culture; Scirocco Drama; Alison Sealy-Smith; Don Shipley; Amela Simic; Sugar 'n' Spice; Dawn Stephenson; Sally Szuster; Theatre Fountainhead; Theatre Passe Muraille; Greg Tjepkema; Toronto Reference Library/Toronto Public Library; Iris Turcott; University College, University of Toronto; Cylla Von Tiedemann; Guillermo Verdecchia; Viking Press Inc.; Rinaldo Walcott; Winsom; Philip Yan.

DEDICATION:

To the future: my neices and nephews:
Qwyn, Kyla, VaNessah, Djustice, Donny, Sherie and Danielle.
May their voices grow full and loud and strong.

INTRODUCTION

by Djanet Sears

...Testifying... is not plain and simple
commentary but a dramatic narration and a communal
reenactment of one's feelings and experiences. Thus one's
humanity is reaffirmed by the group and his or her sense
of isolation is diminished.

—Geneva Smitherman

Testifyin' is to "tellin' it like it is", what gospel is to the blues.

Can I get a witness?

African Canadian playwrights are the soul of Black theatre in this country, and their craft is remarkably representative of the African diasporic experience. For many Black playwrights, dramatic writing is a union between, on the one hand, the western literary tradition of the written word, and on the other hand, the African oral tradition: ripe with stories and cultural histories, constructed for the voice, permeated with the drama of expression, sound and language, created to be spoken aloud in the presence of others, an audience, a community. The African oral tradition is also one of the few items that Africans in the Americas were able to carry with them across the middle passage, unperceived by their abductors. Black playwrights are modern day griots, verbally witnessing onto paper their feelings, their experiences and their truths, in story.

Contrary to popular ideology, there is a remarkable legacy of Black theatre in this country. Unfortunately, the history of people of African descent in Canada is barely detectable in the annals of Canadiana, even as we begin the 21st century and can claim residency in this country from as far back as the early 1600s. Consequently, any informal examination into Canadian Theatre will likely reveal the absence of African Canadians as contributors altogether. So while Canada continues to congratulate itself, and exploit its position as the last stop on the underground railroad for enslaved Africans in the United States more than two centuries ago, there is still little or no documentation of their cultural activities. In fact, Canada suffers from a kind of "historical amnesia". It has forgotten the "racist laws, policies, practices, and ideologies that have shaped Canadian social, cultural political and economic institutions for three hundred years." (Tator, p.10) As a result, there are serious patterns of omission in the documentation of African Canadian cultural production. The effect, more often than not, is erasure, which forces contemporary practitioners in the arts to continuously reinvent themselves, often unaware that there are already footprints on the path that they are now clearing, as if for the first time.

Tell it like it is!

Testifyin': Contemporary African Canadian Drama, Volume I, is more than an effort at mere cultural anthropology. *Testifyin'* is a celebration of African Canadian playwrights and their plays. It is an opportunity to bear witness to their enduring spirit and a testimony to their survival in the face of extraordinary opposition. It is not an attempt to create a canon. There are many wonderful plays that were not included in this collection, due in great part to space limitations and or previous contractual obligations. For instance, there is no representation by a playwright from the western provinces. Hence the need for volume II, which is already well underway. Nevertheless, each of the plays in this collection is accompanied by a forward penned by some of the most noted cultural scholars in the country. There were many reasons for structuring the book in this way, the most important of which was my desire to give the reader a context for the plays that could be used as a springboard to further study. Also, since people of African descent are not homogeneous, one introduction could not sufficiently comment on all of the works contained here. The plays in this collection are a sincere reflection of their authors. We are a diverse people from differing regions, with distinct politics, particular sexual preferences, and cultural characteristics; some are born in Canada, and some are not. This diversity is also resonant in the breadth of content, style and structure – from ahdri zhina mandiela's rhythmically powerful choreodrama *dark diaspora... in dub*, which uses the rich percussive elements of reggae as its foundation, to the lyrical eloquence of George Elliott Clarke's *Whylah Falls: The Play*, where language and melody are one. *Riot*, by Andrew Moodie, is a wonderfully crafted contemporary drama, which challenges the idea that Blackness is a monolithic experience, by following the lives of a house full of roommates at the time of the Rodney King riots in Toronto. h. jay bunyan's *Prodigals In a Promised Land* is a remarkable examination of a Caribbean family in Toronto struggling to stay whole. Well-drawn characters challenge each others aspirations in an effort to attain their own dreams and define their own realities. In contrast, *Come Good Rain* is an incredible autobiographical account, set against the tyrannical backdrop of Uganda's brutal military regime. It is a miracle story of sorts, since George Seremba should never have survived to tell it. *Tightrope Time: Ain't Nuthin' More Than Some Itty Bitty Madness Between Twilight & Dawn* is also a one person show, but in this drama, Walter Borden presents a remarkable array of characters that preach and strut and weep and sing. In contrast, *Coups And Calypsos* is an exquisite tale of love which relentlessly mines those soft and brittle spaces that bridge and yet divide Caribbean people of African and South Asian descent.

When He Was Free And Young And He Used To Wear Silks is a superbly paced story, set at a wedding reception in Toronto. The play is an adaptation by Austin Clarke based on his acclaimed book of short stories of the same title, and is the only work in the collection that has not yet been produced. In the early eighties, I was part of an extraordinary reading of the script, presented by Theatre Fountainhead. Jeff Henry, founder and artistic director of the company had planned to produce it in the following season.

Unfortunately, when the recession of the early eighties swept the country and cutbacks became a reality, Black theatres took the first big hit from the arts councils, forcing the theatre to extract several major pieces from the season – *When He Was Free And Young And He Used To Wear Silks* would be one of them. Nearly seventeen years later, I found a copy of the script in my parents garage, alongside a pile of personal effects long since forgotten.

sistahs, by maxine bailey and sharon m. lewis, is a woman's play. A play about nourishment. A play about healing. A play where the cauldron takes centre stage and the wonderful cast of characters provide the dramatic ingredients for the powerful brew. I have also included one of my own plays, *Harlem Duet*, a non chronologically itinerant prequel to Shakespeare's *Othello*. This rhapsodic blues tragedy recounts the tale of Othello and his first wife Billie. As we enter the world of the play, Othello abandons both Billie and Harlem, for Mona (a colleague at Columbia University) and the affluent Upper West Side. *Harlem Duet* is Billie's story.

Look out now!

Finally, *Testifyin'* is an attempt to challenge allegations of the absence of African Canadians in the theatrical arena. The publishing of Black literature is surprisingly still a new frontier for many Canadian publishers. The first play by a Black writer to be published in this country was a piece titled *The Captive* by Lennox Brown, in 1966. Since that time, hardly a dozen other plays have been set to print. In *A Primer of African-Canadian Literature: George Elliott Clarke's Short But Filled-to-Bursting History*, Clarke points out the reluctance of publishers to print the writings of African Canadians in general. However, he asserts that "the one literary mode that lags well behind the others... is drama." (p.9) Even when examining historical reference texts, if Blacks are mentioned at all, we are often presented erroneously. In *A Stage in Our Past, English-language Theatre in Eastern Canada from the 1790s to 1914*, Murray Edwards maintains that, "because the number of Negroes in Canada was relatively insignificant," there was neither an indigenous Black theatre and what is more important, no evidence of a Canadian minstrelsy (p.144). Edwards' assertions, however, are wholly untrue.

Go head!

Canadian minstrelsy is a well-documented phenomenon. While at first White men in Black face were indeed imported from the United States, later companies of "Ethiopian Delineators", as they were often called, were most certainly homegrown, even in the face of intense African Canadian opposition.

> The black population petitioned Toronto's mayors in 1840, 1841, 1842, and 1843 to forbid licenses to circuses and menageries that allowed "certain acts, and songs, such as Jim Crow and what they call other Negro Characters" (Lenton-Young, p.176-177).

Reminiscent of the subsequent protests against Livent's Showboat, nearly 150 years later, the city ignored the petitions of their own Black population. In fact, the minstrel show in Upper Canada became so popular that by the end of that century, there was a resident minstrel troupe in every Ontario town.

Ain't that some sh-t!

Quite possibly as a result of the failed protests against the minstrel invasion, in February of 1849, one of the earliest documented theatrical productions by an African Canadian theatre group took place in Ontario when The Toronto Coloured Young Men's Amateur Theatrical Society rented the Royal Lyceum for three nights (Saddlemyer, p.14). The Royal Lyceum accommodated a capacity audience of nearly 1500, and was located in the heart of downtown Toronto, on King Street, between Bay and York.

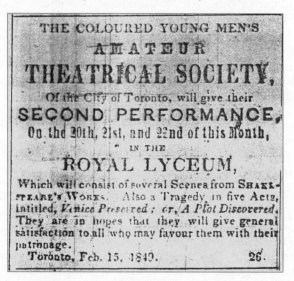

An advertisement in the *Toronto-Mirror* (9 February 1849), noted that "the group would perform for three nights on 20, 21 and 22 February, and that they would be presenting *Venice Preserved* by Thomas Otway (1652-1685) along with selected scenes from Shakespeare. Although the advertisement stated that this was the organization's second Toronto appearance, no record of their first performance has yet been found (Breon, p.217).

Furthermore, according to the *Oxford Companion to Canadian Theatre*, one of the few inclusive resources I discovered, "Black theatre groups have existed since the early nineteenth century in Vancouver and Halifax and in small communities, such as Ontario's North Buxton and Amherstburg (Benson, p.355)." There were also touring African Canadian variety troupes in Ontario. Robertson Davies, in his essay, "The Nineteenth-Century Repertoire," suggests that by the 1870s there were several Black companies including The Great Slave Troupe of Jubilee Singers, who presented "slave songs" and "spirituals" (p.114). Still, many questions remain unanswered. Were these professional choruses, or were they locally-based church choirs? I am also reminded here, that no examination of African Canadian theatre is possible without acknowledging the role of the church as a centre of Black cultural activity. For most African communities in the Americas, the "Church was school, forum, political arena, social club, art gallery, [and] conservatory of music. It was lyceum and gymnasium as well as sanctum sanctorum (Shad Shreve, p.40)." Many Black performers still get their first taste of performance in churches. In more rural communities, the church may have been the lone public gathering place. Unfortunately, few personal accounts remain, and without expeditious efforts to document those accounts as oral histories, there will be no-one left who remembers actual events, or even tales of those events.

I hear you!

In 1941, ninety years after the theatrical presentations by the Toronto Coloured Young Men's Amateur Theatrical society, what is likely the first professional African Canadian theatre company, came into being. The Negro Theatre Guild was formed by a group of young people in the basement of the Union United Church, in the Little Burgundy district of Montreal. Their mandate:

> To utilize the enthusiasm, sincerity and native talent of colored youth, in the presentation of plays of social value, is the principal aim of our organization. We feel that in the common struggle against fascism and Hitlerism, the Negro has not only his blood and labor to contribute, but has a distinct cultural contribution to make (Breon, p.221).

The Negro Theatre Guild's first major success came the following year with its production of Marc Connolly's *The Green Pastures*, produced at Victoria Hall to wide acclaim and eventually transferred to the larger Her Majesty's Theatre. Apart from a four year hiatus during the Second World War, the Negro Theatre Guild, later known as the Negro Theatre Arts Club of Montreal, continued to produce plays until the early 1970s. Its repertoire would include dramatic selections from the classical and contemporary canon, as well as original African Canadian plays.

Montreal is also home to Canada's largest African Francophone population. Nevertheless, the community's desire to produce Haitian Francophone dramas on a regular basis has never been fulfilled. While there is apparently an enormous pool of theatre practitioners to draw from, and an abundance of good material, the primary difficulty appears to be a lack of access to adequate arts council support (Fouche, p.28). While this is a popular complaint, even among mainstream organizations, the relative degree of difficulty is multiplied when the artists are Black. Fortunately for bilingual Haitian artists, there is Black Theatre Workshop, which has become their principal outlet for theatrical activity.

Teach! Teach!

Black Theatre Workshop has taken up where the Negro Theatre Guild left off, and has been producing theatre in Montreal for nearly 35 years. Still its longevity belies the many obstacles it faces. Like the African francophone artists, and most minority cultural organizations in Quebec, Black Theatre Workshop finds itself securely in the margins of the French/English debate. The company is often overlooked as outside of the main concerns of Quebecois cultural agencies. As a result, the company suffers from inadequate financial support, and since such support is based on market performance, the theatre's already inadequate funding will not allow for the development of any large-scale marketing practices (Bayne, p.25). The entire issue becomes a huge catch-22. Nevertheless, Black Theatre Workshop has remained committed to producing dramas, albeit on a shoestring budget, that not only reflect its communities, but has also continued to pledge itself to the development and training of Black theatre artists in Montreal. Lorena Gale, a Montreal-born playwright and actress describes her experience of professional development as a member of the Black theatre community in Montreal as extraordinarily nourishing.

> Black Theatre Workshop provided an abundance of opportunit[ies] to explore each element in the theatre and amass a valuable store of practical experience. It furnished an environment where the mistakes, so necessary to the developmental process, could be made without fear of it reflecting on all members of one's race. It opened my mind to the myriad of black cultural perspectives and representations—african, caribbean, american—all of which, as a canadian-born black, I had been woefully ignorant (sic). It was a safe space in which I could gain empowerment through investigation and knowledge of self. A home (p.16-17).

Gale's perspective on her experience is based on a 20-year career as a professional theatre practitioner in this country, and more recently on her ultimate migration to British Columbia to seek a larger palate of possibilities as an artist.

Speak on it!

Historically, Vancouver has maintained a small but fluctuating population of Africans since the mid 19th century. This is in part due to the northerly migration of African Americans from California after the abolition of slavery in the British territories in the 1830s. At one point Blacks outnumbered

Whites on Vancouver Island; however, many returned south after the Emancipation Proclamation at the end of the American Civil War. From a contemporary perspective the population has remained relatively small.

> What do you call two black people standing on a street corner in Vancouver? A riot (Gale, p. 16).

In theatrical terms one Black company, Sepia Players, has had the charge of serving the entire community since the early 1970s. Unfortunately the theatrical service it provides has not been consistent. "Sepia Players – which in its irregular course of twenty-five years, rises from the ashes like a Phoenix to provide a window of hope and opportunity, only to catch flame and crash back into oblivion... (Gale, p.16)." The only alternative is for African Canadian theatre artists to seek employment and artistic fulfillment in Vancouver's White theatrical establishment. This option, however, can be filled with adversity, in part due to the lack of quality roles White theatre has to offer. The forces of cultural exclusion leave African Canadian theatre artists in Vancouver with the unenviable choice of either working for nothing or being nothing when you work, and leave Black audiences in Vancouver with little or nothing at all.

> What do you call five black people on a stage in Vancouver? Ain't Mis Behavin' (Gale, p.16).

Nevertheless, there is a small but burgeoning community of Black theatre artists in Vancouver who have endeavoured to create their art, regardless. Rejecting silence, they write, produce and present their own work, and often have their plays included in small West Coast Festivals. Among them are Celeste Insell, Mercedes Bains, Erskin King, David Ohdiambo, Siobhan Barker, Liza Huget and Lorena Gale herself. "They have dared to take charge of their [own] artistic destinies and create their own opportunities to access growth and development – from within (Gale, p.19)."

That's right! That's right!

On the opposite side of the country, the Africadians (a neologism coined by George Elliott Clarke that refers to the indigenous Black populations of the Maritimes), unquestionably comprise Canada's oldest Black population. Mathieu d'Acosta accompanied Champlain on his expedition to eastern Canada in 1604, and is the first recorded African in the region.

> Since that time, the people of African descent who came to Nova Scotia have been runaway slaves and free Blacks from the United States, loyalists, Trelawny Maroons from Jamaica, refugees or more recently, immigrants from Africa and the Caribbean (Mortley, 30).

The earliest of these communities, a population of approximately 3,000 people, consisted of free and enslaved United Empire Loyalists who came to Canada between 1766 and 1776, both during and after the American Revolution (Thomson, p.96-97). One might assume that documentation of Black theatrical activity in the Atlantic provinces would be quite extensive. Although cultural scholars like George Elliott Clarke are currently examining the Africadian literary legacy, considerable work remains to be done. Much of this type of analysis is dependent on written and published documentation, or first-hand recollections that have survived the rigours of time. In this case, notwithstanding the lack of available historical sources, a brief examination of the contemporary Africadian theatre scene may offer some remarkable insight.

Look out!

In the early eighties, Kwacha Playhouse was the only Black theatre company in the Atlantic provinces. Founded and led by one of Nova Scotia's most distinguished theatre artists, Walter Borden, Kwacha Playhouse was an undertaking that attempted to counter the established mainstream theatre fair that had until then only reflected "the racist and segregated make-up (Mortley, p.31)" of Nova Scotian life. While Kwacha Playhouse only lasted two years, in 1991, Borden, with his sister, Gloria Borden, established the Portia White Arts Centre, intended to address racism and other problems facing African Nova Scotians through theatre and the arts (Mortley, p.31). As far as Borden is concerned, "...African Canadian artists need their own facilities," and while he has continued to seek financial support for his endeavours, he has sadly had little success in this area (Mortley, p.31). This difficulty in acquiring the equivalent financial support usually granted to non-Black arts organizations is echoed by David Woods, another prominent Africadian theatre practitioner.

> The people who can make things happen are not interested in Black theatre. You might get money for an anti-racism project, but the people in the bureaucracy do not see the connection between arts and life. They just don't appreciate the importance of theatre (Mortley, p.32).

Most arts agencies cite the current era of restraint and cut backs as the reason for this lack of support. Woods, on the other hand, suggests that there has never been any official support for Black theatre in Nova Scotia.

While it is unacceptable that Canada's oldest Black community has no established theatre organization, Africadian theatre continues to exist and flourish (even if actors and directors are rarely paid, the sets makeshift or borrowed, and the flyers photocopied and distributed by hand). In 1990, Woods formed Voices, an amateur theatre company, consisting of more than 25 performers, actors, story-tellers, dancers, musician, singers, RAP artists and technical assistants. Voices hopes to reflect Africadia, "a deeply rooted culture with an oral tradition, a multitude of stories and a distinctive use of language." The company itself is keenly "dedicated to the exploration, development and celebration of the African Canadian experience in Nova Scotia." For Woods, "it's a labour of love... we practice at the limited outlets available, mostly schools. We can do many different things that don't require huge budgets (Mortley, p.30-33)." There is some Africadian drama being presented at smaller theatre establishments such as Eastern Front Theatre, under the artistic direction of Mary Vingoe. In recent seasons, this tiny company has produced the work of George Boyd and George Elliott Clarke to both popular and critical acclaim, while the Neptune theatre, the largest regional theatre in the Atlantic provinces, tries to play catch-up, with only brief runs of dramas by Black playwrights in their studio space, rarely presenting the works of Africadian writers. There are many bridges to build in regards to the presentation of Black work by mainstream companies in this region, but the solution lies in two main areas. First, mainstream companies must endeavour to program seasons that reflect their community in its entirety. Second, Black artists must be allowed access to financial support from cultural agencies, as well as from within their own communities, in order to produce work for, by and about themselves.

You on the case, now!

By far the largest African population in Canada resides in Southern Ontario. One hundred and twenty years following the performances of The Toronto Coloured Young Men's Amateur Theatrical Society in 1849, the eradication of the "preferred nationalities" immigration policy in Canada, and the introduction of the "points system" in the 1960s, brought about a significant increase in the population of Caribbean immigrants, most of whom were Toronto-bound. With them came their artistic aspirations and in the early 1970s Black Theatre Canada, founded by Vera Cudjoe, and Theatre Fountainhead, founded by Jeff Henry, emerged as the primary sources of Black theatre in the city. At first the offerings were generally Caribbean in nature, but in the nearly twenty years these two companies were in operation, they produced numerous plays, and toured copious schools, presenting dramas that included the works of Africans from both Canada and around the world.

Not unlike The Negro Theatre Guild in Montreal almost half a century earlier, Black Theatre Canada proclaimed as its mission: the establishment of a platform for the expression of Black culture in Canada and the creation of an environment that could offer training to the many talented actors, performers, writers and directors who came from the Black community (Breon, p.224). Its commitment to training, on-going workshops, drama classes, and hands-on experience in the productions for the new and emerging artists, developed into a central component of its activities. Many of Toronto's Black theatre artists can trace their theatrical roots directly to Black Theatre Canada and/or Theatre Fountainhead; most Black theatre artists in Toronto are part of the legacy these two companies struggled to establish.

While both companies ended operations in the late 1980s, a brief lull in the very early 1990s belied what was to come. There are currently more than a dozen small independent artist-run theatre companies, developing and producing plays in an itinerant manner around the city. Among them are: The AfriCanadian Playwrights' Festival, b current (sic), Caliban Arts Theatre, Jones And Jones, Luther Hansraj Dramatic Theatre, Sugar 'n' Spice, Theatre Wum, We Are One Theatre, and the newly formed Obsidian Theatre Company. The Obsidian Theatre Company, of which I am a founding member, is an extraordinary gathering of established theatre professionals brought together by a passionate sense of artistic responsibility. A responsibility to tell their own stories, to develop their own voices and to present the work of Black playwrights on the world stage. There is a groundswell of Black theatrical activity in this city, as African Canadian theatre artists are presenting their work more frequently than at any time before. In fact, what is being witnessed in Toronto may be what can only be described as initial signs of a widespread African Canadian theatre movement.

Black theatre artists in Toronto have, on the whole, also been able to eke out a meager living, albeit inconsistently, working for established White theatre organizations. Several mainstream companies have not only hired Black actors to dress their stages in an attempt to offset criticism about racism in the organization, but they have also produced work by African Canadian playwrights. Still, Toronto is the third largest theatre centre in the world. The dozen or so Black companies, like their fellow theatre artists across the country, operate on very little financial support. Moreover, when an established White company does produce African Canadian work, it rarely focuses its marketing "expertise" on the Black community, which is often the drama's intended audience. "...Black audiences... are the best kept secret in Canadian theatre," Winston Smith wrote in response to the once popular mainstream notion that there aren't enough Blacks in Toronto to warrant a Black theatre facility. According to Smith, Black audiences are "Ralph Ellison's 'Invisible' men and women, writ large (p.84)." When one considers the volume of mainstream theatre offerings, the percentage of Black theatre produced in Toronto could be considered minuscule.

Got that right!

A few years ago, I came across the text of an extraordinary speech by renowned African American Playwright, August Wilson. In particular, he called for a gathering of playwrights of African descent to "confer with one another, to come together to meet each other face to face... (Wilson, p.73)" Encouraged and inspired, I sought out the names of other African Canadian playwrights across the country. By the end of that year, I had identified 74 Black playwrights in Canada.

In the summer of 1997, the First AfriCanadian Playwright's Festival, gathered nearly 50 Canadian playwrights of African descent for a celebration of Black playwriting in Canada. The festival, sponsored by Canadian Artist's

Network: Black Artists In Action (CAN:BAIA) and the Canadian Stage Company, in association with b current and Young People's Theatre, included a Keynote Session with Ricardo Khan, artistic director of Crossroads Theatre, the largest Black theatre company in the United States; Yvonne Brewster, artistic director of Talawa Theatre, the largest Black theatre company in the UK; and George Elliott Clarke, Africadia's most prolific scholar, poet and playwright. There was a week-long playreading series, as well as panel discussions and a celebratory evening where the playwrights, representing communities nationwide, including the Northwest Territories, British Columbia, Nova Scotia, and several places in between, each read a brief excerpt from one of their works for the stage. It was a remarkable and magical event.

Yeah! Oh yeah!

Clear patterns emerge as one compares the efforts of African Canadians across the country to form a theatrical tradition. The most important of these concerns remain the need for financial support from the cultural agencies at all levels of government. This is not to say that Black theatre receives no support, it merely receives very little. Furthermore, those with means in the Black communities must themselves begin to take larger financial responsibility if the arts sector is to flourish. Black Canadian theatre practitioners want a home, a building, a place to call their own. However, while the cultural agencies have for more than thirty years continued to debate the relevance and suitability of a permanent regional theatre facility for African Canadians, the fact still remains:

> There is no Negro Ensemble in Canada. There is no Black Theatre in Canada, there is no Free Southern Theatre in Canada. There is no Black theatre that has the financing, for a permanent place [for] an audience in Canada (Hood, p.23).

Yet these same cultural agencies appear to have effortlessly awarded Livent, chaired by Garth Drabinsky, the exclusive contract to manage the Ford Centre for the Performing Arts, newly built at a cost of $31 million in public funds (Tator, p.173).

My, my, my!

I had intended to fully examine African Canadian theatre in the prairies. There is currently an organization in Winnipeg called ACAN (Afrocentric Cultural Artists Network), led by Sonia Hinds and an artist known as "7" (Anthony T. Barrow). Among other cultural activity, ACAN develops and presents theatre by Black playwrights in Manitoba. There was also a Black theatre company in Winnipeg, called the Caribbean Theatre Workshop, which produced the works of new Caribbean playwrights (Benson, p.356). However, further investigations has turned up not much more than a brief mention in the *Oxford Companion to Canadian Theatre*.

Nevertheless, Black theatre is thriving in this country. There is once again talk of a national Black theatre facility, and while actors or directors often spearhead these kinds of projects, there is little drama without the dramatists, who continue to create the extraordinary dramas their fellow theatre practitioners long to present. And while the testimony contained in this record harbours substantial omissions, this will not render it worthless, merely incomplete. Perhaps armed with information on the enduring legacy of Black theatre in Canada that is just now coming to light, Black theatre practitioners can be inspired by and take strength in the knowledge of their forbearers. Further endeavours to document the activity of African Canadian theatre artists on whose shoulders we now stand will go a long way in eliminating the overwhelming isolation we often feel. On-going endeavours to chronicle the efforts of contemporary Black theatre artists to express their joys and their sorrows in dramatic form, from their own perspectives, ensures us that African Canadian theatre will continue to be, for practitioners, readers and theatregoers alike, a remarkable drama still unfolding.

Can I get a witness?

Djanet Sears
Barker Fairley Visiting Professor
University College
University of Toronto
February, 2000

Djanet Sears is the Barker Fairley Visiting Professor at University College, University of Toronto. She is a writer, actor and director for both stage and screen. Her plays include *Afrika Solo* (Sister Vision Press, 1990), *Who Killed Katie Ross*, in *Taking The Stage: Plays by Canadian Women*, (Playwrights Canada Press, 1994), *Double Trouble*, and *Harlem Duet* (Scirocco Drama, 1997). Djanet's other published works include: "Naming Names: Black Women Playwrights in Canada", *Women on the Canadian Stage: The Legacy of Hrotsvit*, Rita Much, editor, (Blizzard Publications, 1991); and "Notes Of A Colored Girl", in *Harlem Duet*, (Scirocco Drama, 1997). She is the recipient of several distinctions, amongst them are the Governor General's Literary Award, the Floyd S. Chalmers Canadian Play Award, a Harry Jerome Award, and Dora Mavor Moore Awards for both writing and directing.

NOTE:
Black and hence White are used as proper nouns in this introduction when referring to Black or White people. The proper nouns are also used in some of the forwards as well as in the plays themselves. This usage is not uncommon in some circles, and is reminiscent of the shift in the spelling of the word negro, to Negro.

WORKS CITED:

Breon, Robin. "The Growth and Development of Black Theatre in Canada: A Starting Point." In *Theatre History In Canada*. Vol. 9, No. 2: (Fall 1988), P. 216-228.

Benson, E., Conolly, L.W.. *The Oxford Companion to Canadian Theatre*. Toronto: Oxford University Press, 1989.

Clarke, George Elliott. "A Primer of African-Canadian Literature: George Elliott Clarke's Short but Filled-to-Bursting History." In *Books In Canada*. v.25(2): (March, 1996), P. 7-9.

Clarke, George Elliott. "Black Culture: From the West Indies to Canada's East Coast." In *The Chronicle-Herald*. Halifax: Nov. 19, 1993. P. D3.

Clarke, George Elliott. "Contesting a Model Blackness: A Meditation on African-Canadian African Americanism, or the Structures of African Canadianite." In *Essays on Canadian Writing*. No. 63: (Spring 1998), P. 1-55.

Davies, Robertson. "The Nineteenth-Century Repertoire." In Saddlemyer, A., Ed. *Early Stages – Theatre in Ontario 1800-1914*. Toronto: University of Toronto Press, 1990.

Edwards, Murray D.. *A Stage in our Past, English-Language Theatre in Eastern Canada From the 1970s to 1914*. Toronto: University of Toronto Press, 1968.

Gale, Lorena. "Into the Margins." In *Canadian Theatre Review*. No. 83: (Summer, 1995), P. 16 - 19.

Hood, Sarah. "No Place to Go: Black Theatre in Canada." In *Canadian Theatre Review*. No. 56: (Fall, 1988). P. 23 -24.

Lenton-Young, Gerald. "Variety Theatre." In Saddlemyer, A., Ed. *Early Stages – Theatre in Ontario 1800-1914*. Toronto: University of Toronto Press, 1990.

Mortley, Basil. "Silent Screams of the Invisible, Visible Minority: African Nova Scotian Theatre." In *Canadian Theatre Review*. No. 83: (Summer, 1995), P. 30 -35.

Saddlemyer, A., Ed. *Early Stages – Theatre in Ontario 1800-1914*. Toronto: University of Toronto Press, 1990.

Shad Shreve, Dorothy. *The Afri-Canadian Church: A Stabilizer*. Jordan Station: Paideia Press, 1983.

Smith, Winston. "Toronto – Serious, Yes; Theatre Fountainhead." In *Canadian Theatre Review*. No. 60 (Fall, 1989), P. 84 - 85.

Smitherman, Geneva. *Talkin and Testifyin: The Language of Black America*. Detroit: Wayne State University Press, 1977.

Tator, Carol. *Challenging Racism In The Arts*. University of Toronto Press: Toronto, 1998.

Thomson, Colin A. *Blacks in Deep Snow: Black Pioneers in Canada*. Don Mills: J. M. Dent & Sons, 1979.

Wilson, August. "The Ground on Which I Stand." In *American Theatre*. Vol. 13, No. 7.: (Sept.,1996), P. 14-74.

TABLE OF CONTENTS

Riot

by Andrew Moodie

Andrew Moodie has appeared in many theatres across Canada as an actor. His first play, *Riot*, garnered him a Floyd S. Chalmers Canadian Play Award for Best New Play in 1996. His other play *Oui* was produced at Factory Theatre in 1998.

RIOTOUS BLACK CANADIANS

by Rinaldo Walcott

"And you know what, if you stay really, really, still, after a while, it almost feels like Canada is hugging you back. And I miss that feeling. I really do".
—Alex: *Riot*, Andrew Moodie

"Riot triumphantly transcends racial issues and becomes a useful metaphor for what it means to be a Canadian in the 90s".
—*The Toronto Star*

In North America Black people are always causing a riot. We cause riots because of how we dance, dress and sing; and when we are really aggrieved we even take to the street. In 1992 two riots in North America got the attention of some of us, if not many of us. The LA riots in the aftermath of the acquittal of police officers in the Rodney King beating; and the similar, but smaller outbursts of riots on Yonge Street in Toronto, which was both a response to LA and a frustration with a similar tactic of acquitting officers who shoot Black people in the Canadian context. In 1992 Black people were loudly announcing their marginality in North America. It is within this context that Andrew Moodie's (1995) *Riot* first came to audiences: in the aftermath of both riots and a renewed Black boisterousness.

It is my contention that Andrew Moodie's much celebrated and Chalmers award-winning play *Riot* does not occupy the site or the space of the special effect in Canadian theatre even though that is how Canadian theatre tends to work on or for blackness. I say this at the expense of the assumption that Black Canada theatre is proliferating and causing a riot – and it is not. And, yet, Moodie's play does not occupy the site of marginality, even though the play concerns itself with what it can mean to be a "not-quite-citizen". The play is concerned with and set in the context of the 1992 LA and Toronto riots. The focus of the Toronto riot is important to the play not because it localizes its discourse but because it forces the audience to immediately consider the Toronto riots in relation to the world-wide media spectacle of the riots in LA. Thus the riots south of the border are the backdrop or diasporic over-coat of the play. But the main attention is on the local (Toronto) and the national (Canada) context. It brings the issues home and ask for a response by posing questions as opposed to answers. As well, because Moodie's dramatic strategies do not speak in any direct way to various versions of Americanism, *Riot* was received in a fashion which led to a momentary elaboration of the nation and its narratives. Let me elaborate.

All the characters in Moodie's play are Canadian. But their relationship to the nation bares the traces of different and competing histories, sometimes-even antagonisms.

WENDLE, a student, 20s, from Halifax, Nova Scotia
ALEX, a student, 20s, from Ottawa
HENRY, owner of electrical repair company, 30s, from Uganda
KIRK, a student; late teens, from Kingston, Jamaica
EFFIE, a student, 20s, from Vancouver
GRACE, a student, 20s, born in Jamaica and raised in Montreal, Kirk's sister

The play thematises a range of passionate attachments to the nation demonstrating that to be Black Canadian does not have one historical path for belonging but many. In this sense, the play constructs a Black diasporic Canada which is fraught with the tensions, contradictions, disappointments and pleasures of "home" and homelessness. The play works across the mantra of gender, class and sexuality and seeks to map a Black community that can only be intelligible when it is made on its own terms, retaining its internal differences and competing histories, but holding on to identities of passions as channeled through two riots – one at "home" and another elsewhere.

The reason why I read the play as elaborating Canadian-ness is not simply because the play is able to negotiate between a deterritorialized discourse and its own productive locality, but because the play generously assumes Canadian-ness as internally complex and places blackness within that complexity too. The play's dynamic is one whereby the audience is left having to ponder their understandings of citizenship and what it might mean when defined and acted upon from different sites. Moodie is able to articulate in his play a move, which is not a response to an already configured set of circumstances. Rather he paints a process of how various circumstances both impacts on and is used by those it marks to fashion selves that must constantly be worked on. The play is then able to avoid the space of marginality and respond to the nation and beyond, in ways that elaborate what the nation might be for Black people.

Let me elaborate with two specifics from the play. One of the characters, Henry, described as an owner of an electrical company, who is in his thirties, and formerly from Uganda, is a good example of how Moodie elaborates the nation without the recourse to marginality. This is not to say that practices and processes of how one becomes marginal are outside the play. Rather, Moodie demonstrates how those practices and processes work by centering his characters in a world in which sociological explanations of their lives are not the place from which we encounter them. In fact, Henry suffers at the hands of police harassment (not unexpected or surprising) but he is not entirely clear about how to negotiate that experience. Henry's uncertainty plays itself out in terms of how he understands his relationship to the nation. His disinterest in filing a complaint for an unlawful search is positioned as being not afraid of the police and has to be understood in light of the history of some contemporary migrations from Uganda. Henry's final word on the issue is "The police in this country don't scare me" (p.18). A possible signal of greater terror encountered elsewhere frames Henry's response.

Now Henry is the "successful" immigrant Canadian who achieves the "dream": he owns a company. On the other hand, Henry is the kind of immigrant who has left certain kinds of terrors behind that positions his relations to police harassment differently from Black people born in the Americas. Moodie's writing characterizes a relation to the nation, which asks us to consider the ways in which blackness is both formed within specific nations and always understood beyond the specificity of nation. Henry's response to filing a compliant lies in a history beyond the Canadian nation, just as the insistence from Alex that he file a complaint lies within a particular response to the Canadian nation and a different history of relating to the police than Henry. No assumed outcome of a potentially shared experience of brutality suggest unanimity on the issue of what is to be done about it.

Grace and Kirk's relationship is another case in point. Grace, who is cast as a kind of mother figure, is forced to negotiate between a certain kind of responsibility for her younger bother Kirk and her own desires for "success". The relationship and her role of "parental" responsibility is not however one where a set of pathologies come to characterize the figures and signifiers of blackness in the play. Despite, Kirk's "criminal" or more accurately rebellious behaviours he is not a "menace to society". Rather, we have the working out of a complex relation of teenage rebellion and separation, in the context of Grace's attempt to figure out the rest of her life. The tensions are raw and the characters are over the top, but they nonetheless articulate a sense of self, which is far removed from the economy of stereotype. Grace and Kirk will resolve their differences in a way that works for both of them.

Riot offers a complex range of Black characters and Black cultures, along with a wider range of collective and individual responses to the everyday living of blackness in Canada. The play's insistence on Black difference, while sometimes didactic, makes clear that it is impossible to attempt to articulate a singular Black Canadian-ness. The privileging of Black difference in the play means that audiences view a complex range of cultures which makes the repeated case for blackness as multiple and polyvalent. In this regard *Riot* is a play which criss-crosses an inquiry into racism with other forms of discrimination, for example homophobia. In the aftermath of *Riot*, Black Canadian theatre can never be the same—no singular Black community is possible but an acknowledgement of Black plurals allows for a more honest assessment of the desire for achieving a possible Black community—that is the project that *Riot* loudly announced, articulated and that was lovingly performed for its audiences in 1995.

Rinaldo Walcott is a Professor of Humanities at York University and the author of *Black Like Who?: Writing Black Canada*.

From top left: Andrew Moodie, Layne Coleman, George Seremba
Seated on chairs: Bryan James, Karen Robinson, Richard Yearwood
On the ground: Conrad Coates, Catherine Bruhier

photo by Andy Moro

Riot was first produced at Factory Theatre in 1995 with the following cast:

GRACE	Karen Robinson
HENRY	George Seremba
WENDLE	Conrad Coates
KIRK	Richard Yearwood
EFFIE	Catherine Bruhier
ALEX	Andrew Moodie

Directed by Layne Coleman
Stage Manager   Bryan James

<u>**CHARACTERS**</u>

GRACE
HENRY
WENDLE
KIRK
EFFIE
ALEX

<u>**SETTING**</u>

A house in Toronto.

ACT I

SCENE I

Lights come up on stage to reveal GRACE at the dining table studying. EFFIE is on the couch, wrapped in a blanket, watching tv, eating Doritos. EFFIE slowly stands, points the remote at the TV. The lights and music fade.

WENDLE   Fuck Quebec!

Lights up. The table is cluttered with their text and note books. EFFIE is laying on the couch. The TV is off.

GRACE   Quebec is a distinct society!

WENDLE   What the fuck makes them a distinct society?!

GRACE   The French language and culture.

WENDLE   Being a black man from Nova Scotia, does that not make me distinct?

GRACE   Yes you are distinct, but that doesn't stop them from being distinct.

WENDLE   Look, you know me; I voted for Brian Mulroney, he's from Quebec. It's not that I don't like people from Quebec, it's just that when they try to tell me that they are better than me, I get pissed off.

GRACE   They're not saying they're better than you, they are looking for the tools to protect their culture.

WENDLE   Jean Chretien is French! He's from Quebec! He doesn't seem to think that we are destroying French culture.

GRACE   Look, I have friends back in Montreal who would tell you that Jean Chretien is a brown nosing two-faced Uncle Tom opportunist who will lick English Canada's asshole so that one day he will become Prime Minister, okay?

WENDLE   You are seriously fucking deluded.

GRACE   I'm just telling you what some people are saying.

WENDLE   Well look, if you're french and from Quebec at least you have a shot at becoming Prime Minister. They're ain't going to be no Black Prime Minister here in Canada within my life time and you know it.

GRACE   You got me there. Fine.

WENDLE   Maybe they should stop thinking about their own culture for a moment and think about other cultures, like what they're doing to Native people!

GRACE   Oh come on!

WENDLE   The French are the most racist, bigoted people in the world.

GRACE   Bullshit!

WENDLE   You go to those people in Oka, you go tell the Mohawks how wonderful Quebec culture is!

GRACE   Don't you dare try and tell me that the people in Quebec are so racist, but hey, Nova Scotian's love Native people, Nova Scotian's don't have a racist bone in their body!

WENDLE   Quebecers are more racist than people in Nova Scotia.

GRACE   (*yelling*) You've never lived in Quebec! You have no idea...

WENDLE   (*yelling*) They had slavery in Quebec!

GRACE   (*yelling*) They had slavery in Nova Scotia!

WENDLE   Okay, look, you want me to feel sympathy for Quebec, why should I feel sympathy for Quebec?

GRACE   1804 to around 1805 there was a crop failure in Lower Canada...

WENDLE   Here we go.

GRACE   This lead to lumber production becoming the number one export to England. With increased export there came with it increased immigration from England. These newly landed...

WENDLE   Look, I don't have a problem with...

GRACE   Just shut up and listen to me for a second.

WENDLE   Don't tell me to...

GRACE   These immigrants were shocked that the French played such a large role in the civil service, and the French were shocked that the English came to dominate the economy. Pierre Bedard, leader of the Canadian party was arrested for... this is what drives me crazy about you Canadians! You should learn your own friggin history!

      WENDLE turns to EFFIE.

WENDLE   I am so glad I am no longer going out with that woman, I swear to god.

      GRACE smacks him on the back of the head. The cordless phone rings.

EFFIE   If it's my mom I'm not here.

WENDLE   Neither am I.

GRACE   So... what, I'm supposed to answer the phone for y'all.

EFFIE   Answer the god-damned phone.

WENDLE   Language...

EFFIE   The fuck do you mean, "language"! You're f-this and f-that...

WENDLE   You don't have to slander God, keep God out of it.

EFFIE   Don't make me get up, just don't... Grace get the phone!!!

      She does.

GRACE   Yo. Hello. Yes she is.

      EFFIE mouths, "who is it." GRACE hands the phone to her.

EFFIE   Hello? Hey ma.

      EFFIE gives grace the finger. GRACE blows her a kiss. ALEX walks in the front door and goes upstairs. EFFIE's line overlaps with GRACE and ALEX.

EFFIE   I'm sorry. I know. How was your day?

GRACE   Get back down here.

ALEX   What did I do?

GRACE   The computer ate my paper.

ALEX   What!?

> *ALEX stops, looks at EFFIE.*

EFFIE   I'm on the rag. Oh yeah. Did you see him again?

> *ALEX mouths "who is she talking to?". GRACE mouths "her*
> *mom." ALEX nods. WENDLE leaves his room with a small*
> *plant. The rest of EFFIE's speech overlaps with ALEX and*
> *GRACE's dialogue.*

EFFIE   What did he say. Oh yeah. No. No it doesn't. Because I just...
no. Because I know. Because in my little experience as a
human being on this planet, I've been there. Mom... Mom...
Mom... listen to me for a sec... Mom? Yes he is. Yes he is.

GRACE   I was in WordPerfect, I imported a graphic into my paper, I
workin' on it not more than 5 minutes and boom she gone and
I ready to smash de rasclot ting pon de wall.

ALEX   One more time in English please.

> *WENDLE goes to the backyard. GRACE pulls out a piece of*
> *scrap paper. ALEX finds it hard to keep his eyes off of EFFIE.*

GRACE   It said, "segment load error; a500:679078" then it said it was
going to shut down if I... if I pressed "yes" and it did.

ALEX   Either there is a problem with the microprocessor or we need
more RAM.

GRACE   I want my paper back.

ALEX   Don't you have it on disk?

EFFIE   Alex.

GRACE   Not most of it. Not ten pages.

EFFIE   Alex.

ALEX   What...

EFFIE   You need to use the phone.

ALEX   What?

EFFIE   You need to use the phone.

ALEX   I need to use the phone.

EFFIE   Ma, someone needs to use the phone.

> *KIRK runs in the front door and up the stairs.*

ALEX   It's an 286 processor right? And the program is supposed to be able to run on a 286 with one Meg RAM, but I hear it works better on a 386 with 4 Meg RAM.

GRACE   RAM.

EFFIE   Alex... he's fine.

ALEX   We've got two, I could try getting four or eight.

GRACE   Right.

ALEX   I thought getting the Quarter-deck memory manager would help. It manages the 640K below the first megabyte. Now TSR programs like the mouse driver...

GRACE   I don't know what you're saying to me right now. I just want my paper back.

ALEX   Okay.

GRACE   I don't care about RAM or any of that stuff...

> *EFFIE hands the phone to ALEX. He takes the phone.*

ALEX   Hey Fiona.

GRACE   Kirk, there's a house meeting tonight...

ALEX   Go on. Anything at all, go ahead. Oh yeah. Well... he should wear a condom.

EFFIE   (*for mother to hear*) Wad I say!

> *WENDLE goes to the kitchen.*

ALEX   He should anyway. It doesn't matter... you don't know that. Because men lie sometimes.

EFFIE   Ha!

ALEX   She's fine. Sorry? I think your daughter is a wonderful per-
        son. She is very pretty. Yes. I have to use the phone. Yes.
        Yes. Sorry. Okay. Nice... nice talking to you. Bye. Bye.

        He hangs up.

EFFIE   I can't believe my mom talked to you. That's too hilarious.

ALEX   Yes it is.

EFFIE   I mean it's just too funny.

ALEX   Now I know where you get it from.

EFFIE   Get what.

ALEX   Your theatricality.

EFFIE   So men lie eh Alex?

ALEX   I guess they do.

EFFIE   I think there's some irony floating around somewhere.

        WENDLE returns with a peanut butter sandwich.

ALEX   So what happened again?

GRACE   The machine ate my paper.

EFFIE   Alex? Any irony?

ALEX   When are you moving out?

EFFIE   Not soon enough.

        WENDLE sits at the table.

WENDLE Peanut butter sandwich anyone?

GRACE   No thanks.

ALEX   Is that my peanut butter?

WENDLE No it's not your motherfucking peanut butter, shut the fuck up.

        EFFIE goes upstairs.

GRACE   Is that it?

ALEX   Check it out.

> *ALEX goes to the kitchen. There is a knock at the door.*

WENDLE   Who is it!

> *ALEX looks at WENDLE, chastising him for not getting the
> door. HENRY enters.*

HENRY   Is Grace there?

GRACE   I'm not ready.

HENRY   Oh, okay.

WENDLE   My brother.

HENRY   Hey Wendle.

GRACE   You want to sit with Wendle for a while?

HENRY   Well if we want dinner, we have to leave soon.

GRACE   I know, I know. Sit with Wendle. This won't take too long.

HENRY   I didn't want to go through this again today.

GRACE   It's something that happened with the computer...

> *KIRK jumps down the stairs and out the door. ALEX steps out
> of the kitchen with a generous shot of scotch and some ice. He
> leans against the couch.*

GRACE   ...hey, there's a house meeting, Kirk!

> *KIRK peeks his head back in.*

KIRK   What.

GRACE   There's a house meeting.

KIRK   When.

GRACE   Five minutes.

KIRK   A'ight.

He runs off. EFFIE takes a few steps down the stairs and looks around, sees ALEX and goes back into her room. ALEX sees her do this and goes to the back yard.

HENRY   How long are you going to be?

GRACE   Just a bit longer.

HENRY   What do you mean just a bit. How long is just a bit.

GRACE   Don't start. Please do not start.

HENRY   But this always happens! Why do you always leave things to the last minute?!

GRACE   I'm sorry.

HENRY   I hate rushing around. I really do.

She goes over to him and hugs him.

GRACE   I know I said I wouldn't do this...

HENRY   Don't talk to me right now. Just get the work done. Go. Work.

GRACE   We don't have to go out at all.

HENRY   Just go to work.

She goes back to the computer.

WENDLE   So how you doing.

HENRY   Fine. What happened to the sound.

WENDLE   I don't know.

HENRY goes to the television and looks at it. He fiddles with the sound knob.

WENDLE   Were you here when the sound cut out... Grace?

GRACE   What?

WENDLE   Were you here when the sound cut out?

GRACE   No. Ask Effie. She knows all about it.

WENDLE   Aww, forget about it. Sit down man. Come on.

        He does.

WENDLE   How you doing.

HENRY   Hard day. Hard day.

WENDLE   What.

HENRY   Nothing. Just a hard day.

        ALEX comes back in from the backyard, grabs a newspaper, and sits at table.

GRACE   Tell him.

WENDLE   Tell me what.

HENRY   I was stopped by the police.

WENDLE   No way.

HENRY   I made an illegal left turn and the guy, he comes up behind me and tells me that he just wants to look in my van.

WENDLE   You're kidding me.

HENRY   He searched my van. When I started to argue, his partner pulled out a gun and searches me. I don't know what he was looking for, but...

WENDLE   I mean what the fuck... every black man is hiding drugs in his car. Fuck! Fuck that!

ALEX   So what happened?

HENRY   Well, they searched me and I got a ticket and they left.

ALEX   Well you've got to file a complaint.

HENRY   No no.

ALEX   You have to. Do you remember what the two cops looked like?

HENRY   Alex... I am not going to do anything.

ALEX   You have to.

HENRY   The police in this country don't scare me.

ALEX   The Metro Toronto police force is not here to scare you. You are a business person. You own a very successful electrical company. You pay your taxes, you employ Canadians, the Metro Toronto police force should at least, at the very least apologize! Am I right? They should at least say that you are a valued person in this community, and there was obviously some terrible mistake, and you should be made to feel welcome here.

WENDLE   Alex, let me tell you a story. One summer I went to live with my uncle, and out east, they've got this thing called "Broom the Coon" and what that is... a bunch of white guys get in a car late at night, they take a broom with them, and when they see a black person on the street, they step on the gas, they stick the broom out the window, and they smack him on the head.

GRACE   You're joking.

WENDLE   So, I'm walking down the street one night, going home. This car goes by, then pulls a u-ee, and when a car does that late at night, and you're black, you know you're in for it. So I run towards the car, grab the broom, start pulling, these two humongous white guys get out of the car and proceed to beat the living shit out of me. Somebody calls the station, tells the police that two white guys are being attacked by a crazed Negro with a knife. The cops arrive, take *me* to the station. The commanding officer? I'm all covered in bruises right? I try to tell him my story, but he doesn't want to hear it. He turns to the arresting officer, goes, "did you get a statement" the arresting officer goes, "no" and that's it. On my record I have an assault charge. I'd contest it but it looks so good; I kicked the shit out of two white guys, single handed.

GRACE   It's like the police are some kind of occupying army or something. You know? It's like; don't look them in the eye, don't make any sudden movements when you walk by.

ALEX   But I think that feeling is pretty universal. I mean, white people feel just as nervous around cops as we do.

GRACE   Yes, but because I'm black I feel like when I step out that door and I see a cop, my life is at risk.

WENDLE   This country is racist from top to bottom. From the police force, to the military, to the business sector, to the CBC... I mean the fuck is it with this Road to Avonlea shit? There's not a single black person in sight! My ancestors fucking fought and died to help found this country. They settled right in that part of the world. I have never seen a black face on that show!

ALEX   How the fuck do you know, you never watch the fucking program!

WENDLE   Philip Rushton is supported by big business.

ALEX   Oh please.

WENDLE   It's true! That's why they refuse to fire him. His research helps to discourage employment equity.

ALEX   If I wanted conspiracy theories, I'd call Oliver Stone.

WENDLE   The government created the Heritage Front.

ALEX   (*yelling*) Oh come on!

WENDLE   They did.

ALEX   Yeah yeah.

GRACE   A friend of mine who works in the Anti-racism League told me that CSIS started the Heritage Front and funds its rallies.

ALEX   Do you have *any* evidence whatsoever to back this up.

GRACE   Well my friend says...

ALEX   No no no no, do you have any evidence to back this up.

GRACE   No but...

ALEX   Then how am I supposed to believe what you're saying?!

WENDLE   Because this country is run by white people and that's just the way white people are. It's in their nature. It's in their genetic make up to try and fuck us over every opportunity they get.

ALEX   That's racist!!!

WENDLE   Yeah, but it's true!!! In the States you can fight racism because they're so open about it. That way, black people have more opportunities. Canada is ten times more racist than the States but they hide it here. Every aspect of this country is racist. They just hide it.

ALEX   Then what do you expect me to do? Do you expect me to live my life in fear of some unseen form of... of oppression or something.

WENDLE   Just open your eyes Alex. Stop living in a dream world.

HENRY   Maybe Madonna was right.

WENDLE   What.

HENRY   Maybe Toronto is a fascist city.

GRACE   The police won't even leave Madonna alone. "Damn."

WENDLE   When is this notorious house meeting?

GRACE   We should get this thing on the road. (*shouting*) Alex!

ALEX   I'm right here.

GRACE   I mean Effie. (*shouting*) Effie!

          GRACE goes to the computer.

ALEX   Hey. What happened to the sound?

          ALEX pounces on WENDLE in an attempt to steal the remote. He is unsuccessful.

WENDLE   Hey.

ALEX   The Rodney King trial is on CNN.

WENDLE   Oh right.

HENRY   Can I see the paper?

          The newspaper is in a mess on the floor.

ALEX   Sure man, what section?

HENRY   Just entertainment.

ALEX gives HENRY the section. HENRY looks over GRACE's shoulder, she motions for him to go away.

GRACE   Did you go to any classes today?

No response. WENDLE taps ALEX.

GRACE   Alex.

ALEX   Yes.

GRACE   Did you go to any classes today?

ALEX   No ma.

GRACE   Just asking.

ALEX   Bite me.

GRACE   It's your life.

ALEX   And I can do what I want.

GRACE   (*shouting*) Effie!

EFFIE   (*off-stage*) What!

GRACE   (*with a Jamaican accent*) House *meeting*!

ALEX jumps off the couch.

ALEX   Let's get this party started right!

WENDLE gets up, they both go to the table. EFFIE comes down the stairs and sits.

EFFIE   Grace.

GRACE   I'm just shutting down the computer. It takes a while.

ALEX   Shouldn't Kirk be here?

GRACE   He said he'd be back.

WENDLE   Should we wait for him?

GRACE   No.

GRACE shuts down the computer and sits.

GRACE   Okay.

HENRY   Guys. You might want to see this.

WENDLE   What.

HENRY   The trial.

ALEX   Is it over?

HENRY   They're just about to read the verdict.

EFFIE   Could we get this done now?

ALEX   It'll take two minutes.

EFFIE   You're going to hear it on the news anyway.

ALEX   Can we just take two minutes to watch this please.

EFFIE   Aww, come on guys. They're guilty, they're going to jail.
                What's there to see.

ALEX   Shhh.

EFFIE   Don't shhh me. There's no sound. What the hell do you want
                to shhh me for? Idiot.

            They all stand in silence for a moment.

HENRY   I don't understand. Is the jury reading the verdict or no.

WENDLE   I think they're doing it now.

ALEX   What just happened?

GRACE   Why are they smiling?

WENDLE   They won.

            EFFIE joins them at the TV.

ALEX   Yeah, I think they did.

EFFIE   No.

GRACE   Waitwaitwaitwait, guys. Here it is.

            On the screen, a written transcript of the jury's findings.

WENDLE   Not guilty. Not guilty.

> *They all move away from the TV set. WENDLE goes to the kitchen. There is a twenty-five second silence.*

ALEX   Where was the trial held?

GRACE   Something valley.

EFFIE   Where were the black people on that jury?

GRACE   I didn't see any.

HENRY   I mean, what... do they not see a human being? Laying on the ground, bleeding! Being beaten to death?

GRACE   There's got to be an appeal.

EFFIE   Think so?

GRACE   They have to. I mean, come on.

ALEX   I know this isn't the best time to play devils advocate, but... the jury was not asked if it was inhumane, they were asked if it was within the law... within police procedure.

HENRY   How can you say that beating some one like that is police procedure!

ALEX   I'm not saying it's right or wrong, I'm just saying that... yeah, the way they treated Rodney King has been police procedure, in America, for quite some time. And if it wasn't for that video tape, we wouldn't even be talking about it.

EFFIE   As a matter of fact, it took a long time for the video to even make it into the news. A lot of stations refused to play it at first.

GRACE   Shhh. They're playing the video again.

> *They watch together in silence for a while. They react to the video.*

ALEX   Okay, now... Someone shows that to the jury and says, "look, you're a cop. An LA cop. You don't know if he's on crack, PCP, whatever. You don't want him to get your gun..."

WENDLE   That's a black man Alex.

ALEX I know.

WENDLE This is what they do to keep us down. To keep you down. To keep me down.

ALEX Okay.

WENDLE I swear to God I try not to hate white people. I swear to God I try to turn the other cheek, but as the God I love is my witness, I only have so many cheeks. And I swear by the Lord that I love, they will not treat me like an animal. But they turn around and do something like this and you can't do anything. You can't do anything. I mean...

> *WENDLE exits. KIRK runs in the front door as WENDLE runs out.*

KIRK What's the matter with him.

EFFIE The guys who attacked Rodney King got off.

KIRK No.

> *GRACE goes outside to see about WENDLE.*

HENRY Yup.

KIRK Racist cops.

ALEX What?

KIRK The cops, they racist.

HENRY Yes they are.

> *ALEX joins GRACE.*

EFFIE So where were you.

KIRK Me?

EFFIE Yes you.

KIRK Out.

EFFIE I figured that.

> *EFFIE goes to the kitchen. KIRK heads for the stairs.*

HENRY   Kirk.

KIRK   Yo.

HENRY   Don't run off. Sit with me for a second.

          KIRK sits next to HENRY.

HENRY   How's school.

KIRK   Fine.

HENRY   Good marks?

          HENRY pulls out a pen and paper.

KIRK   Always.

HENRY   I want to thank you again for helping me out last weekend.

KIRK   No problem.

HENRY   I want you to give me the number of your parole officer. I
          want to tell him about the great job you did.

KIRK   No, don't do that.

HENRY   Please, I want to.

KIRK   I know you want to help, but, they... they're not impressed
          with... I mean... it doesn't mean anything to them. It's nice, but
          it doesn't help.

HENRY   Okay. Okay... you know, I need some help again this weekend.

KIRK   Oh yeah, what kind.

HENRY   Same sort of thing. Lifting boxes, a bit of painting this time.
          Same money as last time. You do a good job, you get a bonus,
          but only if you do a good job.

KIRK   Oh man. I just remembered, I got to go with a friend of mine
          to see his parents.

HENRY   When.

KIRK   Saturday.

HENRY   Then you can come in on Sunday.

KIRK	I was going to stay the whole weekend.
HENRY	The whole weekend?
KIRK	The whole weekend.
HENRY	Okay. I understand.
KIRK	Look man, I know you trying to hook me up and everything, but, what you do... is not my ting, you know?
HENRY	I see.
KIRK	But, you know, it's great that you trying to hook me up and everything.
HENRY	Okay.

KIRK gets up and starts for the stairs. GRACE, ALEX and WENDLE come in.

GRACE	Stop right there.
KIRK	I just have to go to the washroom.
GRACE	You can go later. Effie! Come nuh!
EFFIE	(*from the kitchen*) Coming!
ALEX	Who called this meeting?

EFFIE comes back in with a bowl of ice cream.

GRACE	That's one of the things I want to talk about. We all ready?

Everyone answers.

GRACE	Good. Now. First I want...
ALEX	Is that my ice cream.

EFFIE smiles.

GRACE	Can I please start this now.
ALEX	Sorry.

GRACE   Okay. Now first, I want to say that I called this meeting, but maybe we should just have one every two weeks or something.

No one answers.

GRACE   It doesn't matter to me, I just want to know how you feel.

EFFIE   Well, I know for a fact that if we tell everyone to meet at a specific time and place, none of us are going to do it.

ALEX   I think if there was some money involved...

EFFIE   Don't be an ass.

WENDLE   I think the way we meet now is fine.

GRACE   Everyone agree?

All agree.

GRACE   Great. Now. Rent. Here it is, the last day of the month and again I have three people who have yet to pay.

WENDLE   I paid.

GRACE   No you didn't.

WENDLE   I did. Yesterday. You forgot.

GRACE   Uh huhn.

GRACE goes for her wallet and looks through it.

WENDLE   Henry was there.

HENRY   I'm sorry what?

WENDLE   I pay my rent?

HENRY   Yup.

She finds his cheque.

GRACE   Oh, okay.

EFFIE   Henry, could you toss me my purse.

GRACE　　　Look, I don't want to sound like a tyrant, but y'all know that the landlady is just looking for a reason to kick us out.

EFFIE　　　It's under the chair.　There.　That's it.

ALEX　　　You know that legally she can't do anything until the fifteenth.

　　　　　　HENRY tosses EFFIE's purse.

GRACE　　　Look, I don't want to get angry with you, alright.　Especially because you, out of all of us have the means to pay it on time.

　　　　　　EFFIE pulls out her cheque book and starts writing a rent cheque.

ALEX　　　So.

GRACE　　　So why don't you do it?

ALEX　　　It's not you, it's her.

GRACE　　　Yes, Alex, we all know the landlady a crotchety old racist white cunt...

WENDLE　　Woah.

GRACE　　　We all know that she never does any repairs, we know that she thinks this is a crack house for illegal immigrants.　We know. Just pay the fucking rent.

ALEX　　　I say if she ever fucks with us we take her to court.

　　　　　　EFFIE hands GRACE a cheque.

WENDLE　　Just pay the fucking rent and pay it on time!　It's not too much to ask!

ALEX　　　Fine.

EFFIE　　　Next item?

GRACE　　　Oh and Kirk, you still owe for the phone bill.

KIRK　　　How much?

GRACE　　　Thirty dollars.

　　　　　　WENDLE and ALEX both "ooooo".

WENDLE   You're not calling those phone sex lines or nothing are you?

ALEX   I think junior here's got himself a girlfriend in Buffalo.

GRACE   It's none of your business guys.

WENDLE   Aren't you going to Buffalo this weekend?

KIRK   No.

ALEX   I think junior's got himself a steady lay in Buffalo.

WENDLE   I don't think so because junior here don't even got no pubic hairs man.

KIRK   Who needs pubic hairs, when I just work it boy.

> *KIRK humps the air, the couch, the ground. ALEX and WENDLE go apeshit.*

EFFIE   Could you men please do this at another time and place.

GRACE   Are you finished?

> *KIRK nods.*

GRACE   Does anybody else have anything to say?

> *EFFIE and ALEX both speak at the same time.*

EFFIE   I... Sorry... You go. No you go.

ALEX   I... Sorry... You... No no you go.

GRACE   Effie?

ALEX   Go.

EFFIE   Go. It's alright.

WENDLE   One of you fucking go.

EFFIE   Okay... I don't know... who's doing this and I don't want to know. I don't want to make a big deal out of this but... someone is jerking off into a Kleenex and tossing it in the bin in the bathroom upstairs. Now, I don't care if people jerk off, but if you leave the Kleenex in the bin it leaves this smell... it's like... it's disgusting. I don't want to... anyway... I said what I wanted to... to say.

Silence.

ALEX   It's not me, but do you really notice a smell?

**EFFIE &
GRACE**   Yes.

WENDLE   I've noticed it too.

All eyes turn to ALEX.

ALEX   It wasn't me. (*he notices EFFIE is staring at him*) it wasn't, okay. It wasn't me!

EFFIE   I don't care. I don't want to know who it is, just stop doing it.

GRACE   Alex.

ALEX   It wasn't me!

GRACE   You wanted to say something.

ALEX   Oh. Right. Uhm... I was going to say two things: the computer needs some repairs.

GRACE   What does that mean.

ALEX   Well. The latest version of the word processor, that I was soooo happy to get, isn't functioning properly. I'm going to take it into the shop...

GRACE   Should we all chip in some money?

ALEX   No no I'll cover it. Until that time, constantly save your stuff on disk while you're working on it. Okay?

EFFIE   Anything else?

ALEX   Everyone, stop eating my food!!!! I know that I, out of all of us, have the means to pay the rent on time, but I'm not a food bank. If you're really desperate, ask. That's all.

EFFIE lets her bowl fall on the table.

GRACE   Is that it?

ALEX   Yup.

GRACE   Okay, so...

ALEX   Oh uh...

GRACE   What.

ALEX   I was just messing with you. Sorry.

EFFIE   Oh for fuck's sake.

GRACE   Anything else? Any body?

ALEX opens and closes his mouth just to piss EFFIE off.

GRACE   No? Okay. (*KIRK tries to leave, GRACE grabs him*) Before we all go I want to officially welcome my brother KIRK to the house.

Everyone says "welcome KIRK".

GRACE   And uh... it's your second week here, how do you feel...

KIRK   It feel alright.

EFFIE   It's good having you here.

KIRK   Feels good to be here.

GRACE   Okay. That's it. Kirk? Can I talk to you?

Everyone starts to get up. GRACE pulls KIRK to the backyard.

WENDLE   Effie. Effie. You still want to go see "White Men Can't Jump"?

EFFIE   Uh, well... not today.

WENDLE   I know not today but... I've got some friends going on Saturday. I thought you might like to go... along.

EFFIE   Uh, okay. We'll see. Okay?

WENDLE   Right. Okay.

EFFIE   Cause I...

WENDLE   That's okay. Just thought I'd... I'd let you know.

EFFIE   Right.

KIRK jogs out of the backyard and heads for the stairs.

ALEX   Yo Kirk. Come here man.

              KIRK stops.

ALEX   Everything okay?

KIRK   Yeah yeah. Hey, we going to play pool tonight?

ALEX   Not tonight. Maybe tomorrow night.

KIRK   Come on man, you gotta give me a chance to whip your ass.

ALEX   You couldn't whip my grandmother's nasty old ass motherfuc-
              ka.

KIRK   Bring it on. Let's go.

              *They play-fight a bit. KIRK wins. They say "see ya later" to
              each other. KIRK goes upstairs. ALEX sits on the couch. He
              grabs the converter.*

HENRY   You two seem to be good friends these days.

              ALEX looks around for GRACE.

ALEX   I took him to the Bovine Sex Club last night.

HENRY   Oh yeah.

ALEX   He freaked man. The women with the leather things pushing
              things everywhere. He loved it.

HENRY   What is it called again?

ALEX   Bovine Sex Club? It's just a place to listen to loud music, wear
              dead cows, look cool. I should take you there sometime.

HENRY   Well, somehow I don't see Grace being too keen on my going
              to someplace place called the Bovine Sex Club.

ALEX   Why not.

HENRY   Oh I don't know.

              *GRACE comes back in from the backyard with some laundry.
              They try to look innocent. GRACE notices this. HENRY grabs
              the rest of the newspaper. She goes over to HENRY and hugs
              him. Kisses his cheek.*

GRACE I'll be down in a second. Okay?

HENRY Okay. Okay.

GRACE I'm sorry I yelled at you.

HENRY It's okay. I'm sorry too. Hurry up.

She walks upstairs. WENDLE sits.

ALEX Is he going to work for you?

HENRY Sorry?

ALEX Is he going to work for you this weekend?

HENRY No. No I don't think so.

ALEX You know I'd help you, but that old Korean war wound, it's been giving me hell lately. Oh, cripes there it goes again.

HENRY I'll be fine. I think what's most important is what you guys are doing already.

ALEX What are we doing?

HENRY I think that it really will help him to be with his own people.

ALEX Oh, I see.

WENDLE It's a really good idea but... it should be happening more often.

HENRY I have been saying for years that what we need is a program where if you hire a young person, someone who has committed some small offense, if we put him in our businesses, you get him off the street and learning a skilled trade. That way, he will have a greater respect for himself and therefore he won't commit any crime. And in return, you give small business some tax breaks.

WENDLE I am telling you, white people will never let it happen. They would rather see us killing each other than helping ourselves.

ALEX Does it need to happen?

WENDLE What?

ALEX   Is there a big problem with black youth and crime, or is it a media creation. Is it our responsibility to eliminate all black crime? And if we do, then what, we move on to white crime or something?

> *KIRK walks down the stairs. He stops to listen to the conversation.*

HENRY   We're not trying to eliminate all black criminals.

ALEX   Then what are we talking about?

WENDLE   So, what should we do about Kirk? Should we just kick him out? Make him fend for himself?

ALEX   Look, I think Kirk is a great guy, okay? I'm glad he's here, I think it's important that he's here, but be honest, if he wasn't Grace's brother, if we didn't know him, none of us would want to have anything to do with him.

WENDLE   You know Alex... we've known each other for three years now, and this is something that I've always wanted to say to you.

ALEX   Shoot.

WENDLE   With all respect, because you are a good friend, you are one of those rich niggers who doesn't believe that racism exists.

ALEX   Oh really.

WENDLE   Where I come from, you know it exists. You see it. You feel it. It's all around you...

ALEX   I will be the first to admit...

WENDLE   Nonononono, let me finish. Where I come from, you learn that white people are white people.

ALEX   What the hell is that supposed to mean?!

WENDLE   It means that they like to keep to themselves. They don't like strangers. They like to keep what's theirs to themselves. You know this.

ALEX   So what are you saying...

WENDLE   We have to stick together. This is the reason why I have the greatest amount of respect for the Jews, I really do; everybody swims, or everybody sinks. They help each other out, they know that together they can survive. Everybody swims or everybody sinks. It's that simple. That's why I will do anything for Kirk. Anything. We all have to stick together. This is the most racist country...

    KIRK goes to the kitchen.

ALEX   Oh please!

WENDLE   ... in the world! It's true Alex!

    GRACE walks down the stairs. She is almost ready. EFFIE pokes her head out from the top of the stairs.

EFFIE   Could you guys keep it down, I'm trying to get some sleep.

HENRY   Are you ready to go?

GRACE   Yeah. Let's go.

    HENRY stands. Walks over to GRACE. Holds her. KIRK walks out of the kitchen and sits on the couch. He flips through the channels.

WENDLE   I respect you okay. You know that I respect you. But sometimes all I hear from you is that you're trying to please some invisible white man in your head.

ALEX   Oh man. The reality of what's going on in my head is by far more dangerous than that.

    GRACE and HENRY open the door and are about to leave.

KIRK   Grace, look at that.

ALEX   What the...

    On the television they watch as a group of white youth destroy a parking lot cubicle. HENRY and GRACE are drawn to the television.

GRACE   What's going on?

KIRK   Look at that. Look look... BOOM!

ALEX   Holy shit.

GRACE   Effie!

EFFIE   (*shouting off-stage*) What!

GRACE   You want to see this?

EFFIE   (*off-stage*) What is it.

GRACE   I think a riot has started in Los Angeles.

EFFIE   (*off-stage*) Oh yeah.

GRACE   You want to see this?

> *EFFIE leaves her room wrapped in a blanket, she walks down the stairs and joins everyone in front of the television. Something happens on the television screen to make them all react.*

WENDLE   Where is this. Is it just outside the courthouse?

GRACE   I don't know.

ALEX   Yeah I think it is.

EFFIE   Holy shit.

> *GRACE sucks her teeth.*

ALEX   Look at that.

WENDLE   Fuck.

HENRY   My God.

> *Lights fade as they watch the screen.*

ACT II

SCENE I

Lights up on EFFIE. She lays on the couch trying to memorize terms from a text book. KIRK walks in and goes upstairs to his room. He steps out of his room, bare chested, onto the landing at the top of the stairs and he starts working out with a dumbbell. EFFIE doesn't notice. He starts coughing, clearing his throat to get her attention. Nothing. He takes the weight back to his room and starts to head down the stairs. He stops, sniffs his armpit then heads back to his room. He comes out again, hops down the stairs. He goes to the kitchen. Once in the kitchen, EFFIE looks up from her book. Towards the kitchen. She gets up and creeps over to the kitchen door. KIRK is grabbing a yogurt cup from the fridge. EFFIE makes a dash for the couch. KIRK walks out of the kitchen and heads for the stairs.

EFFIE   Kirk?

KIRK   Yo.

EFFIE   Have a couple of seconds? I need help with something.

KIRK   Sure.

EFFIE   I just have to... sit. Sit.

          He sits at the end of the couch.

EFFIE   I just have to see how well I memorized something. Could you...

KIRK   Alright. Let's see here.

          He takes the book from her.

EFFIE   Just read out the terms with the marks next to them. See if I get it right.

          She stretches out on the couch, absentmindedly putting her feet on his lap.

EFFIE   First one. Go for it.

KIRK   Circular reaction.

EFFIE   Circular reaction refers to a type of interstimulation wherein the response of one individual reproduces the stimulation that has come from another individual and in being reflected back to this individual reinforces the stimulation... well?

KIRK   Yeah.

EFFIE   Yeah what?

KIRK   It's right. It's right.

EFFIE   Next.

He surreptitiously places his hand on her knee.

KIRK   Characteristics of social unrest.

EFFIE   A) random behavior. B) excited feeling...

He slowly moves his hand down her leg.

EFFIE   ...usually in the form of vague apprehension, aroused pugnacity...

KIRK   What's that?

EFFIE   What's what?

KIRK   Aroused pugnacity?

EFFIE   That's a good fucking question.

She moves towards her bag to grab a dictionary, taking her leg away from him. She finds the term in her dictionary.

EFFIE   It means, like a... a readiness to fight.

KIRK   Oh.

EFFIE   C) the irritability and increased suggestibility of the crowd. How am I doing there.

KIRK   Just fine. You're doing just fine.

EFFIE   Last one. Go for it.

KIRK   Okay. What is left here now? Characteristics of the acting crowd.

She's stumped. She wriggles around trying to find the answer. She puts her foot on his thigh. It moves closer up his leg as she struggles to find the answer.

EFFIE I know this! I know it. Don't tell me. Don't... I know this... it's spontaneous... ah fuck. I give up. What is it. What is it.

KIRK leans over towards her to kiss her.

EFFIE What.

Just before they kiss, GRACE and ALEX enter. KIRK jumps to his feet and rushes upstairs. GRACE walks in just in time to catch him bounding up the stairs. GRACE is carrying her knapsack, poster board and wooden sticks. ALEX is carrying two big bags of groceries and a newspaper. He goes to the kitchen.

ALEX I mean, if you lose nine zip to the Royals, nine points to the worst team in baseball, it means Jack Morris has got to go, is what it means.

GRACE What's going on?

EFFIE Nothing. Why.

EFFIE goes to the backyard. GRACE follows her.

ALEX What. What is it. (*no response from GRACE*) Yo Kirk. Kirk!

KIRK (*off-stage*) Ya man.

ALEX Bovine tonight!

KIRK (*off-stage*) I don't think so boy.

ALEX Hey hey hey... what's going on here. You avoiding me or something?

KIRK comes out of his room.

KIRK No. No I'm not.

ALEX Come on now. What's up.

KIRK Nothing. I'm busy. That's all. Alright?

ALEX Alright.

>*KIRK goes back to his room. EFFIE and GRACE step back inside.*

EFFIE   Alright. Fuck off.

>*Upstairs, KIRK sings. EFFIE goes upstairs.*

KIRK   (*off-stage*) "She love me now. Boy, she love me now. Ooo yeah. She love me now."

>*GRACE starts working on placards. ALEX pours himself a scotch.*

ALEX   So what's up?

GRACE   How do you mean?

ALEX   Does Effie want to fuck Kirk or something?

GRACE   Yes she does.

ALEX   Is it really any of your business?

GRACE   He's eighteen.

ALEX   He's in his sexual prime.

GRACE   Kirk has been placed in my care.

ALEX   Is Effie going to corrupt him?

GRACE   No. That's not the point.

ALEX   Then what is the point.

GRACE   He is not here to have fun and get laid. He's here to go to school, get good grades and find a job.

ALEX   Grace, I don't know if you're aware of this but you're his sister, not his mother.

GRACE   (*shouting*) I know I'm not his mother!

ALEX   Okay.

GRACE   (*shouting*) I'm not doing this because I want to be his damn mother!

ALEX   Okay.

GRACE   Kirk is living here with me because he got into trouble and I take that responsibility very seriously.

ALEX   So... so your mom... she still lives in Jamaica right?

GRACE   Yes.

ALEX   And is he gonna stay here, or is he going back eventually, or...

GRACE   Our mother is an alcoholic. My mother's sister took me in when I was young but whenever she couldn't handle Kirk she would send him back home.

ALEX   I see.

GRACE   He has spent most of his life bouncing back and forth. Last time he was sent back home, last Christmas, he had to pull Mummy out of some bar where some woman tried to cut her in half with a machete. She spent the night throwing up. Kirk waited up all night with her; cleaning her, making sure that she lay on her side, so that she wouldn't choke on her own vomit. When she woke up, you know what she did? She slapped him around because there was no rum in the house. That was his Christmas last year.

ALEX   Okay.

GRACE   So I feel... I feel that he needs some stability. That's what I want for him... if... if that makes me into some kind of a mother figure... I don't think I am but...

ALEX   Do you ever go back, visit your Mom?

GRACE   No. No not at all. My mother and I... we don't get along.

ALEX   Okay.

GRACE shows ALEX a scar.

GRACE   See that? That's from a kitchen knife.

KIRK   (*off-stage*) "She love me now. Boy, she love me now. Ooo yeah. She love me now. Boy she love me now."

GRACE   Kirk needs... he needs to start thinking about a career, about school, his future. I don't want him to end up some drug dealer, beating the shit out of his girlfriend, wasting his life away. Do you understand?

ALEX	Yes I do.
GRACE	His marks are terrible. If he had a job, I'd feel better.
ALEX	I could start working on him if you like.
GRACE	Could you?
ALEX	I'll be discreet.
GRACE	And if you could kind of put it in his head that Henry is looking for someone part-time.
ALEX	Sure.
GRACE	He wants to put Kirk in the office, making good money but we can't tell him okay?
ALEX	Okay.
GRACE	Because if he knows...
KIRK	(*off-stage*) "I gonna walk like a champion, talk like a champion..."

She gets ALEX to come closer.

GRACE	Because if he knows, then...
ALEX	Then he won't work hard. I got it.

He tries to kiss her on the neck. She pulls away frantically.

GRACE	You're not going to make a pass at him either, are you.
ALEX	No.
GRACE	Have you told him about...
ALEX	My sexual proclivity? No. He's a bit too straight. Know what I mean. You have to be careful. But who knows. Maybe he's checking me out. (*GRACE laughs*) And he sure does have a mighty fine ass...
GRACE	Alex.
ALEX	It was a joke. I was just kidding.

KIRK jumps down the stairs.

ALEX   Yo Kirk. Come on over here!

> *KIRK goes over to ALEX.*

KIRK   What's up.

ALEX   Look, I want you to tell me the truth and I don't want you to lie to me okay! You lie to me, I'll kill you, you understand me!

KIRK   Okay okay, what up.

ALEX   Was that you singing upstairs or was that the radio or something?

KIRK   You really think it was the radio?

ALEX   No, I'm just fucking with you. But it sounded good though.

KIRK   Thanks.

ALEX   So pull some out. Let's see it.

KIRK   No no.

ALEX   Come on. You got to give your sister over here a taste. You got to.

KIRK   No.

ALEX   Here look... I know you must be a little nervous. Tell you what, I'll do the drum machine part. Okay? Join in any time. You ready? Here we go. One, two, one two three four...

> *ALEX demonstrates that he has no rhythm. KIRK and GRACE laugh.*

ALEX   Come on man. Quick, join in. Whicky whicky whicky.

GRACE   Alex... Al... (*shouting*) Alex! There's a white man inside you just dying to get out.

ALEX   Har de har har.

GRACE   Go on Kirk. Let's hear it.

> *KIRK gets up and pulls a tape out of his pocket.*

KIRK   Alright, alright. I just so happen to have a tape here.

He puts the tape into the stereo. Music starts.

KIRK   This selection is goin' out to all de stations in Toronto. It goin' out to 102.5, 106.9 and what's your favourite station?

GRACE   (*you can improvise a different response every night or...*) 66.5.

KIRK   88.1! Here we go now. "There was a girl. And she make me want to... wind my body down so low. She make me want to..."

> *KIRK notices that EFFIE is sitting and listening at the top of the stairs.*

KIRK   That's all ya gettin' fa now.

> *ALEX and GRACE applaud.*

GRACE   It good still Kirk.

ALEX   That was great!

KIRK   Thanks.

ALEX   So, you have a stage name or something?

KIRK   Ya man. Captain Kirk. You know, like "Star Trek".

ALEX   Right right.

KIRK   The first CD, check it. "Enterprise".

ALEX   You know what?

KIRK   What.

ALEX   I don't know if you're aware of this, but I've got another computer in my room, it has a slot for a sound card...

KIRK   Uh huhn.

ALEX   Now a sound card... think of it as a... a mini recording studio.

> *EFFIE goes back into her room.*

KIRK   Right right.

ALEX   If you want to get one, I can install it for you and then bingo, there you go man. Your own instant recording studio. You can record whatever you want, whenever you want. Four tracks, CD quality sound...

KIRK   That would be a bonus you know. Cause as it stand right now, I have to truck my equipment all the way across town just to get to my friend's studio.

ALEX   Well?

KIRK   And how much do these sound cards cost.

ALEX   Around four hundred bucks. But what you can do is, you can give Henry a call, tell him you want to earn four hundred bucks real fast and bingo... sound card's yours.

KIRK   I see. Alright. Alright.

ALEX   And if you get it, and I install it for you... you can keep the computer cause I never use it.

KIRK   No, I couldn't do that.

ALEX   Hey, look at me. Hey look, look right at me; don't worry about it.

KIRK   I see. I see. Alright.

ALEX   The offer's there. Think about it. All I want from you is when you accept your little Grammy award, I want you to look in the camera and I want you to thank me.

KIRK   Alright, we'll do, we'll do.

         ALEX starts to go upstairs. EFFIE comes downstairs. ALEX stops in his tracks, turns and goes to the kitchen, grabbing his newspaper as he goes. KIRK eats the yogurt that he started eating before. EFFIE looks for a newspaper. KIRK stares at her. GRACE stares at him.

GRACE   Is that all you eat now?

KIRK   Sorry?

GRACE   Is yogurt all you eat now?

KIRK   No.

GRACE   You eating properly?

KIRK   Yeah.

GRACE   I don't see you buying food with the money I give you.

KIRK   Alright, alright.

EFFIE   Did you get today's paper?

> KIRK stares at EFFIE. GRACE grabs her paper from her bag, smacks KIRK on the head with it, hands her newspaper over to EFFIE. EFFIE looks at the front page.

EFFIE   Holy fuck.

GRACE   What?

EFFIE   When did this happen?

GRACE   What?

EFFIE   Some white guy got beaten up.

GRACE   Yeah, I saw that.

EFFIE   Pulled out of his car and...

GRACE   Yeah.

EFFIE   Oh this is great.

> EFFIE grabs her textbook and notebook.

GRACE   What?

EFFIE   Everything is dove-tailing so perfectly for my course.

GRACE   Oh yeah.

EFFIE   You've got to hear this.

GRACE   What.

EFFIE   "Characteristics of the acting crowd: instead of acting on the basis of established rule, it acts on the basis of aroused impulse. It is not strange that much of the crowds behaviour should be violent, cruel and destructive because impulses that would ordinarily be subject to a severe check by the individual's judgment, now has a free passage to expression."

GRACE   Hmmm.

EFFIE   That's what's happening right now. This guy that was pulled out of his truck. That's what's happened to him.

GRACE   You want to help me with these slogans? I need like four slogans.

EFFIE grabs some posterboard and a large magic marker.

EFFIE   Isn't it wild though that we're like living through this really tumultuous time. Doesn't it like...

GRACE   No.

WENDLE walks in the front door. He has his text books. ALEX enters with a bottle of Scotch and a glass, and sits at the computer.

EFFIE   Is it "No Peace No Justice" or is it "No Justice No Peace".

GRACE   I think it's "No Justice No Peace".

EFFIE starts writing.

GRACE   Do you think there's going to be violence?

EFFIE   Where?

GRACE   At the rally?

EFFIE   Probably yeah.

GRACE   You think so?

EFFIE   All the symptoms are there. General restlessness, feeling of unease... aroused pugnacity.

KIRK laughs.

ALEX   There isn't going to be any violence.

EFFIE   You don't think so?

ALEX   This is Canada for crying out loud.

WENDLE   Nova Scotia has had a long history of racial strife my friend.

GRACE   There were riots here back in 1933. A group of Jewish people were playing softball when they were attacked by some jocks from an upper-class yacht club. The Christie Pits riot.

EFFIE   In Montreal they riot over hockey.

GRACE   Are you going to the rally?

ALEX   I was thinking about it but the organizers are trying to make this recent police shooting on the weekend into some kind of Canadian Rodney King...

WENDLE   Tell me something, why do you hate black people so much?

ALEX   I don't hate black people, I just have a hard time equating the shooting of a knife-wielding drug dealer in Toronto with the beating of Rodney King!

WENDLE   Aww get the fuck out of my face right now...

ALEX   Wendle! I know the kid was a black youth and that we all have to sink or swim, but he was a drug dealer!

WENDLE   (*shouting*) He was holding a knife.

ALEX   (*shouting*) What do you expect a police officer to do!

WENDLE   (*shouting*) Why the fuck do you have to shoot someone holding a knife!!!

ALEX   (*shouting*) A knife is still a deadly weapon Wendle!

WENDLE   Oh just fucking go back to those white people... you love white people so much just fucking go back to them. If you didn't hang around those people you wouldn't be the way you are!

ALEX   What did you just say?

WENDLE   Nothing.

ALEX   What the fuck was that supposed to mean.

WENDLE   You know I didn't say what I said. Alex, you know I didn't mean...

    ALEX exits.

WENDLE   Oh fuck off Alex! You know I didn't mean what you thought I meant. Alex... Alex. Fuck you man. Fuck you.

    WENDLE grabs his books. He turns to EFFIE.

WENDLE   I didn't mean it the way it came out.

GRACE   I need a slogan.

EFFIE   Yeah.

    WENDLE sees he is being ignored. Goes upstairs.

GRACE   I can only take so much of that man.

EFFIE   He reminds me of my father. It really pisses me off.

GRACE   Okay. Think think think... slogan.

EFFIE   Can I turn on some music?

GRACE   No. God I don't want to hear no more o dat damn Trini music in this house...

EFFIE   What's wrong with Trini music?

    GRACE stands and moves her hips.

GRACE   "Cent, five cent, ten cent... Loonie."

EFFIE   Sit.

GRACE   It's not my fault people from Trinidad can't write good music. Why should I have to suffer to listen to it.

    EFFIE hits her with the newspaper.

GRACE   That hurt!

EFFIE   Good.

    GRACE points to the cardboard and marker.

GRACE   Get to work!

EFFIE   Didn't you just go to a rally like, yesterday?

GRACE   Don't get me started.

EFFIE   Started on what?

GRACE   It was a rally organized by the black community because there had been another shooting of a black youth by the police. Bob Rae showed up because he has always shown up even before he was Premier. I don't see *nobody* from the Liberal party, *nobody* from the Conservative party. He opens his mouth, not two seconds later, you have these white men screaming, "Hey Bob, what's the story, why you acting like a Tory."

EFFIE   Really.

GRACE   You have a bunch of white men from the so-called labour movement shouting down the only provincial leader that has promised to strengthen employment equity...

EFFIE   Did...

GRACE   And the white men on Bay street are paying for big billboards ridiculing him, and they don't give a damn that a young black man is dead. Let the man do his work before we tear him to pieces.

EFFIE   Why don't you write "I love you Bob".

GRACE   Alright alright.

EFFIE   Seriously. In big block letters "Bob, do me."

GRACE   Alright already.

EFFIE   You'd fuck Bob Rae wouldn't you.

GRACE   I think he's cute. I don't know if I'd go all the way but yeah, I think he's cute.

EFFIE   Get the fuck out of here.

GRACE   What?

EFFIE   Get the fuck out of here.

GRACE   What.

EFFIE   You need serious help.

GRACE   As if you should talk, going after my eighteen-year-old brother.

EFFIE   So.

GRACE   So you're the freak.

EFFIE   Well you better tell him to stop walking around without a shirt on. I swear to God one day...

GRACE   Effie...

EFFIE   I know I know, he's not here to get laid, I know. It's just... After Alex fucking jumped out of the fucking closet, I need... you don't want to know what I need. So Bob Rae: do you think he's...

She motions with her hands to imply he has a large penis.

GRACE   Huge. You know the CN tower? Bigger.

EFFIE   Do you think it's bigger than Henry's?

GRACE says nothing.

EFFIE   No.

GRACE   Effie.

EFFIE   Henry has a small... no.

GRACE   Don't you dare tell anybody!

EFFIE   Awww, honey.

GRACE   Well it's not like... it's kinda... well...

GRACE tries to show EFFIE exactly how small it is.

EFFIE   But is it like...

GRACE   No, it's still pretty thick.

EFFIE   But he's got such a deep voice.

GRACE   Effie, you can't tell anybody. I'm serious. Don't.

EFFIE   Sure okay. Don't worry. You must really love him.

There is a knock at the door.

EFFIE   Who is it?

HENRY   Is anybody home?

EFFIE   Come on in Mr. Stubbs.

> *GRACE slaps EFFIE. HENRY opens the door and steps in. He is carrying a tool case. GRACE runs over to him and hugs him.*

HENRY   Sorry?

GRACE   Hello honey!

> *She kisses him.*

HENRY   What did I do wrong?

GRACE   Nothing...

HENRY   Hi Effie.

EFFIE   Hellooo.

HENRY   Could you help me with... I still have some tools to get out of the truck.

GRACE   Sure. Sure thing.

> *HENRY leaves. GRACE points at EFFIE on her way out. EFFIE grabs a paper towel roll and holds it to her groin. KIRK bounds down the stairs. EFFIE hides in the kitchen. He is carrying a knapsack and talking on the cordless phone.*

KIRK   I coming just now. You follow me? A'ight junior.

> *He returns the phone to the base and pulls a post it note off of it. He knits his brow and crumples it up. He thinks for a second and then opens the knapsack. EFFIE sneaks up behind him and jumps on his back.*

EFFIE   Where do you think you're going?

KIRK   Hey...

> *He carries her around the couch.*

EFFIE   You think you can just waltz out of here without telling me where you are going to and when you'll be back?! You've got another thing coming buster!

KIRK   I can do whatever I want.

EFFIE   Oh you think so do you.

KIRK   Get off me.

EFFIE   No.

KIRK   Get off me.

EFFIE   Make me.

KIRK   Get off!

He tosses her on the couch.

EFFIE   I can't believe you just did that!

KIRK   Oh yeah.

EFFIE   Help me up.

He takes her hand and helps her up. She hits him really hard in the abdomen. He is winded a bit.

EFFIE   Are you okay? I didn't mean to hit you that hard. Honestly. Are you okay?

KIRK   You wanna box with Kirk eh?

He circles the couch, she follows him.

EFFIE   I wouldn't want to hurt you.

KIRK   You can't hurt me.

EFFIE   Don't make me hurt you.

KIRK   Come on. Let's go.

EFFIE   I'm warning you.

EFFIE takes a Jujitsu stance.

EFFIE   Don't make me hurt you. Take your best shot. Go ahead.

> *KIRK tags her shoulder with an open hand.*

EFFIE   Oh that really hurt. Have you met my side kick?

> *EFFIE makes a well placed martial arts kick to his thigh. He tries the same. She grabs his leg and strikes out with her fist, stopping ever so near his groin.*

EFFIE   I could have got you! I didn't, but I could have. Are you scared?

KIRK   A little.

> *KIRK does a Bruce Lee battle cry and tries to dazzle her with improvised Kung Fu moves. EFFIE laughs, grabs one of his arms and holds him close. She kisses him. She shoves him on the couch. He grabs her and they kiss passionately. A truck door closes outside. EFFIE pulls away. KIRK tries to continue, EFFIE shoves him away. We can hear GRACE and HENRY talking outside.*

GRACE   (*off-stage*) So I couldn't go to that class.

HENRY   (*off-stage*) Oh yeah.

EFFIE   Go. Go. Get going. Quick.

KIRK   No don't do that.

> *EFFIE grabs his knapsack, as she picks it up, the contents fall out, a video cassette, a walkman, and a gun. They both see it. KIRK grabs everything and stuffs it all back in his knapsack. The door opens. EFFIE and KIRK look at each other. GRACE and HENRY walk in carrying boxes of tools.*

GRACE   Then, I was late for my aerobics so I didn't go to that either...

HENRY   Didn't you read that book I gave you about prioritizing?

GRACE   No, not yet.

> *KIRK leaves, pushing past them.*

GRACE   What's going on?

EFFIE   Nothing.

GRACE   What did you just do.

EFFIE　　Nothing.

　　　　　EFFIE goes to the backyard. GRACE knits her brow and shakes her head.

HENRY　　If you want things to happen you are going to have to prioritize.

GRACE　　Look, I know I'm not the most prompt person in the world.

HENRY　　Why don't you drop your aerobics class, I mean, I like you big anyway.... I mean I like you the way you are... I mean... could you pass me that box?

　　　　　She does. EFFIE walks back in and sits on the couch.

EFFIE　　Guys.

　　　　　They both look at EFFIE.

EFFIE　　I have to talk to you.

HENRY　　Are you okay?

EFFIE　　Grace.

　　　　　EFFIE motions for them to sit on the couch. They do.

EFFIE　　Kirk has a gun.

GRACE　　What?!

EFFIE　　We were goofing around and I saw it in his knapsack.

　　　　　ALEX stumbles into the room with a bunch of videos. He's been drinking.

ALEX　　Is the sound fixed yet?

HENRY　　No not yet.

EFFIE　　Alex come here.

ALEX　　What. What's wrong? What?

GRACE　　Effie found a gun in Kirk's knapsack.

EFFIE　　We were play-fighting and I saw it.

ALEX   Fuck.

GRACE   (*in a Jamaican accent*) Stupid. Stupid. Fucking idiot.

ALEX   What are we going to do?

EFFIE   I think we should call a house meeting right now.

GRACE   Good idea. Is Wendle here?

EFFIE   He's upstairs. I think he's taking a nap.

>   *GRACE jumps up and goes upstairs.*

ALEX   Henry, is the sound fixed yet?

HENRY   No, not yet. I may have it fixed by tonight, don't hold your breath.

EFFIE   Why? What'd you get?

>   *WENDLE walks down the stairs with GRACE. ALEX does his best Marlon Brando.*

ALEX   "On the Waterfront" and "Guys and Dolls". It's a Marlon Brando extravaganza this evening ladies and gentlemen...

WENDLE   So what's going on.

EFFIE   I was goofing around with Kirk and I found a gun in his knapsack.

>   *Another moment of silence.*

ALEX   Well I think we should talk to him. Find out what's going on...

WENDLE   I want him out of this house and that's it.

>   *WENDLE stands up to leave.*

ALEX   Now hold on a second...

WENDLE   Don't hold on a second me! I don't want to have to worry about some niggers driving by and plugging my body full of holes! I had enough trouble with fucking white kids beating the shit out of me all through high school, I don't need to worry about some fucking dumb nigger with a fucking Uzi ripping apart my fucking living room!

ALEX   I don't think what's needed here is a lot of anger.

WENDLE   I'm not angry. No. I'm hurt. I welcomed him into my home. I treated him like a brother. No. Send the fucking nigger back to Jamaica.

GRACE   What the hell is that supposed to mean?

WENDLE   You heard me. If he doesn't want to live and abide by the laws of my country, send the fucking nigger back to Jamaica.

GRACE   (*shouting*) What the hell do you mean your country? I'm Jamaican and this is just as much my country as it is yours.

WENDLE   The hell you mean you're Jamaican. You were raised in Montreal since you were three! I don't give a fuck where you were born. I don't give a fuck about that little accent you pull out every now and then, you as Jamaican as fucking Henry.

HENRY   What about all the things you said about swimming together. I mean Kirk is a stranger to this country. He is an immigrant like me and...

WENDLE   You ever pick up a gun?

HENRY   No, but I mean, it's not easy being an immigrant in this country, especially if you're black they don't respect your education your training...

WENDLE   Have you ever picked up a gun?

HENRY   No but surely we have to try harder to reach out to him...

WENDLE   (*shouting*) Have you ever fucking picked up a motherfucking gun?!

HENRY   No.

WENDLE   No. No you haven't. And I know it's going to be hard for you to hear me say this, but it's the way I feel; I am sick and tired of these fucking Jamaicans coming into this country and doing crack and shooting each other and shit!

GRACE knocks over a chair and goes into the backyard.

ALEX   Wendle.

WENDLE   I'm sick of it. Every news report; you don't see any Somali's shooting each other do ya. Why? Cause they are grateful to be in this country, as they damn well should be.

        HENRY leaves.

EFFIE   You're such a fucking asshole.

WENDLE   I'm not going to lie about the way I feel.

ALEX   So what do you think we should do.

EFFIE   I think you had a good idea. I'll see if I can talk to Kirk. Find out what's going on.

ALEX   Meeting adjourned?

EFFIE   Yeah, I'll tell Grace.

WENDLE   You understand where I'm coming from right?

EFFIE   It's okay Wendle.

WENDLE   I mean, I can't be untrue to what I feel.

EFFIE   I know.

WENDLE   You're not mad at me are you?

EFFIE   Why would I be mad at you Wendle.

WENDLE   If anybody calls, I'm taking a nap.

EFFIE   Okay.

        WENDLE gets up and goes upstairs. EFFIE realizes that she is alone with ALEX. She heads for the stairs.

ALEX   Can we call a truce for five minutes.

EFFIE   Sure.

ALEX   Grace wants you to slow down with Kirk.

EFFIE   If Grace has anything she wants to say to me, she can say it to my face.

ALEX   I think you should slow down with Kirk.

EFFIE	It's none of your fucking business.
ALEX	I don't think that was five minutes.
EFFIE	Guess not.
ALEX	I want to stop this antagonism. I find it incredibly childish.
EFFIE	You lied to me. You put my life at risk...
ALEX	I didn't put your life at risk!

ALEX (*shouting*) Oh for fucks sake, everything that I did with him was absolutely safe, I made sure that everything we did was absolutely safe. I would never...

EFFIE (*shouting*) You could have infected me with... how do you expect me to... how do I know that! How do I know that!!!

Silence.

ALEX	Being gay doesn't mean you have AIDS.
EFFIE	I don't want to talk about this with you anymore. I get sick. I find it... I find it disgusting. It makes me ill.
ALEX	When are you moving out?
EFFIE	Not soon enough.

She walks away.

ALEX I don't want you to move out. I don't. I'm sorry about what happened and the way you found out. I am. I am very very sorry. I want... I want to be your friend.

EFFIE No.

EFFIE goes upstairs. ALEX sits on the couch. KIRK walks in the front door without his knapsack.

KIRK Alex?

GRACE and HENRY enter the living room. She sees KIRK.

GRACE You. Come here.

ALEX   Uh, Grace, maybe you should talk to Effie first.

GRACE   Why the hell would I want to talk to Effie? You. Come. Now.

          He walks towards her.

GRACE   Move yer ass. Move it!

          GRACE shoves him outside. ALEX pours himself a stiff drink.

GRACE   (*off-stage*) What the hell you mean you don't know... because you've embarrassed me, you embarrass me in front of me friends.

HENRY   Are you going to the rally?

ALEX   I don't know. Are you?

HENRY   Unless I can find a really good excuse.

GRACE   (*off-stage*) Listen now Kirk, I don't want to hear anymore of ya nonsense! Lord give me the pillow and take the case!

HENRY   How are you doing? Are you okay?

ALEX   Yeah I'm fine. Do you mind if I turn the TV around?

HENRY   No. Go ahead.

          ALEX turns the TV around. Turns it on.

ALEX   Anything in particular you want to watch?

HENRY   No, no. I've been thinking about filing a complaint with the police.

ALEX   And...

HENRY   ... if I went, would you go with me?

ALEX   Sure. Of course.

HENRY   Because I... I would like you to go with me.

ALEX   Sure.

HENRY   You're from Ottawa right?

ALEX   Yup. Born and raised.

HENRY   Did you have to deal with a lot of racism when you were growing up?

ALEX   Not really. No. I had some kids make fun of my hair in grade school, but that's just... kids being kids.

HENRY   What about your parents?

ALEX   I don't know. I don't think so. If they did, they never told me. Then again, I spent a lot of time in boarding school so... why do you ask?

HENRY   Just curious.

ALEX   Oh.

Short pause.

HENRY   Sometimes I think that after three hundred years of revolt and riots and discussion and reconstruction and Martin Luther King and Rosa Parks and Marcus Garvey and Mandela and all the others, we... I wish we could just stop. We could just stop and we could just make our own way and not have to struggle all the time to prove that we are equal. And when I see a black person has committed a crime in the newspaper, I don't feel that he is jeopardizing three hundred years of hard work. And if that one person commits a crime, it's because he's human, and sometimes, that's what human beings do. Know what I mean?

ALEX   Yes.

KIRK and GRACE come back inside.

GRACE   Kirk has something he wants to say.

KIRK   I just want to say how sorry I am. I know that you all care for me and if you give me one more chance, I know I won't let you down.

HENRY   Okay.

ALEX   Okay.

GRACE   I'm going to get Wendle and Effie. You stay here.

GRACE goes upstairs. Once she is out of earshot...

ALEX   She took a chunk out of you didn't she.

KIRK	Booooy ya don't know.
ALEX	You don't mess with Jamaican women man.
KIRK	I know it. I know it.
ALEX	So... you know you fucked up right?
KIRK	Yes sir.
ALEX	Don't call me sir.
HENRY	Was it your gun or what's going on...
KIRK	No, no, see... I got this friend, he's not really a friend... I just know him right? He give me this bag to hold for him. I don't know what's in it and I don't want to know. But upstairs, I get kinda curious. I look in it, I see the gun, boom. I call him up right away, ya following me? I tell him, "Junior, I don't want this thing here in my possession" and as I'm taking it to him, Effie find it in the bag. I don't blame her for being shocked right? Cause I was shock just the same way. But I am telling you... I have nothing to do with that gun, you understand? You understand?
ALEX	Yeah I understand, I just don't think you should hang out with this guy anymore.
KIRK	True, true.
ALEX	You want to go out, you want to go for beer or play pool, give me a shout, alright?
KIRK	Cool.

> *ALEX shakes KIRK's hand. KIRK puts his arm around ALEX in a semi-hug.*

ALEX	It's alright.
KIRK	And Henry, I really appreciate what all you done for me.

> *He shakes HENRY's hand.*

HENRY	I still need some help, if you...
GRACE	(*off-stage*) Kirk, could you come up here please.
KIRK	I'll be back.

KIRK rushes upstairs.

ALEX   So what do you think.

HENRY   What do you think?

ALEX   I don't know. I... I don't know.

HENRY   Well, we all have to stick together.

ALEX   That's right. Yeah.

Blackout.

ACT III

SCENE I

WENDLE sits studying at the dining table with a calculator and notebook. HENRY has pulled apart the television and is putting it back together.

WENDLE So how are the repairs coming. Henry? Henry. Henry.

HENRY Yes.

WENDLE How are the repairs.

HENRY Fine.

WENDLE Need a hand? Henry.

HENRY What?

WENDLE Need a hand?

HENRY No.

WENDLE Alright.

GRACE walks in the front door.

WENDLE How was the protest. Grace. Grace.

GRACE Hmm?

WENDLE How was the protest.

GRACE Great.

WENDLE Was there any violence?

GRACE No.

WENDLE Well that's good.

GRACE starts walking up the stairs. She stops.

GRACE Don't talk to me like there is nothing going on. I hate that.

WENDLE Alright.

GRACE   My aunt and uncle are from Jamaica. They worked their finger to the bone trying to make it in this country. My aunt worked as a maid and my uncle worked as a trolley car porter because in Montreal in those days, those were the jobs they gave to black people. They saved every penny they had to give me the education they felt I deserved. And they are not alone. All over this country there are Jamaicans just like them, and even though I was raised in Montreal, I was born in Jamaica and I am proud to call it my place of birth just as I am proud of the people who come from it.

She walks towards the stairs.

WENDLE   Grace. Don't go. Listen, when I get angry I say stupid things.

GRACE   I know.

WENDLE   I guess I've been reading the *Toronto Sun* too much.

GRACE   Don't read the *Sun*.

WENDLE   I read it for the sports page.

GRACE   You know the Heritage Front says that most of the things you hear on its phone line you can read in an editorial of the *Toronto Sun*.

WENDLE   So? The fuck do I care, they have a great sports page.

GRACE   Have mercy.

    GRACE goes upstairs. EFFIE and ALEX burst in the door. ALEX has a bloody piece of cloth and is pinching the bridge of his nose.

EFFIE   Help somebody! Quick!

ALEX   I'm alright. Really.

WENDLE   What the fuck!!!

HENRY   Grace!!!

    HENRY and WENDLE run to help EFFIE and ALEX.

ALEX   It just looks bad, that's all.

HENRY   I'll get some ice. Grace!

ALEX   No nonono. I think it's dried. See?

        He stops pinching. GRACE enters.

HENRY   Come to the sink and get cleaned up. Grace.

ALEX   I don't need to be cleaned up.

EFFIE   Wendle, go to the kitchen, fill a bowl with warm water and grab a clean towel.

GRACE   I'll get the towel.

        WENDLE and GRACE leave.

HENRY   How did this happen?

ALEX   Someone started a fight. I stuck my nose in there, got a little love tap. I'm fine.

HENRY   People are fighting each other?

EFFIE   Henry... there's a riot on Yonge street.

ALEX   I don't know if I would call it a riot. It is definitely a melee.

HENRY   Where's Kirk?

        EFFIE and ALEX look at each other.

ALEX   Well, I thought he was...

EFFIE   We don't know where he is.

        GRACE and WENDLE return with towel and bowl. ALEX cleans himself.

WENDLE   So what happened man, are you okay?

HENRY   There's a riot on Yonge street.

GRACE   Where's Kirk.

HENRY   Grab your jacket, lets go look for him.

        HENRY and GRACE jump up and get ready to leave.

EFFIE   Wait, I'm going too. Let me just get my camera.

EFFIE grabs her camera from the bookshelf.

GRACE   Where did you see him last?

        They head out talking. WENDLE closes the door. ALEX
        cleans himself and pours himself a drink.

ALEX   Man.

WENDLE   So what happened?

ALEX   Uh, there was the protest in front of the US embassy. There
were some Nazi skinheads across the street shouting stuff.
Then a black woman leaves the crowd, runs across the street
and does a flying leap kick at the biggest Nazi skinhead of
them all. He falls, they all just scatter, like that.

WENDLE   Major props to our beautiful black sisters.

ALEX   Here here.

WENDLE   So that's when the fighting started?

ALEX   No nono. So we got up to Queens Park. People started to sit
in the middle of the intersections. And then the cops came.
Some people got really roughed up. We headed down... let's
see, I think that's when we got split up. I went down Bay
street. And then someone threw a rock through a window...

WENDLE   That's when it started?

ALEX   Well, kinda. It's like... it was sort of scary, but it was still kind
of Canadian, you know... it's like, there was violence, but it
was still kinda polite violence. I don't know.

WENDLE   Were there a lot of black people?

ALEX   Well... the crowd was mixed... I don't know...

WENDLE   How'd you get the nose?

ALEX   Oh! Then I crossed over to Church street. I just caught a
glimpse of what was happening on Yonge and it looked a lot
more violent. A lot of young kids, angry, smashing store windows and just grabbing stuff. I just got a glimpse of what was
happening. I'm passing through this parking lot on Church
and this Global cameraman is standing there, black guy starts
shoving him around. I pull him off and he cold cocks me.

WENDLE   Oh.

ALEX   I couldn't believe it. Some motherfucker starts going, "You oppressive white bastard." Right? But who does he hit, he hits me. You've got to go out there. It's wild out there.

WENDLE   No it's okay.

ALEX   No I mean it man, you got to.

WENDLE   It wouldn't be a good idea for me to go out there right now.

ALEX   Hey I understand. You're being responsible. That's good. Well I'm going back out there.

WENDLE   Alex. Be careful.

> *ALEX leaves. KIRK runs in through the backdoor. He is carrying a brand new Camcorder in his hand. He is out of breath. He drops the Camcorder on the couch and catches his breath.*

WENDLE   Don't you move. Everyone is looking for you.

KIRK   Wendle.

WENDLE   What's that you got there?

KIRK   Someone smash a window on some store on Yonge street. Then a whole crowd just start passing the stuff out...

WENDLE   No no no no no no...

KIRK   I didn't steal it, I swear! I swear I didn't steal it! I'm not in for stealing or nothing, but when it is put in you hand you know you can't refuse.

WENDLE   Tomorrow morning you are going to take that back. Stay right here till Grace gets back.

KIRK   But...

WENDLE   No. No no no no. Fuck you. No buts.

KIRK   But...

WENDLE   You have any idea who you're talking to? You are talking to a man who is going to own a store like that one day. You're looking at a man who is going to own a whole chain of stores just like that. Your taking it back tomorrow.

KIRK   Yes sir.

WENDLE   You understand me?

KIRK   Yes sir.

KIRK is about to step out the front door.

WENDLE   (*shouting*) Hey!

He stops.

WENDLE   You stay right there and don't move till Grace gets back.

KIRK sits, one hand on his crotch. WENDLE shakes his head and goes to his room. EFFIE walks in the front door.

EFFIE   Are you okay?

EFFIE puts her camera on the table. While her back is turned, he shoves the video camera under a cushion of the couch.

EFFIE   What, you're not talking to me? Hey.

She touches his head. He sharply pulls away.

EFFIE   You know what? I'll tell you a secret. And this is a... I used to be a really fat and ugly kid. It's true, I know you find that hard to believe. And uh... I grew up in Vancouver... it was just my Mom and me and in the early eighties she lost her job, so we had no money. She had a nervous breakdown, I have to take care of her, I'm fat, ugly, and... I went through a thing that... that was so painful. And I wanted so much to... for someone to reach out and put their hand on my shoulder and reach out to me, but I didn't trust anyone. I couldn't because I had so much pain inside that if I let someone touch me they could hurt me too. People tried to reach out to me and I lashed out at them. And then I wanted to destroy myself. I just wanted... I wanted...

EFFIE slowly places her hand on his shoulder.

EFFIE   Shhh.

These next two lines overlap.

KIRK   But you don't know, you don't know...

EFFIE   Yes I do. Yes I do.

> *WENDLE walks down the stairs with a textbook and calculator in hand. He stops when he sees them in an embrace. He continues down the stairs. KIRK and EFFIE pull apart.*

EFFIE   Want a glass of water or something?

> *KIRK shrugs. EFFIE goes to the kitchen. WENDLE walks to the table. Stands there.*

WENDLE   So, things are crazy out there.

KIRK   Yeah man.

WENDLE   You didn't do any fighting did you.

KIRK   Some faggot try to rough me up but I...

WENDLE   Watch the language.

KIRK   Yes sir.

> *WENDLE stops working and looks up from his books at KIRK. EFFIE returns with the water.*

WENDLE   Don't use the word faggot around Alex.

KIRK   Why.

WENDLE   Cause he's gay.

KIRK   What!

WENDLE   He's gay.

KIRK   You joking.

WENDLE   No. No I'm not.

KIRK   Alex a faggot?

WENDLE   Just thought I'd let you know.

> *GRACE, HENRY and ALEX return. GRACE rushes over to KIRK. ALEX goes towards his bottle.*

GRACE   Are you okay? I was worried there for a moment.

KIRK   I'm fine.

ALEX   That's what I told them.

KIRK   I'm fine.

EFFIE   Alex is a hero, he saved a white man.

ALEX   Oh it was nothing, really.

> *WENDLE walks over to the couch. He looks for the Camcorder.*

WENDLE   Where is it?

GRACE   What...

> *WENDLE rifles through the cushions. Finds the Camcorder. Hands it to GRACE.*

GRACE   What is this?

KIRK   I can explain.

WENDLE   He's taking it back tomorrow morning.

GRACE   What the hell is this?

KIRK   I can explain. I was walking through the crowd, somebody walk up to me and shove it in my hand, I swear I didn't steal it. Don't look at me like that! I'm telling you the truth! You're just like Auntie June, you never believe me! I am...

GRACE   Shut up.

KIRK   I swear I swear I swear...

GRACE   (*shouting*) Shut up!

EFFIE   I think...

GRACE   Shhhh!

> *She puts the Camcorder down. She takes a finger and pokes his head.*

KIRK   Don't do that.

GRACE   You don't like that?

KIRK   I telling you, don't do that.

GRACE   I am supposed to be looking out for you...

KIRK   I...

GRACE   Shut *up*! I don't know what to say to you anymore. Are you stupid?! Are you insane?! All these people working hard, for you. Do you not care?

ALEX   Grace...

GRACE   *Shut the fuck up*... you are on probation for one crime and you commit another. What are we supposed to do for you now. Are we supposed to lie to your probation officer when he finds out that you were looting, do you want us to lie? Is that what you want!? Let me ask you something Kirk, do you think that I had all of this? Hmmm? Do you think I had all this?!

> *She shoves him.*

ALEX   Grace...

GRACE   Do you think I had people caring for me willing to give me chance after chance after chance!!!

> *She starts slapping him around. She unintentionally shoves him towards ALEX. ALEX tries to pull KIRK away from her.*

KIRK   Don't touch me!

EFFIE   Grace!

ALEX   Come on, Grace!

> *She continues to shove him. ALEX touches KIRK's shoulder.*

KIRK   Don't touch me!

> *ALEX tries to step in between KIRK and GRACE. He holds KIRK's shoulders, in the process. KIRK shoves ALEX down violently.*

KIRK   Just get your faggoty hands off me! Fucking faggot. Right.

> *He pulls out a gun. He fires it twice in the air.*

KIRK   Y'all pretend but ya don't give a damn about me. What, you think I don't know? You think I don't know shame? Eh?

> *He places the gun to ALEX's back.*

KIRK   Hear me? You think I don't know shame? I gonna ask you one more time, you think I don't know shame?

ALEX   Yes you know shame.

> *He backs away and spits on ALEX.*

KIRK   Check it. I gone.

> *He exits. Silence. EFFIE goes after him.*

WENDLE   Well, if the landlady had any doubts that this was a crack house, the two bullets in the ceiling will definitely help.

> *EFFIE goes to the phone. HENRY goes to GRACE and hugs her.*

HENRY   You okay?

WENDLE   We should all go. The police are going to be here. Alex.

EFFIE   Hello? Yes, I'd like to talk to... who's in charge of uh... of uh...

WENDLE   Henry, we should get out of here in case the police get here with their guns out. Henry?

> *HENRY looks at GRACE. She nods. HENRY and GRACE stand and walk out the door.*

EFFIE   Well it's just that a couple of fire crackers went off in my house and I just wanted to tell them in case they... but I just want to tell them in case...

WENDLE   Alex. We should leave for a while. Alex.

EFFIE   Have you had a report of gunfire?

WENDLE   Come on. Alex. We have to go. We have to go now. Effie?

> *WENDLE pulls ALEX towards the door.*

EFFIE   It was just a couple of firecrackers. I know but... but why. Okay... I understand but... but...

> *Blackout.*

> *Lights up. ALEX enters, pours himself a Scotch, sits on the couch. Bags of luggage at the base of the stairs. GRACE enters from the front door and goes upstairs. ALEX looks for the remote. He finds it, but does not turn the TV on. HENRY enters as GRACE walks down the stairs with EFFIE's stereo in a box.*

HENRY　You okay?

GRACE　Yeah.

> *She struggles with it.*

ALEX　Henry, is the sound fixed?

HENRY　No, not yet.

GRACE　You could give us a fucking hand here.

> *ALEX jumps up, and walks over and takes the box from GRACE. HENRY goes to EFFIE's room.*

HENRY　Actually I don't think there is anything left.

ALEX　I could help take the stuff to the car?

HENRY　The trunk's not open yet.

GRACE　Open it.

HENRY　Is that a command?

GRACE　It's not a command, but why do something half way. Open the trunk so that we don't have to stop. You do things and then you don't finish them. It drives me crazy.

HENRY　Here.

> *HENRY gives the keys to ALEX and goes upstairs.*

ALEX　I'll go open the trunk.

> *ALEX leaves. WENDLE enters with some groceries. He goes to the kitchen. EFFIE walks down the stairs.*

EFFIE　Thanks a lot for helping me.

GRACE　No problem.

EFFIE   So call me tonight. We'll go out.

GRACE   All right.

EFFIE   Promise?

GRACE   Promise.

EFFIE   No you won't.

GRACE   I will, I swear.

        The phone rings. GRACE gets it.

GRACE   Hello. Effie?

        EFFIE shakes her head.

GRACE   She's not in right now can I take a message? Okay. Right.
Okay. Yes. Bye. That was your Mom. She wants you to call
her with your new number.

EFFIE   I fuckin' gave it to her already. She's such a ditz.

        ALEX returns.

ALEX   Is all this stuff going too?

EFFIE   Actually, leave that. Henry?

HENRY   Yes?

EFFIE   Before we move anything, could you drive me to a hardware
store? I have to get some keys copied before they close.

HENRY   Sure no problem.

        EFFIE hugs GRACE.

ALEX   Well, see you later.

EFFIE   I'll be back in a half hour.

ALEX   But I might not be here when you get back so...

EFFIE   All right. Well... all right.

        *ALEX hugs her. She doesn't hug back. ALEX goes to the
        couch and turns on the television.*

EFFIE   Good-bye Wendle.

WENDLE   What!

EFFIE   I'm heading out.

WENDLE   All right.

EFFIE   Are you leaving in the next twenty minutes?

WENDLE   No.

EFFIE   Then I'll say good-bye when I come back.

WENDLE   Hey, fill your boots.

EFFIE   What?

WENDLE   Do what you have to do, I'll be here when you get back.

> *EFFIE nods, grabs her purse and heads out the door.*

ALEX   Bye Henry.

HENRY   See you in a bit.

> *HENRY blows GRACE a kiss and leaves. WENDLE goes to the backyard, reads a magazine. GRACE starts walking upstairs to her room. The phone rings. ALEX gets it.*

ALEX   Hello. Hello. Hello Kirk.

> *GRACE stops.*

ALEX   I think she's here. Hold on a second.

> *GRACE takes the receiver. ALEX goes to the kitchen.*

GRACE   Hello? Hi. Yeah. I'm okay. How are you... where are you. I see. I see. No. Well, I feel that I want a second chance. Uh huhn, no but you see. Well... well if you think that's what's right for you... I said if you think that's what's right for you then I can't really argue can I. No I can't. Okay. Right. Well, it would be good if your stuff was gone by the end of the month because... because Henry is moving into your room. Yeah. Okay, well the sooner the better. Right. Okay. Okay. Bye. Kirk... remember when Grandma stayed with us? It was the Easter just after you had the chicken pox.

GRACE   (*continuing*) Yeah... and she would sit there watching televi-
          sion... an she would take out her teeth and chew on the apples
          and spit out all the skin into a Kleenex... and then she would
          get me to carry the skin to the garbage... *me*. You lie... Oh
          Lord I can still remember the feel o dat mush in me hand. An'
          it all mix up wid de spit. (*she sucks her teeth*) my hand drippin'
          wid it. *You did not.* Oh that is such a lie. That is such a lie.
          Anyway, I was just thinkin' about her yesterday, and I just
          thought I'd tell you. What?... okay. Yes. Thank you for call-
          ing. Bye.

ALEX   What'd he say?

GRACE   He's fine.

ALEX   Where is he.

GRACE   Buffalo.

ALEX   Buffalo?

GRACE   Yeah.

          *GRACE sits on the couch. ALEX looks to refill his drink but
          the bottle is empty.*

ALEX   I remember when I was a kid, we had a big house; two-car
          garage, big backyard, pool, barbecue, the whole bit. Some
          days when I was sick, or when there was a PD day or some-
          thing, I would get to leave school early. And I would run
          home and my Nanny would be there to look after my little sis-
          ter and she would have the ironing board set up right in front
          of the television, smoking her Craven A cigarettes eh, watching
          like... "Coronation Street" eh, or news reports about guerrillas
          hijacking planes to Cuba. And Pierre Trudeau was the coolest.
          We had no idea why, he just was, he was the coolest. And on
          those days when I was in a bad mood or something, I would
          go out into the backyard, and I would lay down on the grass
          and look up at the big blue sky and... and I'd just get these gig-
          gling fits right? Cause it would just strike me that Canada is
          so big. I mean, it's huge right? So I would jump up and try to
          see all the way over to Halifax but it was too far. Okay, so I'd
          jump up and try to see all the way over to Vancouver, but it
          was too far. Okay so I would stretch my arms out and try to
          touch the edge of Canada, but it was way too big. So I would
          flop on my stomach and grab fistfuls of grass and I would hug
          Canada. And you know what... if you stay really really really
          still, after a while, it almost feels like Canada is hugging you
          back. And I miss that feeling. I really do.

> *He looks at her. He holds his arms out. She leans into his arms, he hugs her.*

ALEX   Shhh. Hey, Grace. Hey look. Look. See? We made CNN.

> *Curtain.*

Coups And Calypsos

by M. Nourbese Philip

M. Nourbese Philip is a poet, novelist, essayist and play-wright who lives in Toronto. Her short stories, essays, reviews and articles have appeared in magazines and journals in Canada, the United Kingdom and the United States of America, and her poetry and prose have been extensively anthologised. M. Nourbese Philip has written two plays, *The Redemption of Al Bumen* and the 1999 Dora award finalist, *Coups and Calypsos*, which was produced in Toronto and London in 1999.

Introduction to Coups And Calypsos

by Ramabai Espinet

M. Nourbese Philip's play, *Coups And Calypsos*, created quite a buzz in the diasporic Caribbean community in Toronto when it was first staged by Cahoots Theatre as a workshop production in 1997. People were curious and expectant. This was "us" being dramatised on stage—our secrets and lies, our neuroses—a dramatisation of one of our most hidden areas, that of racial mixing or "douglarisation" in the Caribbean.

"Douglarisation"[1] refers to racial mixing in a reproductive context in Trinidad and Tobago where Indian and African populations are concentrated in almost equal numbers. The children of such unions are called "dougla," which is simply the extant Hindi variety for the word "two," but various negative connotations have evolved over time including the stigma of bastardisation. "Douglarisation" itself is a singularly nuanced term depending on which group uses it. It is fair to say that to a great extent in the Indian community its usage is tinged with regret and in extreme cases, fear and even horror, while in the African sector its register is more muted.

As one early anthropologist put it, both races hold each other in "hearty contempt." Such contemptuous attitudes are, of course, deeply inflected by the region's history of colonialism, slavery and indentureship, resulting even to the present day, *malgre tout*, in the continuing reinforcement of the European phenotype as the ideal, European institutions and ways of seeing as the norm, and all other approximations evaluated on such a scale of value.

The play situates itself within a dialogue about these racialised responses to douglarisation, dissected within the intimate space of a failed marriage. It is set in the island of Tobago. The protagonists possess highly educated minds, and function within a sophisticated racial discourse which is by no means common to the citizenry of Trinidad and Tobago. Presumably unions such as theirs occur in the twin-island state with regularity, and along a continuum of familial and societal responses which may range from acceptance to tolerance to downright hostility, but their present outsiderhood allows them the liberty of engaging in an anatomy of why their love could not survive, without reference to contemporary racetalk in Trinidad & Tobago.

The framing of this play within the context of the historical 1990 coup where people are actually killed, and at a stage in the action when the resolution is entirely unknown, provides occasion for an oblique commentary on the lack of awareness and social consciousness of the society. [Mis]information about the coup and the actions of the revolutionaries is broadcast sporadically, punctuated by episodes of calypso music. This presentation of frivolity in public response is further underlined by Elvira's disgust at "curfew parties" and Mrs. Samuels' continued references to the "coup" as "coop," a wire-enclosed fowl-run. The protagonists' status as visitors to the islands of their birth distance them from the immediate repercussions of the coup. Unanswered questions arise though, about its political implications, especially since voice is given to the history of labour activism and workers' riots in the country through the ubiquity of Mrs. Samuels, who was personally present at each of these events.

Frequently, the teasing expostulations of the principals take us to just that point of rupture where an insight can burst through, but at such moments recoil is the chosen option and the intensity breaks. Such avoidance tactics mimic the dialogic resonances of race relations in Trinidad and Tobago which, in contrast to its South American neighbour Guyana, takes pride in the fact that with similar populations and competition for resources and political power, race riots have not broken out in the twin-island state between these two ethnic groups still managing to coexist in uneasy alliance with each other.

Certain facts and a continuing public debate about their significance are vital to understanding Philip's background for this play. In the author's notes she gives a brief history of the settlement of these islands. After the the abolition of slavery in 1834 in the Anglophone Caribbean, indentured workers from several countries were imported to provide cheap plantation labour. Indians (Hindus and a smaller percentage of Muslims) proved to be the most suitable and were brought to the Caribbean in large numbers between the years of 1838 and 1917. Conversion to Christianity (real or dissembled) and the embrace of the denominational (Presbyterian) system of education offered them in the Trinidad context proved to be a fruitful source of social mobility for Indians. The Canadian missionary, John Morton, arrived in Trinidad in 1867 and his ministry was directed almost exclusively to Indians in the south of the island, a fact commented upon bitterly by Elvira. The Christian connection is further underlined by the fact that one of Rohan's Christian names is Morton. Elvira's idiosyncratic appraisal of Morton's preferential treatment of Indians is not connected to any widespread African discontent in the Trinidad and Tobago context about this phenomenon since there were already several Christian missionary groups in the island ministering to Africans, but is uttered more as a personal comment meant to emphasise Rohan's parents' objections to their union on racial grounds.

The distancing of both protagonists from a live community mired in the workings out of a racial imbroglio, as it were, allows them a dizzying freedom in their analysis because there is no sounding board for testing their insights or the validity of their personal rages. Mrs. Samuels cannot serve that function because, as thorough as her experience of the history of a grassroots class struggle in Trinidad appears to be, her experience in race relations is not apparent. As well, her long residency in Tobago is likely to make such experience lean, since Tobago's native population is almost exclusively African. The lovers, when young, are situated in a very different environment, that of a rural racially mixed setting of working-class and peasant families, all of roughly the same social status. Their romance is an idyllic and deeply romantic village pastoral which seems to be set in the period of the mid sixties, and which coalesces into maturity and breakdown in a foreign place, England, only to be anatomized in another place, Tobago, to which they are now foreign.

Defining the context is a major issue in this play. The peculiarities of the socio-political context must be delineated if the dilemma of the characters is to provoke real engagement. The playwright rises to the challenge of performing this difficult task, while leaving the vexing question of "douglarisation" as unsettled as it is beyond the fourth wall.

Notes:
[1] A biracial individual of African/Indian origin in Trinidad and Tobago is known as a "dougla." The term "douglarisation" erupted in the late 1980s as part of a heated political (and very public) discussion of race. The term carries connotations of forced racial mixing and the fear of dilution of a "pure" racial stock on the part of Indians. On the other hand, such associations are defused by the irony and picong by which the calypso culture exists. The usage of the term is far from denotative.

Ramabai Espinet is an academic, a poet and a writer of fiction and essays. She is a Professor of English at Seneca College in Toronto and also teaches in the Caribbean Studies and Women's Studies programmes at New College, University of Toronto and in the English Department at York University. Works include: *Nuclear Seasons* (1991), *Creation Fire* (1990), *The Princess of Spadina* (1992), *Ninja's Carnival* (1993), and *Indian Robber Talk* (Performance: 1994).

Left to right:
Karen Robinson
Peter Deboran
Kathy Imrie

photo by Greg Tjepkema

Coups And Calypsos was first produced by Cahoots Theatre Projects in 1999 with the following cast:

ELVIRA JACKSON   Alison Sealey-Smith

ROHAN SANKAR   Errol Sitahal

MRS. SAMUELS   Denise Jones

Directed by Diane Roberts

CHARACTERS

ELVIRA JACKSON   An African Caribbean woman from Trinidad.

ROHAN SANKAR   A South Asian Caribbean man from Trinidad.

MRS. SAMUELS   An African Caribbean woman from Tobago.

Playwright's Notes

The islands of Trinidad and Tobago, lying to the northeast of the continent of South America, share a history of being owned by various European powers and play an integral part in the holocaust carried out by the Europeans against the Aboriginal and African peoples. The Europeans repopulated both islands with large numbers of Africans who had been forcibly removed from their homelands in Africa, stripped of their languages and cultures, and made to work in the production of sugar.

After the abolition of slavery in British colonies in 1834, plantation owners in Trinidad, unwilling to pay adequate wages to freed Africans, imported large numbers of indentured workers from India. These Indians were of Hindu and Muslim backgrounds and their life under indentureship was harsh.

While the Africans and Indians, constituting the two largest ethnic groups and virtually equal in size, share the land, theirs is not an easy relationship and tensions between the groups have been manipulated, if not exploited, by the politicians and religious leaders. Political parties have traditionally formed along the racial fault line.

Canadian Content

In 1987 the Reverend John Morton of the United Presbyterian Church of Canada established the first mission to the Indians of Trinidad. These Canadian missionaries saw "the Coolie system" as "the salvation of this Island." Their perceived role to elevate the Indian "to a position of true manhood" was based on their belief that "negroes are of a much lower type, and do not seem to have the genius for anything more intellectual or spiritual than drawing their breath."

1990

On July 27, 1990 the Jamaat al Muslimeen, comprised mainly of African Trinidadians, led by one Abu Bakr, attacked the Parliament and held the primarily African-based government hostage for six days. On August 1, 1990, the Muslimeen surrendered and were imprisoned. Since that time there have been lawsuits and counter suits between the government and the Muslimeen as to whether or not an amnesty deal had been made and which of the two parties would pay compensation for damage to property.

ACT I

SCENE I

The sea–side village of Black Rock, Tobago, 1990. Mid-afternoon. A wooden, one-bedroom house, compact and simply furnished. Shuttered windows. There is a small front porch with railings and steps which lead down to the beach. On the porch are two wooden rocking chairs facing out to the sea. There are two pieces of luggage, an overnight bag and a large suitcase.

A radio plays calypso music. ELVIRA is pacing up and down the room holding her passport and ticket.

ELVIRA   You were the last person I expected to see at the airport!

ROHAN   Something like your worst nightmare.

ELVIRA   Please don't start, Rohan.

ROHAN   Elvira, it's not every day I get the chance to rescue a damsel in distress. At the risk of being cliched – all's well that ends well – you're here now.

ELVIRA   You are being cliched, Rohan, and there's nothing that's "well" about this. It's a real piss off, that's what it is.

ROHAN   Why not make the best of it.

ELVIRA   I have to be back at work. I scheduled a meeting weeks ago for Monday.

ROHAN   The hospital will understand–

ELVIRA   I'll tell you what I don't understand, Rohan. I don't understand how you can have a confirmed ticket and still not be allowed to board your flight.

ROHAN   Didn't you show them your passport?

ELVIRA   The bloody idiots wouldn't even look at it! They said they were only taking tourists.

She puts the passport and ticket near to the telephone.

ROHAN   The place is a bit small, El, but–

ELVIRA   That's all right. There may be a flight out this evening. At worst
          there'll be one tomorrow.

ROHAN   I thought you could have the bed.

ELVIRA   And where will you sleep?

ROHAN   I can rough it – I brought my sleeping bag.

ELVIRA   I really don't want to inconvenience you. I would go to a hotel,
          but with so many people caught here there isn't a spare room in
          all of Tobago.

ROHAN   Elvira! I'm happy to have you here and I insist, you must have
          the bed–

RADIO   We interrupt this program to bring you an update on the events
          surrounding the coup. The Muslimeen have set fire to the police
          headquarters. The Army and the Muslimeen continue to
          exchange gunfire. As you know our own station TBS has been
          under siege since Wednesday, but we want to assure you that we
          are all safe. We will continue to broadcast for as long as we are
          able to. We are told that there are several casualties but we are
          unable to let you know–

          ELVIRA abruptly turns off the radio.

ELVIRA   I still can't believe this is really happening.

ROHAN   Can I get you something to drink? You must be hungry.

ELVIRA   A glass of water – as cold as you can make it. Please.

          *ROHAN leaves. ELVIRA turns on the radio. There is a sound
          of calypso music. ROHAN returns with two glasses of water.*

ROHAN   Leave it off, Elvira.

          She lowers the volume.

ELVIRA   How else are we going to find out what's going on?

ROHAN   Not from the radio. You heard them say the station's under
          siege. They're only able to broadcast information that people
          call into them.

ELVIRA   It's better than nothing.

ROHAN   The fact that the radio mentions something, Elvira, doesn't mean that it has happened. Nor does the fact that it doesn't mention an event mean that it isn't happening. Hasn't happened. Or won't happen for that matter.

ELVIRA   I'm not interested in lessons in logic, Rohan.

         He hands her the glass of water.

ROHAN   Why don't we go on the porch.

ELVIRA   I have never in my life heard so many prayers since the start of this coup – priest, pundit, minister, meditationist, levitator. All praying for deliverance while the bloody radio plays calypso! Yesterday one of them even suggested we should become concentrated points of light.

ROHAN   Given the options we have at present, that's as useful an action as any.

ELVIRA   You're not bothered by any of this, are you?

ROHAN   Look, I didn't get turned back at the airport – you have every right to be upset.

ELVIRA   I am not upset, Rohan, I am – hell what does it matter. There's no point taking it out on you.

ROHAN   That's a relief.

         She laughs.

ROHAN   What's so funny?

ELVIRA   The look on the ticket clerk's face when I told him that I would personally write to the Muslimeen and suggest that they come for him and all his co-workers when they were done with the politicians.

ROHAN   You did what?

ELVIRA   You heard me.

ROHAN   And they let you go?

ELVIRA   I'll always remember the look on that man's face. He was scared. Something I had said made him frightened. And guess what? I enjoyed it. I felt so powerless – so humiliated by what they had done to me. It was either that or using some racial epithet or insulting his mother. You know what I mean – you get to the point where you just want to lash out – to hurt back as much as you've been.

ROHAN   I'm surprised they didn't have you arrested.

ELVIRA   They called the soldiers for me – had me escorted out of the waiting room. In my own country – soldiers manhandling me–

ROHAN   You can't have it both ways, Elvira, you did say you were a tourist.

ELVIRA   I don't have it any way, Rohan. I don't get the advantages of being a tourist, and when I object to being treated unfairly I get handled like a common criminal. (*pause*) Are you going to spend all day on the gallery rocking and watching the sea?

ROHAN   What else is there to do, Elvira? (*pause*) And the word is porch not gallery.

ELVIRA   *I* grew up calling it gallery – and gallery it will remain.

ROHAN   Come on, El, sit with me. Look at the sea; look at the waves.

ELVIRA   You do believe there's a coup in Trinidad, don't you?

ROHAN   I most certainly do.

ELVIRA   And that it started the day before yesterday?

ROHAN   Yes.

ELVIRA   You got that through the radio, didn't you?

ROHAN   I've also seen troops in and around Scarborough *and* I called the police station. They assured me that something was, indeed, happening. In Trinidad.

ELVIRA   Rohan! Port of Spain is going up in smoke, people are being shot and you – you look at waves!

ROHAN   What else is there to do, Elvira? When Port of Spain is going up in smoke. (*pause*) We might as well consider beauty. Just look at the different blues out there: I've counted five so far.

ELVIRA   There's a coup, Rohan, a coup! and–

ROHAN   Elvira, what do you think about my resurrecting the – er my book?

ELVIRA   What book?

ROHAN   What book, she asks. Only the one I spent the better part of ten years researching and working on.

ELVIRA   Oh, that book! The one that I spent ten years on supporting you through your depression. Right? You said you burnt the bloody manuscript.

ROHAN   I didn't know you felt that way about it.

ELVIRA   What way? That it hurt me to see you hurt by rejection after rejection from publishers who wouldn't take the subject seriously. "Dear Mr. Sankar, we read your manuscript with great interest but..."–

ROHAN   I know, Elvira – I remember.

ELVIRA   I don't think you do, Rohan. That you could even be thinking of putting yourself through that again!

ROHAN   The climate has changed. Publishers are far more receptive to this sort of work now. Besides, it's all post-modern today – it should fit quite nicely, I think. Anyway, that's what I'm spending my sabbatical doing.

ELVIRA   You're more of a sucker for punishment than I thought, Rohan.

ROHAN   I've made some changes – introduced the political element. I think it's going to go quite well, El. I've done quite some interviews since I've been here and I have a few more lined up. One of my neighbours has even agreed to let me interview her.

ELVIRA   We put off starting a family because of that – don't count on me being there to see you through this time around.

ROHAN   I hadn't asked.

ELVIRA goes to the phone, dials and listens and hangs up.

ELVIRA   The lines are all busy.

RADIO   This is a public service announcement – once again (*ELVIRA turns up the volume*) we are warning everyone to remember the curfew that starts at 6:00 p.m. Soldiers have orders to shoot on sight anyone caught breaking the curfew. We will continue to bring you news throughout the day and night. In the meantime, for your listening pleasure we are bringing you some of the best calypsos of the last season.

         Calypso music starts again.

ELVIRA   It's Friday today, Rohan! I have to be back in London on Monday! What if the fighting spreads here and I can't leave. What if–

ROHAN   What if, what if, what if! What if it all just peters out, El, as it most likely will. You forget this is Trinidad and Tobago where, as they say, "de rum cheap and de living sweeter still." I hear that people are throwing curfew parties in Trinidad. They party till it's close to curfew time, then rush home trying to beat the curfew.

ELVIRA   Sun, sea and sex! Isn't that what all the tourist brochures promise you? They don't say anything about coups and soldiers. They should all bloody well be sued.

ROHAN   We've got sun and sea, El. Two out of three. That's not doing too badly. Why don't we take advantage of being marooned? Do you remember our first time here – that little beach at Bacolet where–

ELVIRA   All hell is breaking out around us–

ROHAN   Not here in Tobago.

ELVIRA   I am dog-tired, Rohan.

         ROHAN fetches her luggage from the porch.

ROHAN   Look, why don't you change into something comfortable and rest for a while. You've had an exhausting day. (*pause*) Elvira, you still haven't learnt to travel lightly.

ELVIRA   You should have seen what I started out with.

ROHAN   I meant what I said about your having the bed tonight.

ELVIRA   No, no, I won't hear of it–

MRS. S. (*off-stage*) Hullooo! Hullooo! Anybody home?

ELVIRA Who's that?

ROHAN Sounds like Mrs. Samuels from next door.

ELVIRA The last thing I want now is to be sociable.

ROHAN You don't have to be – she's a good neighbour. You'll like her.

> *MRS. SAMUELS enters. She is a dark-skinned, older woman. Throughout her conversation, she pronounces coup as coop.*

MRS. S. Is me, Mr. Rohan – Mrs. Samuels.

ROHAN Hello, Mrs. Samuels.

MRS. S. Lord, me tired!

ROHAN Mrs. Samuels, this is Elvira.

MRS. S. Is your wife dis, Mr. Rohan?

ROHAN Yes, well I only have one wife, Mrs. Samuels.

MRS. S. But – pardon me manners, Miss Elvira but me very pleased to meet you. Mr. Rohan tell me plenty bout you, but – pardon me, Mr. Rohan, but you did never tell me Miss Elvira is African.

ROHAN I thought I had.

MRS. S. Don't worry, Miss Elvira, he didn't let out no secrets. You do right to come to Tobago. Is God own land dis. Except for dis craziness dem Trinidadians starting. Me don't know what coming down in dis here island. From nine o'clock dis morning me standing waiting for transport to go in town to get some gas and me cyant get nutting. Neither bus nor taxi – because of dis damn coop. But see me crosses nuh! Me did sure it was a gangster movie when me see it on TV – big big and bold dem Muslimeen men wit dey gun pointing at people. You did see it?

ROHAN We don't have a television.

MRS. S. Me say me cyant believe it – right dere in Port of Spain dese Muslimeen holding up de Prime Minister and de Parliament. You ever hear anyting like it, Miss Elvira? You have ting like dis in foreign, Mr. Rohan?

ROHAN Not quite, Mrs. Samuels. What do you think of their leader – what's his name?

ELVIRA   Ali Khalid.

MRS. S.   Huh! Ali Khalid, Khalli Alid, if dem had proper names none a dis would be happening.

ROHAN   Do you agree with what he's saying?

MRS. S.   Agree? How me could agree when de man talking so much foolishness and turning me life topsy turvy. See me here, I'se a woman who don't like violence, but violence does come in plenty different ways and dem yard fowl in Parliament getting a taste of dey own medicine. All a dem not doing nutting for people, only running dey mouth all over de place while people waking up hungry and going to sleep hungry. Dem shoulda lock dem up in another kind a coop long time ago and save we a whole set a trouble. Huh.

ROHAN   Is that what you think caused the coup?

MRS. S.   Huh. Sometimes people does live with a problem day in and day out and den suddenly one day braps! jus so dem does catch a vaps and dey cyant stand it no longer. Huh. Me see it happen plenty time in man and woman business. All you know what me mean. Could be dey don't sleep well de night before. Mind if me take off me shoes, Mr. Rohan, me been on me foot since early morning. (*pause*) All me know is that talk don't feed hungry belly and nutting hurt as much as when you have pickney you cyant feed.

ROHAN   So Ali Khalid's right about–

MRS. S.   Nuh say me say! All me know is dat me have ten cake to bake for de hotel for day after tomorrow, and me don't want no damn Muslimeen wit dey coop stopping me earning a decent living, because as far as me see all a dem *and* de politicians earning some damn indecent living – pardon de language. All a dem! If dey ever had to do a real day's work, dey wouldn't have no time for all dis commotion. But see me crosses nuh! Lord, me hot for so. Trouble you for a glass of water, Mr. Rohan.

ELVIRA   I'll get it.

        ELVIRA leaves.

MRS. S.   Mr. Rohan, you is Indian and me hear is Indian religion dese Muslimeen following, what dis word Muslimeen mean?

ROHAN   (*laughs*) I know as little as you do.

MRS. S.   Me did tink since you come from foreign you might a know.

ROHAN   Foreign! (*laughs*) You know I'm from Trinidad, Mrs. Samuels. What I do know is that Ali Khalid and his followers are not Indian. They're African – Black Muslims. And it looks to me like all they've done is add e-e-n to the word Muslim. Muslim – Muslimeen.

MRS. S.   Dat supposed to frighten we or someting? (*she sucks her teeth loudly*) By de way, Mr. Rohan, you hear dem Muslimeen send a whole planeload of dey women and children over here? Dey hiding out somewhere on the Windward side of de island. Outta de comess dem making in Trinidad.

ROHAN   It probably means we're safe here then.

ELVIRA returns with a glass of water.

MRS. S.   Safe? You never safe nowhere, Mr. Rohan. Not wit de evil in dis world. De only protection is living right. (*pause*) What we needing now is a man like Butler. He would a straighten dis mess out.

MRS. SAMUELS takes the glass of water and drinks.

MRS. S.   Tank you, chile, tank you. Me can still see it like it was yesterday. In dose days Mr. Samuels – God rest his soul – working down South in de oil fields in Trinidad, and when he telling you how dem wicked bosses treating de workers, it making water come to yuh eye. Uh uh. Is like slavery never done and a whole set a white South African just squeezing de life blood outta Black people – until Butler put a stop to it. Yes man, Tubal Uriah Butler – Buzz dey used to call him – saviour of de working man. And me – Altruda Samuels – only twenty years old, me was right dere in dat march! (*pause*) Back den Mr. Buzz Butler really showing dem a ting or two – yes sirree! – when he calling dat strike! An he making we Black people feel proud – real proud. June twenty-third, nineteen hundred and thirty-seven! We setting off from La Brea down South and we start walking all de way to Port of Spain. Sun hot and de pitch melting under we foot but we still walking. Den we hearing dey wanting to arrest Butler. We deciding dat if dey coming for he den is we dey having to deal wit. (*she sips the water*) Tings getting hot in more ways dan one when we getting to Fyzabad junction because is dere we meeting a police officer name Charlie King, who say he goin to arrest Butler—you hear me—arrest Butler! Well who tell he say dat?

MRS. S.   (*continuing*) Hear Butler – Lord me still remember de words – "Go and tell your bastard bosses that if de workers don't get dey dues, God and Uriah will turn de British Empire upside down!" Ha! – You hear dat? "turn de British Empire upside down!" Huh.

ROHAN   Mrs. Samuels is the neighbour who is going to let me interview her, El. For the book.

MRS. S.   Me still tinking bout it, Mr. Rohan.

ROHAN   It would mean a great deal to me, Mrs. Samuels.

MRS. S.   You can't lock up a man like Butler in no chapter or book, Mr. Rohan.

ROHAN   I know, Mrs. Samuels, but to talk to someone who was actually there–

MRS. S.   Me tinking, Mr. Rohan, me tinking. But wait, is how plane flying when de airport close down.

ELVIRA   When did you hear that, Mrs. Samuels? It wasn't on the radio.

> *She tries to find a station which will give her information. All she hears is music.*

ROHAN   I told you not to rely on the radio.

MRS. S.   Is so me hear when me was waiting for transport on de road.

ELVIRA   But they said there were going to be flights out this evening and tomorrow morning. They wait-listed me for both of them.

> *ELVIRA tries the phone.*

ELVIRA   The phone's dead!

ROHAN   What you saw back then, Mrs. Samuels, is really important. If I interviewed you, what I would do is–

MRS. S.   Is not just what me *seeing*, Mr. Rohan, is what happening back den. All like you and Miss Elvira so coulda never get together. No sir! Somebody woulda dead already–

ROHAN   That's the sort of insight I'm–

MRS. S.   Is like Butler setting fire to de whole island. From way down south all de way up north to Port of Spain de strikes spreading. Even some of de Indians on de Caroni sugar estates going on strike and joining in we march. And you better believe me when me telling you dat in dose days Indian and African not doing nothing together. Huh. Except what dem shouldn't be doing.

ROHAN   That's exactly what my research confirms, Mrs. Samuels and–

MRS. S.   All you never hear bout dougla children?

ROHAN   Of course we know what dougla means, don't we, Elvira – part Indian, part–

ELVIRA   The word means bastard in Hindi.

ROHAN   Part African.

MRS. S.   All *me* know is dat Indian and African not really setting horses, if you take me meaning. Indian one side, African another side. But de Indian life in sugar not much better dan de Africans working in oil. Is suffering on both sides. And one boss man. Huh. When we getting to Jumbie Bridge in Barataria, de police arresting plenty a we, but Mr. Samuels and me run and manage to get way.

ROHAN   And you think we need a man like Butler today.

MRS. S.   He worth all dem yard fowl in Parliament and all dem Muslimeen all wrap up together.

ROHAN   Perhaps Ali Khalid is a modern day Butler.

MRS. S.   Bite yuh tongue, Mr. Rohan! You cyant call Butler name in de same breath wit dese jokers. You hear Ali Khalid talk? People say he went all de way to Canada for an education. Huh.

ROHAN   The newspapers report he went to Ryerson College. In Toronto.

MRS. S.   Same ting me tellin you. Canada! Is what dis world coming to? Every Tom, Dick and Harrilal say he going foreign for education. Huh. Somebody waste a whole heap a money paying for he education. If me was head of dat Rayerson–

ROHAN   Ryerson.

MRS. S.   Ryerson, Rayerson – whatever! If me was head of dat college, is no way me tellin anybody he went dere for an education. All de same maybe is dere he picking up dese damn fool ideas bout holding up Parliament.

ELVIRA   Rohan! What do you think we should do?

ROHAN   Nothing right now, Elvira. I'm sure the airport's going to be open soon. If it's closed.

MRS. S.   Dis life is a funny business. Butler struggle and bring changes to stop white people exploiting we and today is we own Black people who putting de squeeze on we. Massa does come in all colour – oh yes. And bullet don't know no colour and gun don't care who shooting it – it doing what it have to do and dat is kill.

RADIO   We wish to interrupt this program to bring you the following information.

ELVIRA picks up the radio and turns up the volume.

ROHAN   Elvira!

MRS. S.   Is alright, Mr. Rohan – sometimes you must be hearing de lies to know what true.

RADIO   Two Members of Parliament have been shot and the Muslimeen have allowed an ambulance to take them away.

Calypso music in the background.

MRS. S.   Same ting me saying bout bullet just doing it job.

ELVIRA   Ministers have been shot, Rohan!

MRS. S.   Miss Elvira, pardon me, but is forces higher dan you dat putting you here now and when dat happening you have to go wit it. Is just like when me did find meself in de Black Power marches back in–

ROHAN   Nineteen seventy!

MRS. S.   Tank you, Mr. Rohan. You have a chapter bout dat in your book? What it call again? You did tell me but me forget.

They both answer

ELVIRA   The Tropical and the Sublime.

ROHAN   The Sublime and the Tropical.

MRS. S.   It sounding real important. I understand de Tropical part of it, but what is dis ting you calling Sublime?

ELVIRA   That's where Rohan gets to show that we Black people are no different from white people. Like them we have our beauty, our awe-inspiring nature—just look at the blues out there in the Caribbean Sea, Mrs. Samuels. How many can you count? And like the whites we also have our terror. Which is just another name for the sublime–

MRS. S.   Huh! De only terror me knowing in dese islands is what people doing to each other. Especially politicians. White politician. Black politician. Indian politician. Is all de same.

ELVIRA   I think that's what Rohan's been trying to say, but nobody's listening.

MRS. S.   Mr. Rohan, you have to have a chapter bout how all like you, Miss Elvira, couldnta work in no bank before de Black Power marches, cause your skin too black! Only fairy fairy people gettin de jobs.

ELVIRA   He will have a chapter on the Black Power marches, won't you, Rohan?

ROHAN   The title of the book is *The Sublime and the Tropical.* Not *The Tropical and the Sublime.*

MRS. S.   Miss Elvira, if me did lose me head and try to get way, dat day when me get trap in de Black Power marches who know what might a happen – who know? When me looking round is people for so and all a dem except me having someting red tie on dey head, or dey hand or dey foot and me one have nutting red. Me seeing people looking at me funny. Me tinking tank god me skin black because dat bound to count for someting, but me worried dey tinking me spying on dem, because is not every Black person what agreeing wit dem. (*pause*) Den suddenly dis little girl who holding she mother hand and marching, reaching up and taking off one of she red ribbons and giving it to me – me tying it round me hand and marching proud proud, you woulda tink me was somebody important. If is one ting me learning in life is dat you cyant run from what you ha fe find out. It still going find you, wherever you hiding. Mr. Rohan, trouble you for a little more water, please.

ROHAN   Would you prefer some lemonade?

MRS. S.   No tanks – me have to watch de sugar.

> *ROHAN leaves with the glass.*

MRS. S.   Miss Elvira, you notice how woman nowhere in all dis bacchanal and tankalan?

> *ELVIRA nods.*

MRS. S.   So, Miss Elvira, you enjoying Tobago?

ELVIRA   Not since this coup.

MRS. S.   Miss Elvira is not you I did see last week when–

> *ROHAN returns with a glass of water.*

MRS. S.   Mr. Rohan, beg you a lift in town to get some gas. Me have to cook some food, or me going take wind bad bad and is days me suffering. And me have a whole set a cake to make–

ROHAN   But of course – I should have offered – I'm sorry–

MRS. S.   Is how you to offer if me don't ask. You live too long a foreign.

ROHAN   Elvira, come for the ride!

ELVIRA   No.

ROHAN   We should hurry, Mrs. Samuels – we don't want to be caught in the curfew.

> *She puts on her shoes slowly.*

MRS. S.   You right, Mr. Rohan. You know what me don't understand, Miss Elvira—is how come dese Muslimeen all wanting more dan one wife? A whole set a gun and grenade and more dan one wife. What self-respecting woman want to be wife number two, three or four eh? Or even wife number one? Mr. Samuels coulda never bring any of dat stupidness to me. Me know man does run woman on de side and does want to say dat is how God make dem, but at least dey having a little shame and dey hiding de outside woman. But dese Muslimeen big and boldface saying dey having more dan one wife and dat is god will. Huh. Since me coming to understand how dese tings does go between man and woman, and dat is a long time now, me know de only will dat driving man when it come to woman is de will between dey legs. You agree, Miss Elvira?

ELVIRA Mr. Rohan can better answer that question.

ROHAN   Mrs. Samuels! – we must go. Elvira, I'll see what I can find out about the airport.

MRS. S. Bye, Miss Elvira. You mustn't worry too much – everyting going to be all right.

> *ROHAN and MRS. SAMUELS leave. ELVIRA paces. She tries the phone.*

RADIO   We are asking listeners not to call the radio station. We would like to keep the telephone lines free so that we can get news of the hostage situation. (*ELVIRA sucks her teeth loudly over the sound of the radio*) The following is a public service announcement. The following flights have been cancelled: Air Canada – Flight three zero one to Toronto; American Airlines – Flight four five six to Miami and British West Indian Airways – Flight two five seven to London. For further details please call your airlines. And now for your listening pleasure.

> *The radio plays calypso music. ELVIRA closes the shutters.*

SCENE II

> *Two to three hours later. Throughout the scene there are sounds of crickets, frogs and surf. ROHAN sits in the same chair. A book is in his lap.*

ROHAN   Elvira! Elvira! Come quickly – come and see this!

> *She enters quickly.*

ELVIRA What is it? What's happened?

ROHAN   I wanted you to see the sunset – look at it, it's really spectacular today.

ELVIRA Rohan! You woke me.

ROHAN   I'm sorry, but you like sunsets.

ELVIRA I thought something had happened – I must have fallen asleep.

ROHAN   Something *has* happened. Look at the way the red streaks across the sky there. And the grey over there, with just that hint of violet or purple. Look, Elvira – look!

ELVIRA   It is beautiful. How can you relax at a time like this? Do you think it's because you're a man?

ROHAN   (*he laughs*) I hadn't thought that my sex had anything to do with it.

ELVIRA   Don't make fun of me, Rohan. What's it like out there?

ROHAN   Nothing to report really – a few soldiers. People seem to be going about their life much the same as usual. The line-ups are longer, that's all. (*pause*) The airport's closed, El – indefinitely. And even if it is opened, there's no guarantee that airlines will fly in until they're sure the violence is over (*pause*) What about the ferry services? There might be something on Sunday.

ELVIRA   Oh god – that's two days away.

ELVIRA leaves and returns with the radio.

ROHAN   We're safe here. You heard what Mrs. Samuels said – they sent their women here for safe-keeping.

ELVIRA   Since when do you accept gossip?

ROHAN   Gossip? I would wager Mrs. Samuels is a much more reliable source of information than that radio you listen to.

ELVIRA   What have you told Mrs. Samuels about us?

ROHAN   Not much – that we're separated.

ELVIRA   She seems to know a lot. She said she thought she recognized me.

ROHAN   Did she? El, turn off the radio. It doesn't help to listen to all that.

She lowers the volume on the radio.

ELVIRA   I am trying to find out what is going on.

ROHAN   Speaking of what's going on, what were you doing in Tobago, El?

ELVIRA   I had a job interview in Trinidad – the General Hospital is looking for someone to head up their pathology department. I decided to come over for a few days – you know, lie on the beach, drink a rum and coca cola and relax. And here I am trapped and going nowhere fast.

ROHAN   All the more reason to stay here, Elvira, until the coup is over. Let's make this the holiday we had planned to take. Before you left. There is nothing happening here. It's calm, beautiful – sublimely tropical, in fact. Or, is it tropically sublime?

ELVIRA is silent.

ELVIRA   Have you forgiven me?

ROHAN   For what?

ELVIRA   Don't play games, Rohan.

ROHAN   I'm not. I don't know what I have to forgive you for.

He takes her hand.

ELVIRA   For leaving you like that.

ROHAN   Like what?

She pulls her hand away.

ROHAN   Come on Elvira, lets play the finger-tip game!

He reaches out his hand. After a small delay she brings her finger-tips to his.

ROHAN   Remember? Come on, you're cheating, El, close your eyes. What are you feeling?

ELVIRA   What are you feeling?

ROHAN   I asked first.

She takes her hand away. He reaches out and holds it. He brings her hand to his lips and kisses her fingers gently.

ROHAN   I had never seen hands quite like yours before – the way your fingers tapered to slender points. And when you talked! You moved them so they looked like butterflies – black butterflies.

ELVIRA   That was years ago – we were kids.

ROHAN   We used to send each other energy and thoughts.

ELVIRA   Don't Rohan–

She pulls her hand away.

ROHAN   Sometimes it helps to remember, Elvira.

ELVIRA   Remember what, Rohan? That your family didn't want no little nigger girl for their great son who was going to be a doctor, or a lawyer.

ROHAN   Well, I disappointed them on both counts, didn't I? (*pause*) But your family didn't want no coolie boy either, Elvira. And they had plans for you too – you were going to become a teacher – the first in your family! (*pause*) Now look at us – I'm the teacher – and not any old teacher either, but a professor of English literature. And you, Elvira, of the butterfly fingers, you are the doctor.

> *He leaves and returns with a bowl.*

ROHAN   I got a treat for you when I was out.

ELVIRA   Mangoes!

ROHAN   Some Julic, some Starch – that's all they had.

> *ELVIRA smells and gently tests the mangoes. ROHAN watches her. He laughs.*

ELVIRA   What's so funny?

ROHAN   You – watching you choose a mango. It takes me back to when I used to come and buy mangoes from you and your granny? Do you remember? I would take a long time to choose one and I'd ask you to test it for me – to see if it was ripe enough. God – the hard-ons I used to get, just standing there watching your fingers touching and testing the mango's flesh, so gently, so lightly. Just like you're doing now.

ELVIRA   Is that why you got me these mangoes?

ROHAN   You would be feeling and feeling the mango and I would be imagining your breasts round and firm like the flesh of the mangoes–

ELVIRA   Not like Long mangoes, I hope.

ROHAN   No – like big, juicy Calabash mangoes – those round, creamy-tasting Calabash mangoes–

ELVIRA   Stop it, Rohan – you're turning me on–

ROHAN   Then there's no reason why I should stop.

She bites a hole in the top of a mango and sucks the juice.

ELVIRA   Hmmm, this is good. What I could never understand was why you were coming to buy mangoes from us, when your parents had their own vegetable stall? Want a taste?

She offers him the mango.

ROHAN   Only a taste?

He sucks the mango and passes it back to her.

ELVIRA   I asked you once and you–

ROHAN   I said we had run out of mangoes and Ma had sent me to get some for a customer. I was lying.

ELVIRA   I know. (*pause*) I had forgotten how quickly it gets dark here.

ROHAN   Yes – there's no in between, is there. It's like the islands themselves – black or white, light or darkness, no shades of grey. (*pause*) Would my forgiving you change–

RADIO   Attention! Attention!

She turns up volume.

ELVIRA   Shhhh!

RADIO   Would all doctors, nurses and health workers report immediately to the Port of Spain General Hospital.

ELVIRA   Did you hear that, Rohan? Do you think I should go?

ROHAN   Get a hold of yourself, Elvira. You can't go anywhere.

After the announcement the radio plays calypso music.

ELVIRA   You don't have to rub it in. They're calling for medical personnel – something must be going on.

ROHAN   Something is going on, Elvira – a coup.

ELVIRA   I mean something more than usual – more than what they're telling us.

ROHAN   I'll make you some dhal! – you always liked my dhal. And I bought some red fish on the way back from town with Mrs. Samuels.

> *ROHAN cooks throughout the conversation with ELVIRA. She searches for a station.*

ROHAN   Turn off the radio, Elvira.

ELVIRA   I want it on.

ROHAN   Turn it down at least.

ELVIRA   Why are they playing calypso music? There's a bloody coup in the goddamn country and they're playing calypso music! This place is crazy!

ROHAN   What should they be playing, Elvira? Classical music? (*pause*) A requiem, perhaps? For a dead or dying country.

ELVIRA   You never take what I say seriously!

ROHAN   But I do – I'm merely trying to show you that there is another way of looking at it all. Maybe they—the authorities, the government, the army, whoever *they* are—have decided that calypso will make the people feel better: bring back memories of good times – Bacchanal and all that. You know how Trinis love to fete and party.

ELVIRA   It just seems inappropriate somehow.

ROHAN   Actually, I disagree with you. Calypsos and coups – there's something strangely right about the connection – apart from the alliteration, I mean. You could have calypso coups which this one has all the makings of. And then, of course, there are coup calypsos which I'm sure you'll have hundreds of–

ELVIRA   Rohan!

ROHAN   Maybe that's what they should do, El! Blast the Muslimeen with calypso music and not just any kind of calypso music, but some good wine and jam calypso music. Word has it that they're opposed to the "good time" Trini mentality. (*pause*) Can't you see it, Elvira?!–

> *He goes to the radio and turns up the music. Laughing, he pretends to hold a gun above his head in the gesture of surrender and dances over to ELVIRA, wining his pelvic area.*

ROHAN   The Muslimeen wining their way out of the Parliament building to the tune of a Sparrow or Kitch calypso, holding their weapons high above their heads.

ELVIRA pushes him away.

ROHAN   Maybe they could even export the technique – as a means of solving hostage-taking situations. It could earn them some much-needed foreign exchange.

ELVIRA   (*ELVIRA sucks her teeth loudly*) You are taking serious thing to make joke with, Rohan.

ROHAN   What else is there to do, Elvira? We should cry if we didn't laugh.

ELVIRA   I know why you're treating this whole thing so lightly?

ROHAN   Tell me.

ELVIRA   You feel you don't belong here any more.

ROHAN   I never belonged here, Elvira. (*pause*) Neither did you for that matter. The fundamental difference being that we Indians always felt that we didn't belong, whereas you Blacks believed you did—no, you believed you owned here. And guess what, Elvira, that was as much of a myth as those Indians who felt they didn't belong. (*pause*) You didn't even own the land, Elvira, so how could you belong. And it wasn't us, coolies, that owned it either – contrary to the common belief that "coolie own everyting." No, Elvira, it was the French Creole – the *French Creole*! And here you are talking about belonging. The situation was always clearer for us Indians – we never had the luxury you people had.

ELVIRA   Luxury!

ROHAN   Once we got here we were coolies, and coolies we remained. Until we left or died – those who were lucky enough.

ELVIRA   And weren't we niggers once we got here? At least you had your Hindi and your Gujerati! Do you hear anybody speaking Yoruba or Ga in Trinidad, Rohan? And *your people* are still practising their religion today. You forget the government used to lock up the Shouter Baptists like Granny, because their worship – their *Christian* worship, mind you, was too African! Anybody Indian ever got put in jail, Rohan, because they practised their religion?

ROHAN   And your people have political power and you run the government – seems to me you're doing pretty well.

ELVIRA   You yourself said that it was the French Creoles who owned the
          land and ran this country! You can believe what you want,
          Rohan, I know that in my soul I am–

ROHAN   What, Elvira? What are you? You now have to *apply* for your
          Trinidadian citizenship? Isn't that a qualification for the job
          you've applied for. And didn't I hear somewhere that you have
          to be finger-printed—those beautiful finger-tips of yours, Elvira,
          pressed into inky pads. And don't forget proof that you're not a
          criminal. As for your soul, there is no exam that I know of yet,
          Elvira, that can test the contents of yours or anyone else's for
          that matter.

ELVIRA   I will never stop being Trinidadian.

ROHAN   Why? Because you eat creole food like pelau a few times a year
          and wine–up in a carnival band in Notting Hill? Aren't you the
          same person who wants to flee this damn forsaken place? Eric
          Williams was right. If you didn't have a British passport, where
          could you run to, Elvira? You would have to stay here and real-
          ly *be* Trinidadian. Taking the tropical licks and the sublime
          perks, whatever they may be, like everyone else.

ELVIRA   I didn't have a choice about giving up Trinidadian citizenship,
          Rohan. You know that. You did it too. I had to become British
          to qualify for grants and loans.

ROHAN   You have entered one of the most select and prestigious clubs in
          the world – you own a British passport and you quibble about
          losing Trinidadian citizenship! Once you start waving that pass-
          port around you'll be on the next plane out of here.

ELVIRA   I did wave it this morning, Rohan. You forget. And I'm still
          here.

ROHAN   I take your point, Elvira, but do you know how many people
          like us – Trinidadians, Bangladeshis, Nigerians – would give
          their eye teeth and more for British citizenship?

ELVIRA   Don't you feel anything?

ROHAN   Do I feel anything? (*pause*) I don't know. I like certain things
          about the Caribbean. I like certain things about England. Both
          places are hell to live in and so you choose the hell you prefer to
          live with. I choose the English hell.

ELVIRA   Your attitude's so cold–

ROHAN   Not about you, Elvira. The only belonging I care about is us belonging to each other. And that passport which you value so lightly – the British one? – that's the one that's going to get you out of this tropical hell, if the going gets rough.

ELVIRA   That's what began to get to me – that nothing seemed to matter to you. After your book. That was the one thing you felt passion about.

ROHAN   Not the one thing. You forget Elvira. Of the butterfly fingers.

ELVIRA   You have an image of me – It's like the Caribbean – the Tropical, whatever you call it. You are trying to force it into some mold and it doesn't fit, Rohan. Didn't you hear Mrs. Samuels? It's not everything you can put into a book, force into your words – The Sublime and the Tropical don't fit. They never have–

ROHAN   Mrs. Samuels just needs to get comfortable with what I'm doing.

ELVIRA   You've been here what? Three, almost four, months and she's still "tinking bout it", Rohan. You don't get it, do you?

ROHAN   What don't I get, Elvira? That we are the products of one of the biggest fuck-ups in history? And the only thing that fuck-up has birthed are crazy, confused people like us—you and me—Elvira and Rohan—who talk about belonging, when we don't even have a pot to piss in. And remember, Elvira, it was *your* hero, the Black man's saviour – "De Doc", who said you couldn't be loyal to massa and massa. (*pause*) Why don't we have some wine, Elvira.

    He takes a bottle of wine out of the refrigerator.

ROHAN   What a way to sit out a coup! Pan-fried red snapper on a bed of freshly-cooked, Basmati rice alongside dhal, fried plantains and served with a chilled German Riesling. I'm surprised this sort of thing hasn't been marketed yet – "Come and see Beirut burn while you savour succulent lamb kebabs and fragrant cous cous."

ELVIRA   You are a sick man, Rohan. *Very* sick.

ROHAN   (*opening the bottle of wine*) No sicker than CNN bringing to us fortunate Westerners our daily dose of death and dying. I'm only rationalizing it – isn't that what they say these days? You rationalize a situation.

    He takes two wine glasses from the cupboard.

ELVIRA You've got to admit there was a certain logic to what Williams was saying – back then.

ROHAN You mean that he was rationalizing a situation too?

He pours the wine.

ELVIRA What he *said* was that if you took out citizenship in another country, you couldn't keep your Trinidad and Tobago citizenship. (*pause*) What he *meant* was that you had to be loyal to your country – he just didn't realize that sometimes people had to take out citizenship in other countries simply to survive.

ROHAN That's what I mean by the choice between massa and massa. (*pause*) He was telling us "Massa day done," but he and his cronies were busily setting up another class of massas – Black ones.

ELVIRA That's your race speaking – not you.

ROHAN (*tasting the dhal*) Damn – the garlic's cooked too much. If I speak through my race, Elvira, it doesn't always mean what I'm saying is not true. It's like the radio – sometimes it is, sometimes it isn't. True, I mean.

ELVIRA And you've told me that I should disregard the radio for that very reason.

ROHAN Come, El, I want to show you something.

He takes her over to where she can see the beach.

ROHAN You see that beach down there? I've been watching the fishermen pull seine every day since I've been here. It's hard work and with all this tourism it's only going to get harder. How many of their children are going to make it to university? You and I come from families like those. The only way we could have gone to university was to win scholarships. If Williams had understood the plight of people like us, he would have known what taking out citizenship in another country meant. The last thing it meant was that we didn't want to be Trinidadian. (*pause*) Meantime the real, bona fide Trinis with Trinidadian passports were busily siphoning off money to Canada and the States. Not to mention their Swiss bank accounts. That's passport patriotism for you, El. (*pause*) Let's toast.

ELVIRA What's there to toast to?

ROHAN   There's us – we could always toast to us.

ELVIRA   I suppose so...

ROHAN   You don't have to be so enthusiastic.

ELVIRA   (*sipping the wine*) Hmm, this is good.

ROHAN   God, El, how I miss these conversations. When I saw you at the airport– (*pause*) For one brief moment I thought you had come to see me.

ELVIRA   Would you have preferred if I hadn't come?

ROHAN   Why did you come?

ELVIRA   You asked me, Rohan.

ROHAN   You know what I mean.

ELVIRA   What do you want me to say, Rohan.

ROHAN   I never thought you would consider a job in Trinidad? You always said you wouldn't work back here–

ELVIRA   I wanted a change – then I heard about this job and decided to apply. I've lost all interest since this coup, though.

ROHAN   Is that the only rea–?

RADIO   There has been massive looting in Port of Spain.

ELVIRA turns up radio.

RADIO   Many business places have been set on fire and from where we are the city looks like a huge bonfire. Do not, under any circumstances, leave your homes – the army has instructions to shoot on sight.

ROHAN turns the radio off.

ELVIRA   What are you doing? (*she tries to turn radio on again, but he stops her*) We don't even know what's happening in Tobago. What if there is looting here?–

ROHAN   At best of times, Elvira, you don't get news about Tobago, why do you expect to get news now? And even if there were looting here, it'll take place in the town – Scarborough, not out here in Black Rock.

ELVIRA   You don't know that, Rohan – you don't know, I don't know. We don't know anything!

ROHAN   You win, Elvira, you win.

          He turns on the radio and returns to the kitchen. Calypso music is heard.

ROHAN   Damn it! The plantains are burnt after all that.

ELVIRA   I like them burnt.

ROHAN   Since when?

ELVIRA   Since always – you've forgotten.

ROHAN   Well, I aim to please and burnt is how you'll get them.

          He takes dishes out of a cupboard.

ELVIRA   Nothing about all this affects you, does it? It's like you're not here, or it's happening in another country.

ROHAN   My mother's in Trinidad and I *am* worried about her. (*he begins to dish out food*) I'm also worried about racial violence, although you don't think it's likely.

ELVIRA   There you go again–

ROHAN   Yes, there I go again – my race is speaking. But I'm very very happy that I am sitting out this particular example of Trinidadian madness here in Tobago and not there.

ELVIRA   This coup has nothing to do with race, Rohan – the government is Black and the Muslimeen are Black, even though they are Muslim.

ROHAN   And half the country is Indian. Please set the table so we can eat.

          He arranges food on plates.

ELVIRA   And when I set the table, Rohan, what food are we going to be eating? Not African food like float and accra. Not creole food like pelau. What food do most Trinidadians eat most often? Roti and doubles. And curry chicken. Indian food!

> *She moves back and forth between the kitchen area and the table putting first plates and cutlery on the table and then the dishes of food.*

ROHAN Well, they say you are what you eat. That would make most Trinidadians Indians, right? More wine? (*he refills their glasses*) And what about candles? – yes, candles! A candle-light dinner – how's that, Elvira? I saw a couple of candle holders and some candles around here somewhere.

> *He opens cupboards and drawers. He takes out two candles and candle holders. He takes them to the table and lights them with a flourish. He turns off the light. The candle-light casts long shadows in the room.*

ROHAN How's that for atmosphere?

ELVIRA It does make everything seem a little more distant.

ROHAN Good, then let's eat! Elvira, the sight of that radio ruins my appetite – can you at least move it?

ELVIRA (*putting the radio on the floor next to her*) Happy?

ROHAN Very.

ELVIRA Hmmm. This is good, Rohan.

ROHAN Even if it is Indian food.

ELVIRA You haven't lost your touch.

ROHAN I could say something.

ELVIRA Go ahead – I'm beyond being shocked.

MRS. S. (*off-stage*) Good night! Hello – anybody home?

ELVIRA Sounds like your favourite neighbour.

ROHAN Hope everything is O.K.

> *He stands. Mrs. Samuels enters.*

MRS. S. Night, Miss Elvira, night, Mr. Rohan. Me know young people don't like cook dese days and since Mr. Rohan so kind as to take me in town, me bringing some food for you.

ELVIRA Thanks, Mrs. Samuels. What is it?

ELVIRA takes the bag from MRS. SAMUELS. She takes out two covered dishes.

MRS. S. Me did make some conch bunyah wit dumpling and some rice and peas and some dasheen.

ROHAN I fried some fish and made some dhal, Mrs. Samuels. Would you like some?

MRS. S. Tank you, Mr. Rohan but me done eat – and anyway is only de fish me could eat. Indian food never agree wit me.

ELVIRA uncovers the dishes.

ELVIRA What's bunyah, Mrs. Samuels?

MRS. S. You never hear bout bunyah? Is when you cooking down someting in coconut milk—you ever hear bout come down or oil down? Same ting. Is ole time Tobago cooking.

ELVIRA Hmm, this is delicious, Mrs. Samuels. Jamaicans call it run down.

MRS. S. Me don't care what Jamaicans calling it—*me* know it as bun-yah—is a African word dat—and is good Tobago food—make you and de pickney dem strong, and Lord know we needing some strengthening in dese times. Ole people use to say when man and woman eat conch bunyah together and conch shell blow, dey living does come sweet sweet. Heh heh! You and Miss Elvira better watch it, Mr. Rohan. Nine months from now you might have a nice bunyah baby. Lord, me going rest me tired bones. Night Miss Elvira, night Mr. Rohan. Eh eh, is how me forget? Me hear on de TV dat dey will open de airport tomorrow.

ELVIRA Do you hear that Rohan? Maybe I'll be able to leave after all.

She checks the phone.

MRS. S. Dem say you to call de airlines, but me don't know how you can do dat when de phones dem dead. Dead dead – all it leave now is for dem to bury.

MRS. S. Night, Miss Elvira, night, Mr. Rohan.

She leaves.

ROHAN Your food's getting cold.

ELVIRA   Will you take me to the airport tomorrow?

ROHAN   Anything you wish, Elvira.

ELVIRA   *Finally* something's happening.

> *They eat in silence after MRS. SAMUELS leaves.*

ROHAN   Are we going to hear the conch shell, Elvira?

ELVIRA   What *I* want to know is who blows the conch shell, where they got it from, and must it be blown while you're eating the bun-yah.

ROHAN   Always the scientist.

ELVIRA   Conch shell or no conch shell, it's delicious.

> *She feeds him some bunyah.*

ROHAN   Hmm. Hadn't realized I was so hungry.

> *He helps himself to more bunyah.*

ELVIRA   That's what I liked about you. You always seemed so hungry.

ROHAN   Hungry! You mean I was a skinny, little coolie boy.

ELVIRA   There was a hunger that clung to you. You were so... so fragile, I just wanted to gather you up, cradle you in my arms and just rock you and rock you... (*pause*) Do you remember the day you came round to our stall selling goat's milk?

ROHAN   How could I forget?

ELVIRA   (*acting it out*) Granny put her hands on her hips, fi you with her eye and say: "Boy, you test de goat yet."

ROHAN   I didn't have the slightest idea she meant a test for TB.

ELVIRA   And you said: "No, Miss, is I who take de test. Yesterday, in school. De goat too stupid."

ELVIRA   Then Granny give this long suck-teeth – "Huh, Elvira, dis boy trying to make a fool outta we."

ROHAN   When did our living stop being sweet sweet, Elvira? (*silence*) Would it help if I blew the conch shell? (*silence*) Close your eyes, El.

ELVIRA   Rohan!

ROHAN   *Please.* I'll close mine too. It's Saturday—mid-morning. I've been studying since six a.m. Exams are coming up, but I'm tired, want a break, and mangoes are always a good enough reason to take a break. (*pause*) First you beat the clothes against the rock then you rinse them out in the water, wring them out and put them in the tub.

ELVIRA   (*opening her eyes*) The river!

ROHAN   You look around, making sure there is no one, then you take off your clothes, slip into the water and swim out to the rock. Your skin that morning, Elvira, so black and shining with the water, the droplets in your hair – like so many stars – your breasts! I want to reach out, to touch you – to be blessed... I also want to dry the drops of water from your body... one by one by one...

ELVIRA   I always thought I had that place to myself – I used to leave offerings... flowers, earrings... on the rock.

ROHAN   Have I spoilt it for you?

ELVIRA   Why are you telling me this? Now? After all these years?

ROHAN   I can describe every leaf, every stone... as if it were yesterday, Elvira. And the feeling I've lived with all these years.

ELVIRA   What is it, Rohan?

ROHAN   My shame.

ELVIRA   At spying on me?

ROHAN   That too. Shame at finding a Black girl beautiful. For my family it was absolutely taboo. And wanting her like I had never wanted anything before. Or since. In loving caste or colour, Elvira— your colour—which was so much a part of you that day – I was also breaching caste. (*pause*) It was after that I started coming around to your stall. (*pause*) Why do you want to know if I've forgiven you?

ELVIRA   I don't know.

ROHAN   You want absolution.

ELVIRA   Something like that.

ROHAN   Only a priest can give you absolution, Elvira, and only God forgive you. I am neither.

ELVIRA   Then don't, Rohan.

ROHAN   That's why you came, isn't it? So you could feel better about yourself.

ELVIRA   I couldn't get on my flight and didn't have a hotel room. That's why I came, Rohan. I came because when I saw you, I couldn't believe my good luck. I came because I was hurt and knew you would never hurt me deliberately. I came because I was feeling so much shame at how I had been treated. I came, Rohan, because – Do you know what month this is?

ROHAN   August. Why?

ELVIRA   August seventeenth – one year ago.

ROHAN   Shit!

ELVIRA   She would have been–

ROHAN   Elvira, I'm so sorry, I didn't remember – you must think–

ELVIRA   I stopped thinking a long time ago, Rohan.

> *The radio crackles. The music is interrupted by a woman's voice.*

RADIO   There have been running battles between the army and looters. (*ELVIRA puts the radio on the table and turns up the volume*) Many people have been injured or killed. Looting is widespread. Many of the people looting, we have been told, do not appear to be poor people. We are pleading with all citizens to stay indoors and refrain from illegal acts.

> *ROHAN turns away abruptly, walks to the doorway and looks out into the blackness. The sound of calypso music comes up again.*

ACT II

SCENE I

Living room. ROHAN watches ELVIRA. She gazes out towards the sea. The radio plays calypso music in the background.

ROHAN   (*chanting*) "Mary, Mary close your door..."

ELVIRA   "Mary Mary close your door...
Police coming to hold you."

ROHAN &
ELVIRA   "Mary, Mary close your door, police coming to hold you."

He is standing very close to her. She moves away.

ROHAN   I'm not the police, Elvira, and you aren't Mary Mary.

ELVIRA   What do you think Mary did?

ROHAN   What do you mean?

ELVIRA   Why were we always telling her to close her door against the police? I used to spend hours as a child trying to figure out what it was she could have done. I always thought the police were the bad guys. Because Mary Mary was so pretty. And the way she closed herself up, (*she gestures*) when you stroked her. It was like a prayer. That was no door she was closing.

ROHAN   I want to stroke you, Elvira. Stroke all your pain away–

ELVIRA   I used to spend hours planning what I would do to the police when they came for Mary Mary. I was going to pour hot oil on them. Shoot them. I watched too many cowboy movies.

ROHAN   But I'm afraid–

ELVIRA   Maybe she was running away from her husband. What do you think, Rohan? Or, maybe she had done something to her husband? Or her lover? Maybe she killed them. Maybe that's why the police–

ROHAN   Elvira, it's only a plant.

ELVIRA   Did you close the back door?

ROHAN   We're perfectly safe here. There's only the beach down there and unless you're expecting Muslimeen frogmen to emerge from the Caribbean Sea, there are only the stars, the fireflies and you and me—Elvira and Rohan. (*ELVIRA shuts the shutters*) Elvira! Please – don't close the shutters – it'll make it too hot.

ELVIRA   People can look in on us.

ROHAN   Which people?

ELVIRA   You know – the ones with penises and two balls – the same ones who go around raping women. Do I make myself clear?

ROHAN   You most certainly do.

ELVIRA   Maybe I just know too well how much damage can be done to a human body. Maybe, I've listened to too many news reports about what happens to women when men start their wars.

ROHAN   We're not in a state of war yet.

ELVIRA   I'm shut in on this damn island, where if you're not careful and run too fast, you land in the sea; shut up in this damn house; shut up in this body of mine that's only a liability at a time like this. Why the hell doesn't America invade and put an end to all this?

ROHAN   (*he laughs loudly*) Wash your mouth out, Elvira. I never thought I would live to hear you contemplate, let alone voice, such a wish.

ELVIRA   Forget you heard me say it. I feel like I'm living in a fucking nightmare dreamed up by Naipaul.

ROHAN   So he does get credit for some prescience.

ELVIRA   He probably planned it all. (*ROHAN laughs*) It's the waiting I find so impossible!

ROHAN   It is sometimes the hardest thing to do. Waiting. (*pause*) I used to repeat some lines of poetry to myself whenever I felt hopeless, filled with despair... I don't remember it all now, but it was something about waiting and the darkness. (*pause*) By Eliot. Poetry always helps, El.

ELVIRA   Go on, tell me we doctors are badly educated, not knowing about Eliot and the likes.

ROHAN   But you are—focused entirely on the body with no attention given to the soul—I suppose because you can't dissect it—put it under a microscope.

ELVIRA   Who was it that said there was no exam for the soul?

ROHAN   It doesn't mean that I don't believe the soul should not be nurtured. It should be mandatory for doctors and lawyers to study poetry. "The darkness shall be light." How many times did I repeat that to myself? (*pause*) While I waited, not knowing whether you were coming: "the darkness shall be light." Would you accept my offer of marriage? Two years, Elvira! Two years I waited for you.

ELVIRA   It was only 18 months. (*pause*) And I was doing my exams.

ROHAN   Twenty two months to the day – waiting and going slowly mad —"the darkness shall be light"—more mad than I knew I already was for leaving my law studies to do a degree in English literature. "The darkness shall be light" and London was never drearier, uglier, or more grim.

ELVIRA   Is this supposed to make me feel guilty?

ROHAN   Guilty!? No – The only two things I remember from that time is that quotation and the woman in the bus queue.

ELVIRA   The one who put a good West Indian cussing on you. Who told you to go and touch the woman?

ROHAN   You make it sound like I was sexually molesting her. I only touched her on the shoulder. The way she moved her head – she looked so much like you. You know how in winter everyone looks the same all bundled up against the cold.

ELVIRA   But, Rohan, how could I have come to London and not told you? I was coming to join you.

ROHAN   Oh, I don't know. That's what I believed.

ELVIRA   Serves you right for not trusting enough. You're lucky she didn't call the police for you.

ROHAN   What she did was worse. She traced my ancestry right back to before time itself, punctuated by a few raases and bumba cloths. And the longer my genealogy grew, the more questionable it became.

ELVIRA   What I remember from those days is how your family didn't want me for their great son. I was here, Rohan. In Trinidad. You forget that. I heard the talk: "You hear what happen to dat nice Rohan – Sam and Vena oldest boy? Dey used to have a stall on de Main Road. He marrying dat nigger girl from up Brown Trace. And you should see she – she black for so. She must be give him some good stoop down obeah. Is a good ting dey have other children."

ROHAN   Stop it, Elvira!

ELVIRA   Dis douglarisation must stop – Indian should marry Indian and African marry African. Dove and corbeau should never mate although both a dem is bird. And how about "dog have straight hair, and cat have straight hair, is only nigger people don't have straight hair." While *you* waited and read poetry, *that* is what I lived with.

ROHAN   I said stop it!

ELVIRA   They all blame you for killing your father – the shock of your marrying a hanoman – a monkey.

ROHAN   Enough, Elvira! Enough, I said!

ELVIRA   You started it.

ROHAN   Maybe I want that innocence we had back then.

ELVIRA   What innocence, Rohan? You romanticise everything to compensate for all the pain you caused your family over me.

ROHAN   That's a cruel thing to say, Elvira—my leaving my law studies was equally stressful for him—for all of them. They had sacrificed so much–

ELVIRA   We live in cruel times, Rohan. I didn't lose my family because of you.

ROHAN   Your family wasn't exactly overjoyed–

ELVIRA   All Granny wanted was for me to be happy, you know that. Ma and Pa were worried about my getting hurt, but as long as I qualified and got a degree, they would support me in my decision. Whatever it was.

ROHAN   I felt they would get used to it. Eventually.

ELVIRA   Only your sister speaks to you. Your two brothers pretend you're dead – Your mother won't give up on you—her beloved first born. (*pause*) Your family buried you, Rohan. Because you loved a Black woman—a nigger woman—and weren't content just to fuck her behind the bushes. Like all your friends were doing. Everyone knows that we're loose and that's what we do. No, you had to go and marry her. I can't ever compensate you for that.

ROHAN   I haven't ever asked you for compensation, Elvira. (*pause*) Only your love.

ELVIRA   You've always had that.

ROHAN   Then for fuck's sake, Elvira, why did you leave me? Why?

         ELVIRA is silent.

ELVIRA   I really need a drink, Rohan. Something strong.

         He leaves and returns with two glasses.

ROHAN   When I was out with Mrs. Samuels I got some cognac – it's expensive, but I know how much you like it. Come on the porch and talk to me.

ELVIRA   Only if you call it a gallery.

ROHAN   Come on the gallery and talk with me.

ELVIRA   What are you having?

ROHAN   A rum as usual. I'm still a Trini in that respect.

ELVIRA   Hmmm – hits the spot. I would much rather be here with you than alone in my hotel room being worried. At least I can get angry with you.

ROHAN   It's good to know I have some uses.

ELVIRA   I'm suffocating, Rohan, I just want out.

ROHAN   Is that us or the coup?

ELVIRA   I didn't—don't—want any heavy scenes...

ROHAN   Elvira, you walk out of a fifteen-year marriage without so much as a goodbye and–

ELVIRA   I didn't know what to tell you. I wanted time – needed space – that's all I knew.

ROHAN   Why, Elvira?

ELVIRA   There wasn't even anyone else–

Silence.

ROHAN   Was my loving you so burdensome?

ELVIRA   You sacrificed so much for me.

ROHAN   And for that you leave me? It's the baby, isn't it. I'm sorry I didn't remember the date–

ELVIRA   Nothing affects you, Rohan. Look at how you've been through-out this coup.

ROHAN   Thank god one of us is calm.

ELVIRA   I always think of death as frozen. A sort of solid state. Never as something active, or alive. It must have to do with being a pathologist. You get to look at cells, diseased cells all neatly arranged on slides. (*pause*) Her dying was so bright – so red! All that blood flowing down my legs and I couldn't stop it. If I could just gather it all up, I remember thinking, put it back inside me, inside her–

ROHAN   El!

ELVIRA   If I follow it—the blood, the trail—it'll lead me to her, I know it will. No neat, tidy death here, contained on little slides. Only a very bright, very red ribbon of death – from my chair to the door. My body still remembers her, you know, Rohan. Each cell–

ROHAN   You were working too hard, Elvira.

ELVIRA   My body has a memory of her. And yet there's just an empti-ness where she used to be. I dream of her sometimes and when I come awake – it's as if where my body was has become one big ache–

ROHAN   We could try again.

ELVIRA   You made the break so cleanly, Rohan. With Trinidad. You were
           born here, you grew up here, then you leave, go to England and
           it's like nothing happened. No wound – nothing – or if it was
           there, it's healed. Cleanly. With barely a scar. (*pause*) Where
           does it hurt you, Rohan? Where on your body do you carry the
           pain of losing her. Here? (*she touches his head*) Or Here? (*she
           touches his chest*) Or maybe you feel it in your wrist. Your little
           finger, perhaps? Or is it that you truly don't feel anything?

ROHAN   You were in bed for two weeks, Elvira. One of us had to
           continue.

ELVIRA   I always feel as if I'm bleeding, Rohan. Oozing. And the ques-
           tions: should I go back or should I stay in England. Am I
           coloured, Negro, or Black? Afro–Saxon, or Afro–English? Or
           just plain African? West Indian or Caribbean? Depending on
           whom I talked to I could be all those things in one day. You
           don't see them, Rohan, but there are these cuts. All over me.
           (*pause*) None of them has healed. Or if one heals, another one
           opens.

MRS. S.   (*off-stage*) Hello! Night Mr. Rohan! Night Miss Elvira!

           MRS. SAMUELS comes up the steps.

MRS. S.   Sorry for bothering you, Mr. Rohan, but me fuse just blow and
           me whole house in darkness. You have any me could borrow.
           Me have some candles, but me always worry bout fire.

ROHAN   I think I might know where some are.

           ROHAN leaves the porch and goes indoors.

MRS. S.   (*pause*) Miss Elvira you always looking so sad.

           She sits. ELVIRA is silent.

ELVIRA   I just want it all over and done with.

MRS. S.   It cyant be over until it over, Miss Elvira. An if is one ting me
           learning in dis life, is that whatever you running from, you
           bound to buck up. And when you tink you holding secret one
           way, it bussing out another way.

ELVIRA   I hate feeling afraid.

MRS. S.   Miss Elvira when me was having me first chile me was living in de country and Mr. Samuels, Lord rest his soul, wasn't nowhere round. Is nobody but me one. Lord when de pain lick me so, I staring death right in it face and me frighten for so – but you have to learn to hold onto dat fear inside, otherwise you dead. You have to ride it nice and easy. Sometimes you so busy being frighten you cyant do what you have to do. But if de fear not dere, chile, den someting wrong – because when you come through to de other side of dat fear – ah ha! – braps, just so de chile born.

ELVIRA   My baby girl died. A year ago–

MRS. S.   She go come again, chile. When de time right.

ELVIRA   Sometimes I don't believe the time will ever be right.

MRS. S.   Is only you one can make it right, Miss Elvira.

ELVIRA   At least I'll be out of here tomorrow.

MRS. S.   But you don't hear dem say de airport not opening tomorrow. De news just come over de TV. Before me fuse blow. Is how you don't hear it on de radio.

ELVIRA   I wasn't listening. You said the airport was going to be open.

MRS. S.   Chile, you cyant believe nutting dese damn criminals telling you. Miss Elvira, me know is none of me business, but is not you me did see last week in Scarborough. You was in a white car outside de market. It was de car me did notice because me son have one just like it.

ELVIRA   Yes.

MRS. S.   Miss, Elvira, de man driving de car – it wasn't Mr. Rohan. It was a African man.

ELVIRA   Yes. He's a friend.

MRS. S.   Miss Elvira, you know dis man?

ELVIRA   A bit.

MRS. S.   Sometimes a bit does be too much and sometimes it not enough. Nuh say me say, Miss Elvira, but me would take time with a bit.

ROHAN returns.

ROHAN   I found two fuses, Mrs. Samuels.

ELVIRA   Mrs. Samuels says they're not opening the airport tomorrow. I think we should still go.

MRS. S.   All you like de bunyah?

ROHAN   It was delicious.

MRS. S.   Me did cook some bunyah for dis friend once. She and de husband having some real problem and she say she want to make him feel good and how he like conch but she could never cook conch good. You know after dey eat de bunyah tings come good between dem and guess what? Both a dem start showing me bad face. Husband and wife business is a funny business. When de living turn hard dey does come to you and when you done helping, dem make back up sweet sweet and throwing cut eye at you. Mr. Rohan you should have a chapter in your book on man and woman business because plenty time what happening in politics all wrap up in what happen de night before – in de bedroom. Or what don't happen.

ROHAN   Shall I come with you, Mrs. Samuels?

MRS. S.   Tank you, Mr. Rohan, but me can do it meself. Miss Elvira, take heart.

ROHAN   Well at least take this torch.

MRS. S.   Is OK, Mr. Rohan, me know de darkness better.

> *MRS. SAMUELS leaves.*

SCENE II

> *ELVIRA is twirling the dial trying to find a news report. All she can get is music. They're both drinking.*

ELVIRA   If I told you I was only with you because you're Indian, what would you say?

ROHAN   I should have gone with Mrs. Samuels, it's so dark.

ELVIRA   What the hell were we doing together?

ROHAN   I thought it was because we loved each other. Sometimes that happens you know – we manage to break from our tribes to see each other.

ELVIRA   Our tribes are very different. Maybe if the baby had lived, I would have felt like I belonged to something larger. Something we had created. Together. That dish Mrs. Samuels brought for us–

ROHAN   The bunyah?

ELVIRA   She said it was a good African word, and before tonight I had never heard it. It's stranger to me than any French or Spanish word. Or even Hindi word for that matter.

They are silent.

ROHAN   I don't know much about Hindu culture either Elvira. Beyond what I saw as a child. I don't even speak the language. You forget I was raised Presbyterian. Ma was a good, god-fearing Presbyterian.

ELVIRA   And every year at Divali she would hide and light the deeyas out the back – I've heard that story so many times, Rohan. You *had* deeyas to light.

ROHAN   You may have heard the story, but do you really understand, Elvira? I can still see Pa's face getting darker than it already was with anger. And his eyes! as if they were going to pop out of his head with fear: "What if dey take away de boy scholarship, when dey find out that he not really Presbyterian." And all the while my grandmother was silently cursing them both with her eyes. Do you have any idea what that does to your head? Maybe it was the deeyas that began it all. This desire to have my pleasure tinged with danger. Like loving you. (*pause*) They seemed to burn even brighter in the darkness for all the fear and anger and resentment swirling around them. (*pause*) And my name – Rohan Morton Grant Sankar! Rohan for a famous Indian cricketer, and Morton and Grant for racist, Presbyterian missionaries from Canada.

ELVIRA   It beats Elvira Jackson. And those missionaries the racist, Presbyterian ones from Canada whose names you have – didn't they come to civilize Indians and not Africans, because they thought we were incapable of being civilised.

ROHAN   What do you want me to do, Elvira? Prove that I understand the struggle of Black people? And how that struggle has made things easier for others? How do you want me to prove it? Tell me, Elvira. I've done the marches and the demonstrations. I've yelled and shouted anti–racist slogans with the best of them. Faced down the National Front. What more do you want me to do?

ELVIRA   How many of you think like you do?

ROHAN   I can't carry that burden for my people, Elvira. The ones my parents saddled me with are enough.

ELVIRA   Back there, Rohan—in the white man's country—they'd take one of you any day over one of us. You know that when the going gets rough the browns and the pinks hang together. Particularly against the Blacks.

ROHAN   Are you blaming me for that?

ELVIRA   They're modest, hard-working and quiet – not like those aggressive Blacks who cry racism at the drop of a hat.

> *She leaves and returns with a tape and puts it in the tape deck. Bob Marley music is heard. She begins to dance.*

ELVIRA   When I listen to that, when I dance, I know there's something else there – I know it's not all emptiness. I feel it here. (*she takes his hand and puts it to her stomach*) And here. (*she puts his hand to her heart*) I feel connected to something larger – but most of the time with you, I just feel unequal.

ROHAN   I don't belong any more than you do, Elvira.

ELVIRA   If you wanted to you could.

ROHAN   We can still work it out.

ELVIRA   You mean like therapy? Some things need more than therapy, Rohan. There are some pains, some injuries that only new histories will fix, and history is never new.

ROHAN   That hunger you saw when you first met me. We all have it, Elvira – those of us let loose in this part of the world to rattle around without roots.

ELVIRA   If you say you're without roots, what do you leave for me to say?

ROHAN   Let's not get into comparing rootlessness.

ELVIRA   Why not?

ROHAN   Because it's the same disease – some of us just have it worse than others. If I go to India, I'm just as confused, just as much a stranger.

ELVIRA   And if I went to Africa where should I visit? East Africa? West Africa? And which group. Fon? Ibo? Ashanti? Yoruba?

ROHAN   I know, Elvira, I weep for your loss.

ELVIRA   I'll do my own weeping, Rohan. Weep for your own loss. (*silence*) "She trying to get a little soft hair and high colour for she children."

ROHAN   El – that was bigotry and stupidity.

ELVIRA   Have you ever thought that was true?

ROHAN   No.

ELVIRA   I wanted my family to insist on racial purity and sticking to one's own and not having doves marrying corbeau! I wanted a letter threatening to cut me off! To bury me! Never to speak to me again! I'm pissed to hell that what I got was support, understanding and generosity. (*mimicking a high voice*) Rohan was always a nice, well-behaved boy.

ROHAN   Didn't they say coolie boy?

ELVIRA   No, they didn't. Although Pa did say he wouldn't hold it against you that you were Indian. And being Christian helped.

ROHAN   So they had a problem too.

ELVIRA   There are problems and there are problems.

ROHAN   We survived so much in England together. You know what they call us. Wogs! It doesn't matter to them that you're African and I'm Indian, we're both wogs.

ELVIRA   In the white man's country we can pretend we're both the same – both Black. Back here that lie becomes very clear.

ROHAN   We don't live here, Elvira.

ELVIRA   Never being let in. That's what belonging means to me.

ROHAN   Let in where, El? What do you think you'll find there?

ELVIRA   If I find myself that'll be enough. I have to begin with the little Black girl from Brown Trace. The one who felt so sorry for Mary Mary and wanted to protect her from the police. If I begin there with her–

ROHAN   Why didn't you tell me this before?

ELVIRA   There were so many lies, to myself, Rohan. Each one built around the other. Like those Russian dolls. And way at the centre of the smallest one – nothing. "Rohan loves me, Rohan loves me." Or, sometimes for a change, 'Rohan loves Elvira." That was a little mantra I made up.

ROHAN   Rohan does love Elvira.

ELVIRA   But what does Rohan love? There's nothing, just this great emptiness. "Rohan loves me – Rohan loves Elvira," and everything rights itself again. When I lost the baby I couldn't pretend any longer.

ROHAN   We have each other.

ELVIRA   It's the "each other" that's causing the pain, Rohan. (*pause*) I couldn't even become English like you did.

ROHAN   I didn't become English, Elvira, and your accent's still more English than Trinidadian.

ELVIRA   It's not the accent – it's how you never looked back, and the more you didn't, the more I wanted to. It was bad enough when Granny died, but then losing the baby... (*silence*) I bet when you saw your mother in Trinidad, the first thing she wanted to know is if you're still with that hanoman. And whether you had cursed their house by bringing any little dougla bastard grandchildren into the world.

ROHAN   She's had a stroke, Elvira, she can't talk.

ELVIRA   Shit! Shit! Shit! I'm sorry.

   Silence.

ROHAN   One night shortly after you left, El, I couldn't sleep and decided to go for a walk – to clear my head. I was so caught up in my thoughts, I didn't realize I was being followed by some National Front thugs—young, white punks with those army boots that can strike fear into the most stalwart heart. I started walking faster and faster and so did they. I felt the sweat break out on me—god, was I afraid, Elvira. Afraid and scared shitless, as they say, and running, running – just one scared and frightened Paki running for his life.

ROHAN (*continuing*) Why don't I turn – fight them? At least die like a man. I know the area well – there's a Greek take-out restaurant that's open late and my heart is pounding this refrain: "if I can just get there," "if I can just get there"... And then – there's a moment, Elvira—such a brief duration of time—but it will stay with me for the rest of my life. Between the "am I going to make it," and the "I'm not going to make it," as the sweat is pouring down my face, or is it tears? As I hear my lungs wheezing, and my heart pounding – a moment in which I feel a great and overwhelming revulsion. For this brown body of mine. This Indian body. Source of so much pain, so much anxiety, so much fear. And hard on the heels of that feeling, a profound shame at having those feelings. (*pause*) I did make it into the restaurant. They stood outside laughing at me.

> *ROHAN moves into the bedroom. ELVIRA follows, unsure of how to comfort him. She sits on the bed. She is reaching out to touch him when we hear the radio.*

RADIO We now join the BBC for the world news.

ROHAN Elvira, don't you think–

ELVIRA Shhhh! It's the BBC–

RADIO The coup, begun two days ago on the island republic of Trinidad and Tobago by a radical group of Black Muslims continues. Members of Parliament are still being held hostage by armed members of the group while negotiations continue. This morning Iraqui forces invaded Kuwait by land and air.

ELVIRA Is that all? I thought I would hear something new–

> *ROHAN walks up and down.*

RADIO All British subjects in Kuwait have been asked to report to the British Embassy...

> *She turns the radio down.*

ELVIRA If sugar were still king we would be in a very different position. We'd be getting a lot more attention – like Kuwait. America's sitting up and taking notice because oil's involved.

ROHAN Elvira, forget the radio.

> *She looks down at radio in her hands. She turns the dial. We hear rock steady music.*

ELVIRA   Here we go again – more music for our listening pleasure.

ELVIRA &
ROHAN   (*simultaneously*) Shepherd's Bush!

> *She closes her eyes and rocks a little in one spot.*

ELVIRA   We used to have some good times, didn't we. Come nuh man – come leh we rent a tile.

> *They dance, becoming more physically intimate, nuzzling, laughing and kissing each other. They make love.*

ELVIRA   God, it's so hot! Open the shutters, Rohan!

ROHAN   Did I hear you right?

ELVIRA   I don't give a damn any more– (*ROHAN goes to the windows and begins opening the shutters*) Not too far! Ah that's better. What this damn country needs is a good sweeping out with a Black Sage broom – to clear out all the bad vibrations. "There's very little that a Black Sage broom can't fix in a house or a yard," Granny used to say.

ROHAN   And you a scientist too.

ELVIRA   Science can't fix everything, Rohan. (*she turns on her side, away from him – he sits up in bed watching her*) She would have boiled up something for me to drink.

ROHAN   Is that what you believe?

ELVIRA   She would have stopped the bleeding.

ROHAN   I never thought it mattered that much to you, Elvira – You recovered so quickly

ELVIRA   How could it not matter?

ROHAN   You never talked about it–

ELVIRA   Words always matter so much to you–

ROHAN   Let's try again, El – we're still young–

ELVIRA   Never want anything too much – Granny always used to say that. I wanted it so much – (*pause*) I couldn't even bear to look at her – me the big pathologist. Did you see her, Rohan? I should have – I didn't think I could look at her – and continue–

ROHAN   Oh, El–

ELVIRA   How can I believe Granny would have helped and still be a scientist?

ROHAN   I wouldn't worry about being a scientist, Elvira. You're turned on by the smell of Bunsen burners and formaldehyde is an aphrodisiac for you.

ELVIRA   Do you remember when you told your parents that you couldn't bear to cut up anything.

ROHAN   And that I couldn't stand the sight of blood and wasn't going to become a doctor. My god, it put them into deep mourning. I rallied them with a promise of law. (*silence*) You don't know that your Granny would have saved the baby, El.

ELVIRA   I believe it. (*pause*) What did she look like – the baby?

ROHAN   Elvira – you mustn't dwell on it so much.

ELVIRA   What did she look like?

ROHAN   Well, she had good hair–

        They laugh.

ELVIRA   Did you want the baby, Rohan?

ROHAN   Of course, I did.

ELVIRA   (*she mimics his tone*) Of course I did.

ROHAN   You were the one who kept putting it off.

ELVIRA   Only because I sensed you didn't want it. You had to finish your great contribution to literature, didn't you

ROHAN   Why wouldn't I want our child?

ELVIRA   To make your parents feel better – as long as you didn't bring any dougla children into the world it would be easier to leave.

ROHAN   If I wanted to make my parents feel good, Elvira, I wouldn't have married you. I wanted our child – a beautiful dougla girl or boy. Why did you want it?

ELVIRA   To keep us together – maybe that's why I lost it.

ROHAN   That's rubbish, Elvira, and you know it.

ELVIRA   Then maybe it was punishment.

ROHAN   For what?

ELVIRA   For offending. Straying outside. Why bring a child into the world to be even more confused than we are – part Indian, part African, and all nothing.

ROHAN   You're beginning to sound like my parents.

ELVIRA   Maybe they were right, Rohan.

RADIO   I wish to interrupt this broadcast to make the following announcement. We have been asked by the government to assure citizens and residents that, contrary to earlier reports, the water supply is not poisoned – we repeat, the water supply is not poisoned.

ELVIRA   Poison! Rohan, can you believe this? I don't know whether to laugh or cry – when was the water supply supposed to have been poisoned?

ROHAN   I'm sure sales of Carib beer have skyrocketed.

They laugh. A pause.

ELVIRA   Tell me a story, like you used to.

ROHAN   What kind of story – a true true story or a story story?

ELVIRA   Don't tease. Tell me the one about Anancy and the calabash.

ROHAN   I'm not sure I remember that one – *(pause)* Once upon a time, there was a god called Rama–

ELVIRA   I like this one, but you're supposed to say–

**ROHAN &
ELVIRA**   Crick crack.

ELVIRA   And I say–

**ELVIRA &
ROHAN**   Monkey break he back.

ELVIRA   Start over, Rohan, and do it right this time.

ROHAN   Crick crack–

ELVIRA   Monkey break he back.

ROHAN   Once upon a time, there was a god called Rama and he had a most beautiful wife, Sita. Rama loved Sita and Sita loved Rama.

ELVIRA   Rama loved Sita and Sita loved Rama – say that again.

ROHAN   Rama loves Sita and Sita loves Rama.

ELVIRA   Do you think Sita wants to be rescued?

ROHAN   Elvira – do you want me to tell the story or not?

ELVIRA   Go on.

ROHAN   Rama loved Sita and Sita loved Rama and they were very, very happy. Then one day the wicked, demon king Ravana heard about Sita's beauty all the way across the ocean in Lanka and he was jealous. Very, very jealous. He decided he would steal Sita away from Rama who loved her so much. So he left Lanka, went to India and stole the lovely Sita away. (*pause*) Who is he, Elvira?

ELVIRA   Who's who?

ROHAN   The man you're seeing.

> *She is silent.*

ELVIRA   I was going to tell you – I was waiting for the right time.

ROHAN   Aren't you going to ask how I know?

ELVIRA   No.

ROHAN   When you were talking—on the porch—your hands stopped moving when you said you couldn't even tell me there was someone else. (*he takes one of her hands*) They do flutter and dance on your words you know – except when you hold back. You should be careful if you ever have to give evidence in court. (*she pulls her hand away*) And you've never liked burnt plantains before. When was the right time going to be? As you got on the plane?

ELVIRA   When I left you there was no one, Rohan. I didn't lie about that.

ROHAN   But there is now.

ELVIRA   Is this the fifth degree?

ROHAN   And he's Black, he's well built and he's handsome – right? That's what all this African and Indian shit is all about.

ELVIRA   Fuck off, Rohan. Do you want to know if he's well hung? Isn't that what all women want – big dicks.

ROHAN   If it's more than twelve inches long, Elvira, I can't compete.

ELVIRA   I don't believe you!

ROHAN   I do have cause to be worried, Elvira, and least of all because of the size of his dick.

ELVIRA   What are you talking about?

ROHAN   I was always afraid of coming back here with you. I can't compete, Elvira.

ELVIRA   Compete! With whom? – Black men!

ROHAN   Yes – like Mikey.

ELVIRA   Mikey? You mean Lone Ranger? Your friend? From all those years ago. What's there to compete with?

ROHAN   A kind of vitality–

ELVIRA   Vital! Do you *hear* what you're saying? What about loose Black women? You believe that too? You believe that shit, don't you.

ROHAN   I don't believe you're loose.

ELVIRA   That's not what I asked you.

ROHAN   What you asked has nothing to do with us.

ELVIRA   You bloody shit – you can't even say it – after all these years and all your bloody talk about beauty and love.

ROHAN   It's all true. (*pause*) El–

He touches her tentatively on her shoulder.

ELVIRA   Don't you touch me!

ROHAN   Are you going to curse me? Trace my ancestry like that woman years ago. (*pause*) I love you, Elvira. (*pause*) Rama loves Sita.

ELVIRA   What if Sita doesn't love Rama, Rohan. What if she doesn't want to be rescued?

ROHAN   Why didn't you tell me?

ELVIRA   I didn't want to hurt you – I was afraid–

ROHAN   Of what? Did you think I would chop off your head with a cutlass. Like some jealous coolie husband?

ELVIRA   Don't be stupid, Rohan. Last time I checked husbands killing wives was not exactly the monopoly of any one racial group. (*pause*) I met him last year—December. When I came home for Christmas to see Ma and Pa. I came to Tobago for a few days. I was lying on the beach. At Pigeon Point. There was a man – he was beaching his boat. He had just come back from fishing and we got to talking.

ROHAN   He's a fisherman!

ELVIRA   Is there something wrong with that?

ROHAN   No, just surprised. Do you like him?

ELVIRA   What do you think?

ROHAN   And he's good in bed?

ELVIRA   Rohan! What is this? He's OK. (*pause*) I had been lying on my bed at the hotel one afternoon and I came awake very suddenly. The radio was playing Eddy Grant. Do you know his song "Neighbour, Neighbour?" (*she hums the refrain and he shakes his head*) There was something in the timbre of his voice–

ROHAN   So, I've got Eddy Grant to thank for this?

ELVIRA   It was the first time I'd ever felt like that.

ROHAN   Like what? Are you having an affair with Eddy Grant? For Christ's sake, Elvira, stop talking in riddles.

ELVIRA   Have you ever been with an Indian woman?

ROHAN   What are you asking?

ELVIRA   Have you slept with anyone since we separated?

ROHAN   What does that have to do with anything?

ELVIRA   Have you?

ROHAN   Have I what?

ELVIRA   For fuck's sake, Rohan, have you fucked anyone since I left?

ROHAN   Yes.

ELVIRA   Was she Indian?

ROHAN   No.

ELVIRA   You haven't told me whether you've ever been with an Indian woman.

ROHAN   No, I haven't. Told you, that is.

ELVIRA   Have you noticed, Rohan, how black skin comes alive in the sun? After dreary old London with all those white folks, it is such a joy–

ROHAN   That I can understand.

ELVIRA   No, you don't, Rohan! I wanted to be with a Black man. I need-ed to–

ROHAN   So you heard a song by Eddy Grant, you felt the need to fuck a Black man and you went and found one.

ELVIRA   I'm not going to talk to you any longer if you–

ROHAN   You are not going to talk to me! You are screwing around on me–

ELVIRA   I left you. *Then* I met a man.

ROHAN   Why did you sleep with me? You wanted to compare, didn't you. So how did I rate, Elvira? On your racial sexual scale.

ELVIRA   I wanted to sleep with you, Rohan, because I still love you.

ROHAN   You're here to see him, aren't you? All this talk about coming to Tobago to relax is just so much bull-shit isn't it?

ELVIRA   Yes, but it's not–

An announcer's voice interrupts the music.

RADIO   We have received reports that there have been several incidents in the San Juan, Santa Cruz, Saint Augustine area. Roving bands of African and Indian youth are reported to be–

She goes to the radio and turns it up.

ELVIRA   Wait! (*ROHAN picks up the radio*) What are you doing?

ROHAN   What does it look like I'm doing?

ELVIRA tries to take the radio from him. ROHAN walks out of the bedroom carrying the radio.

ELVIRA   You can't do that. There's racial violence–

ROHAN   Just watch me, Elvira. All day long you've been listening to this crap – the stupid lies, it's all lies – lies! Driving everyone crazy! Tell me you want to be with another man – any man! But what's this wanting-to-be-with-a-Black-man shit? It's like those T-shirts that proclaim – "It's a black thing, you won't understand." No, I don't fucking understand, Elvira – this black thing.

ELVIRA   It's mine – Rohan! (*she tugs at him*) Give me my radio! (*he wards her off, goes onto the porch*) No – don't, Rohan!

He hurls the other radio off the porch.

ROHAN   It's too late, Elvira!

ELVIRA   (*she strikes at him with her fists*) You son of a bitch! (*they struggle*) How could you! How could you!

ROHAN   "Wait, Rohan, wait" – that's all I've had from you. Every fucking time I try talking to you about us, you let that goddam radio get in the way. I'm not waiting any more, Elvira!

ELVIRA   You fool, didn't you hear about the racial violence on the radio? We could be in danger.

ROHAN   No, I did not! The only African and Indian I care about—no—to use your language, the only nigger and coolie I care about is you and me. We—you and I—have a relationship, and you care more about the crap that's being broadcast on that radio than about us. I don't give a fuck about racial violence. I care about us. Me, Rohan and you Elvira. And I don't see you as Black – you are Elvira!

ELVIRA   That's your mistake. Not seeing me as Black. And no amount of your love will change the fact that I am.

ROHAN   What are you doing?

ELVIRA   What does it look like I'm doing. I'm leaving that's what I'm doing.

    She takes off her night shirt and puts on a pair of jogging pants and a t-shirt. She puts her clothes in the overnight case.

ROHAN   Elvira! Where can you go at this time of the night?

ELVIRA   Anywhere where I don't have to be with you. I wish to hell Columbus had never discovered these islands – then I would never have met you. You said it right – we are the result of one big fuck-up and you know what? We're fucked, Rohan, fucked – you and I.

    ROHAN pulls on a pair of trousers. He puts the passport and ticket in his pocket.

ROHAN   Calm down, Elvira.

    She picks up the suitcase.

ELVIRA   Oh I am calm, Rohan – very calm.

    He pushes past her. He blocks her exit.

ROHAN   You can't let this madness get to you, Elvira. I won't let you go–

ELVIRA   *You* won't let me go?

ROHAN   I can't let you go! Where are you going?

ELVIRA   Back to the hotel—to Mrs Samuels—I don't know and don't much care.

ROHAN   Your luggage, Elvira! How are you–?

ELVIRA   My luggage! "Elvira, why do you have to pack so much?" How many times have you told me that? I've got everything that I need here, Rohan. I'm travelling light for a change.

ROHAN   There's a curfew – think of what can happen to you.

ELVIRA And what's that, Rohan? You've been making light of my fears all day – but what can happen to me? Tell me. I get fucked – I get raped and maybe killed. That might not be too bad after all this hanging around not knowing what's going to happen next. I'm tired of all this shit, Rohan – tired of history, tired of politics, tired of men shooting other men because – because they don't like the way their dicks hang, or some such equally stupid reason. I want out Rohan. This country is fucked – and as you told me earlier – I have a British passport. The British look after their own, don't they, so move.

ROHAN But you're not British – you'll never be British. You're not kith and kin. You are Wog.

ELVIRA I know that Rohan. I'm surprised you didn't say hanoman. But the passport means something. It'll get me out of here.

ROHAN This passport? Are you're going to wave it at the soldiers and yell that you're British subject. Like you did this morning.

ELVIRA Don't fuck with me, Rohan. Give me my passport.

ROHAN Elvira! – I am Wog too!

ELVIRA What are you going to do – throw it away like you did the radios? That won't stop me leaving.

ROHAN You and I are Wog, Elvira! That's the only country we belong to – you wanted a land of belonging – that's our land of belonging – Wogland!

ELVIRA My passport!

ROHAN Elvira! You must hear what I'm saying. For now at least. You'll be safe here – you belong to me. Oh shit! I don't have – I love you, Elvira, that much I know – I don't have the words to keep you here – all I know is... you are my history, my politics– (*he slides down the door*) My music, my literature – You're Elvira! (*the passport falls to the floor next to him*) Elvira with the butterfly hands – Rohan loves Elvira, Rohan loves Elvira–

> ELVIRA *watches him, still holding the suitcase. She puts it down, goes to him and crouches in front of him. She kisses him full on the lips.*

ELVIRA   Rohan loves Elvira. (*she kisses him*) Elvira loves Rohan. (*she kisses him*) I have to learn to know the darkness. I want to learn to love the darkness. I must go.

The stage darkens.

Prodigals in a
Promised Land

by h. jay bunyan

HECTOR BUNYAN AND THE HYPHENATED CANADIAN
AN INTRODUCTION TO THE PLAY PRODIGALS IN A PROMISED LAND
IN THE FORM OF A DIALOGUE

by Patricia Keeney and Don Rubin

RUBIN: I remember seeing this play when it was first produced at Toronto's Theatre Passe Muraille in 1981. Very few plays by black writers had appeared on Canadian stages to that time. So this was a special event. Unfortunately, the production was not a very good one. What struck me then was that the script was better than the playing. It had some strong characters and a strong situation – two people from Jamaica with a dream of bettering themselves by moving to Canada. Canada was to them the land of milk and honey. Racism never seems to enter their minds. But the play, I think, was ultimately hurt by a very realistic, nearly a naturalistic, production. That style kept slowing the play down. The script wanted to fly from scene to scene. But the real tables and the real chairs kept getting in the way. The real world of the play was beyond the kitchen sink. The realistic approach taken by the director really did lock it in an unfortunate way. Reading it again today, I think I was right. The dreams need to fly; the sun and snow, the past and present.

KEENEY: I'm not so sure how much dream is in it. It seems to me there are the dualities you talk about but they are real and it's these realities which clash. And both realities in the play are ultimately restrictive. Both are claustrophobic. They ultimately are about what people think they should want rather than what they really want, what they think they should be rather than what they are.

RUBIN: This doubleness is the play's real strength. It's what a production needs to capture. Both the husband and the wife say things not necessarily because they believe them but because they think they should believe them. The audience needs to see that. They are buying into attitudes that they think they should be buying into. The closer they get to the reality of particular situations, however, the further they get from the dream. The Canada presented at the beginning of the play, for example, is not a real Canada but a dream Canada. A land of milk and honey covered by a thin layer of pristine snow. But once they are in Canada and they see the reality, the Caribbean becomes the land of dream. They forget the unemployment problems and the social problems. In that sense, they can never reach their goals because their goals must, by definition, remain in dream. That, I think, is part of what Hector Bunyan, the playwright, is really saying about first generation immigrants, wherever they come from. Certainly a realistic production (as this play got) would lock in the reality and would keep it from flying as I think it must to really work.

KEENEY: I still don't think there's an active dream dimension as I read it. Whether they are in the Caribbean or in Canada, it's reality that stifles them. The dream dimension that they are all groping for but that they can't quite reach is vague. The play for me really comes alive about halfway through when Theo, the husband, starts to realize that he, in fact, has to face reality, that he has to stop buying into attitudes toward Canada, toward education. Theo's wife has turned away from him and eventually takes up with another man. That's when the daughter, Atiba, starts to hear two different versions of reality. That's when she says she doesn't know whose reality to believe in anymore. And for me that's where the play really starts to come alive and that's where the questions in the play start to become really interesting. That's when the situation of the struggles of the immigrant family start to become meaningful.

RUBIN: You bring up another interesting point. Whose play is it? It starts out as the husband's play, it evolves into the wife's play for a time and then ends up as the child's play. The focus wanders in that sense. That allows the reader's focus, the audience's focus to wander as well. Ultimately, I think the focus is not to be found in any of the characters specifically but rather in the family as a whole. That's much harder to make work on a stage.

KEENEY: The mother-in-law comes in at the end and tells the family that what they really need is to use some common sense. The real decisions here are also ultimately made by the women. The sense of the matriarchy is significant.

RUBIN: Yet Theo, the husband, is the most dominant character. Even so, his intellectuality is a false one. He thinks a doctorate, any university degree, will make him into a better human being somehow. He does come to realize this, however, and that saves his character. He comes to realize that what he has been searching for all along is freedom at some deep level. The freedom to choose his own way to live. Did he have to leave Jamaica to find that? I think there's a doubt in his mind. Is Canada the place to find his freedom? He begins to doubt it in the same way that he begins, near the end of the play, to doubt that the answer is to be found simply in university degrees. One finds ultimate freedom in the self. One finds one's real identity in the self. You have to go far to go deeply. The world outside doesn't necessarily have better answers. These are also very Canadian questions, perhaps questions that grow from smaller countries. Do you have to leave home to define your self? Ibsen was never so Norwegian as when he left Norway. Perhaps the Caribbean sense of identity is not so far from the Canadian sense of identity. Theo begins by thinking that Canada and a Canadian education will ultimately tell him who he is. He comes to realize that the answer to the question has more to do with roots and family and personal integrity than geography. I agree it's the mother-in- law who has it right. She says you find yourself in your self and you don't have to go far to get that answer.

KEENEY: Theo keeps looking for himself in all the wrong places. He goes away from himself to find the self. He realizes that he has to go back to his own values. That's where the answers will be found. And those places are where his own intellectual thirst has come from. The light dawns at the end of the play. His desire to return to his wife is a recognition that he needs to return to roots, to self. She is ahead of him, however, and they can't quite return to their former relationship. She is already back there. Theo says to his daughter that he understands that her mother, his wife, is at least two women – the one he constructed and the one who was there all the time. Maybe that need for identity is just a male thing. He doesn't even know who his wife is. But by the end he is on the right path. Finally.

RUBIN: So the play is about cultural identity. That's clear. It's also about the immigrant experience, an experience that is in some instances not such a pretty one. In this play, those from the Caribbean find Canada a very "white" country, a very cold country, a land where you can get fired even from lousy jobs, a land where you can't make love in the morning for fear of showing up at work late.

KEENEY: It's the unrealistic preconceptions that are the real problem. Milk and honey do not flow in any country. Jobs are jobs wherever they are. Responsibilities are responsibilities. When Theo hears from family back in the Caribbean saying that they want to share in the Canadian dream he gets frustrated. By that time, he understands the need to be realistic. The immigrant is never walking into wonderland. The process of emigrating, immigrating and integrating into any new society is a difficult one and Hector Bunyan is saying precisely that. And he is suggesting that it may take more than one generation to accomplish it. Atiba may do it. Atiba has a future in a way that neither of her parents do.

RUBIN: Could we go back to the differences in male and female experience for the immigrant? He wants to go to university. That's where he feels the future is. His wife wants a child. Education doesn't seem to be an issue or an interest for her.

KEENEY: Those are the stereotypes he was dealing with in the 1980s and earlier. I think he does get past those stereotypes in the play. It's the women who really know things. I think both Theo and Gloria are locked in attitudes at the beginning of the play. As their journey progresses they both grow as people and as dramatic characters. As a writer, Hector sees that growth quite clearly.

RUBIN: Is it a play of its time then?

KEENEY: No doubt. And that makes it problematic in some ways for today's audiences.

RUBIN: I also think it's a dramaturgical problem to have a play take place over more than a decade (as this one does). The characters have to grow a lot more than they do.

KEENEY: I would agree. The flashback scenes are intercut quickly and I don't think the reader notices much character distinction in them.

RUBIN: The ending is a bit like Ibsen's *Doll's House* where the wife leaves hoping to find a miracle that would allow her marriage to go on. She returns home with hope. The prodigal Theo though remains in Canada still trying to work it all out.

KEENEY: With Atiba caught between the two worlds of her parents.

RUBIN: Perhaps Atiba is on her way to becoming a truly hyphenated Canadian.

KEENEY: Perhaps. As for the ending, I think it's meant to be ambivalent. The answers can't be easy. Atiba may well become a hyphenated Canadian and that may be inevitable. The old dreams are gone by the end of the play. They all finally understand how to understand themselves. They all have a sense finally of where the romantic dream has to end and where reality has to set in.

RUBIN: I was struck by how the dialect changes as they acculturate through the course of the play. In the beginning Theo's dialect is often so thick as to be almost indecipherable to the non-Caribbean ear. But as he Canadianizes, as Theo spends more and more time in Canada, the accent changes. It's quite well-done.

KEENEY: The change is almost imperceptible. You accept it without even noticing it.

RUBIN: What does this play ultimately say to a Canadian audience, an African-Canadian audience, an immigrant audience?

KEENEY: All the things we've been saying. The difficulty of assimilation. The natural resistance to assimilation. Cultural loss. The need to take your rightful place within a culture. The problems of leaving your own culture. Disappointments in dreams. It's the eternal struggle of every immigrant. It has a lot to say. And I don't think it's limited to just the black immigrant community.

Patricia Keeney is a poet and novelist and for several years was theatre critic for the *Canadian Forum*. She teaches Creative Writing at Toronto's York University. Don Rubin, former chair of the Department of Theatre at York, was the founding editor of the quarterly journal *Canadian Theatre Review* which he edited between 1974 and 1982. Since that time he has been the General editor of Routledge's six-volume *World Encyclopedia of Contemporary Theatre*.

Prodigals in a Promised Land was first produced at Theatre Passe Muraille on March 12, 1981.

Directed by Clarke Rogers

Cast:

THEO	Ardon Bess
GLORIA	Diane Nqui-Yen
ATIBA	Eva Maximea
STELLA	Joy Bullen
ARNOLD	John Blackwood
THEO'S MOTHER	Pauline Thomas

Set & Lighting Designed by Terry Gunvordahl
Music Composed and Played by Marsha Coffey

Stage Manager	Sarah Wakely
Costumes	Arron Moses
Lighting Operator	Tom D. Lux

Prodigals in a Promised Land was developed by New Works & Theatre Passe Muraille as a part of the New Play Series.

CHARACTERS

THEO
GLORIA
ATIBA
STELLA
ARNOLD
THEO'S MOTHER

Left to right: Dian Ngui-Yen, Ardon Bess

photo by Joël Benard

PROLOGUE

THEO   (*solemnly to Gloria*) Because dis country can't offer me the education I want. That is why Oscar left and Malcolm left and so many young people leaving by the planeloads, because the future waiting for us in the outside world.

GLORIA   But w'at about dis university here?

THEO   (*scornfully*) Dis university? Nobody beyond the West Indies knows too much about it, and what they know ain' too flattering.

GLORIA   Well, if yuh have the money to pay for yuh studies, I can't stop you from goin'.

THEO   But I wasn't planning on goin' without you.

GLORIA   Although yuh know I happy right here?

THEO   But...

GLORIA   I ain' want anyt'ing they got in dih outside world, yuh know. And I quite contented to continue talking with dis same accent up to dih moment dat they tighten the screws on mih coffin. You asking me to give up everyt'ing dat makes me happy...

THEO   But w'at about me?

GLORIA   I goin't miss yuh.

THEO   Well, if dat is dih way yuh feel...

GLORIA   I hear dat place so cold dat even the people living deh is tell West Indians dat they stupid fuh leaving their own country; I love dih sun, Theo; and ah have mih mother and brothers and father and all mih family here; and ah happy with mih job (*she wipes her eyes*) and yuh know dat once we board dat plane we might never come back to dis place.

THEO   I know dat a lot uh people who leave here ain' come back, but we can be different.

GLORIA   I ain' so sure about dat, Theo.

THEO   But dem people went into the world aimlessly. They didn't have a plan.

GLORIA   You asking too much from me, Theo.

They sit in silence, each in his/her own thoughts.

GLORIA   W'en yuh want to leave?

ACT I

SCENE I

GLORIA and ATIBA, her ten-year old daughter, are looking at the TV in a room, the decor of which comprises a three-piece chesterfield suite, its upholstery protected by plastic, two book shelves tightly stacked, a stereo component set, a telephone on a little table, one large centre table on which is an elegant cut glass vase resting on a stiffly-starched crocheted doily. There are two tables beside the large sofa, on each of which is a large lamp. Drapes are drawn all around this room. Portraits rest atop the TV. The walls are decorated with ceramic and copper ornaments. A dining table cluttered with books and papers is situated between the living room and the kitchen. The carpet is bordered with plastic about three feet in width and covers most of the living room.

THEO enters, a briefcase in one hand and quite a few books in the other. He kicks the door shut, stumbles over to the dining table, drops the books and collapses onto a chair. ATIBA runs over to him.

ATIBA   *(her hands outstretched)* Daddy, give me a piggy-ride; a long one.

THEO   *(a fatigued expression)* Girl, ah dead whey yuh see me lay.

ATIBA   *(sulks)* But you promised and every time you are always tired. Boy! I wish I had another daddy.

GLORIA   *(jumping to her feet)* What did I hear you say? *(shaking her finger at ATIBA in an admonitory gesture)* Don't you ever let me hear you say that again.

ATIBA bows her head. THEO places his arm around her waist drawing her closer to him.

THEO   Leff dih girl nuh. She ain't mean anyt'ing.

GLORIA   You could let shih say anyt'ing shih want, but not w'en I around. If she believe shih goin' grow like these children hey, shih lie, 'cause ah goin' kill shih with blows.

THEO   Den yuh bettah stop sending shih to school.

GLORIA   W'at nonsense you talking?

THEO   (*sarcastic*) Well that would be the only way to ensure she isn't influenced by the bad ways of the children around here.

GLORIA   She will be influenced anywhere she goes. She will just have to learn to leave the bad influences outside the door.

THEO   Yuh say some senseless t'ings before, but dis is really stupid.

> *GLORIA returns to her chair, picking up a book which she will try reading. ATIBA sits on THEO's legs.*

THEO   (*sucks his teeth*) Tell me, do you feel threatened by this child?

GLORIA   Is threatened yuh call it, eh? I see. It is heartening to know that when you try to give children proper guidance you are doing so because you feel threatened by them.

THEO   I ain' quarrelling about you trying to give her proper guidance. (*scornfully*) Every time dis girl seh anyt'ing, yuh shout at shih and mek shih feel like dih little dog dat shit pun madam sofa.

GLORIA   (*emphatically*) Well she is my child and I am going to do whatever I want with her.

THEO   Yes, sweetheart. You can do anything you want with her. But just a tiny favour I will ask you: don't ask her to meet you at the door wagging her tail with your slippers between her teeth.

GLORIA   (*hostile*) Favour denied! Don't forget you just called me stupid.

THEO   (*sarcastically*) And yuh mean to prove me right, because all you doin' fuh yuhself is vegetating in front of the TV and reading the kind of literature that can only poison yuh mind.

GLORIA   (*loudly*) W'at I read mek me stupid and w'at you read mek you an ass. So which one uh we better off?

THEO   Time will be the judge of that. One t'ing ah know fuh sure is dat I comfortable with mihself because ah putting somet'ing in mih head and the world ain't a mystery to me. But the world needs people like you to walk in the shadows of the accomplished and to applaud the successes of the winners. Yuh might burst yuh hand clapping but yuh goin't have to keep on doin' it because dat will be yuh only claim to recognition. Ha, haaa! (*his accent changes*) What skills do you possess Mrs. McAllister? (*accent reverts to normal; parodies a bashful woman*) Well, sir, I am a good hand-clapper. (*previous accent; imperious*) But we already have a multitude of coloured women who are excellent at giving applause. Is there anything else you can do?

GLORIA   (*lowering her book, continues in the same bashful tone*) Well, ah can wash perspiration stains from dih armpits of mih husban' shirts, and ah can wash he shorts till they look like new, and ah can cook, and ah can bring in money to mek sure dat dih house run properly, and ah can give he sex to relieve he frustrations, and w'en ah get careless ah can breed fuh he.

THEO   I'm sorry, my dear. I was wrong about you all along.

GLORIA   (*feigning surprise*) But eh, eh! I ain' hearing' mih ears right at all. You? Wrong? No! It can't be! (*her eyes cast to the ceiling*) Lawd, tell mih wuh yuh have in store fuh me and stop playing games.

THEO   The unfortunate thing is dat the skills you mention are so primitive dat they are as good as obsolete, because ah can always carry mih shirts to dih laundry...

GLORIA   (*interrupting*) And pay extra for fumigating the washing machine.

THEO   (*ignoring her*) And ah can cook mih own food.

GLORIA   And starve?

THEO   And sex is no problem because ah can get crotch at a dime ah dozen.

GLORIA   And at dat price yuh can get clap by the ton.

THEO   (*sarcastic*) Comin' to t'ink of it, dat might be a lot more exciting dan anyt'ing I can get from you.

GLORIA   (*angry*) Thank yuh! Ah goin' mark yuh words and, by Christ! I ain' goin' allow yuh to forget dem.

ATIBA gets off THEO's legs, looks enquiringly at both of them then goes off to the living room.

GLORIA   Yuh see! You have no consideration for dis child.

THEO   Hear who talking.

GLORIA   But you started it first with yuh dam nonsense.

THEO   And of course ah was carrying on all by mihself.

GLORIA   So w'at! You expect me to sit down and listen to all the bull you gotta say? No! The days fuh dat pass and gone! I use to allow you to upset me and mek me cry like a dam fool. But dat over now! Any crying I doin' now is fuh me and mih chile. I done shedding tears for you.

THEO   If you talking so powerful and you ain't get anywhere in life yet, I hate to hear how you goin' sound w'en yuh really get somewhere.

GLORIA   Get somewhere? Love, I am not like you, living somewhere in the clouds. I have arrived because I am comfortable in my world and I don't need a thing from you. Yuh know what dat means? It means you are serving absolutely no purpose in this house, none whatsoever.

THEO   So much for gratitude! If I used to treat you like a dog you woulda run and deafen the ears of the world with the good word dat God bless yuh with a considerate and loving man.

Gloria walks, slams door.

(*sarcastic*) Good night, my love.

ATIBA   Was she always like that?

THEO   It's hard to say. I ask myself that question many times and still can't arrive at an answer.

ATIBA   Maybe you don't want to know the answer.

THEO   Maybe I want to protect the memories.

ATIBA   Were they good?

THEO   Yes. The best.

ATIBA   So what went wrong?

THEO   Things changed after we came here, perhaps because your mother remained behind.

ATIBA   Why don't you say what you mean?

THEO   Ten years ago when we came here, life wasn't as easy as we thought it would be; our dreams were too big for a tiny room.

FLASHBACK ONE

The clock-radio alarms. GLORIA moans, stirs, stretches and stumbles out of bed. She shakes THEO. He groans and stirs, raises his head slowly.

THEO   Wuh time is it?

GLORIA   Six thirty.

THEO   Ah t'ink ah goin' sleep for a few more minutes.

GLORIA   If yuh don't get up now yuh goin' be late.

THEO   (*rolls over and hugs her*) Yuh know wuh dis mean?

GLORIA   It means we don't have enough time.

THEO   Fifteen minutes ain't enough time? Man we gotta adjust to dis new way of life or we goin' suffer.

GLORIA   So what you suggesting?

THEO   We can spend five minutes on foreplay, five minutes copulating, and five minutes to savour.

GLORIA   Sex on a bun to go, eh? (*she pushes him off*)

THEO   You crude woman! You just killed the urge!

GLORIA   Oh, sorry darling.

THEO lurches from the bed leaving her behind. He dresses hurriedly. Off-stage, he makes himself a cup of tea. He returns sipping from an enamel cup.

THEO   This is nothing like the Sundays we used to spend back home.

GLORIA   You shouldn't remind me of that w'en you have to go to work.

THEO   Yuh right. I should never put the idea in your head.

GLORIA   Well, if the idea become too annoying, I can always invite a man. (*in a deep male voice*) Lots of lonely men walking the streets.

> *THEO clears his throat then gathers some books, placing them into a shopping-bag. He pauses, looks at her questioningly and asks:*

THEO   You would ever do something like that?

GLORIA   What do you think?

THEO   You should always reassure a man when he is leaving for work.

> *GLORIA gets up from the bed and pushes him out of the room. THEO playfully resists.*

GLORIA   OK. You're reassured.

THEO   Of what?

GLORIA   Look, go on to work.

> *They kiss. He slaps her on the backside.*

THEO   Ah gone.

GLORIA   Call me w'en you get there. (*she locks the door*)

THEO   (*from the other side of the door*) If you ever do dat to me I'll fracture yuh balls!

SCENE II

> *GLORIA is attired in evening dress, her face is made up, hair in curls, bejeweled. ATIBA sits at a table in her pyjamas. She is drawing. A knock at the door.*

GLORIA   (*to ATIBA*) Get that please.

ATIBA   But I'm doing something.

GLORIA   I don't care what you are doing. W'en I give you an order I expect you to act immediately.

ATIBA   It just isn't fair.

ATIBA (*at the door*) Who is it?

VOICE Is me.

GLORIA (*bellowing*) Is who?

ATIBA Somebody name me.

GLORIA (*shouting*) Don't be an idiot! Who is me? What is the person's name?

ATIBA What is your name?

VOICE (*argumentatively*) Is me, man. How come yuh don't know mih voice?

GLORIA (*to ATIBA as she unlocks the door*) Yuh mean yuh don't know Stella voice or yuh just playing stupid.

STELLA (*enters*) The man ain' come yet? I ready fuh go to sleep. (*catches sight of GLORIA*) Eh, eh! Look at yooooou! Dressing like a fashion model now.

GLORIA Now tek a good look at dis furniture. (*she sweeps her arm around the living room*) Even a dog won't pee pun it.

STELLA Well I know some people who won't only pee pun it, they would even try to add to the world population pun it.

GLORIA With dih service I get from these chairs, I should retire dem with a pension. Well I done decide to change mih furniture because ah need a change in mih life. I wukking too hard and ah don't have a t'ing to show for it. Is time I start brightening up mih life.

STELLA Well, darling, yuh have a husban' and dat would make t'ings easier.

GLORIA But I ain' tell he.

STELLA So wuh yuh waitin' for?

GLORIA I don't intend to tell he because he goin' give mih a lecture and w'en he done ah goin' feel like a fool fuh ever t'inking about it. Yuh know how many t'ings I wanted to do with mih money and I allow dat man to talk me out uh dem?

STELLA   Girl, don't lemme say anything before yuh say I interfering, but some women playing Jesus on the cross, just to wring a few cents out of a man, and here you turning up yuh nose at what you can get without a fight. Some of us arrive already.

GLORIA   Girl, sometimes it better to walk naked than to walk in rags.

STELLA   (*gets up from the chair*) Come, Atiba, yuh sleeping by me tonight.

    ATIBA gathers her crayons and drawing and heads for the door.

GLORIA   (*a hand at her hip, she fumes as she watches ATIBA leave, then she shouts at her*) Wait, yuh leavin' without saying anyt'ing to me?

ATIBA   (*stops in her tracks, turns around*) Good night.

GLORIA   Come here. (*ATIBA walks to her dejectedly*) Aren't you goin' to kiss me?

    ATIBA inclines her head forward, kissing her on the chest.

GLORIA   (*pushes her away*) Look, go!

    ATIBA runs out of the door, crying.

STELLA   Girl, ah gone.

    Heavy footsteps approach the door.

THEO   (*outside, speaks to ATIBA*) Why you crying?

    No reply from ATIBA who turns around confusedly pointing.

STELLA   Look, don't point at me. Is she and shih mother kyetch a case.

    THEO enters with briefcase and books in his hands, followed by ATIBA and STELLA.

THEO   (*to GLORIA*) Wuh wrong? Why dis girl crying?

    ATIBA runs off to her bedroom. STELLA looks on with interest at the proceedings.

GLORIA   (*ignoring his question*) Weh you been till all dis time?

THEO   (*interrupts*) Look, I ask you a question because ah want an answer, not another question.

GLORIA   (*facetiously*) Sorry, daddy, but yuh see, ah can't help being a West Indian. (*becomes forceful*) And the next time you want to know why she is crying, yuh better stay home to find out.

THEO   (*sucks his teeth and goes to the kitchen where he opens pots in search of food*) So yuh stop leaving food fuh me? (*he reappears in the living room*)

GLORIA   Well be sensible now; why would I cook w'en we are supposed to be goin' to dinner (*voice crescendos*) which is probably over by now because we shoulda been there since nine o'clock and it is now ten-thirty and you ain' dressed yet.

THEO   So what yuh call dis? (*brushing his hand down the front of his shirt and pants*) Undressed?

GLORIA   It might as well be because you look like the closest thing to carrion.

THEO   (*an irritating grin*) Ah want to feed the scavengers tonight.

STELLA   Den they goin' have a proper feast. Ha, haaa!

GLORIA   (*blurts out*) Tell he fuh mih, girl.

THEO   What' wrong with the way I look? Nobody told me I was goin' to a costume party.

GLORIA   (*to STELLA*) Yuh hear the shit dis man talking?

STELLA   Man, yuh should dress nice w'en yuh goin' to a dinner party. Yuh should wear a...

THEO   (*interjects*) I have all that I need to wear: I have mih mouth, and a stomach dat fulling up with gas by the minute.

GLORIA   So why dih hell yuh don't go naked?

THEO   Dat ain' no problem. (*he starts pulling off his shirt and loosens his pants at the waist*)

STELLA   But why you like to be so difficult?

GLORIA   Yuh know wuh I can't unde'stand with he, Stella? He always complaining: "dih white man is a racist muddah-fuckah; dih white man is a muddah-fuckah of a muddah-fuckah," and, by Christ! (*she slaps the chair on which she is sitting*) I would run far from anybody dressed and smelling like he.

THEO   (*to GLORIA*) Fuh Christ sake! Get one t'ing straight. It is what yuh have in yuh head that makes a big difference in yuh life, not the costume yuh wear. We used to be comfortable in our nakedness until they decreed that nakedness is disgusting in the eyes of God. So we start covering up in their clothes and dressing our feet in their shoes, only to get bunions for we troubles. And we started painting we armpits and spraying we bodies with chemicals only to smell like whores on the prowl. But they never decreed that we nourish the mind. Yuh think they will ever tell us that the mind has been neglected too long? Aaah! Wake up woman!

STELLA sucks her teeth and leaves.

GLORIA   Why dih hell yuh didn' tell mih yuh had no intention of goin' tonight, rather...

THEO   (*interrupting*) I was getting worried that you would never come to dat realization.

GLORIA   But yuh coulda try being a man just for one small moment and tell mih to mih face. I woulda respect you fuh dat, Theo.

THEO   It is difficult being a man w'en dih woman yuh livin' with refuses to allow you to grow.

GLORIA   Correction. It is difficult being a man w'en you are in love with the idea of being an ass.

THEO   At least I'm a proud self-respecting ass. Claudette is typical of so many black women who squander their energies on parties and gossip from morning till night and indulge in an endless search for an excuse to keep their legs apart. They lead blind, aimless, empty lives! That's why I have no intention of going to her place tonight.

GLORIA   Yes, you got pride and self-respect, but only fuh using people. Before you get into university, dem same empty people use to be good enough company fuh you. Now, all of a sudden, they are shit.

THEO   It was inevitable I woulda drop dem because I constantly assessing my life. Dat is dih vast difference between me and you.

GLORIA   No, honey. Dih difference is dat I accept people for themselves, not for what they can do for me.

THEO   But soon ah goin' drop dem all because ah don't want any hin-
                drance to mih vision. Yuh better take a page from my book
                and start sweeping dih cobwebs out of yuh life.

GLORIA   (*shouting*) I would prefer to be dead before I tek a page from
                your book because you are the worst example anybody can
                follow. And if yuh was any kind uh man, yuh woulda move
                out and spare me and dis child the ordeal of putting up with
                you every Jesus day.

THEO   If you believe I would move out and leave dat child behind to
                have you damage her mind, then yuh lie! One empty life is
                enough of an injustice upon the world.

GLORIA   (*jumps to her feet and approaches him menacingly*) Yes, ass! It
                empty! It empty for a real man dat can make mih feel like a
                woman; a man ah would feel proud to walk with; a man ah
                can talk to without cringing for fear dat he would make mih
                feel like a retardate. Not some half-mad, half-celibate man car-
                rying the cares of the world on he shoulders and smelling as if
                he got a quarrel with deodorant.

THEO   (*belches*) Brrrrrrrp.

                GLORIA sucks her teeth and turns away in disgust.

                FLASHBACK TWO

                *THEO returns home wearing a dour expression. He collapses
                onto the bed.*

GLORIA   (*puzzled*) Wuh you doin' back so soon? (*pause*) Yuh get in
                trouble with dem? (*pause*) Wuh happen?

                THEO sits up in bed, hangs his head dejectedly.

GLORIA   Yuh go late and get fired, eh?

                THEO nods affirmatively.

GLORIA   Well I warned you about goin' late.

THEO   It ain' got anyt'ing to do with goin' late.

GLORIA   Well den, wuh happen?

THEO   I was doin' mih homework and they seh I wasn't being vigi-
                lant enough.

GLORIA   Before yuh get so upset, why yuh don't talk to that supervisor who used to treat you with a little decency?

THEO   He is the fucking hypocrite who ordered me fired!

GLORIA   Yuh mean dat same man who say yuh use to work so hard.

THEO   Yes, that same son-of-a-bitch.

GLORIA   Well sweetheart, dat is something else yuh dear friends didn't tell you about this promised land. (*silence*) On the other hand, yuh shouldn't get upset. Yuh never hear that man appoints but God disappoints? (*pause*) It could just be that this happen for the best.

THEO   How could you say dat after you know it took me three months before I got that job, day and night, listening to people tell me that I ain' got Canadian experience. I couldn't even get the job as a floor-cleaner, probably because the floors are Canadian and I would clean them with a different accent.

GLORIA   Don't worry yuh head, man. We ain' got a single bill to pay. What yuh woulda do if yuh had to pay a mortgage? We should be the happiest people in the world! (*pause*) And yuh know w'at? (*she comes up behind him and wraps her arms around his neck*) This is the first Sunday in three months that we at home together. (*with a wicked grin, she says in a polished accent*) So what will it be, mih Lord?

THEO   You don't understand, eh? Even though the job was so terrible I used to feel useful doing something and knowing dat ah could bring home some money.

GLORIA   OK. So you will get another job soon.

THEO   That is easy for you to say. You ain' got my problem, yuh know.

GLORIA   (*becomes apprehensive*) Wuh yuh mean?

THEO   Well one look at you and they would gladly hire you for any office job because you can easily blend... (*pause*)

GLORIA   (*she recoils in anger*) Say it Theo! Don't stop now! And listen to yuhself w'en yuh saying it!

THEO   Say what?

GLORIA   Don't play that game with me, man! Be a man and admit to your intention! You know dam-well that yuh want to say I would be hired at a glance because I can easily blend in with the majority.

> *THEO hangs his head in embarrassment.*

Ah, boy. Yuh see how easy you can lose your perspective? Yuh see how a person's skin can blind him to another's misery?

THEO   Sorry.

GLORIA   I don't want any apologies. I only want you to recognize how dangerous it is to feel sorry for yuhself.

> *THEO gets up and walks away from her. He stands looking through a window. GLORIA gets up from the bed, removes a packet from under the mattress and drops it on a table beside him.*

GLORIA   I was going to buy yuh birthday gift with dis. Use it to enroll in full-time school tomorrow.

THEO   (*opens the packet, not believing what he sees*) Where you get this from?

> *GLORIA returns to bed and gets under the blanket.*

How you get all dis money? (*he stands over her*) If you don't tell me where you got all this money, I won't touch a cent of it. I insist that you tell me!

GLORIA   (*in disgust*) I have exciting legs, Theo.

SCENE III

> *New furniture has just been delivered. The pieces are covered with plastic. GLORIA leans against a wall, wipes her forehead with her head-tie and surveys the task before her. The door to the apartment is ajar.*

STELLA   (*peering into the apartment*) I hope madame supervisor will invite me to the party.

GLORIA   (*climbing over the furniture, she goes to the door*) What party, may I ask?

STELLA   Yuh mean you ain't goin' to acknowledge yuh promotion with at least a drink?

GLORIA   Girl, I don't get excited by rumours.

STELLA   Darling, this is no rumour because Margaret tell...

GLORIA   Margaret?

STELLA   Ah know Margaret mouth rip from ears to ass, but shih friend who is tek minutes at the executive meetings, tell shih, so everybody know.

GLORIA   Girl, whether I get that promotion or not, I intend getting up in this world.

STELLA   (*now in the apartment, she covers her eyes quickly*) Lord, I am blinded! I am seeing strange visions! (*uncovering her eyes*) For a woman who don't get excited by rumours, what do you call this? (*she points at the furniture*)

GLORIA   A modest gesture.

STELLA   Well honey, this goin' to be the first time I enjoy sitting on modest.

GLORIA   Look, stop trying to make mih feel important and give mih a hand.

STELLA   (*tears off the plastic covering a chair*) Lord Jesus!

GLORIA   What's wrong?

STELLA   (*stroking the upholstery*) You have entered the world of velvet!

GLORIA   Lift dih darn t'ing.

STELLA   You have entered the world of royalty!

GLORIA   Hurry up and lift. I have work to do.

STELLA   Do you know it is Jesus who made velvet popular?

GLORIA   Yes?

STELLA   That's right! What yuh t'ink he was wearing when he rode the jackass into Jerusalem on Palm Sunday? It was a custom-tailored velvet dress with no underwear.

GLORIA   Lift!

STELLA   (*as they move the chair into place*) Ah come all the way to dis country to get a hernia.

GLORIA   This chair look nice here?

STELLA   No.

GLORIA   Give me a good suggestion, then.

STELLA   Put it in the bedroom.

GLORIA   Stop joking, man.

STELLA   I don't ever joke about matters relating to the bedroom. The mere thought of that place and my heart (*she clutches her chest and breathes deeply*) starts to palpitate.

GLORIA   I don't intend to join that group of women who spend their lives trying to hold on to a man.

STELLA   And ah don't blame yuh because a lot of women fussing over men who have less class than a box of cat shit. But your husband is different. Soon he will have his Ph.D.

GLORIA   Oh, that rare disease! Girl, if yuh don't live in the house yuh can't know where the roof leaking.

STELLA   Well at my age, I won't allow even a tidal-wave to discourage me from my vision of the good life. That's why now, before I encourage a man into mih house, I check his credentials to mek sure I ain' picking up shit.

GLORIA   What about the man with the bible yuh introduce me to the other day?

STELLA   That son-of-a-bitch was just using the bible as a front.

GLORIA   He looked so quiet and decent.

STELLA   Mih mother use to warn me about men like dat. During his first few visits, he couldn't seh fart. But after couple weeks I was still holding on to the goods. Well you shoulda see the change dat overcome that man: he wouldn't only seh fart, he would do it and leave a stench that could change mih complexion, and w'en he go to pee, he would miss the porcelain and make sure dat every last drop of pee hit the water so hard dat yuh would t'ink a riot was goin' on in the toilet bowl.

GLORIA   (*laughing*) Look, leh we lift dis other chair.

STELLA   You would never imagine how much trouble I had getting rid of dat man. Even w'en I tell him I have another man, he would still keep coming back and fart more stink and piss against the bathroom walls.

GLORIA   But yuh never tell me dis.

STELLA   I was too embarrassed.

GLORIA   So what yuh do?

STELLA   I would wait until he knock at mih door and tell he, "hold on please, sweetheart", and ah would run fast and sprinkle some ammonia around the edge of the toilet bowl and leave the toilet seat standing up. The poor fool probably seh to heself dat any man who could piss dat stink, got to be a rass of a man. Look, he fly out of dat apartment never to return again. (*pause*) Of course on his way out the door he said goodbye with a fart that killed all my plants.

GLORIA   (*laughing*) He left you fond memories.

STELLA   Yuh see, you ain' got anything to complain about. You can at least show something for dih years you in dis country. But me, what do I have to show. I had three abortions, the man I was engaged to turned out to be married and left me in ten thousand dollars debt, and when ah try to collect just a few hundred dollars, he put me in hospital for three months. That's why when I think about you and Theo ah is have to say, "Gloria complaining, but shih don't know w'at it is to feel the sting of a man's brutality."

GLORIA   You talking about the kind of brutality dat leaves visible scars. But there is another kind of brutality dat leaves invisible scars and ruins people permanently. That is how Theo brutalizes.

STELLA   But dat don't make too much sense.

GLORIA   I know. That's why I can't afford to discuss my problems, because the first thing people say is "where are the bruises and the lumps and the scars." They don't seem to realize that people can die from internal hemorrhage.

FLASHBACK THREE

The table is laid for two with her best utensils. Everything glitters in the candlelight. GLORIA greets THEO at the door, throwing her arms around him with the gaiety of her ebullient spirit.

THEO   (*rigidly*) What happen to the lights?

GLORIA   We have all the light we need.

THEO   Come on. Let me go.

GLORIA   What's the hurry?

THEO   Lots of work.

GLORIA   Well, you'll have all the time you need after dinner.

THEO   I'm not hungry.

GLORIA   (*arms fall from around his neck*) But it's your favourite meal, Theo.

THEO   I have too much work to do.

GLORIA   But I laid the table for us to have a good meal together.

THEO   Well I'll sit down with you but I won't eat.

GLORIA   But I can't eat by myself. Plus I want to tell you something.

THEO   OK. Tell me quickly.

GLORIA   No. Let us both sit down and I'll get you a drink (*she mixes a drink*) then I'll tell you. This is good news.

THEO   What is it? Did we get a letter from home that isn't asking for money.

GLORIA   (*dishing out her food*) Nah. The best news.

THEO   What?

She links her arm in his and brings him to the table. He walks stiffly. She sits him down before his drink.

GLORIA   (*sits down and pours herself a drink*) I went to the doctor today.

THEO	What did he say?
GLORIA	He says you can father a child.
THEO	That means you won't be able to go to school.
GLORIA	This is more important than school. Don't you think so?
THEO	And I'll have to leave school and get a job, and...
GLORIA	No man. We goin' manage.
THEO	How?! Raising a child requires lots of money and right now we barely making ends meet.
GLORIA	You worry too much.
THEO	But we had agreed you were going to wait until I'm finished with school before we decide to bring a child into this world. What's the rush?
GLORIA	I'm getting older, Theo.
THEO	You allowed a stupid, romantic idea to overrule your better sense.

GLORIA in tears stops eating, her head bowed in her drink.

What will be that child's future. Did you ever think about that? Well let me tell you: it will be that of a victim, the victim of a father catching his ass at menial jobs and a mother who couldn't wait, because she had to justify the sole reason for her existence: that she could breed.

GLORIA	(*gets up from the table*) You go have your education and I'll have my child.
THEO	You prefer to unlock your pelvis before you unlock your mind. What's wrong with getting an education?
GLORIA	I have the best education in the world because I didn't go to a university to have my mind fucked up like yours. I want to remain a simple woman.
THEO	You'll die of an overdose of simplicity.

GLORIA   (*picks up a handful of papers*) That's right. So don't you bring
         another of these brochures home. (*starts ripping them to shreds*)
         I don't want what they can offer me, and I want nothing from
         you where this child is concerned. Do you hear me?! I will
         carry it proudly! And if God is ever to be so unjust to me as to
         have it become like you, I will kill myself! Do you hear me?! ·

SCENE IV

THEO   (*to GLORIA*) I'm home.

GLORIA   So I see.

THEO   (*places the books on the table and looks around searchingly*) Where
         my books?

GLORIA   I put them away.

THEO   Ah didn' ask yuh dat. I just want to know where yuh put
         dem, then after you answer dat, wc can deal with the next
         question.

GLORIA   No. I answer both questions at the same time.

THEO   Please, don't do me any favours.

GLORIA   Interpret it however you like, but understand one t'ing: I don't
         want any books and papers hanging around dis place now.
         I want to have a proper house, not a library.

THEO   Woman, where are my books?

GLORIA   You can find your intellectual nourishment in a box under the
         bed.

THEO   The voice of independence! Arrogant and self-indulgent, yet
         ever so protective of its insecurity. You don't want my books
         in here because to see them is to be reminded of your crippling
         inferiority complex. (*he walks toward the bedroom*)

GLORIA   And if yuh want to do me a big favour, you can stay there with
         them.

THEO	Yuh know, I have a friend whose wife laughs at him whenever he says he will get the best education and escape the misery they left behind. She ridicules his idea because she feels poor people are not supposed to entertain exalted dreams. Nevertheless, she wants the good life but without sacrifice, she wants the product but not the process by which it is realized, she can't free her mind to see beyond her obsession with expensive clothes and fancy furniture, and worst of all... they have a child. Christ! She is going to ruin that child's delicate mind! Goddamit! That woman is a criminal! She should be shot!

GLORIA gets up and turns on the radio to a deafening volume.

ATIBA	(*runs out of the bedroom, looks at them perplexedly, then turns down the volume*) You guys deaf?
GLORIA	(*in the voice of a command*) Stay there, and if your father starts talking again, turn it up loud.
ATIBA	But that's not good manners...
THEO	Out of the mouth of babes and...
GLORIA	Anything is good manners w'en you have to silence a pompous ass.
ATIBA	What is "pompous"?

FLASHBACK FOUR

GLORIA	(*home from work*) Ah come.
THEO	Uh hum.
GLORIA	(*removing her shoes*) Any letters come?
THEO	Nah.
GLORIA	(*opens the refrigerator, removes a carton of milk and pours herself some*) Yuh goin' out tonight?
THEO	I ain' sure yet. (*short pause*) Why?
GLORIA	Just asked.
THEO	Something wrong?

GLORIA   Not particularly.

THEO   (*looks in her direction*) Wuh?

GLORIA   Well... today is six months.

THEO   (*his eyes back in his books*) Yuh only have three months more.

GLORIA   From here on is touch and go.

THEO   Yeah. Ah know. Don't lift anything too heavy.

GLORIA   The doctor ask me what kind of delivery ah want and if you want to witness it.

THEO   Nah.

GLORIA   Yeah, I know. (*sighs*) I told him you don't like the sight of blood. I even told him you're afraid to feel the movements of the child.

THEO   Because I don't like it.

GLORIA   But it is your child, Theo.

THEO   I never doubted your fidelity.

GLORIA   It is one way to show interest.

THEO   Believe me, I'm interested.

GLORIA   You coulda fooled me.

THEO   I don't have to do it because others do. Yuh know how I hate being part of the crowd.

GLORIA   So you have become the worst example of indifference.

THEO   W'at yuh mean?

GLORIA   Ah, forget it.

THEO   No. If yuh have somet'ing on yuh mind, say it.

GLORIA   What's the use? I'm never listened to.

THEO   OK. Then I'll listen to you.

GLORIA   Don't patronize me: I detest it.

THEO	See how difficult it is to please women?
GLORIA	I don't want you to go out of your way to please me.
THEO	Then what you have to say couldn't be too important.
GLORIA	Believe me, whether you listen or not, it is very important.
THEO	I assure you, whatever it is, it wouldn't upset me.
GLORIA	Yes. I know *(pause)* you are too proud.
THEO	Right.
GLORIA	And angry.
THEO	Anger has been a good companion.
GLORIA	And you are destroying yourself.
THEO	That's a measure of my freedom.
GLORIA	You use to be gentle and considerate, Theo. You use to be a good friend. Now I don't know the person that lives inside you. You are without feeling, Theo. You are a man of stone.
THEO	I would probably be wasting my time to tell you I disagree.
GLORIA	Your attitude toward me became progressively worse since I started carrying this child. You never ask how I feel, not once. Many nights I lie down in pain, my stomach empty from vomiting, and you never even ask if I want a cup of tea, and now dat I tell you the next three months goin' be touch and go, you just dismiss my fears. Why, Theo? Is there no room in your world for a little tenderness or understanding? Do you believe it will make you less of a man.
THEO	*(pounds the table)* Hell, man! Do you know what I have to endure every day just trying to keep my sanity? If I'm unfeeling, it is because I've had to become a predator to survive.
GLORIA	Predator? Dat too good fuh you, Theo. You just confused, that's all.
THEO	*(approaches her slowly, menacingly)* I see. I have to compromise my ass to pieces to give more wealth to the wealthy, and I have to take fucking shit to put bread on the table, and I have to sacrifice my dignity that one day I may be able to say, I am dignified, and you tell me I am confused?!

GLORIA   Well only someone who is confused would fight something he cannot change.

THEO   (*outraged*) I refuse to join in the celebration of impotence which characterizes the immigrant. I despise that thinking and I will fight it with every passion that's left in my body.

GLORIA   And what is to become of me?

THEO   I'll fight the negative aspects of your thinking; I didn't say I'll abandon you.

GLORIA   It would be better if you did, because you ignore me; you don't talk to me; you are insensitive to my needs; you (*she hesitates*) you treat me like a leper; (*shrill voice*) I'm your wife, Theo, not your dam patient!

THEO   Look, it is a waste of time trying to have a decent talk with you. You need to justify your opinions of me and you will jump like a vulture at anything I say.

GLORIA   Do you blame me?

THEO   No, I blame myself, but...

GLORIA   (*interrupts*) No buts, Theo. I hear too many buts and I know you will say, once again, that the society put you this way. Well I don't feel like listening to that tune again because you always act as though you have been wronged more than any-one else.

THEO   It's a question of sensitivity.

GLORIA   (*sharply*) So I am insensitive when people cough in my face on the elevator? Or when I have to stand on a crowded bus with my large stomach, to the point where I could faint, while young healthy people bury their heads deeper in a book or a newspaper? Or when I have to work like a mule at my job just to keep my position at the bottom? Or when the looks I get from people tell me I don't belong here? Perhaps I am insensi-tive because I have never come home and tried to turn this house into a living hell.

THEO   Have I?

GLORIA   (*sharply*) Yes! A silent and menacing hell!

THEO   You will never understand, eh.

GLORIA   I understand one thing, and that is my need to have my presence acknowledged; to know that I am alive; to feel I'm worth something to someone. I never did many things because I used to think about your feelings. But no more. (*pause*) So after this child comes, it will be my turn to be reborn and to live the life you never allowed me to live. Now you will know what it feels like to be alone in someone else's presence.

THEO   (*sits down before his books, fingers papers as he talks*) Yuh know, when a wise man doesn't understand a process, he perseveres. When the fool doesn't understand that same process, he focuses his energies on destroying it.

GLORIA   (*scans THEO from head to toe*) So try not to get hurt, eh.

SCENE V

THEO and ATIBA are seated at the dining table where he is assisting her with homework. A radio plays quietly.

THEO   (*pointing to her book*) Look w'at yuh do here. Does this look right?

ATIBA   (*flippantly*) Looks OK to me.

THEO   Then show me how you arrived at this amount.

ATIBA   Oh! That's the one you are talking about. Eight times nine.

THEO   Yes, Atiba.

ATIBA   Well what do you want me to put? I had seventy-two and you said that was wrong.

THEO   Why would I say it is wrong? I'm not mad you know.

ATIBA   Then answer me honestly: should I believe you or mommy?

THEO   About what?

ATIBA   Well she often says you're mad, and now you say you're not. It's like when she says, "Eat all your food," and you say, "Just eat the liver"; or when she says, "Go to bed at eight o'clock," and then you tell me, "Read until nine and do your math". Who should I listen to?

THEO   Ah see yuh dilemma.

ATIBA   Well?

THEO   OK. As she is not here, listen to what I tell you now.

ATIBA   But when she is here and you are here too, who should I listen to?

THEO   (*pause*) That's a tough one.

ATIBA   (*insistent*) Well, answer me.

THEO   You must listen to your mother.

ATIBA   Because you know she would shout and yell and hit me if I didn't do as she says?

THEO   Not really.

ATIBA   Then why?

THEO   She needs it.

ATIBA   The same way she needs food and sleep?

THEO   Yes. It doesn't make sense, but it is true.

ATIBA   Even if what she says isn't fair, I should still do what she wants?

THEO   Ah (*pause*) yes, even...

ATIBA   (*upset*) But that's not fair...

THEO   (*bangs the table with his fist*) Dammit! I know. (*he gets up and goes to the cupboard*)

ATIBA   Do you have to shout at me?

THEO   (*pouring a drink*) Sorry.

ATIBA   Do you have to drink?

THEO   Right now, yes.

ATIBA   Why?

THEO   It's the only way to tolerate an unfair life.

ATIBA   I don't understand.

THEO	Yuh too young to understand. Look, lemme tell you something: You're lucky I am not like your mother, otherwise you'd be like many children who have to exist in the midst of total terror, scolded and beaten by both parents.
ATIBA	But mommy doesn't scare me. She makes me mad sometimes, and I cry. But she doesn't scare me.
THEO	That's a relief.
ATIBA	You scare me.
THEO	(*surprised*) W'at! Why... ah mean, how yuh can say dat?
ATIBA	That scared you, eh?
THEO	Yes. Yuh shouldn't make jokes like dat.
ATIBA	You know why it scared you?
THEO	I didn't expect it.
ATIBA	Right! You see, I know what to expect from mommy. But I never know what to expect from you.
THEO	What do you want to expect other than what you see? You t'ink I'm hiding some awful surprise from you?
ATIBA	No. But you get angry. I've heard you.
THEO	I don't get angry with you though.
ATIBA	Will you promise never to get angry with me?
THEO	I can't do that.
ATIBA	But why not?
THEO	Christ, girl! Ah kyan't win? Anyhow, let's get back to basics.
ATIBA	What is basics?
THEO	Math.
ATIBA	I don't think so.
THEO	W'at do you t'ink about eight and nine?
ATIBA	(*feigning disdain*) They're only figures.

THEO   Come on now. Stop playing. (*he tickles her and she reciprocates*)

ATIBA   You see, people who tickle are ticklish.

> *The door is opened. GLORIA enters.*

GLORIA   It is way past your bedtime.

ATIBA   I have some work to do... (*music drowns her last words*)

GLORIA   (*abruptly*) Well you can go to your room and finish it.

ATIBA   (*to THEO*) We can finish it tomorrow night. (*she kisses him*) Good night.

> *ATIBA goes to her room. THEO gets up from the table. He is surly, packs some books in his bag and goes to ATIBA's room where he picks up a set of keys.*

ATIBA   (*under the covers, she turns to him*) Dad.

THEO   Yes.

ATIBA   Where are you going?

THEO   For a long walk.

ATIBA   Are you coming back?

THEO   Do you want me to?

ATIBA   Only if it makes you happy. (*THEO sits down on the bed next to her, staring vacantly*) Dad.

THEO   Yes?

ATIBA   Would you promise me one thing?

THEO   What?

ATIBA   Don't get mad with mommy.

> *THEO sits in silence for a while longer, then he kisses her and leaves.*

SCENE VI

*THEO is visiting a friend, ARNOLD. He is seated at a table in
the midst of paintings, an unmade bed, pillows on the floor, and
a bookcase stacked to the limit. On the floor are other books and
the pages of a newspaper at the base of an easel on which there
is a canvas with a jumble of colour. A bottle with a partly melted candle stuck in the mouth, rests on a carton converted to a
table. Paintings and enlarged prints hang on the walls.
ARNOLD is shirtless, his pants are rolled up to the knees.
Blotches of paint mark his hands, and a pencil sticks out of his
hair. He pours himself a drink then places the bottle before
THEO.*

ARNOLD   (*encouraging THEO*) Tek a good drink, mastah.

    THEO pours a drink. ARNOLD holds up his glass to THEO.

Cheers, man.

THEO   Cheers to w'at?

ARNOLD   (*to the audience*) Wuh sort of t'ing is dis I hearing at all? (*to
THEO forcefully*) Wait, ah hope you didn' come hay expecting
pity, because if you t'ink I goin' allow you to spread gloom
over dis room, den yuh bettah t'ink again; because dis is me
world, and w'en yuh come into it I don't expect yuh to disturb
the light yuh meet here.

THEO   Then yuh expect me to be a hypocrite and pretend dat every-
t'ing OK?

ARNOLD   No. But if your woman is giving you shit and she's driving
you crazy, you must find a way to get even. Now if I was in
your position, yuh know what I would do?

THEO   What would you do?

ARNOLD   I would do something to hurt her, and in Gloria's case that is
not too hard to do.

THEO   What would you do?

ARNOLD   Yuh see that velvet sofa shih buy the other day?

THEO   You would rip it to shreds.

ARNOLD   Nah. Dat too energetic. I would do something more poetic.

THEO   What?

ARNOLD   I would make love to it.

THEO   (*puzzles*) W'at yuh mean?

ARNOLD   I would deposit my come on the goddam thing.

THEO   Man, you're perverse.

ARNOLD   I know, but I bet you she would respect me after that and will go and tell her friends, "Although he was bad, he was a propah man". He left a good impression on my life. That's right! Being a man is where the struggle is at, mih friend. Look, we come into dis world to be men, and no matter how poor we be, we must always mek sure dat dih world, the whole, stinking rass-hole world, remember we as men. (*he jumps to he feet and starts gesticulating furiously*) Dat is wuh cutting we niggas' ass in dis country: we leff home as men and come here to be transvestites, strutting around the place like peacocks in high heel shoes and big hats, with we hair curling and twirling, and the front of we shirts open down to the navel, even pun the coldest day, and wearing some pants that would arrest yuh blood circulation, because we have to accentuate we cock size. But w'en yuh pause to a-na-lyze; yes, mih friend, analyze, because analysis is where it muddah-cunt is at, (*he sips his drink quickly*) you will come to one inescapable conclusion. (*bending close to THEO's face*) Yuh know what dat is?

THEO   You talking.

ARNOLD   Ah doin' more dan talking; ah sermonizing, and ah don't want any interruption. So lemme tell yuh, pardna, the only conclusion you will come to is dat the costumery and the advertisements to virility dat we niggas flashing about the streets, all amount to one t'ing: *Illusion!* Niggas befriending illusion and scorning substance just to be labelled as "hip." I ain' right? Of course I right, because I already t'ink about it. (*short pause*) Tek a drink before the spirits go to sleep and lemme tell yuh somet'ing, lemme school yuh and yuh can quote me as your source. Tell dem Arnold La Pierre seh (*he ponders for a while*) but dat name fuck up, eh? "La Pierre." Nothing to the name though; is the man behind the name. So go and tell dem dat dih man with dih funny name seh dat too many uh we niggas deceiving people with the flanges we have boring through our pants, because plenty uh them cock can't get hard no more!

THEO   Dat is a dangerous allegation.

ARNOLD   Correction, it is a dangerous truth, because it doesn't genuflect to the myth of the black male's sexual vitality.

THEO   Ah shit!

ARNOLD   Look, I got a friend from home who we used to call the Teenager, because dis man is endowed with a piece of equipment of exaggerated proportions. When it was being casual about the business of getting erect, it would measure in the teens, and dat was before conversion to metric. Women use to tell him dat God created the jenny ass with he in mind. Yuh know what we call him now? (*pauses for reply*) Traffic Hazard.

THEO   Why? He like to expose himself in public?

ARNOLD   Ah coming to dat. Ha, haaa! Boy, dis story got melody. Look, dis man (*whispers to THEO*) according to the consensus among adventurous ladies, (*normal tone*) he can't function normally, because w'en he get an erection, his equipment becomes most erratic in its conduct and assumes a series of angular formations. According to these ladies, (*he demonstrates with his arm*) this t'ing might look as if it doing a zig-zag; den it might make a sudden bend or a U-turn; and w'en the heat of passion really get up into it, it would make a complete about turn and hang its head in shame. Ha, haaa! Oh, lawd!

THEO smiles and sips his drink.

ARNOLD   Now, this man, this ex-prince of the woods is perennially depressed, but in deference to his past glory, I still address him as "Teenager." And every time I t'ink about dih niggah, ah is have to t'ink about the Teenager, because we concentrate all our energies on igniting an image of ourselves, not as people of industry and intellect, but as walking symbols of fuck. But w'en yuh get down to the nitty gritty, we cannot reconcile performance with image because the equipment is no better than a museum piece; just the kind of thing that engages the attention of anthropologists.

THEO   W'at yuh getting at.

ARNOLD   Ah getting at the business of being a man! Ah saying, go out there and be a man and stop cowering behind yuh problems. We all got problems, yuh know, because we livin' in a pressure-cooker that is intent upon squeezing everyone into a faceless, soulless pulp, and dis is why tension and depression cuttin' ass here. Lemme tell yuh, sometimes I get so depressed dat I is have to look to big "G" and seh (*his eyes to the ceiling*) "Hey, big G, why dih ass yuh putting me through dis misery?"

And den ah would ask mihself, "Yuh see any ugly people for dih day? Yuh get any letters from home singing dih blues?" And w'en ah realize dat ah can't answer the reason for mih depression, guess wuh is happen? (*short pause*) I became more depressed. (*short pause*) Is a rass of a t'ing, eh? So now I realize dat depression is like lust; once you can't satisfy the hunger of your curiosity, it becomes more persistent and punishing. I can write a book about that dam subject.

THEO   I know about depression too.

ARNOLD   Yes. I would also be depressed if I allowed an unreasonable woman to shit all over me.

THEO   I was merely being patient.

ARNOLD   When yuh balls in a juicer? Bull-shit to dat, McAllister!

THEO   Fuck man! Because you don't agree?!

ARNOLD   I can live with my disagreements, but what I can't live with is this impotence you're encouraging... this liberal, intellectual faggotting.

THEO   Get off my fucking case because I don't live there anymore.

ARNOLD   Wait... yuh mean yuh move out? Well why the (*Jamaican colloquialism*) yuh never tell mih. Well, yuh see? It wasn't that difficult. Now you're on the road to recovery, and to celebrate your coming to manhood, I will get out my special book of chicks and broads (*he searches frantically in a box of books*) and arrange a meaningful one-night stand for you. (*he locates his book and starts flipping the pages*) Now tell mih which of these women yuh want... Dolores, she is a good fuck but kind of proper. With her you don't come, you arrive.... Denise, she is into yoga and ESP. She believes in administering reciprocal enemas before sex.... now, Joan, she has these quiet nervous break-downs at the moment of orgasm (*an effeminate scream*) then she swears at her mother and father. Oh let me call...

THEO   Don't waste your time.

ARNOLD   If we keep the women waiting they will explode from spontaneous combustion.

THEO   I don't want to see anybody.

ARNOLD   (*Jamaican colloquialism*) Well why the fuck yuh come here to poison my room with yuh depression?

THEO   Sorry. I'll leave.

ARNOLD   That's right! Take your depression elsewhere! Try being a fucking man and stop feeling sorry for yuhself, because dis muddah-fucker ain't got no sympathy to waste!

> *THEO gets up in anger and walks to the door. ARNOLD walks behind him.*

That's right. Go on and do what yuh have to do because I have to preserve mih energies for my program. (*the door slams behind THEO*) Yuh hear mih, McAllister? It goin' be wicked and destructive. Tell them make way fuh dih man with dih funny name. (*he slaps his fist into his hand and leaps into the air exultantly*) Ha, haiiiii!

ACT II

SCENE I

> *THEO brings ATIBA to visit with him. As they approach his room, he stops.*

THEO   (*nervously*) Atiba.

ATIBA   Yes?

THEO   Ahm.

ATIBA   What?

THEO   How do you feel about me?

ATIBA   What do you mean?

THEO   You hate me, eh?

ATIBA   Why? Because you ran away and left me and mommy?

THEO   Sort of.

ATIBA   Well, are you happy?

THEO   It's hard to say.

ATIBA   What's so difficult about that? Either you're happy or you're not.

THEO   You see, sometimes you're happy only when other people, who mean a lot to you, are happy with the things you do and the way you live.

ATIBA   What do you do? (*pause*) And how do you live? (*pause*) Anyway what does this have to do with making people happy?

> *THEO opens the door and shows her in. The room is in darkness.*

What smells so funny? (*the light goes on*) Jeeze! This place is the pits. Do you have to live here? Why didn't you tell me you live in the dumps instead of asking me all those silly questions?

THEO   I didn't know how to tell you.

ATIBA   It was easy. All you had to say was, "I live in the dumps; my apartment is the pits; (*she lifts the bed sheet*) with a sheet full of holes; and no proper chairs for my guests to sit on; and (*she looks under the bed and emerges coughing*) it is full of dust and..."

THEO   Alright, alright. You succeeded in embarrassing me so I'll start to clean up immediately. (*he looks around the room surveying the task, scratches his head*) I have a good idea: what about if I take you to a nice restaurant for lunch.

ATIBA   But you said you don't have much money.

THEO   That's true.

ATIBA   Can't we be happy here?

THEO   In this dump?

ATIBA   Well, I can help you clean it.

THEO   OK. I won't refuse a good offer. (*he goes for a broom*) But remember, it will never become as clean as your mother's house.

ATIBA   Good.

THEO   Wuh yuh mean by that?

ATIBA   Well hers is so clean, you would believe nobody lives there. If I just leave something on the floor, she starts to scream and shout (*mimicking her mother*) "Atiba, what did I tell you about leaving your things around the house. Remove your books from here, and fix your shoes properly, and do this and don't do that." She's always yelling all the time.

THEO   (*pause*) I want you to know that you can bring your problems to me anytime you feel like it. And when you come here on weekends, make as much mess as you want; it wouldn't make any difference to this place. Have all the fun you want, and tell me whatever is on your mind. I might not be able to do anything about it but it is always good to have a friend you can talk to.

ATIBA   (*buries her head in a pillow*) I don't know. I just don't know.

THEO   (*places his arm around her*) You can't give up now. Look at me.

     ATIBA removes the pillow slowly from her face.

     I haven't given up. Yuh know why? (*silence*) Because of you. That's right. You! You are the one who is keeping me alive, and if you can keep someone else alive, then you have more than enough strength to survive your dark moments and become a whole lot better than I.

ATIBA   You think so?

THEO   I know so.

     ATIBA rests her head on his shoulder and they sit in silence for a while.

ATIBA   You know, if you didn't marry her I wouldn't be here complaining.

THEO   If I didn't marry her you might have had a father who would've been worse that your mother.

ATIBA   Then I would've been really alone.

THEO   Right!

ATIBA   But why did you marry her?

THEO   I suppose I was in love, and w'en you are in love, your heart does your thinking and seeing.

ATIBA	(*pause*) You still love her, eh?
THEO	(*hesitates*) It's hard to forget.
ATIBA	(*impatient*) Well, don't you?
THEO	Love is a strong word.
ATIBA	Why don't you answer me?
THEO	I never use that word.
ATIBA	There is nothing wrong with it.
THEO	I know. But there is a lot wrong with many people who use it.
ATIBA	So what do you feel for her? Be honest.
THEO	I don't know.
ATIBA	(*irritated*) But you should know, after all they are your feelings. Do you or don't you love her? Yes or no?
THEO	(*barely audible*) She has a man.
ATIBA	(*scornful*) And he is the pits.
THEO	(*mild protest*) I don't want to know.
ATIBA	He is stupid and loud and...
THEO	Please, I don't want to...
ATIBA	He's a show off and shouts a lot and...
THEO	W'at!
ATIBA	Yes, I hate it when he shouts at mommy.
THEO	(*hands grasping his head*) Jesus Christ! Same t'ing ah seh...
ATIBA	And when he visits mommy always sends me to buy something fancy to cook for him.
THEO	But w'at dih rass is dis ah hearin' at all!
ATIBA	Is he really my uncle?
THEO	(*shouts*) W'at! Of course not!

ATIBA   That's why my friends at school laughed at me when I said my mother sleeps with my uncle.

THEO   Don't you ever call him uncle!

ATIBA   But mommy said I must.

THEO   (*erupts*) Dih fuckin' nerve! (*he tugs her by the hand and heads for the door*) We goin' and put an end to dis shit!

> *The door slams behind them. THEO reappears after a few moments and changes out of his bedroom slippers, uttering curses to himself.*

Uncle, mih rass! Mih back ain' even turn yet and shih want to frig up dih chile head. (*he rushes out of the room, slamming the door*)

SCENE II

> *GLORIA, with a drink in her hand opens the door for THEO and ATIBA. She bends over to kiss ATIBA.*

THEO   (*as ATIBA condescends to kiss her mother*) Since when you pick up with drinking?

> *GLORIA walks into the living room with THEO closely behind. He sees a burning cigarette.*

And smoking?

GLORIA   Are you asking because you are interested in me or because you have forgotten that you are no longer entitled to question what I do with my life?

THEO   (*enraged*) I can question you about anything, especially when it concerns this child.

GLORIA   (*retorts*) Not even then.

THEO   (*furious*) Bull-shit!

GLORIA   (*calmly*) When a spouse moves out of the matrimonial home, he loses certain privileges, Theo.

THEO   Oooooooh! I see.

GLORIA   I'm happy you see my point.

THEO   (*blurts out*) You have no point! All you have is a responsibility to nourish the child's life by exposing her to healthy influences.

GLORIA   (*retorts*) Look, get it through your knowledgeable head, fella, you can't call the tune if you don't pay the piper.

THEO   So now it's a question of money?

GLORIA   (*same tone*) Always was. When last you been to the store to buy a pair of drawers for dis child? W'en last you buy her a pair of shoes, or a dress, or pay her ballet fees, or pay her dental bill? If you can work dem miracles with the paltry fifty dollars you give me every month, then I would start praying to you rather than some mysterious stranger.

THEO   You ever thought for a moment that my paltry fifty dollars might accomplish a lot more if it didn't have to cater to your recently acquired appetite for liquor and cigarettes?

GLORIA   Thank God, w'en yuh left dis house yuh didn't take mih pride with you. And if you must know, I pay for my liquor and cigarettes with my supplementary income.

THEO   Also known as child support.

GLORIA   Except that it was enclosed in an envelope with a letter thanking me for my services.

THEO   (*sarcastic*) You lost your job? Impossible! I never thought you would be so calm when your loved ones finally decided to let you go.

GLORIA   I would never give you the satisfaction of seeing me depressed and helpless.

THEO   That's good because I have no sympathy for people like you who embrace their enemy and spit in the face of their ally. The way you fraternized with the people in your office, one woulda get the impression that racism is just another offensive cliché.

GLORIA   (*calmly*) My poor, estranged husband; still hating, eh?

   THEO turns away, sucking his teeth.

   It seems that is all you are capable of doing.

THEO   (*piqued*) You were just kicked out on your ass by the people for whom you worked yourself to the brink of exhaustion and you telling me dat all I am capable of doing is hating? What will it take to open your idiot's eyes?

GLORIA   (*sharply*) Don't call me an idiot Theo!

THEO   What do you want me to call you?

GLORIA   You're the idiot! You and people like you who waste your time searching for more reasons to accuse white people of racism, conveniently forgetting that we come from a part of the world where racism is subtle, but a lot more brutal. We love to jump up in the streets and at parties and shout, "all ah we is one!", when we damn-well know that nothing could be further from the truth. You shoulda been fighting racism at home, rather than...

THEO   (*impatiently*) Look, I didn't ask for a rambling account on the existence of racism at home.

GLORIA   (*vehemently*) I don't give a shit w'at you ask for. Yuh goin' hear it whether yuh like it or not because that racism follow me to these parts. That's why I out of a job now.

THEO   Wuh?

GLORIA   Ah saying dat it is a home-grown racist who responsible for me being without a job today, Theo.

THEO   (*shocked*) Wuh yuh saying at all?

GLORIA   Yes, Theo. Donald, also known as Don; Mr. Wynter, the chief accountant; ah we-country man; our compatriot, Theo. He is the one who fired me.

THEO   What reason did he give?

GLORIA   He doesn't have to give a reason, but his attitude toward me changed when he discovered that I'm married to a nig-gah.

THEO   (*piqued*) Dat muddah-fucking son-of-a-bitch! He most likely had a nigger for a nanny, and the hand of a nigger stirred his pot and powdered his ass and lulled him to sleep. Goddamit! That son-of-a-bitch was probably raised by a niggah! Do you now understand why I have to hate?

GLORIA   Only lazy people hate Theo, because love needs hard work.

THEO   At least you know the reason for my anger.

GLORIA   And I still feel it is senseless.

THEO   So you pick up a man who will have decent and sensible motives for being angry... that is if he is capable of anger, which I seriously doubt, judging from the kind of job he does for a living.

GLORIA   (*puzzled*) W'at yuh mean by dat?

THEO   Isn't he a goddam salesman?

GLORIA   So salesmen don't get angry?

THEO   Sure they do, when they can't dupe people into buying what they have to sell.

GLORIA   (*overlapping*) You don't need to be jealous, Theo.

THEO   (*overlapping*) His is a job without ethics. They capitalize on people's weaknesses.

GLORIA   You're jealous.

THEO   They sell the squalor and decadence of this system to...

GLORIA   (*raising her voice*) You don't need to be jealous, Theo.

THEO   ...to people like you who need to drown their sorrow in material wares. (*voice lowers*) Wuh yuh say?

GLORIA   I said there is no need to be jealous.

THEO   I don't...

GLORIA   (*raises her hand to silence him*) Look, don't put yuh conscience on trial, I know you well enough.

THEO   You...

GLORIA   Look. The man is my security. He is like a protection against hard times.

THEO   (*calm delivery*) I hope you realize that is the motivation of the whore.

GLORIA   (*offended*) There's a bit of the whore in everyone, Theo!

THEO   (*incensed*) Hell, man!

GLORIA   (*shouting*) Look. I am interested in surviving and giving (*she emphasizes*) your child the best. Do you realize this same man who sells the squalor and decadence of this system is the one who is helping to support (*emphasis*) your child?

THEO   (*livid*) Yuh using that child and I won't allow it!

GLORIA   Good. Then I will write you a list of her needs.

THEO   (*marches off toward the door*) You ain't hear the last uh dis.

GLORIA   (*runs after him, shouting*) Where yuh goin' love? Wait for the list.

>   *The door slams behind Theo.*

SCENE III

>   *Furniture is stacked in a pile in the middle of the room. Sheets of newspaper are spread at the base of the walls. THEO is washing paint brushes. He is interrupted by the phone.*

THEO   (*speaking on the phone*) Who?... collect you said?... yes, that's my brother... OK. (*he waits, glancing at his watch repeatedly*) Michael, wuh wrong?... everybody OK? Uh hum... yes... but... come to the point fas' because ah can only pay for five minutes... you planning what?... here?... fuh how long? How're you going to go to school? Yuh have money for yuh fees?... yes, I know I promise, but... wuh? Yes, I seh a lot of things w'en I first come to dis country but t'ings didn't work out the way I expected... shit, Michael, don't play that game with me... what is dat? But I kyetching mih ass too... you starving?... well where you find the energy to get a clap the other day? You have a car? Look, is pointless telling me dat gas cost four dollars a gallon when I don't even own a bicycle... what's that? You goin' kill yuhself if I don't send for you?... well go right ahead and do it because frankly I had enough of you people... I will gladly contribute to your burial... I hope they cremate yuh ass! Goodbye! (*he slams down the receiver*)

ARNOLD   (*as THEO's alter-ego*) Mack.

THEO   Why do you always bother me at the worst possible times?

ARNOLD   But I am your friend.

THEO   I in a bad mood.

ARNOLD   You and your kiss-mih-ass moods.

THEO   You can talk that way because you don't have a care in the world.

ARNOLD   Ah, the illusion of it all!

THEO   Driving a cab couple days a week and investing most of your time emptying your genes in any available woman, and spending your hours of relaxation splashing paint on a canvas.

ARNOLD   It is called abstract expressionism, dammit!

THEO   Your life is made!

ARNOLD   Only because I left the goddam university.

THEO   They kicked your ass out.

ARNOLD   (*emphatic*) Nobody kicks me out! I made a dignified exit after telling them they could stuff their obscure theories and gibberish up their mumbling asses!

THEO   My brother just called me collect to tell me he will kill himself if I don't send for him?

ARNOLD   He's a serious man.

THEO   I gave that son-of-a-bitch my most sincere blessings.

ARNOLD   But supposing he do it and leave a note saying his cruel brother helped him make up his mind.

THEO   Then his would be the first suicide to be classified as a justified abortion.

ARNOLD   Man, yuh have to go easy with dem people back home 'cause no matter w'at you tell dem, they are receiving images of the metropolitan society from movies and magazines that don't show pictures of people in the unemployment line, or pictures of winos, or the anguish...

THEO   We pamper them too long. For all the years I in dis country,
        not a month go by without me sending money to them, even
        when I wasn't working. And the more I send them, the more
        they complain. Them sons-of-whores believe life owes them a
        living! Listen to the letter I got from my cousin: (*imitating her
        voice*) "We ain' got money fuh pay de daktah 'cause he
        priscript somet'ing wid a lang, lang name, an de dispensah seh
        dat if de name wuzn't so lang, ah wuzn't goin' gat fuh pay so
        much. And, cuzzin T, we kyan' get prapah food fuh eat 'cause
        de gov'ment ban salt fish and sardine and tin-nin stuffs. And
        ah wuz hearing from yuh half-sistah brother-in-law chile, who
        is wuk at de gov-ment bond, dat we ain' goin' get no mo' car-
        nation milk fuh do res' of de year. So I ain' know wuh ah
        goin' do w'en dis cartoon ah have run out. Cuzzin T, you
        must always be grateful and give t'anks to God dih fadah
        almighty and to the white people for the opportunity to live in
        a land of nuffness and plentitude." (*his voice*) Do you believe
        these fucking parasites? Mothers complaining that their chil-
        dren suffering from malnutrition, yet they are bejeweled in
        gold from elbow to wrist!

ARNOLD I see you despise the memory of what you used to be.

THEO   I despise the memory of what we are: we're infants disfigured
        by puberty.

ARNOLD (*pause*) Yuh bitter no rass, Mack.

THEO   I used to anxiously await letters from home. I can't anymore.
        Imagine that woman telling me (*he slaps the letter*) to be grate-
        ful for being here. (*he shouts*) The whole fucking world is clos-
        ing in on me! I work at a job that's fit for imbeciles! For eight
        hours a day I labour in heat and dust, I have to listen to the
        incessant groaning of machines and the depraved jesting of
        men with the minds of morons, who demonstrate their cama-
        raderie by climbing on each other's backsides and sticking
        their fingers up one another's ass.

ARNOLD So wuh yuh goin' do, Mack? If yuh go back home, the para-
        sites will feast on yuh intestines, and if yuh stay here, some-
        body's finger might stray up yuh ass. Man, yuh in bad shape,
        Mack.

THEO   But all the fondest memories that continue to rack the sub-
        stance of my brain, are back home.

ARNOLD (*aside*) Ah goin' to fatigue his rass. Then go back home fast!
        Don't mek anyt'ing stop yuh!

THEO As soon as I get my Ph.D.

ARNOLD Your Ph.D.? Somebody promise you somet'ing?

THEO You couldn't get one.

ARNOLD Look! I chose to be an artist, not an artifact. Man, they ain't goin' allow you to add dem consonants to yuh name until they castrate the native in you.

THEO That's not true.

ARNOLD Oh fuck off McAllister! You know dam well dat Third World students have to kiss ass before they can graduate.

THEO It is a truism of life that poor people gotta kiss ass before they can kick it.

ARNOLD And it is also true of life that if yuh kiss ass long enough yuh wouldn't want to kick it.

THEO I have my integrity!

ARNOLD Integrity mih muddah-ass! It was the absence of integrity that made us run away from home in the first place.

THEO That's not true!

ARNOLD Ask any immigrant about home and he will say, "I don't want to know about that place..."

THEO Only a handful say that.

ARNOLD "...It is a goddam whorehouse..."

THEO No!

ARNOLD "...Its streets are defaced with dog shit..."

THEO You're lying!

ARNOLD "...It is over-run with rum-shops which play deafening music all day long..."

THEO That's a fucking lie!

ARNOLD "...and reek of the stench of piss and last year's puke."

THEO Stop it! No!

ARNOLD   You typical immigrant, Mack.

THEO   Goddamit, no! No!

ARNOLD   Man you help rape your home.

THEO   No! It's these people here!

ARNOLD   Now you copulate with the rapists.

THEO   Fuck, no!

ARNOLD   Now you're part of your poor country's foreign aid to the rich.

THEO   No fucking way! That's the doctors and engineers and businessmen who got their education and their riches at the people's expense!

ARNOLD   But you want to become like them.

THEO   Noo! I have my integrity!

ARNOLD   Bull-shit McAllister! Integrity would tremble before the smile of the hypocrite, but we fleet-footed immigrants return that smile.

THEO   But our smile masks a poisonous rage.

ARNOLD   Then rip away the mask and end the goddam deceit.

THEO   I can't as long as a carefully selected few among us are rewarded with eminent positions, but without political power, for being well-behaved immigrants. I despise that specie of immigrant!

ARNOLD   But wuh they do you, Mack?

THEO   They palliate our anger with our words spoken with our accents. They manage to convince too many of us that we too can achieve positions of privilege in this country.

ARNOLD   Hey boy! Yuh know what is your problem?

THEO   What?!

ARNOLD   You prefer to celebrate an easy passion instead of reaching beyond your misery to see the light of wisdom.

THEO   I feel pain and I will bawl.

ARNOLD   And everybody you just condemned living with pain too.

THEO   What pain?

ARNOLD   The pain of violence we inflict upon ourselves just to keep pace
         with the society in which we live. When the factory worker
         loses his job because he couldn't keep up with the production
         line, yuh know w'at dat is?... I call that violence. And when
         yuh have to bite yuh lip just not to tell yuh boss to fuck off, ·
         that is also violence. And when the executive develops a
         bleeding ulcer just to remain a slave to privilege, what yuh call
         dat?... I call that executive violence. And when yuh must do
         two or more jobs just to keep the shelter over yuh head, what
         yuh call dat?... I call dat violence. When you have to deprive
         yuh children of your presence just to get food for their stom-
         achs, w'at is dat, man?... dat is rass violence. And when yuh
         have to trample people to get to work on time, what you call
         dat?... dat too is violence. Time marches to the rhythm of vio-
         lence...

              *A quiet knock at the door. The knock, a little stronger, accompa-
              nied by a call.*

VOICE   (*outside the door*) Dad.

THEO   (*running to the door*) Atiba. (*He tugs the door open and ATIBA
         enters, walking stiffly, her eyes telling a tale of horror*) Where yuh
         mother? Who bring you?

ATIBA   There was blood...

THEO   W'at you talking about?

ATIBA   They were fighting, dad.

ARNOLD   Is violence...

THEO   Who was fighting?

ATIBA   He hit mommy, dad.

ARNOLD   Ah tell y'all is violence...

THEO   (*sharply*) Shut up! Atiba, tell mih...

ATIBA   (*sits at the edge of the bed, rigidly, staring, as if in a trance*) He hit
         mom, dad... there was blood all over... (*wipes her eyes*)
         Mommy was crying and screaming,... I am scared, dad.

SCENE IV

THEO sits at the table in his room before books and papers scattered all over the table. He scribbles then raises his head to the ceiling taking long pulls on a cigarette. A radio plays softly. ATIBA turns in the bed. He looks over his shoulder at her then gets up from the table. He is about to tuck in the blanket around her when she looks at him.

THEO	Not sleeping?
ATIBA	I'm not sleepy.
THEO	But it is one o'clock.
ATIBA	Then you should be sleeping.
THEO	At my age I sleep when I can, and right now I can't afford to do so.
ATIBA	Why?
THEO	I was just thinking...
ATIBA	What about?
THEO	There are some things parents shouldn't tell children.
ATIBA	Why?
THEO	Because the children might feel responsible.
ATIBA	You talking about mom?
THEO	Yes. I have a plan.
ATIBA	She hasn't called.
THEO	We'll move to a bigger place and...
ATIBA	Why hasn't she called, dad?
THEO	You will have your own room and your own dresser and...
ATIBA	I miss her, dad.
THEO	(*sits up and folds his arms*) Yes. (*pause*) I know.
ATIBA	Is she glad to get rid of me. Is that why she hasn't called?

THEO   I don't think so.

ATIBA   Then why hasn't she? (*no answer*) Is she scared I would hate her?

               THEO shrugs his shoulders.

          You aren't saying anything, dad.

THEO   What can I say?

ATIBA   But you know her better than me.

THEO   (*dejectedly*) I never knew her.

ATIBA   But you lived with her all those years.

THEO   I lived with a different woman.

ATIBA   That doesn't make sense.

THEO   I don't know how to explain it to you.

ATIBA   (*impatient*) I am not a three-year-old, just say it.

THEO   Look, your mother was always a simple woman. She would think simple thoughts, read simple books, talk about simple matters; (*brief pause*) maybe even her dreams were simple. But I always saw simple people as the freaks of nature. And it used to embarrass me to think (*scornful expression*) this is my wife: a simple woman. So you know what I did? I pretended that she was the kind of woman of whom I would be proud; I started to imagine that she was another woman.

ATIBA   (*turns to him*) Why doesn't she call, dad?

THEO   I couldn't say. Now I don't even know the other woman. (*he lights a cigarette*)

ATIBA   Dad?

THEO   Uhm?

ATIBA   Did she yell and scream at you when she was angry?

THEO   No. That was the other woman. Your mother cried.

ATIBA   It was scary dad. She cried and she kept on calling for you; but you wouldn't come. (*pause*) Dad.

THEO	Uhm.
ATIBA	Maybe she is calling for you now. Maybe she's crying.
THEO	Don't think those thoughts, Atiba.
ATIBA	(*louder*) But dad I'm worried.
THEO	She'll take care of herself.
ATIBA	(*louder*) Well maybe not. Maybe she's in trouble again. Maybe he is killing her. Don't you care?
THEO	Go to sleep Atiba.
ATIBA	(*shouting*) Dammit dad! Don't you understand?

SCENE V

THEO is at home. The room is in darkness, intermittently pierced by the glow of a cigarette.

ARNOLD	(*pounding on the door*) Hey boy! Oooi! (*shouting some more*)

THEO gets up slowly. ARNOLD resumes pounding.

Hey boy! Mack!

THEO opens the door. ARNOLD rushes into the dark room.

Turn on the light. (*lights on, he sniffs the air*) McAllister, do I detect the scent of come?

THEO	(*ignores him*) W'happen?
ARNOLD	I bring you glad tidings. The perfect antidote to your depression. (*he shows THEO a paper bag*)
THEO	Who says I'm depressed?
ARNOLD	Well the facts speak for themselves. If I see someone moping around a frowzy room, I would say that person is depressed.
THEO	I just in a mellow mood.

ARNOLD Mellow mih mother-ass! When a man in a mellow mood, he listens to soft music and sips cognac while an adorable woman, who is secure in her femininity, lays her head on his chest and counts his heart beats. Depressed people lie at home in the dark.

THEO I am contemplating.

ARNOLD Then contemplate no more! You contem-fucking-plate too much, that's why Gloria kicked you in your ass.

THEO Whey you been in the last few weeks?

ARNOLD I was around.

THEO I have been battling with the worst depression ever.

ARNOLD Mack, don't bother me with trivialities.

THEO I thought I was hitting bottom, and in desperation I would call the few people I thought were my friends, but they were all too busy being around.

ARNOLD I was journeying into my soul.

THEO The doctor prescribed tranquilizers and psychiatric counselling.

ARNOLD Don't go to any psychiatrist if yuh want to preserve yuh sanity because they goin' throw some ink on a paper and ask yuh what it is, and if yuh ever say it look like dog shit, bam! Just like that! They goin' certify yuh a chronic schizophrenic and enquire about yuh bowel movements.

THEO I have been talking to myself all dis time.

ARNOLD Man, do I have a woman for you! (*whispering to THEO*) She is a nice voluptuous 1943 model with aero-dynamic suspension. A mere glimpse of the undulations of her hips will weave the strings of your manhood into a tight knot.

   THEO moves away and starts reading a book.

   Now I, the prince of charm, the cass of nova, the don of juan, I was stepping, exuding my usual amount of flamboyance, when all of a sudden I descried in the distance, a female of exquisite linear conjunctions gliding gracefully and tenderly padding the side-walk with legs that were sculpted by a god in heat.

THEO breaks into a laugh, approaches ARNOLD with a book.

ARNOLD Yuh like it already!

THEO No. It is a pile of shit!

ARNOLD But she besieged my mind with her sensual poetic seduction.

THEO (*pointing to a page in the book*) It is a quantity of shit! Hear this: "A scheme for the analytical breakdown of individual societies into functional sub-systems has been evolved... this basically consists in the categorization of aspects of societal interaction in terms of the functional exigencies with which it is postulated, all variable social systems must cope." ...yuh know, when I first enrolled in university I didn't understand what those words meant. Now nine years and six thousand dollars later, I still don't understand them.

ARNOLD (*offers THEO a smoke*) Good! Now suck on this joint of wisdom...

THEO But these are the words in which I wrapped myself like an insulation. Now they're cold and unresponsive, because these words are not about people and feelings! They came from the heads of people divorced from their passions.

ARNOLD Okay. Let me continue to tell you about my passionate experiences with this woman...

THEO Look at this room. Cluttered with the substance of an absurd language. Not a book on poetry or good literature! Well I've dwelled by this absurdity too long! (*he shoves the books and papers from the table onto the floor*) I don't want this fucking insubstantial shit around me anymore.

ARNOLD (*offers THEO the smoke*) Now you prodigal!

THEO Look what I've been doing all this time, Arnold. I've been living by a formula I didn't evolve for myself. I allowed my life to be shaped by the dreams of the people back home. I was supposed to get a Ph.D. But that wasn't my dream. Man I never allowed myself to dream my own dreams. Man I fucked myself just so that somebody could say, "He's one of ours and I'm proud of him."

ARNOLD Good! Now. (*he offers THEO the smoke again*)

THEO I should've been a poet. They are more respected than politicians and businessmen.

ARNOLD   (*offering THEO the smoke*) Forward to salvation, brethren.

THEO   Do you see what I was doing to that woman! I called her stu-
          pid because she knew her mind! She understood her universe
          and I insulted her because I didn't understand mine! (*he clasps
          his head*) Jesus Lord!

ARNOLD   Okay. Now get a hard on and let us go...

THEO   But I don't need that man! Don't you see I'm a free man?!
          Free of bull-shit, free of other peoples' expectations, free of
          self-deceptions... but you, Arnold, have you found your free-
          dom?

ARNOLD   Of course!

THEO   Look at you! I was hooked on words, you're hooked on chem-
          icals. Look. (*he starts ripping the pages out of a book*) Throw
          away your chemicals La Pierre.

ARNOLD   They help me to cope with premature ejaculation.

THEO   Yuh can't find your freedom by brandishing yuh cock like a
          credit card, Arnold. (*he gently escorts ARNOLD out of the room*)

ARNOLD   OK. I believe you, mastah.

THEO   But that's it! You don't have to believe me because I know I'm
          right! Thanks, Arnold, you've been a big help.

ARNOLD   Yes, ah know.

THEO   Good. So yuh must go and let me enjoy this mood.

ARNOLD   You not putting me out Mack. You won't do anything so irra-
          tional.

THEO   What it looks like?

ARNOLD   You prefer to stay here and talk to yuhself?

THEO   I need my solitude, man. You must understand.

ARNOLD   Stop being a goddam faggot and come invest your energies on
          the famished women of this restless city.

THEO   Naw. I gotta keep my energies for my programme. (*pushes
          ARNOLD out the door*)

ARNOLD   I promise not to intrude upon your solitude... I'll speak quietly... she splayed her luxuriant thighs at the insinuation of my touch.

SCENE VI

THEO returns home from work, a lunch box in one hand and a coat over his shoulder.

GLORIA   (*meets him at the door, her finger to her lips*) Shhh. Shih just fell asleep.

THEO   (*seems apprehensive at her presence*) Hi... wuh happening?

GLORIA   I OK. How everything with you?

THEO   (*sheepishly*) Well. (*he shrugs*) You can see for yuhself.

GLORIA   Yeah... yuh know, yuh shouldn't leave her by herself.

THEO   Sometimes we have to take chances... yuh want a drink?

GLORIA   Naw.

THEO   I need one.

GLORIA   You still drink so much?

THEO   Only when I need it.

GLORIA   If you ruin your health yuh goin' to deprive Atiba of her father.

THEO   I'm a big boy now.

GLORIA   (*pause*) Shih tell me yuh having a party for her birthday.

THEO   Yeah. Ah hope yuh coming.

GLORIA   Do you want me to?

THEO   You should. After all, you're her mother.

GLORIA   And this is your home.

THEO   So?

GLORIA   I don't have any say in what goes on here.

THEO	Ah! Don't be silly.
GLORIA	Well. (*she shrugs, then a moment of silence*) How things at school?
THEO	Ah taking a year off.
GLORIA	Why?
THEO	Ah gotta reconsider certain things.
GLORIA	Like what?
THEO	That's what ah still trying to find out.
GLORIA	(*smiles*) Good to see you can laugh now... you and Atiba laugh a lot?
THEO	Sometimes. But ah thinking about getting a bigger place so we can have bigger laughs. (*they smile*) She misses you. (*silence*)
GLORIA	(*opens her purse and removes a letter*) We get a letter from home. Mih mother-in-law say she's coming for a visit.

THEO reads the letter.

You haven't told her about us.

THEO	No.
GLORIA	Are you going to?
THEO	That depends on... ahm...
GLORIA	What?
THEO	Yuh get a job yet?
GLORIA	Not yet. But ah get a few good offers.
THEO	(*reaches into his pocket and removes some money*) Look. Take this.
GLORIA	Dat ain' necessary. Use it for Atiba.
THEO	She's OK...
GLORIA	And buy yourself some clothes.
THEO	I ain' interested in clothes.

GLORIA Yuh neglecting your health and ignoring your appearance. Yuh have to take care of yourself y'know.

THEO I doin' OK. And nobody would be interested in looking at me, yuh know.

GLORIA Don't be too sure about dat.

THEO Well, you should know what yuh saying.

GLORIA That's right, Theo.

> *A moment of silence. GLORIA reaches for THEO's hand, holds it. He stiffens, withdraws his hand.*

THEO Now is not the time. We still have a lot to talk about.

GLORIA Words drove us apart, Theo.

THEO Not words, misunderstanding.

GLORIA And how will we ever understand each other if we don't start now?

THEO Look... I...

GLORIA (*almost a whisper*) You're still a cold man, Theo... maybe I've made you hate me too much... funny thing is that you're the only man I ever...

THEO (*enraged*) What only man?! Don't deceive yourself. You know you've had other men...

GLORIA (*in tears*) So what did you expect of me? You rejected me, Theo. You turned me against myself! And now you're rejecting me again!

THEO I'm not rejecting you.

GLORIA (*harsh tone*) Then why don't you talk to me? Tell me how you feel about me? I'm the mother of your child, Theo...

THEO Look, I've taken enough punishment for the day. Don't let's argue.

GLORIA But you're not giving me a chance to...

THEO Please...

GLORIA   OK. Suit yourself.

>   *She leaves, slamming the door. THEO sits at the table, sipping*
>   *a drink and staring vacantly. He lights a cigarette and starts*
>   *flipping the pages of a book. ATIBA stirs in her bed.*

THEO   (*glancing over his shoulder at ATIBA*) Not sleeping?

ATIBA   What was all that noise? (*she looks around, blinking her eyes and*
               rubbing them) Where's mommy?

THEO   She left.

ATIBA   (*sulking*) You had a fight.

THEO   An argument.

ATIBA   (*sits up in the bed*) Why?

THEO   That's the story of our life.

ATIBA   (*serious*) But this time it should have been different.

THEO   Maybe we try too hard to be consistent.

ATIBA   Be serious.

THEO   What's wrong with you now?

ATIBA   How could you fight with her when she tells you she loves
               you?

THEO   (*shocked*) What?

ATIBA   You never listen to anybody!

THEO   Try to understand, Atiba. (*tries touching her*)

ATIBA   Don't touch me! I hate you!

SCENE VII

Clusters of balloons are suspended from the ceiling. The table, from which hangs a colourful tablecloth, is decorated with cups and glasses, cans of juice, fruits and sweets. In one corner of the room are several boxes. THEO is cooking. ATIBA is attired in a dress in which the colours are complementary to those of the room. She sits on the bed with STELLA, displaying her gifts. Cheerful music plays in the background.

STELLA   Which gift yuh like the most?

ATIBA   It hasn't come yet.

STELLA   What yuh talking about? There it is. And yuh better say you like it, because I paid for it with my Chargex.

ATIBA   Yours is OK.

STELLA   Oh, I wuz just wondering.

ATIBA   But my mom's will be nicer. *(there's a knock at the door)* That must be mommy. *(opens door)*

ARNOLD   *(enters)* Happy birthday to you. This is for you. *(gives a painting to ATIBA)* Mack, ah want a drink.

STELLA   Where you been all this time?

ARNOLD   Now, that is the way I love women to greet me. Although I don't know you, I'm ready when you are.

STELLA   Theo, tell dis boy I am a very proper woman.

THEO   Girl, at your age, propriety can be yuh worst enemy.

ARNOLD   I need your leg.

THEO   Rid him of his misery, Stella, please.

STELLA   But wait, did you invite me to entertain your guests?

THEO   It would be a humanitarian gesture.

ARNOLD   All I request is a little charity.

STELLA   Poor man. You're dribbling on my dress.

ATIBA   Arnold, do I colour in the blank spaces on this painting?

ARNOLD	Wat!? Don't you ruin the brush strokes of my genius!
ATIBA	But what's this mess all about?
ARNOLD	Ask yuh father.
THEO	It seems well intentioned, conceptually, but uncertain in its idiom.
STELLA	Jesus lord have mercy! Is wuh dah boy just seh?
ARNOLD	Now one more time Mack.
THEO	It seems like a confusion of angry colours.
ARNOLD	That's better. We minorities have to learn to be more direct in our speech if we wish to be understood.
STELLA	Wuh it mean, sexy?
ARNOLD	Yuh see all these colours? They represent the cosmopolitan nature of the West Indies: the Indian, Chinese, European, Amerindian, the Black man...
STELLA	Dat is right, yuh know. People use to leave they wife and children all parts of the world and go to the West Indies just to have a good time.
ARNOLD	Talk my talk Sweetheart. We know the strokes of all the world's folks, from the north pole to the south pole. Look, some uh we got blonde hair and blue eyes even though a soul brother been stirring the pot a few generations back; and some uh we black like one minute to midnight only because a European intervene sometime back and save we from looking like one o'clock in the morning. Dat's why I is always tell people that it ain't important who mih mother lay down with, but if she enjoy laying down; and talking about laying down, ah hope yuh know I coming by you tonight.
STELLA	Theo, what yuh want to tell us?
THEO	All right. Everybody get a drink.
ARNOLD	Now yuh talking Mack.
ATIBA	Can I drink what you're drinking?
THEO	If you start at this age, you might end up like Stella, climbing walls.

STELLA   I think you talk dis way because I wouldn't allow you to... me.

ARNOLD   Mack, I never know you wanted to... her.

THEO   The woman needs her fantasy.

ARNOLD   Can we marry our fantasies?

THEO   OK. Enough. I must make an announcement.

ARNOLD   Take as much time as yuh want because I haven't hyperventi-lated on a well-preserved woman in a long time.

STELLA   Look, behave yuhself. Hurry up and say what yuh have to say.

THEO   Today is a double celebration. First there is the more obvious celebration...

STELLA   Look, hurry up and come to the point fast.

ARNOLD   God, she's ready. Theo, dispense with the goddam foreplay.

STELLA   Why don't you behave yourself?

THEO   Today is Atiba's eleventh birthday.

STELLA &
ARNOLD   Happy birthday to you.

THEO   Now y'all ready for the big news?

STELLA   Go on.

THEO   I told Gloria we must live together again.

ARNOLD   W'at?

STELLA   What is her answer?

THEO   She hasn't given me an answer yet but she's coming to the party and what do you think her answer will be? That damn woman was miserable without me.

ARNOLD   Mack I though you was goin' forward to salvation but instead yuh really goin' back to dih woman. After all she do to you yuh mean fuh seh you still goin' back?

ATIBA punches ARNOLD.

ARNOLD   Ow. Ah wuz only joking.

STELLA   Good. It should teach you never to get involved in what doesn't concern you.

ARNOLD   Thanks for reminding me. I should be concentrating on you instead of worrying about Mr. and Mrs. McAllister. If only my smoking brush could recreate the splendour of your majestic columns on a hungry canvas.

STELLA   Theo, what should I tell him?

THEO   Put him on hold and test his sincerity.

ARNOLD   If you do dat I'll chew my shorts!

THEO   Come let's have another drink.

A knock at the door.

ATIBA   Mommy's here.

THEO's mother is at the door.

MA   Surprise!

THEO   Ma, why yuh didn't call and tell me when your plane was coming.

MA   Look, I is an independent woman, I took a cab from the airport and turned at your old address, and Jesus Lord Heavenly father, ah come all dis distance to hear damnation descending on dis family. What Gloria do that y'all divorcing?

THEO   We ain' getting a divorce.

MA   Divorce, separation leffing, all is dih same blasted t'ing.

THEO   It is just a trial separation.

MA   Trial separation? Only criminal is be pun trial! Yuh want to tell me dat mih favourite daughter-in-law is a criminal? What shih do? Shih teef? Shih tek man wit' you?

ARNOLD   Dat's right! She had a man!

MA   (*to ARNOLD*) Don't tell me you is another jackass like Theo. (*to THEO*) Theo, did she take a man w'en y'all been together?

THEO No. After we separated.

MA So w'at yuh expect?! I understand from shih mother dat shih wasn't working. Now tell mih, son, would you prefer shih to get the necessities of life by showing shih legs at a street corner?

STELLA He should be happy shih have some morals.

MA Tell dis idiot fuh me, girl.

THEO But we goin' back together.

MA After the damage is done?! If y'all couldn't scale the mountain when yuh been close to dih top, yuh expect to scale it standing at the bottom?

THEO But we had irreconcilable problems, ma.

MA And y'all leff because of a few problems and a big word?! But wait, yuh t'ink yuh goin' go through life without problems?

STELLA He's too hasty.

THEO Stella, why don't you shut up?!

MA No! You shut up! She got more sense dan you and dis jackass put together! (*to STELLA*) Look, me and he father had a million and one problems, but we didn't leff because we didn't want we children taking sides, and we also had enough common sense to know dat problems are to be solved, and if yuh run from them now, they goin' turn up in yuh backside tomorrow. (*to THEO*) Dat is dih problem with y'all young people today. Yuh have education but no common sense.

ARNOLD I say burn down the university!

MA Mek sure mih intellectual son in it w'en yuh burn it down!

THEO But ma...

MA What?! Yuh goin' tell mih why yuh had to lie to me, (*she slaps her chest*) yuh own mother? You know how I hate liars, Theo. I would prefer to know dat one of mih flesh and blood die by the hands of the executioner because he refuse to lie. How good is life with no moral strength?

ARNOLD Morality is where it's at!

MA   Shut up, jackass!

> STELLA elbows ARNOLD.

THEO   Christ ma!

MA   (*stomps her foot*) Dammit child! Show me respect!

THEO   Maybe I lost that too. You wanted me to become somebody so you encouraged me to come abroad. And why yuh t'ink I ain't in some madhouse today? It is because I had to lie and live like a hustler and a whore. So don't tell me about morality man, because it died when I kissed you good-bye ten years ago.

MA   (*sighs and is subdued*) Son, look wuh happening to dis world. Everybody shifting responsibility fuh he life onto someone else. And everybody following the crowd blindly without realizing dat if yuh jump up behind the band, yuh goin' come home smelling as stink as dih multitude. Is dat the example yuh goin' to leave dis child? Yuh mean to tell mih the whole world goin' to go up in smoke because nobody had any integrity? Dat's why we got all dem problems at home: people teefing because they know others who teefing; people tekking bribe because others tekking bribe, then they all raising they voice in one unrighteous chorus and sehing, "Is de gov'ment dat responsible!'

ARNOLD   We must take responsibility for our lives.

MA   Tell dat to yuh friend. (*to THEO*) Son, where will this iniquity end if me and you don't decide to end it in we own life? (*pause*) Yuh know, mama always use to tell mih somet'ing as a child. Shih use to say dat in dis life we have two choices: we can choose dih garden of fragrance, or we can choose dih cesspool. So tell mih, son, how you intend to choose? Take yuh time and t'ink about yuh decision... but t'ink carefully.

THEO   (*moves slowly, puts on his shoes and picks up his coat*) Come, Atiba.

ATIBA   Where are we going?

THEO   To mommy.

ATIBA   (*exultant*) Oh boy!

THEO   (*to his mother*) We gone.

MA   And fuh God sake, treat shih with care.

The door closes behind them. His mother searches in her suitcase and removes a bible. She hums to herself.

On the way to GLORIA's apartment, THEO and ATIBA hurry.

ATIBA   This time everything... will be different... promise?

THEO   Promise.

ATIBA   And I'll have my own room... again.

THEO   Yes.

ATIBA   Can I paper... the walls?

THEO   Anything you want.

They arrive at GLORIA's apartment and knock at the door. No answer. They look at each other curiously, knock again... same result. ATIBA plays with the doorknob and the door yields.

That's strange.

They enter upon darkness and stumble around for a while, searching for the light switch.

Gloria! (*the light goes on*)

ATIBA   (*a frightened expression*) There's no one here.

THEO doesn't answer. He is apprehensive as he wanders through the emptiness of the apartment. ATIBA picks up a gift.

Dad, come see this. (*she gives him an envelope attached to the gift*)

THEO   (*removes a note within and commences reading*) "Dear Theo..."

ATIBA   Where is she, dad? Has she gone away? Has she gone away from me, dad?

THEO   (*puts his arm around her*) Seems so.

ATIBA   (*crying*) Why did she do this to me, dad? Why?

GLORIA   (*off-stage, GLORIA's voice continues the reading of the letter*) It is painful... I must write this letter... maybe the pain will bring some happiness. I have decided to go away from you and Atiba for a while... I need to go back home... maybe it will show us where we went wrong. I also want to give more thought to your proposal... do you really think we could get together again? Your letter sounded sincere and reminded me of our life back home. That is why I want to give some thought to my decision... so I need time. I need to decide whether we are capable of sharing each other's burdens. Most of all I need time to decide whether understanding can replace the love you were always afraid to show but always anxious to accept.

I am also going away for Atiba's sake. She needs the best of both of us, but I can only give her my best when I am sure of myself. I want to love her totally... I want to love her without obligation. Please take care of her during my absence. Let her know that my love for her will only grow more intense.

Don't be angry with me. I need your understanding. In return I can offer no promises, just my sincerity. Take care.

Love, Gloria.

Whylah Falls: The Play

by George Elliott Clarke

George Elliott Clarke was born in Windsor, Nova Scotia, in 1960, *sans* regret. He has authored three books of poetry, including, *Whylah Falls* (1990) and *Lush Dreams, Blue Exile* (1994); two chapbooks – *Provençal Songs* (1993, 1997) and *Gold Indigoes* (2000); an opera libretto (scored by James Rolfe), *Beatrice Chancy* (1998); a second verse-play, also titled *Beatrice Chancy* (1999); and a Clement Virgo-directed, feature-film screenplay, *One Heart Broken Into Song* (1999). Awarded the Archibald Lampman Prize (for *Whylah Falls*) in 1991, Clarke received, in 1998, the prestigious Portia White Prize, honouring all of his work. A literature professor since 1994, Clarke has taught at Duke University (1994-1999), and at McGill University (1998-1999). He is currently teaching at the University of Toronto.

George Elliott Clarke's Redemptive Vision

by Maureen Moynagh

Whylah Falls: The Play at first blush seems a curiously old-fashioned play: it is a play in verse about a poet's quest for love and community; it is a love story with a happy ending; and, despite the tragedy at its core, the play is joyous, celebratory, redemptive. Herein lies its appeal, for while it remains attuned to the rather less than ideal social conditions that obtain for the vision of community it presents, *Whylah Falls: The Play* makes what amounts to a leap of faith and offers its audiences hope at the end of the twentieth century.

The play is set in Nova Scotia in the 1930s, in an economically-deprived region during an economic depression, yet as poet-protagonist Xavier Zachary, or X, arrives home in Whylah Falls from his self-imposed exile in Paris, he enters a space that seems to promise a kind of haven from hardship. The dramatic tension centres on his efforts to negotiate a place for himself in that space, to find a role for his skills, through his courtship of Shelley. Whylah Falls is, nonetheless, not an ideal world. Cora has had her share of domestic violence which she fashions into an instructive wives' tale for her daughter, Shelley; and there is public violence as well, in the form of a corrupt local politician and his lackey, violence that erupts in the murder of Shelley's brother, Othello. Clarke's achievement is to hold in productive tension such harsh realities and a faith in the possibility of a creative overcoming. *Whylah Falls* evokes a blues sensibility, but it sounds a few gospel notes too.

Both the play and the lyric sequence from which it is derived are dedicated to the memory of Graham Norman Cromwell. *Whylah Falls: The Play* was inspired in part by Cromwell's 1985 murder near Weymouth Falls, N.S., and the acquittal of his killer by an all-white jury. Dissatisfaction with the verdict and, especially, with the handling of the case by the justice system led to the formation of the Weymouth Falls Justice Committee which sought an appeal. Clarke became a member of the committee, and while they were ultimately unsuccessful in persuading the attorney general to grant their request for an appeal, the committee rallied community support for its cause and raised public awareness about structural racism. Clarke's participation in the struggle for justice was significant in other ways: by his own testimony, "the creation of the WFJC marked the first time that Black urban intelligentsia has joined potently with the rural population."[1] Key elements of the Weymouth Falls experience are incorporated, transmuted, into the play, including its lessons about the value of community-based resistance and the possibilities for working across social divisions.

In *Whylah Falls: The Play* Clarke deliberately invents a utopian space that nonetheless reflects a history of pain and injustice. "Whylah Falls," Pablo tells us in his opening speech, "ain't undramatically real... . Founded in 1783 by Negro Loyalists seeking Liberty, Justice, Beauty, Whylah Falls be a snowy, northern Mississippi with blood spattered, not on magnolias, but on pines, lilacs, and wild roses."[2] Even as Whylah Falls is identified as a destination for seekers of justice, its kinship to Mississippi and the blood spattered on the landscape suggest the search is not yet over. The quest of its founders is implicitly also the quest of the characters in the play, particularly of X and his fellow expatriate poet, Pablo. The play opens with Pablo seated in a Paris café reminiscing about Whylah Falls and X. We are transported back to the 1930s through him, where we meet X, also looking back to the Whylah Falls he has left behind, homesick and lovelorn. Yet the appeal of Whylah Falls for these two exiled poets turns out to be more complicated, and to have more to do with their experience of diasporic homelessness. Pablo hints at hardship in the merchant marine, and X's exile has not provided the kind of freedom he sought: "My father's life insurance is freedom, / But my name's still 'Coloured,' 'black,' 'nigger,' / And, wincing, I crawl, this barbed globe of pain." (p.226). Since racism follows him everywhere, X decides to pursue a different path to liberty, and Whylah Falls turns out to be his destination.

The search for beauty is as important to the play as the search for liberty and justice, and poetry is an abiding concern as well as the medium for this play in verse. X identifies Whylah Falls as "the cradle of poetry," and while Pablo accuses him of lusting after Shelley rather than longing for artistic inspiration, the play suggests that X's quest for love and filiation cannot be dissociated from his poetic vocation. Poetry needs community, we learn, and at the same time, poetry can serve a vital social function in transmuting pain into beauty. Thus poetry's relation to the crisis of racial violence in the play: in the wake of Othello's death and the acquittal of his murderer, Pablo declares "[n]o death – or poem – is neutral any more" (p.264). Shelley, in her angry denunciation of her brother's lynching by the judicial system, bids "*Poetry* come among us" (p.264) and argues, toward the end of the play, that "Beauty honeys bitter pain" (p.275).

A faith in the social efficacy of poetry may well seem a romantic vision ill-adapted to the dominant sensibilities of the late twentieth-century, yet in fashioning this tale of a cosmopolitan rural community where poetry is both critical and redemptive, Clarke enacts the transmutation of which he writes. In charting the particular terrain of African-Nova Scotia and in remapping its relation to the dominant culture through the poetic transmogrification of Weymouth into Whylah Falls, Nova Scotia into Africadia, Clarke contests the ongoing erasure of black history and culture in the province and the nation. In writing to and from a particular locality, Clarke makes clear how vital to his poetry his affiliation to this community is. And in drawing on vernacular forms – the blues, African-Nova Scotian idioms and, particularly in the second act, the sermon and gospel music – in a verse play, Clarke recombines literary elements with popular forms to create a hybrid genre that is alive to the poetic possibilities of the community he strives to represent. Through these vernacular forms the play celebrates African-Nova Scotia and the diasporic traditions on which it draws. For indeed, not just any poetic form will do: Amarantha makes clear her contempt for "those skinny, / Malnourished poems that professors love" and insists on seeking out "words [that] are rain [she] run[s] through" (p.251).

In centering the play on the quest of a poet for a spiritual and emotional home, then, Clarke insists on the vitality of poetry in contemporary society, provided that poetry speaks its commitment to justice and to a redemptive vision of community.

[1] George Elliott Clarke, "The Birmingham of Nova Scotia: The Weymouth Falls Justice Committee vs. the Attorney General of Nova Scotia," *Toward a New Maritimes*, ed. Ian McKay and Scott Milsom (Charlottetown: Ragweed Press, 1992)23.
[2] George Elliott Clarke and Jeremy Sparks, *Whylah Falls: The Play* (Toronto: Playwrights Canada Press, 1999)13.

Maureen Moynagh is a professor in the Department of English at St. Francis Xavier University, Antigonish, Nova Scotia.

Left to right:
Shakura S'Aida
Jackie Richardson
Dawn McColman
Anne-Marie Woods

photo by Ken Kam

Whylah Falls: The Play premiered at the Sir James Dunn Theatre, Halifax, Nova Scotia, produced by Eastern Front Theatre (with the generous support of David and Margaret Fountain), January 8-11, 1997, with the following cast:

PABLO	*Walter Borden*
X	*Troy Adams*
CORA	*Jackie Richardson*
SELAH	*Shakura S'Aida*
OTHELLO	*Jeremiah Sparks*
SHELLEY	*Dawn McColman*
AMARANTHA	*Anne-Marie Woods*
SCRATCH	*Lucky Campbell*

CHORUS (*Nova Scotia Mass Choir*): *Mary Adams, Kim Bernard, Dan Blunden, Ken Boyd, Novalea Buchans, Linda Carvery, Joe Colley, Rosella Fraser, Lucille Robinson, and Cecily Williams.*

Director	*Paula Danckert*
Set Design	*Emmanuel Jannasch*
Lighting Design	*Leigh Ann Vardy*
Costume Design	*Carna Morton*
Stage Manager	*Lynn McQueen*
Technical Director	*Marçel Boulet*
Assistant Stage Manager	*Ralana Vorters*
Assistant to Costume Designer	*Nicole Johnson*
Original Score	*Joe Sealy*
Musical Direction & Composition	*Jeremiah Sparks & Kim Bernard*

Whylah Falls: The Play was also staged as a dramatic reading at the National Arts Centre, Ottawa, Ontario, as part of its "On the Verge" series, on May 29, 1998, with the following cast:

PABLO	*Walter Borden*
X	*Troy Adams*
CORA	*Jackie Richardson*
SELAH	*Shakura S'Aida*
OTHELLO	*Jeremiah Sparks*
SHELLEY	*Karen Glave*
AMARANTHA	*Karen Robinson*
SCRATCH	*Lucky Campbell*
CHORUS	*The Cast*

Director	*Paula Danckert*
Artistic Coordinator	*Lise Ann Johnson*
Stage Manager	*Chris Hidalgo*
Assistant Stage Manager	*Jennifer Strahl*
Original Score	*Joe Sealy*
Musical Direction & Composition	*Jeremiah Sparks*

DRAMATIS PERSONAE

PABLO — *An old black man in his late 70s; sometimes a young man in his early 30s. An ex-African-American-Cuban sailor. A voice scraped raw by rum, spirituals, and the cutlass of a Spanish accent.*

XAVIER ZACHARY — *A black poet in his early 20s. Mid-Atlantic African speech — tinge of Alabama and Acadia.*

SHELLEY CLEMENCE — *A black woman in her late teens. Her voice is a hoarse sultriness.*

CORA CLEMENCE — *A fiftyish black woman given to frank, no-nonsense, countryish speech.*

SELAH CLEMENCE — *A twenty-something black woman with a raspy, wispy voice.*

AMARANTHA CLEMENCE *A twentyish black woman. Husky-voiced.*

OTHELLO CLEMENCE — *A thirtyish black man with a rough, muscular voice.*

REV. F.R. LANGFORD — *An African Baptist pastor in his 50s. A voice of iron, shrouded in silk.*

S. SCRATCH SEVILLE — *A thirtyish murderer. A voice of shotgun guitar.*

CHORUS — *Revellers, Mourners, and Worshippers.*

THE SCENE

Acadia in the 1930s; Paris in the 1980s.

ACT I

1. A STREET IN PARIS

An expressionist backdrop of blue, tumbling café with a
flower of violet accordion. An old black man, PABLO, medi-
tates on a bottle and a glass. He ogles memory. He wears a
long coat and rainbow scarves. The time is April. Cool. A
dream of music, the melody of "The Nova Scotia Song," per-
formed as a kind of Southern-fried blues, searing and melan-
cholic, saturates the scene. Just emergent from the shadows,
a phantasmal chorus, invisible to PABLO, fleshes out his
interests in song.

CHORUS   He cries of rivers, stars, the moon, and pines,
Saltwater sorrow that descants in lines,
The Long March from Jarvis to Whylah Falls,
A shotgunned man dissolving in petals,
His trialled mother who witnesses in cries
Over his corpse cankered white by lilies,
The history of love that could not be,
Though every lyric sketches liberty.

PABLO orates slowly to the uncaring street.

PABLO   Whylah Falls ain't a real place. You travel there only in
dreams, conducted by an African Baptist choir, a beloved
guitar, and a few swigs of dark rum from Bridgetown,
either Barbados or Nova Scotia. Dulcet rum as terrible and
lethal as love. Goddamn!

Founded in 1783 by Negro Loyalists seeking Liberty,
Justice, Beauty, Whylah Falls be a snowy, northern
Mississippi, with blood spattered, not on magnolias, but on
pines, lilacs, and wild roses.

Remember *Nofaskosha*? Goddamn! Black folks got voices
cut by rum, their hearts break with gypsum.... The sunlight
be chock full of blood, sometimes blossoms, sometimes a
blueness as sharp as some *neo-écossais* eyes.

I remember how Othello got killed and how his killer got
away. It was that clean, that clinically evil. Lemme tell you
what I know about love and death, I mean, Whylah Falls,
where X brought me, back in the 1930s, when I was nursin
poems, when I was young.

> *The sound of wild, giddy, 1930s fast blues, mixed in with a hint of Parisian accordion. PABLO sits again at his table, pours himself a shot.*

PABLO   Everything begins with X, short for Xavier, Xavier Zachary, the solitary dreamer come from Windsor Plains, a strange comrade poet, who always wore black, berets, and was always talkin bout Paris, and then went. But he went too late, cos he'd already spied Shelley Adah Clemence, that vision of Rousseau's *Yadwigha* – same almond-shaped eyes, same sloe-coloured hair – and gifted up his heart. He wanted to woo her with words – desire decanted in deca-syllabic lines. He was crazy for her slenderity, *avoirdupois*, particular what-have-you, and her dreams of birthin a school. He inked her the most desperate lyrics – fiery like the blood-drenched trenches of the Somme. He was here, in the City of Light, for five years, walkin in darkness, cos he was desirin her – the *belle* of Whylah Falls – the whole, unliveable time. He was a voyager, *si*, a mariner, of love.

   That night we met, the stars were on fire. He was a sarto-rial and sardonic Negro, stylin like he had the Muse, sweet Queen a Sheba herself, layin up in his bed *alone*, like he be God's Poet to the World.

> *The stage goes dark. When the light reappears, X, garbed in black, sporting a beret and round-lensed glasses, is sitting at the same table that PABLO had used. Enter YOUNG PABLO, in his suave, sinless clothes; he takes a seat at a table opposite X and begins reading a book titled "The Exile". X eyes PABLO, even leaning across his table to inspect his book. PABLO looks up.*

X   *Parlez-vous anglais, monsieur?*

YOUNG PABLO   It's better than your French.

X   If my French is bad, that book you're reading, *The Exile*, by Webster Oxford, is worse. It's just well-written lies.

YOUNG PABLO   And what makes you a critic?

X   I'm a poet. I know all the good books.

YOUNG PABLO   I'm a poet, too, and I like Oxford and – it's that simple because he's that good.

X   His ass is cleaner than his style.

YOUNG PABLO You don't talk like a poet; you talk like a Nova Scotian: blunt and foul, all piss and saltwater.

X How can you tell a Scotian? What sort of eyes do you have?

YOUNG PABLO A poet's eyes – and a sailor's ears. I've weighed anchor in Nova Scotia, that Latin province of New Darkness. Regard what's darkening your speech.

X Are your words drunk?

YOUNG PABLO On the ugliest, nastiest rum you can buy. You Scotians are well-damned for your Bridgetown rum.

X (*laughing*) So what's your passport to Paris?

YOUNG PABLO A memory I need to forget.

X Ah, a woman.

YOUNG PABLO That's why *you're* here.

X I'm here because of pain no law relieves. I'm here because of Whylah Falls.

> *The music is blues piano. X stands, approaches YOUNG PABLO; his gestures are rich with passionate, undeniable memory. The rival poet listens intently.*

X I can still see that soil crimsoned by butchered
Hog and imbrued with rye, lye, and homely
Spirituals everybody must know,
Still dream of folk who broke or cracked like shale.

For the tyrant sun that reared from barbed-wire
Spewed flame that charred the idiot crops
To Depression, and hurt my granddaddy
To bottle after bottle of sweet death,
His dreams beaten to one tremendous pulp,
Until his heart seized, choked; his love gave out.

I remember my Creator in the old ways:
I sit in taverns and stare at my fists;
I knead earth into bread, spell water into wine.
Still, nothing warms my wintry exile – neither
Prayers nor fine love, neither votes nor hard drink:
For nothing heals those saints felled in green beds.

YOUNG PABLO claps as X sits.

YOUNG PABLO There's no such thing as suffering in my economy. I feed
pragmatism with spoonsful of honey.

X You haven't seen the cradle of poetry.

YOUNG PABLO What? A pair of pear-hard breasts to excite a boy? Is that
what you mean?

X No, no. I mean Whylah Falls, the oasis I just sang, where
lovers are well-shaped, luscious, and pain gives birth to
poetry. But you wouldn't know anything about that.

YOUNG PABLO You don't know *me*. Saltspray corrodes my lungs, dust
chokes my mouth, blood blurs my eyes. When you can
understand more than your pain, you'll find me at the
Hôtel Césaire.

> *PABLO exits. X turns his attentions to his notebook. He
> scribbles furiously, then pulls a photo from his jacket pocket.
> He stands again, but creakily.*

X I seek *you*, Shelley – indelible, pure –
No matter where or how long I wander.
My father's life insurance is freedom,
But my name's still "Coloured," "black," "nigger,"
So, wincing, I crawl, this barbed globe of pain.
I fear there's no love anywhere, Shelley,
Unless you love, Shelley, unless you love.

One rich night, moist with chance, the liquid shock
Of lightning, the river crashed like timber,
You fed me coffee, weiners, beans, and bread;
I tramped ten miles traumatically under stars.
Now I am in Paris, in lonesome Paris.
Five years later, Shelley, I can't forget.
We are our pasts. Nothing is forgotten.

> *X babies his head in his hands. The stage again falls dark.*

2. CORA'S KITCHEN

Dawn. Moan of a steam engine. An oval, maple table glistens under a window. An iron stove heats up coffee and longing. The door looks toward the sun. SHELLEY, 18, wearing a housecoat, walks into the kitchen and begins to tend to the stove. Her brother, OTHELLO, sits at the table. His fingers alternate between the guitar on his lap and the mug of coffee on the table.

OTHELLO   (*singing gruffly*) Mary had a little sheep,
She took it to bed with her to sleep.
The sheep turned out to be a ram,
And Mary had a little lamb.

SHELLEY   Don't you ever contemplate anything else than putting notches on your belt?

OTHELLO   You're just mad, Shelley, cos I'm a better poet than your fancy, dog-tongued man, X.

SHELLEY   He ain't·*my* man.

OTHELLO   He be some black gal's man cos I know he's lookin back here gain.

SHELLEY   Jes because he's lookin at me don't mean I'm lookin back.

SHELLEY prepares the breakfast things as OTHELLO continues to pet his guitar.

3. WHYLAH TRAIN STATION

Wooooooo! Steam. The first passenger to exit from the white marble phantasm of the Whylah train station is S. SCRATCH SEVILLE, dressed immaculately in white. A scraggly beard occupies his face. He brandishes an oily shotgun that he aims, playfully, at the audience. Laughing, he hoists it over his shoulder. The music combines flamenco, blues, and Spanish guitar.

SCRATCH   Ma name is S. Scratch Seville. Ink it well.
            I don't suffer foolishness, don't take guff.
            I'm a taxpayer and a coupled man.
            I come from Jarvis with a shotgun on my knee.
            I think my weapon's brilliant as a poem,
            As fine as my damn-near-white wife, Angel
            (Who sports satanic in our sacred bed).
            I was bo'n hard by this Jarvis County.
            I will slay anything that disturbs me.
            Ma name is S. Scratch Seville. Ink it well.

            *SCRATCH moves into darkness. SELAH, CORA, and
            AMARANTHA pass by the train station. SELAH and
            CORA carry market baskets; AMARANTHA carries a book:
            "The Selected Poems of Shelley".*

CORA   These days, make sure yo man got all his parts.

SELAH   Ain't that the truth.

CORA   Uh huh, mama got a big surprise on her wedding night cos
            when it come time for her and papa to retire, he took out
            his false teeth and put them in the bureau drawer.

            CORA mimes the action.

SELAH   Quit yo lies, mama!

CORA   (*continuing*) That's the truth! Listen up: then, he took off a
            false wig and put it in the bureau drawer. Lastly, he took
            off a false leg and put it in the bureau drawer.

SELAH   No, he didn't!

CORA   (*continuing*) Yes he did! When it come time for mama to
            get into bed, she didn't know what to do. She didn't know
            if to get in bed – or in the bureau drawer.

            The women laugh.

SELAH   I don't know bout you, mama, but I would've chose the
            bureau drawer cos Lawd knows what else was gonna fall
            off!

            The women laugh.

AMARANTHA   (*seriously*) What's love, anyway?

CORA   Nothin you go'n find in a book by some Percy Shelley who's likely as worm-eaten as his poems.

AMARANTHA   But he's a poet of love, of luxurious oxygen.

REVEREND LANGFORD passes by. He clears his throat.

CORA   Well, hello there, Rev. Langford!

LANGFORD   (*authoritatively*) Find Love in the Bible; find Love in the Good Book!

LANGFORD wags his finger at the women, turns on his heels, and leaves.

CORA   Rev. Langford got some nerve. He be talkin bout findin Love in the Bible, when he be findin it with Liana. Every Saturday night and twice on Sunday! He climb in bed and his feet never touch the floor till morning!

SELAH   Sometimes, Reverend gets on my nerves. Actin like his shit don't stink. Some half-baked Baptist! You shoulda been there when he was botherin Eely bout his drinkin.

CORA   And Eely can do some drinkin! He drink till he get miserable and then till he get all sooty and greasy.

SELAH   Ma, I ain't finished! Listen. So Reverend was ridin Eely awful mean, tellin im he should bury all his bottles. And Eely stop and ask im, "Rev. Langford, if I bury a bottle of rum, what'll come up?" Reverend swoll up like a bullfrog, preachin hard, sayin "Gospel of salvation will come up." Eely started laughin, then said, "No, Rev. Langford, you'll come up to steal a drink if you's anywhere's around."

The women laugh.

AMARANTHA   Ma, Selah, you two prove there's nothin more contagious than foolishness.

SELAH   If you provoke me, Am, you might hear some things bout love that'll blush your black purple.

AMARANTHA   We gotta get to market. I mean to digest this book.

CORA   Now, Selah, don't take that gal serious! If she don't start bein wise, she's gonna end up hitched to some backdoor creepin, thigh-digestin preacher!

The women wave into darkness. The lights blush. Wearing a black suit, with a red carnation attached to one lapel, X, accompanied by YOUNG PABLO, persuasively suave in a blue suit, emerges from the station. X bears a satchel stuffed with books, YOUNG PABLO carries a suitcase.

YOUNG PABLO So this is Whylah Falls, X? So this is Utopia?

X Didn't you see the Clemence womens? They was just here.

YOUNG PABLO Don't start on that "Shelley, Shelley, Shelley" rhetoric! Her unprecedented *et cetera*, her delicious *et cetera*.

X She got sisters. Ain't that why you're here?

YOUNG PABLO I'm here for my peace of mind. For my p-e-a-c-e. I'm goin to the Whylah Inn, blow out the candle, and start myself to sleep.

X But, Pablo, it's morning.

YOUNG PABLO For you, it's morning. For me, it's inspiration. I'm gonna sleep even if folks be shovellin an pitchin gravel under my bed. You twenty-year-old men run roads non-stop; us thirty-year-old men rest before we love.

X Catch me later up the hill – at the Clemences.

PABLO exits. Apple blossoms cascade onto the stage.

X (*majestically, longingly*)
I spied Shelley's ma and sisters, just now, not her.
Where she be hiding? Where she be? Shelley!

At eighteen, I thought the Sixhiboux wept.
Five years younger, you were lush, beautiful
Mystery; your limbs – scrolls of deep water.
You hung the moon backwards, crooned crooked poems
That no voice could straighten, not even O.

Apple blossoms blizzard. The garden flutes
E-flats of lilacs, G-sharps of lilies.
Too many years, too many years, are past...

Apple blossoms continue to waft across the stage. The music is a puritanical blues, with shadings of acoustic guitar and operatic voicings.

X   (*singing*)
Blackberry, blackberry, on the vine,
Sweet, bittersweet, blackberry wine,
When will you be mine, all mine?
When will you be mine?

The day comes soft, suggestible; our pines
Are ripe with eloquence, rumours of wings,
While milk and honey burns in the fields,
While milk and honey burns in the fields.

X glides into darkness. PABLO emerges from opposing shadows. The light darkens about him to a halo.

PABLO   "While milk and honey burns in the fields." *Si*, X, was dreamin Shelley eternally, with smooth lines pawned from Castiglione. But she knows words always have somethin to hide. So X was just a Romantic fool in the wrong century for adoration. Can I get an amen?

The stage falls dark again.

4. CORA'S KITCHEN

Sunlight, wet yellow luscious radiant, soaks in the kitchen. A blues voice weeps from the radio. A downcome of roses drenches a wall and spills onto the table. CORA stirs a pot while SHELLEY, carrying an armload of wood, drops it by the stove. Wearing a lumberjack jacket over her housedress and clodhopper boots, she takes a mug of coffee to the table. She flips through a recipe book.

CORA   You know that boy, X, too sweet on you, is comin back here soon. You knows that, Shelley? And I hope he be takin way this fever of roses clutterin up my house. I can't skirt an inch without brushin up gainst prickly, whorish roses. They're in the kitchen, they're in the bathtub, they're in the livingroom. Everywhere is roses!

SHELLEY   Ma, I never asked X to wire me no roses! I've told him nothin lovin. I told him to watch out for living gales and lamb-killin blizzards, and that's all.

CORA   Well, he think you mean somethin more.

SHELLEY   That's him, that ain't me. I study the woman wisdom hidden in letters, diaries, and songs. I don't want no man come talkin stupidness, talkin love, love, love.

Everyone cries for love–
but here's the truth of love:

Men cannibalizing their women,
or just sucking off them like leeches.

Don't you remember how Daddy
was cinematically romantic,

But kept side women, murky women,
cola-coloured and maliciously thin.

CORA   Don't bring that up again, Shelley.
      Don't bring that up again.

SHELLEY I wish I was lying.

CORA   If you can't love, you done cut yourself off from your
      mama's milk.

SHELLEY I ain't shackin up with no man to be beat on and pounded
      on for no good reason – like some tragedian.

CORA   Well, jes do somethin bout these damned roses!

SHELLEY I got a recipe, ma, for "Rose Vinegar."

Stuff a cup with the fresh rose petals;
then, stripping off the heels (the white part),
stir the petals into a quart sealer
and add two cups of white vinegar.
Then, seal the jar and place it on a sun-steeped windowsill
for sixteen days, seven hours,
and nine minutes.
When the vinegar is ready,
strain it through a sieve
and then pour it back into the bottle.

Rose vinegar:
It's especially good on salads.

CORA   Shelley, ya got no romance. But I'll try this recipe!

SHELLEY This vinegar's the answer to desire.

      *SHELLEY picks up a bottle of her vinegar. She daubs some –
      like perfume – on the back of her hand and holds it up for
      CORA to smell.*

CORA

Shell, you're a mad gal, wringin vinegar outta roses. But it does smell kinda sweetly bitter.

SHELLEY

I'll call it "Scent of Love" and sell it as perfume.

SHELLEY daubs some of the vinegar behind her ears.

CORA

Now, Shell, you trespass gainst ma uncommon sense!

SHELLEY

If a man really loves me, he's gotta love me whether I smell of roses or of vinegar.

CORA

Men are dogs, Shelley. They'll jump on anything, even if she smells of shit.

There's a knock at the door.

CORA

Shelley, it's him. It's X!

SHELLEY

Ma, stall him. I ain't even dressed.

SHELLEY runs out of the kitchen. MA turns up the radio. X knocks again.

X

I've climbed to Whylah Falls because I thirst,
Hunger for you. My five-winter exile now melts
To roses gorged where tears once hammered dirt.

X knocks at the door again. CORA turns down the radio and opens the door.

CORA

The radio was up too loud for me to hear you knockin. Ma eyes must be lyin to me! Now come right in.

X

Mrs. Clemence, you are balm for my hurtin eyes.

CORA and X embrace.

CORA

Xavier Zachary, cut this "Mrs. Clemence" noise! The name be Cora. You and your Haligonian fussiness! What do you mean whorehousin my house with all these roses?

X

Roses orate for me like no simple eloquence.

CORA

Well, you've filled out a bit – specially in the jaw. Let me call Shelley in here. Shelley! X is here to see you cos I know he ain't come this far jes to talk to me.

SHELLEY

(*offstage*) Ma, stop talkin nonsense!

SHELLEY enters the kitchen. Carmenesque, she has changed into a white dress and a white blouse. Her hyacinthine hair bears the scent of hyacinth. Her skin is gold leaf; her face shimmers with a light as diffuse as that glimpsed through bees' wings.

CORA Shelley, fix X somethin to eat! You two can hang together for a spell. I'm goin upstairs for a beauty rest – cos I'm where you pick up your looks.

CORA exits.

X When you were thirteen, I thought you could never be more beautiful, but no poet has ever imagined a beauty so lucid.

SHELLEY X, you know you can't expect nothin from me but breakfast.

X Shelley, you are the honeyed light that kisses my eyes – eyes that rest in my face like wishes. You are *Poetry*'s definition of indefinable magnificence – all I want.

SHELLEY What did you say you want? There's eggs and bacon, toast and marmalade, sausages and coffee.

X I just want a chance to be serious with you. You're the grace that makes the heavens shine.

SHELLEY You are too bold, X, to tango in here like some idol out of a lousy picture, with two-penny quotations, and expect me to plop in your arms – like some tossed out bouquet of roses. You left. Don't talk to me of love.

X You were only thirteen, how could I...?

SHELLEY You stayed away long enough –
as if calculated to suffocate any love.
Am I a body to trifle with?

Now, you come down, after five winters, X,
bristlin with roses
and words words words,
brazen as brass.

Like a late blizzard,
you bust in our door,
talkin roses and light and love,
litterin the table with poems –
as if we could trust them!

I can't.
I heard pa tell ma
how much and much he
loved loved loved her
and I saw his fist
fall so gracefully
against her cheek,
she swooned.

Roses
got thorns.
And words
do lie.

I've seen love
die.

X   Shelley, I am like that road that slinks to your door
Like a married lover, sneaking around
To curve his ribaldry about his moll.
Shelley, that's how much, that's how much, I feel.

SHELLEY   All you can say is "I" or "me."
The love you talk about's imaginary.
True love is vinegary.

> *SHELLEY holds out her hand for X to kiss. He does so, then steps back.*

X   You smell – forgive me – of vinegar.

SHELLEY   That's the perfume of reality.

> *The kitchen door bursts open. OTHELLO, clad in woodsman clothes, strides into the kitchen.*

SHELLEY   Othello, X has come back. We was talkin, but I think we's finished now.

OTHELLO   Just as good, lil sistuh, cos I hate all dem skinny-butted players, so-called poets, comin here, layin molasses twixt foolish gals' legs. I's got ma eyeballs out for you, lil sis.

X   Why're you so pugnacious, Othello? After five years, I'm here to confess to Shelley a roseate, illustrious love.

SHELLEY   Your love ain't nothin but a lie in poetry.

OTHELLO   That says it clear. Gimme some white rum, Shelley. I need
               to drink now. Lemme live right now, up to my thighs in
               thighs. Feed me some dried, salty smelts. Water song with
               rum.

               (*singing*)

               Sweet Sixhiboux, run softly, till I end my song.

X   I don't need you to slam my face into the door. I can go.

SHELLEY   You may as well go cos I'm goin to teacher's college.

OTHELLO   (*singing*)
               X, you sure as hell may as well go:
               Shelley don't want you no mo.
               I'll take some rum and a hot white ho.

                    *Another knock at the door. SHELLEY answers: it's YOUNG
                    PABLO.*

YOUNG PABLO This is the Clemence residence? I'm seeking Zachary X. He
               said he'd be here. My name's Pablo Gabriel.

SHELLEY   He's here. Come right in. Where you from?

X   I was about to exit – to demolish bad manners.

OTHELLO   What's young men made out of?
               Whisky and rum and bed-hoppin bums.
               They creep bout in the rain like pouncin – dogs.

YOUNG PABLO You must be Othello. X told me stories.

SHELLEY   Every bit of his wickedness is true.

OTHELLO   Don't listen at her. She squints at fun like a dyin priest.

SHELLEY   Don't pay Othello no mind. Wild words just pour from his
               mouth like stuff that makes you sick. But where are you
               from?

X   Paris. That's where I'll take you, Shelley, if you come with
               me, ebon-sultry *belle* with eyes like rum.

SHELLEY   I ain't gonna depend on no man. I ain't gonna be no pen-
               dant.

OTHELLO   Pablo, you an me can talk cos these two just ain't sober. So where you from?

YOUNG PABLO   I encountered X in Paris. But I'm from Naw Orleens – after some *alluring* years in Cuba.

OTHELLO   If you're X's buddy, you must be here lookin for a woman.

X   We're two poets, craving inspiration.

OTHELLO   Shell, tip these lovers some rum. A little rum!

YOUNG PABLO   Don't mind if I do.

X   I'll have one glass; then I gotta go.

OTHELLO   Give that *dried-up* Scotian two glasses.

SHELLEY   Othello, don't you have somewhere to go?

OTHELLO   Lil sis, I'm the eye of this household. I fix an eye on alien and pesty suitors, and I burn their rotten poems in the stove.

> *As SHELLEY looks for glasses for PABLO and X, AMA-RANTHA and SELAH enter the kitchen. They are in mixed stages of relaxed, late-morning déshabillé.*

SELAH   What is this stylish assembly we got here? These cool, cologned mens, smellin of travel?

AMARANTHA   Welcome back, X. Who's your choice friend?

YOUNG PABLO   Pablo Gabriel. *Enchanté, mademoiselle. Vous êtes très, très jolie. Incroyable!*

AMARANTHA   When they'd start makin men with manners?

OTHELLO   Don't ask cos they're just wasted on you.

AMARANTHA   Othello, why you always gotta be so foolish?

SELAH   Shelley's man got some manners too, eh, X?

SHELLEY   Selah, you don't need to talk for me.

SELAH   Long as it aint weddin night chat, it's legal.

SHELLEY   What do you know bout weddins?

SELAH	Dishevelled mornins of wide-awake beds.
OTHELLO	Most likely some quaking beds too.
SELAH	If you ain't Christ, do I gotta be the Virgin Mary?
	(beat)
	What you say, X?
X	I'm just delighted to see you all again.
SELAH	X talk like he always got a poem on his tongue.
OTHELLO	Mouth of a poet, ass of a dog.
AMARANTHA	Thello, you adore giving unmitigated offense.
OTHELLO	Poetess Amarantha! Am I a man who's shook?
YOUNG PABLO	The sun's pouring forth light.
X	Love is the light.
OTHELLO	There's an ulcer behind it.
SHELLEY	Would you two just quit it! Othello, you should be out supportin your beloved Thomson.
OTHELLO	I do what I gotta do. Only fools vote Tory.
SELAH	You go around with that stuck-up man, Scratch Seville, who's so uniquely ugly, that every time I see him, it's like studyin filth for page after page!
OTHELLO	Never mind, Scratch. He's foolish but he labours hard – sweats buckets like me. We're gettin Jack Thomson elected so we can get a pension at the sawmill.
SHELLEY	You're so deep in Thomson's pocket that you're starting to smell like him.
OTHELLO	I don't mind smellin like money.
SHELLEY	Since when did money smell like an outhouse?
SELAH	Jack got that mangy mutt, Scratch, on a tight chain. When Jack wants to piss on you, he gets Scratch to hike his leg.

OTHELLO	That's why he's a poli-pussy-snatchin-tician.
SELAH	O, your tongue's a rag you use to polish lies.
X	Shelley, why don't we get some fresh air?
OTHELLO	X, you've got to be a snake charmer to win Shelley.
SHELLEY	Go on by yourself, X. Ignore this tumultuous, triflin, and argumentative riffraff.
SELAH	Shelley and Othello just love to fuss and attempt mutual, petty treason. Come on, X, walk me down the road a spell. We'll get caught up, and I'll snatch some nutritious bootleg.

CORA comes downstairs and, hollering, enters the kitchen.

CORA	Would you listen at that fool girl! Always talkin bout buyin bootleg when she ain't got a pot to piss in.
SELAH	I make my own money on the boats, ma, and I'll spend it how I want. Come on, X.
X	Goodbye. Mrs. Clemence.

After giving SHELLEY a significant look and shaking hands with YOUNG PABLO, X leaves with SELAH. CORA turns her attention to YOUNG PABLO.

CORA	And what be your name?
YOUNG PABLO	I'm Pablo Gabriel, Madame Clémence.

YOUNG PABLO kisses her hand.

YOUNG PABLO	Tell me, what is your secret?
CORA	What do you mean, my secret?
YOUNG PABLO	For staying so unparalleledly beautiful, madame.
CORA	Shelley, fix this nice young man whatever he wants to be comfortable. He's welcome in my house anytime. Now, let me go get ready to go to town.

CORA exits.

OTHELLO	Ma's gonna love you forever now, Pablo.

SHELLEY   She likes men who know how to speak; so I don't know
               how she could've birthed Othello.

OTHELLO   Same way she birthed you, cept it was pleasant with me –
               and painful with you.

YOUNG PABLO   You both give birth to poetry – just by what you say.

AMARANTHA   I make poems too, Mr. Pablo. May I show you?

PABLO   It's Pablo, and I'm frantic to see them.

OTHELLO   Watch out, Pablo, it's like chokin on rose petals.

AMARANTHA   Your tongue is just pickled in the stench of cruelty.

SHELLEY   Just one look tells you how nasty O is.

               OTHELLO laughs, downs a shot.

OTHELLO   This rum's warblin a silky vanilla blues with a smoky oak
               chorus. Ma belly likes this opera.

               OTHELLO exits.

5. RIVERSIDE

*X paces along the river. Snow hammers down from the crow-
dark heavens.*

X   The air smells of rhubarb, occasional
               Roses, or first birth of blossoms, a fresh,
               Undulant hurt, so body snaps and curls
               Like flower. I step through snow as thin as script,
               Watch white stars spin dizzy as drunks, and yearn
               To sleep beneath this patchwork quilt of rum.
               I want the slow, sure collapse of language
               Washed out by alcohol. Lovely Shelley,
               I have no use for measured, cadenced verse
               If you won't read. Icarus-like, I'll fall
               Against this page of snow, tumble blackly
               Across vision to drown in the white sea
               That closes every poem – the white reverse
               That cancels the blackness of each image.

               X pulls out a hidden flask of rum, drinks.

X   Shelley's brown eyes outspeak all of Shelley.
But she's quit our love, exiled herself far.
Now Selah sings eyes at me like a blues –
This Ellington *belle* with jazzy scorings.
   Shelley, have you left me Selah, Shelley?
Let me dismantle my brains with this rum.

The lights darken. General blues. YOUNG PABLO comes along and picks X up.

YOUNG PABLO   That ain't the way, brother. That ain't the way.
Put up that flask. Put that dark rum away.

6. SPOTLIGHT

PABLO, solo, addresses the audience.

PABLO   Shelley's iciness cut X to the bone. His longing cankered
into bitter song. But Shelley was not to be seduced, for she
was goin away to serve on the Yarmouth-Boston steamer to
compile cash for teachers's college. Neither knew that each
moment is magnificent. But Selah knew it – and she knew
how to sick kisses on love-weakened lips. But, Shelley, she
took after Cora, that truth-spoutin woman who baked
apple tree leaves, blossoms, seeds, and bark into her apple
pies, whose dandelion wine tasted like Soviet literature
(sunlight shining through birch leaves), and whose husband had a ditch for a heart.

The spotlight fades out.

7. CORA'S KITCHEN

The roses are absent. Instead, bottles of rose vinegar shimmer in a cupboard. CORA is doing SHELLEY's hair.

CORA   Don't give me nothin to jaw bout, Shelley, and I won't have
nothin to holler for! Just sit back, relax, and be black. I'm
gonna learn you bout the mens so you can scape the bitter
foolishness I've suffered. A little thoughtful can save you
trouble.

   Shelley, you gotta lie to get a good man. And after you
gets him, you gotta be set to hurt him to hold him, so help
my chucky! Cos if you don't or won't or can't, you're
gonna be stepped on, pushed round, walked out on, beat
up on, cheated on, worked like a black fool, and cast out
your own house.

> *SHELLEY sucks her teeth. CORA cuffs her upside her head.*

CORA   Don't suck your teeth and cut your eyes at me! I be finished in a hot second. But you'll hear this gospel truth so long you, my youngest, eat and sleep in my house. Best cut your sass!

Pack a spare suitcase, one for him. If he proves devilish, it be easier to toss him out that way. Put one change of clothes into it so he can't beg and bug you for nothin!

If he be too quiet, he'll ruminate and feel his bottle more than he will you.

SHELLEY   Hmm, this rose vinegar's too good to ignore.

CORA   Shut up, Shelley! I ain't finished. As I was sayin, a quiet man will feel his bottle more than he will you. Rum'll be his milk and meat for months. It'll spoil him for anythin. Won't be fit to drive his nail no mo. So when he's sleepy drunk, smack the long-ass son of a gun in the head, tell him to wake his black-ass body up, and drive him out. If the fair fool don't come back sober, he don't come back. Am I lyin?

SHELLEY   I ain't marryin no one like that!

CORA   You don't know who you gonna marry till after you marry him! So either pay attention or pay a lawyer. If a man be sweet lookin, a heavy-natured man, always pullin on women, and he takes up with some spinny woman all daddlied up from the cash he's vowed to bring you, just tell him right and down that you ain't his monkey in a dress, and raise particular devil. Don't give him no shakes. And if that don't work, don't waste another black word, grab yourself a second man.

Shelley, slide me over my rum tumbler. Preachin parches the throat. Sides, ma eyes feel kinda zigzaggy today.

If some woman is grinnin at your man, tell her straight: "If it was shit that I had, you'd want some of that too." Make her skedaddle. If her fresh fool follows, take everything he got, and don't give a single black penny back!

Shelley, life's nothin but guts, muscle, nerve. All you gotta do is stay black and die.

SHELLEY   I wish you'd studied that advice when you met pa.

CORA   Who can tell how love will turn? When I met your pa, I *had*
          to meet him. It were a drastic destiny.

          Mean-minded Saul Clemence, ugly as sin,
          Once pounded, punched, and kicked me cross the floor;
          Once flung me through the second-storey glass:
          My back ain't been right for clear, twenty year.
          But I bore it, stuck it out, stood his fists.
          And he's worms now. How'd I take up with him?

          Uncle was sniffin me, and I'd be damned
          If I lowed him to stir my sugar bowl,
          And I shushed Othello, a tiny doll.
          So when skirt-crazed Saul, who trudged nine miles to pitch
          Gypsum, come courtin me, I swept his house,
          Slept in his bed.

          Why he always beat me?
          I was too jolly scared to run around.
          I was true to him like stars in the sky.

SHELLEY   He smelled ugly of alcohol, and shook.
          His hands were mistaken with the hammer:
          Nails would bumble and break before driven.

CORA   Between my servings of watery tea
          And his helpings of woman on woman –
          Whelping so many bastards I lost count –
          My heart rotted in its cage.

SHELLEY   He was too old to be loved forever.

CORA   He was too mean to be loved forever.
          When, at last, his secret, hidden cancer
          Overthrew him, taking its possession,
          And I had folded him – beige suit – into
          A grey casket, I salvaged my lost poems
          And I began to sing. *Oh how I sang!*
          But what about you and that poem-mad X?
          Don't you feel anything feeling for him?

SHELLEY   How can I? How can I say yes or no when
          I hardly know him.

CORA   You come flyin downstairs when he came in the door. You
          put his letters from Paris under your pillow.

SHELLEY   How do you know bout that?

CORA	Chile, a mother with daughters never sleeps.
SHELLEY	Sometimes I think X just dreams too much.
CORA	Don't cry to me if he cries for someone else.
SHELLEY	He can't love anyone else. He's too much in love with being in love with me.
CORA	You say what you say, but I say what I knows: men respect their danglin part, not their hearts.
SHELLEY	Selah knows that well; she takes a man as quick as he winks at her.
CORA	What makes you think X be any different from a man? Don't you remember this song?

(singing)

A man likes to act a statue –
Bronzen, cold, and hefting a sword.
But a woman knows what is true:
He's a boy, easily injured.

> *The lights darken once again.*

8. WHYLAH TRAIN STATION

> *SHELLEY and SELAH stand before the station. SHELLEY carries a suitcase.*

SELAH	We's all gonna miss you, Shell, lil sis. Specially, I worry, X.
SHELLEY	He's voyaged the globe; I'm just voyagin to Boston. Don't I have the right?
SELAH	And X? There's pain stabbed right into his face.
SHELLEY	Should I throw myself down at his feet, and weep?
SELAH	Your will is strong; but hearts are weak.
SHELLEY	If X is still here when August ends, maybe then ... Until then, treat him like a candidate.

> *The sisters embrace.*

9. WHYLAH TAVERN & RIVERSIDE

PABLO stands before the tavern. Disgruntled music barges into the light, full of angry laughter and bitter piano, frowning smiles and gutter guitar. Evening is hurtling into night.

PABLO Shelley was right to discount X's big-flute romanticism, but that don't change the fact that this Mi'kmaq-Mandingo weren't hard to look at. Once Shelley left for Yarmouth, X learned the fragility of desire. There were two Clemence women to woo. Take Selah, for instance. I call her *Gatito*, Cuban Spanish for *little cat*. She'd soak in bright scents of *chypré*, coconut, and honey so that she'd be consciously sweet. She'd drape her red panties on the edge of a bathtub where a choice explorer could find em. A brash innocent, always she was dying of love for some no-count man who'd abandon her always after a month of epic scandals that'd forever brand him a bastard and the most miserable dog in Jarvis County.

Consider her a modern martyr for love, bearing witness to its betrayal by men who feared their own nakedness. Thus, she made alcohol her one true love. She wedded liquor because men betrayed her sexuality as they betrayed their own. Selah was Beauty oppressed because of its perfection.

PABLO moves into darkness. In the tavern, SELAH, wearing a red dress, begins to dance, grinding her hips to a definite, low-down, dirty blues. Assorted whoops and cackles are heard, along with a laying down of bottles and a picking up of glasses. X watches her performance with 200% interest.

SELAH (*singing*)
Pretty boy, towel your tears,
And robe yourself in black.
Pretty boy, dry your tears,
You know I'm comin back.
I'm your lavish lover
And I'm slavish in the sack.

Call me Sweet Potato,
Sweet Pea, or Sweety Pie,
There's sugar on my lips
And honey tween my thighs.
Jos'phine Baker bakes beans,
But I stew pigtails in rye.

My bones are guitar strings
And blues the chords you strum.
My bones are slender flutes
And blues the bars you hum.
You wanna stay my man,
Serve me whisky when I come.

> *Laughter and applause erupts. The music is chastely lascivi-*
> *ous. The steam engine's whistle cuts through the night. X*
> *exits from the tavern.*

X   (*softly*)
The lean, livid engine plunges through night.
I almost feel moist softness – rain's sheer silk:
A crow wallows in this wet, cool pleasure
Like a man in his tomb, stricken numb, dumb,
By soil, its cool clench, sexual pressure.
I hug cigarette smoke, anticipate
Selah, her dark face upturned full of stars.
Her love's squeezed cotton and muscle. The town
Pulls tight. The train shudders. A sweet spasm.

> *SELAH sashays, sultry, toward X.*

SELAH   Shelley's a garden
enclosed.
She don't trust words:
men lie
to lie on top of you.

X, I know languages–
Music or Silence,
Touch or Absence–
that need no words.

I'm not Shelley.
My gate's open.
My fruits are pleasant.
Come and taste.

> *As SELAH embraces X, they kiss. He picks her up in his*
> *arms.*

SELAH   Where you takin me, X?

X   Down by the river.
......Just over here.
...........Down by the riverside.

X sets SELAH down beside the river. Water courses over the tavern music.

SELAH

Do you love me? Do you love me? Buy me a dream to drink? Let rum sizzle luscious in my stomach.

X

(*singing*)
The butter moon is white,
Sorta like your eyes;
The butter moon is bright, Selah,
Kinda like your eyes.
And it melts like I melt for you
While it coasts cross the sky.

The black highway uncoils
Like your body do sometimes.
The long highway unwinds, sugah,
Like your lovin do sometimes.
I'm gonna swerve your curves
And ride your centre line.

SELAH

(*kissing X*) X, X, X, X, X, X, X!

X

(*singing*)
I'm movin down that soft road
To part your sweet, dark river.
I'm gonna plunge in deep
Til I start to shiver.
Then I'm gonna wade back in,
Make your water quiver.

SELAH

(*laughing*) Bring your tender foolishness right over here. I want you to go down like a hot shot of rum. Warm my heart, my belly, and my beautiful thing. Love me like a saint, X, love me like an apostle.

The lovers kiss.

X

After Howlin Will Shakespeare and London Jack Milton, I'm just one more dreamer to strum Sixhiboux Delta Blues, Selah. Oh yes.

SELAH

Dream with me! Dream with me! Consecrate me! Baptize me! Anoint me! I am. Amn't I? Holy!

The lovers swoon together by the river. Giggles, laughter. Lights out.

10. CORA'S KITCHEN

Let the radio enjoy some complicated fugue as twilight forces
AMARANTHA – vestal virgin – to prepare a lamp of poetry
for her reputed bridegroom. PABLO stretches at her feet as
she sings and reads to him, breathing her words into his hair.

AMARANTHA (*singing*)
Should I die like lightning-stricken pines
Or fall to April's fatal snows,
I'd perish happy if your lips wet mine
With love as glistening as salves,
With love as glistening as salves.

PABLO How can love be so good, Am? Why is it so good?

AMARANTHA It's precious as Christ's blood-lettered words. But I fear for
X and Selah.

PABLO Gatito has found a mouse; yes, but one that'll roar.

11. RIVERSIDE

Daylight. The end of dreams. SELAH and X sit, sterile,
beside the river.

X Selah, all we do is frolic every day. I haven't turned a line
in weeks. Just sit here, in the grass, with you and sorry,
misbegotten rum, watchin ants, watchin clouds. We never
go any further than wastefulness.

SELAH Don't see what you's got to complain bout. Ain't this what
you always talkin bout? "Me an you an a jug of shine,
moanin in the wilderness"? Ain't ma love as needful, bliss-
ful, and undeniable as bread?

X You're too sweet, Selah, and sweet enough. But I need, a
man needs, to cut his kindling.

SELAH You ain't had no problem cuttin my kindlin. We've struck
together, you cuttin in, me grippin you there.

X Selah, your tongue's a little stick you just sharpen and drive
into my heart, so you can use my blood as ink.

SELAH Nigguh, I'm gonna get hot, rear up out this grass, and tear
that thing you call a heart to pieces. Who you think you
talkin to? I ain't no floozie. If you don't like my apples,
why you always shakin my tree?

SELAH jumps up and strides away. X, looking dejected, plunks himself down beside the river. A duet of mutually solitary despairs ensues.

X

I remember how Selah opened
like a complex flower.
I brushed her sleeping breasts
and they startled awake:
two rippling fish.

She said my kisses on her breasts
were "bee stings and cool mist."
After words, I carried her, seared
with grass and kisses, from the river.

From her portion of the riverbank, SELAH continues to excoriate the relationship.

SELAH

X calls me stupid things,
just plain idiocies –
"baroque belladonna,"
"lacy curlicues" –

never dreaming
my womb is gone,
hallowed by scalpels
and Casanova cancer.

I flood myself with rum,
blue smoke, and blues
to try to forget
how I've been cut.

The music here is gentle sorrow, wistful regret.

X

Is love more foolish than wicked?
Or moreso wicked than foolish?
No more wine-dark gals' wine-dark eyes.
No more simpletons' songs and sighs.
The proverbial prodigal, I will go to my father's house
In Windsor Plains. I am lost but I will be found.

X lumbers away from the riverside. SELAH turns in an opposite direction.

SELAH

Once I dreamed love would seed sunflowers, honey.
But wisdom arrives late, while death comes soon.

As SELAH exits, PABLO enters.

PABLO   Why, why, does love got to be so brief? Their affair died
                 before it had a chance to live. Selah ran off with a
                 Jordantown man, Jordan by name, whose diet was white
                 Tory rum, pigtails, while hers became fear, tea, and aspirin.
                 Her Jordan died, pukin up blood, after a three-day wine
                 binge. X retreated to his poetry and hurtful memories of
                 Shelley's iciness.

                 As for me, I was courtin Amarantha – "Am" – the once
                 and future Scallop Queen of Jarvis County. Our love was
                 rich, successful. When we made love, our clothes swooned
                 before the marvellous. We made body poetry and sass. *Je
                 ne me rappelle que son pantalon à dentelles blanches.* We surged
                 in water as if rolling in maple leaves, or as if we were
                 entries in an encyclopedia of water, a fresh garden bed. We
                 exchanged vibrant valentines of being. A gourmet trumpet
                 diced Cajun catfish Bb with Acadian trout G#, stewing a
                 blues callaloo.

                 Blackout.

12. A ROOM

*Dusk. Oil lamp. AM is reading a novel when the door
opens. YOUNG PABLO enters. He is wearing a slanted
beret and rainbow cottons.*

YOUNG PABLO Come, my love, come, this lonely, passionate,
             Nova Scotian night. Your voice trembles like wings,
             Your bones whisper. Under the moon, I stroll
             The shadowed road, awaiting your dark eyes
             And sandalled feet. My love, if I have to,
             I will pace this blue town of white shadows
             And black water all night, if I have to.

AMARANTHA   I'm not ready for you. I'm not ready.
             You bring me silk and sunflowers and Spanish,
             But I'm not ready. No, I'm not ready.

             Ma was torn in the matrimonial bed.
             Coloured girls are everyone's best martyrs.
             Sometimes I think that love is poison.

             Our world's the property of Jack Thomson,
             Who acts canine and rips larger the wounds
             In other people's hearts, to lap their blood.

But I love you, if you can see me for real.
I love you so much, breath aches in my lungs.
I love you, uncompromising promise.

> *AMARANTHA begins to cry as YOUNG PABLO takes her in his arms. Amid tears and quiet breath, they cling together, forming a binary star.*

YOUNG PABLO Thou art black
but comely
like the Sixhiboux River
like Mount Eulah's pines.

Behold, thou art perfect,
yea, *excellent*:
thou hast raven's hair;
also our bed is pine.

AMARANTHA In school, I hated poetry – those skinny,
Malnourished poems that professors love;
The bad grammar and dirty words that catch
In the mouth like fishhooks, tear holes in speech.
Pablo, your words are rain I run through,
Grass I sleep in.

> *The lovers kiss and caress each other.*

AMARANTHA Your mouth reaps, harvests, my kisses.
My lips are bruised from the marks of your teeth.

YOUNG PABLO Our skin is blue and orange. I love you – more than words.

> *The lovers clench together; YOUNG PABLO turns down the lamp.*

AMARANTHA Pablo, there's some news I have to reveal. Jack Thomson, you know, Thello's loved candidate? He's all the time pullin on me. His eyes commit rape.

YOUNG PABLO If you'd told me sooner, his sawmill would already have manufactured his coffin.

AMARANTHA We can do nothing while Thello works for him.

YOUNG PABLO I'll be stealthy. I'll stab his eyes so he won't know who's damaging him. And I'll lacerate him with razors, Am, if he bother you gain. You jes tell me. Hear? Jes tell me.

13. WHYLAH TAVERN

The tavern is festooned with scarlet election posters exclaim-
ing Vote Jack Thomson, Liberal, South West Nova. Enter
SCRATCH and OTHELLO, carrying fresh posters.

OTHELLO   Come on, Scratch. I guess you're too good to work with a
brother, sawmill Negro, but help me get these posters up.

SCRATCH   The problem with country nigguhs, O, is you don't think
fore you mouth off.

OTHELLO   You lice-filled idiot, shut up and lend a shoulder.

SCRATCH   (*first clearing his throat*) No wonder white people spit at
your Negro type. You ain't got the pizzazz of a piss-ass
Picasso.

OTHELLO   Scratch, I suffer your scruffy company only cos I want Jack
Thomson in an that damn Tory out. Once Jack takes South
West Nova, I'll take no mo of your lavishly, heaped-up shit.

SCRATCH   Why don't you diversify your vocabulary.

OTHELLO   Help me get these posters up – if ya can get anythin up.

SCRATCH   What are you digging at?

OTHELLO   Ask your wife, Angel.

SCRATCH   What are you doing with my wife?

OTHELLO   I ain't the one who's doin the doin.

SCRATCH   What do you know about my business?

OTHELLO   I hear that when Angel screws, she sounds like a slaughter-
house.

SCRATCH   I could tell news bout your sister, Amarantha.

OTHELLO   No, you won't, cos my foot'll get stuck goin down your
throat an comin out your ass. Now, nail up some posters,
fool.

OTHELLO glares at SCRATCH who, sulking, begins to nail
up a poster.

14. CORA'S KITCHEN

Sunlight. YOUNG PABLO is reading a newspaper while AMARANTHA sews a quilt. Sunflowers loom into the room.

AMARANTHA Sunflowers are sprouting in the tropical light.
Pablo, I am falling away from words.

The newspaper scares me with its gossip
of Mussolini and the dead of Ethiopia.
The radio stutters of Spain and bullets.
Only the Devil ain't tired of history.

The latest reports from Germany are all bad.

I quilt, planting sunflower patches in a pleasance of thick cotton.
But can any blanket repel this world's freezing cruelty?

And who'll stand against Jack Thomson,
who creeps and fawns like a minister?

YOUNG PABLO stands and approaches AMARANTHA.

YOUNG PABLO Doncha worry, Am, I'll fortress you.
I'll bring you warmth. I'll hold you warm.
I'd be damned if I loved you less than this.
Passion is chanting through my fluted bones.

The door opens and OTHELLO swaggers into the kitchen.

OTHELLO I've been out all day pullin votes for Thomson. We'll get a sawmill pension at last.

YOUNG PABLO *Si*, and Eely's gonna give you free medicine on a company plan. I think they'll both sell out black folk as quick as others hang em in Mississippi.

AMARANTHA Thello, how do you know Jack's gonna do anything for us? Might as well vote Tory as credit his stories.

OTHELLO *(pounding the table)* Cochrane's a Tory; Jack is best! And here's my reason: he let me elect myself a forty ouncer!

OTHELLO removes the bottle from beneath his jacket and sets it on the table.

AMARANTHA   That's why Nova Scotians never get ahead: all they think about is drinking.

OTHELLO   You and Shelley are just the same. I can't wait for Pablo to marry you and take you off my hands.

AMARANTHA   Thomson, Thomson, Thomson. Are liberals supposed to be next to godliness – or even cleanliness? You can correct your logic while I get some kindling. I'll see you after, Pablo.

AMARANTHA kisses PABLO and exits.

YOUNG PABLO   Othello, to you, Jack Thomson's an apple tree in spring bloom, but, to me, he's a rotted-through tree with blossoms of gull shit!

OTHELLO cracks the bottle and takes a swig.

OTHELLO   (*laughing*) It's a good thing I like you, Pablo, or there'd be hell to pay. You're a damn foreigner, anyway. Who cares what you think?

YOUNG PABLO   I may be a foreigner, but I know a fool when I hear one.

OTHELLO   Who you callin a fool? You bes be right!

PABLO   It's a good thing we've both got a sense of humour!

OTHELLO   That may be so, but, goddamn, Pablo, can I drink in peace?

YOUNG PABLO   I'll give you so much peace, it'll break in pieces. But your politics are – how shall I say it? – ass-backwards.

OTHELLO   So what? Tories be droppin like leaves off the trees.

YOUNG PABLO   So what, O? This province is full of bigots: There are churches everywhere.

OTHELLO   I'll build my own church: The Cathedral of the Sacred Rum. Sides, Thomson's comin over here to thank me for all I've done for im.

YOUNG PABLO   That's a pretty cheap *merci* from Thomson. But, *c'est la vie*. *Salut*, O.

PABLO exits. OTHELLO begins to sing.

OTHELLO   (*singing*)
               I come and bam on your door,
               Crack a keg of homemade nails.
               You shake your drawers in my face
               Until each bone in me howls.

               Let's not smudge this thing over,
               Or pretend it's all jes roses.
               I'm drownin in your river,
               I'm carryin all your crosses.

               Damn me or bless me. I'll laugh.
               I'm not afraid to love or hate.
               If I gotta strike a blow,
               I'll hit as boldly as preachers say.

               AMARANTHA's voice looms into the kitchen.

AMARANTHA   OTHELLO! OTHELLO!

               AMARANTHA slams the kitchen door shut.

AMARANTHA   He shamed me; he ashamed me! He pressed himself gainst
               me when I was bent over in the woodshed. He just come
               right in and oiled himself at me fore I knew what he was
               bout. His flesh tried to tear and scissor my undergarments.
               His eyes have tainted me.

OTHELLO   What're you talkin bout? Who did this, Am?

AMARANTHA   Who? Who do you think? He's always lookin down me.
               Givin me Hell-like looks, with his crimson, puffy face. Your
               Jack Thomson. He been botherin me forever. But I ain't
               said nothin cos of your job.

OTHELLO   I work for him! He can't disrespect me like that!

AMARANTHA   It's not you he's disrespectin. He come up, breathin sweat
               an alcohol all in my hair an face, sayin he wants me to help
               him savour his election night. I grabbed a stick of wood an
               hit im in the face. He fled when I called for you.

               CORA comes down stairs and enters the kitchen.

CORA   What's all this commotion? Is the whole Liberal Party
               barged and camped in my house?

OTHELLO   That royal bastard, Thomson, was grabbin at Am. He must
               crave a Nova Scotia of blood. I'll hack im up.

*CORA picks up a knife and moves to comfort
AMARANTHA.*

CORA Am, my sweet chile, as this knife's my witness,
That dog will never pump up your belly.
I'll chop his gristle clean off, feed it to cats.
Doncha worry a bit about a thing.

CORA pulls OTHELLO aside.

CORA If you go after Jack Thomson, you'll have Scratch Seville
tryin to distill trouble for us. He thinks he's the next best
thing to a white man.

AMARANTHA Scratch is nothin but a white man's monkey. White folks
love his clownish, foolish grin.

CORA But he's not the fatal problem, it's Jack.

OTHELLO leaps for the door and runs outside.

OTHELLO You two-faced, piss-ass rat! Get away! If you say a single
black word, I'll bash your false face. I'll mash your dough
face. I'll tear you all to pieces. I'll beat you so much that
you'll get tired and sit down. Botherin my sister – right
behind my back! That's the last time. Don't give me no
looks. No use cloudin up, you can't rain. I quit your service, Mr. Man. If you come back round here, you'll be sorry,
Jack. You'll be messed-up white trash with a bloody face.

15. A ROOM

*AMARANTHA and YOUNG PABLO are in bed together.
AMARANTHA sits up and turns up an oil lamp.*

AMARANTHA Pablo, I dreamed I saw Thello's blood glaring in the grass.
It jumped and writhed like lightning.

YOUNG PABLO Come, Am, I gather you to my warmth.
Sleep, sleep. In my lovin warmth.
Faithful, human, tender. Sleep, sleep.

YOUNG PABLO turns out the lamp.

16. CORA'S LIVINGROOM

OTHELLO is composing at the piano. CORA looks on approvingly.

CORA   I love it when you play, Othello. Is this a new song?

OTHELLO   This one's for you, mama.

OTHELLO begins to play the melody of "Mother weep, mother wait" (which he will reprise in II.14). CORA sits, rocking and listening, her eyes closed. Carrying a suitcase, SELAH enters. She is returning home. She tiptoes over to her mother and kisses her.

CORA   Selah, you're home. Let me look at you, baby.

SELAH   I'm tired of all havoc of love.

OTHELLO   Still gotta voice on ya?

The trio begins to sing "Red, red calico." Applause, whoops, and laughter.

OTHELLO, CORA, & SELAH

(*singing*)
I bought ya red, red calico:
mmmmmmm, ya didn't love me though.

Moon burnt the blue sky orange;
not ripe, plucked stars tasted green.
In its bed, the river tossed, black.

AMARANTHA enters with PABLO.

AMARANTHA   (*joining in*) God made everyone with a need to love:

SELAH   (*singing to AMARANTHA*) wonder who ya be thinkin of?

They laugh and applaud the moment.

ENSEMBLE   (*singing*)
April rain snows white and cold,
I feel so goddamn scared.
You could love me if you dared.
Are you waitin to get old?
Why do you act so weird?
You love me like you never care!

More applause.

OTHELLO   Come on, ma, you choose the next song.

YOUNG PABLO *Si*, Cora, sing "Hurry Down, Sunshine."

CORA   You fellas got some tricks! Lord have mercy! God expects truth, not entertainment.

AMARANTHA Come on, ma!

CORA   Okay, okay, just one elegant verse.

        CORA prepares to sing as the others accompany her.

CORA   (*singing*)
Come and love me, darling one,
In sweetest April rain.
Kiss me until night is done:
Youth won't come again.

        Everyone dances as they sing the song again. The lights fade with the song.

ACT II

1. WHYLAH TAVERN

Assisted by YOUNG PABLO, OTHELLO tears down the Thomson election posters.

OTHELLO   Thomson won't have my vote again.

YOUNG PABLO You okay, O? You've pissed a gallon of ale.

OTHELLO   Day's my birthday. June 6th. I'll drink all I want. I want some white lightnin – shit fanged like cobras – to come back an bite me on the ass.

YOUNG PABLO Do the right thing, Othello. Do the thing right.

As OTHELLO tears down another poster, SCRATCH arrives.

SCRATCH   Othello, you're wreckin private property.

OTHELLO   Scratch, it's best that I tear up these posters than I tear off Thomson's head.

SCRATCH   Thomson's a better friend than enemy.

YOUNG PABLO Thomson don't treat black people like friends, but like sticks of furniture.

OTHELLO   Scratch, if you's still workin for Thomson, remember this: clap an eyeball to your wife.

SCRATCH   I don't worry bout white men; it's black men who tend to tomcat around.

SCRATCH leaves.

OTHELLO   There goes a blight-faced fool.

OTHELLO tears up the last poster.

OTHELLO   Time for me to bust some sweat at the sawmill.

YOUNG PABLO Time for me to see a chestnut mare woman with the body of a poem.

OTHELLO   I figure you gotta be marryin Am, Pablo, the ways you talk.
           See to it, bro.

           OTHELLO exits, staggering liltingly.

YOUNG PABLO Muscular, maddened, and wrecking cornstalks,
           Othell totters, interrogates the crows,
           Keels, and rags his majesty on brambles.
           Felled, green maple leaves tangle in his hair.

           I pray nothing calamitous happens,
           But everything imaginable happens.
           And if something climactical happens,
           I want to remember
           carbon culture:
           how skin and bones
           become diamonds
           after so much pain.
           It is our fate
           to become beautiful
           only after tremendous pain.

           YOUNG PABLO melts into darkness.

2. CORA'S KITCHEN

Enter this scene in media res.

SCRATCH   If ya don't want someone lookin at yer friggin, long-chin,
           hypocrite virgin, store her at home. You Clemences ain't
           nothin but coloured trouble, givin Negroes a black name.
           Jack Thomson ain't done nothin to hurt you or that little
           bitch, Ama.

CORA   Scratch Seville, you've lost your skull to come in my house,
           yellin stupid abuse, you ass-suckin weasel!

SCRATCH   Ya ain't got no sense, ya must be missin half a head. You
           yella-mouthed bitch!

CORA   Get out ma house! Ya usetabe okay but now ya've turned
           the opposite – aggravatin, mean-minded, cross-eyed, and
           grouchy! You just love to wallow in the dirt cos you're very
           comfortable there. Your wife Angel is a pasty-faced whore,
           and you ain't the father of your boy.

SCRATCH   I'm manly, a real man, like a white man. I'll smack you
           silly, Cora, you wanna mess with me.

> *CORA shakes her cane at SCRATCH as OTHELLO enters and suckers him coldly.*

OTHELLO   Scratch, you *knows* you don't ever wanna disrespect my ma. Your blood'll run in the road for rats to lick up.

SCRATCH   I'll make you hurt, Othello. You'll hurt!

OTHELLO   My ma's got a bad back – and you wanna argue with her in her own house? Get out fore I wrap a baseball bat round your face!

CORA   Put him out, Thello, or I'll put my cane up his ass!

3. SCRATCH'S KITCHEN

> *SCRATCH sits at a crippled table in his shack. Garbed in milk-white, he downs a beer, smokes, wipes off sweat. Kerosene lamplight corrodes the kitchen.*

SCRATCH   I've got good cause for homicidin some dead, stinkin meat, specially after what Jack's just told me. He says that tom-cat, Othello, is sniffing around my little three-quarters-white Angel. He says that Othello told Eely that "There must be something in the milk for girls to have asses like that." I'll blast off Othello's head if he even blinked at Angel! Lemme see. First, I'll invite that bastard over for a drink (cos he's sickly tempted by liquor), I'll say I'm sorry, then I'll confess my shotgun. First, I'll shoot him, then I'll smack him, then I'll spit in his face.

> *SCRATCH picks up his shotgun and punches the wall. The lights fall*

4. SPOTLIGHT

> *SCRATCH, his shotgun levelled at OTHELLO, takes aim at his stomach.*

OTHELLO   IT'S A DIRTY FUCKIN LIE!
A DIRTY FUCKIN LIE!
DIRTY FUCKIN LIE!
FUCKIN LIE!

SCRATCH   A "lie," Othello?
A fact: Jack Thomson saw you,
last night, man my wife.

A shotgun blast.

5. SCRATCH'S KITCHEN

*A death march sounds throughout the scene. The kitchen
seems weirdly constructivistic as OTHELLO spills through
the splintering door of the shack into the roadside.
SCRATCH flourishes his shotgun, then sets it aside to look
for a knife in a counter drawer. Palming a hole in his gut,
OTHELLO crawls down SCRATCH's driveway. In half
darkness, the Chorus reveals his song.*

CHORUS   *(plainsong)*
The shotgun splutters loneliness,
Its loneliness, black like the sea.
A guitar breaks, and twenty-four
Yellow butterflies flutter free.
We are but dust.

The Atlantic mutters, then mewls,
Tearing itself from rough gravel.
My blood waters grass and gravel,
My tears baptise stones with the sea.
We are but dust.

Othello's giant hands palm crimson misery,
Try to patch his stomach.
But nothing can stop death.
The wind swoops low to kiss and sponge his brow
And haul a fiery quilt of stars
Over his drooping head.
His history stops on bloodied gravel
While silence whines in the legislature.

His breath goes emergency in his lungs.

Dead silence.

6. SPOTLIGHT

*OTHELLO stands, a bloody mess at his belly. He is dead,
and must look it, but this speech cannot be repressed by the
grave.*

OTHELLO   When I felt the scream as the shot smoked... and saw the
hot, red pain as it tore my stomach, splashing me back
through the soft door that crumpled like thin ice, icy splinters gouging my back, and I flailed under air, I swore
Scratch had drowned me. I was at peace. But that peace
was pissed by terror as I crawled down his thrashing driveway, wanting water. Water. I was leaking from the hole in
my stomach, my face busted, and the sight in my eyes
crazy, blue, red, yellow, I wasn't much able to move, then I
blurred Scratch limping slow after me, cursing his fucked
door, and looming over me (I ain't lyin) with his butterknife
(I know, pretty funny, cept it wasn't very funny for me),
and drove the cold blade into my gut so hard he bent the
tip.

All I could think about was having surgery. But what
happened was horror. Scratch didn't once stop his attack
on me. Quite the contrary. The simple bastard broke my
stomach at very close range. When he feared the shot had
failed, he must have gone to his kitchen, gone straight to
the knife drawer, and got a butterknife, knowing it would
follow the shot into my gut and leave no trace. Does that
sound as though he killed in self-defence?

Make no mistake! Scratch used that knife to stab me.
And when I whimpered, he stabbed me again. And when
blood, instead of words, spilled from my mouth, he stabbed
me again and again, and he would have gone on stabbing
me til I was dead, cept he was scared someone would
come. But it didn't matter cos I died anyway.

Fade to black.

7. WHYLAH TRAIN STATION

*Dressed in black, SHELLEY emerges from the station and
walks away. The lights go black. When the lights blossom
again, X, also dressed in black, leaves the train station.*

8. RIVERSIDE

X and YOUNG PABLO sit together on the riverbank.

X   There is no justice for any Coloured.
What they did to Othello was horror:
It was execution by attorneys
After assassination by shotgun.

YOUNG PABLO I think only of death. The drink we all taste.

X

Crows collapse into a still wind of bones,
Their black, feathered truth stripped to a white dream,
What everything becomes: Roses open
To worms and dust; a woman, impassioned,
Abandons herself to white ash, black oil,
And doubles death upon herself; I, too,
Feel quite unmasked: my hate-galled skull glimmers;
Its grin eases into an earthy leer.
All, all must end: worms plough eternity.

YOUNG PABLO Othello dropped in the garden where he
Had crawled, bowled over, like a dog. Then, bright
Enthusiastic machines stormed his last
Self defence with morphine. In court, Scratch joked,
"Self-defence." His white-wash jury guffawed.

X

I feel like takin a gun and blastin Scratch to bits.

YOUNG PABLO No death – or poem – is neutral anymore.

The two men rise to their feet and walk from the riverside.

9. CORA'S KITCHEN

CORA, dressed in black, is comforted by SELAH, SHELLEY, and AMARANTHA, who are also night-shaded. SHELLEY walks away and smashes her fist into her palm.

SHELLEY

I see the sun hunted down, spooked from hills,
Roses hammer his coffin shut, O stilled
By stuttered slander, judicial gossip,
And a killer's brawling discharge.
Bludgeoned men, noosed by loose law, swing from pines;
Judges, chalked *commandants*, gabble dour commandments;
Their law books yawn like lime-white, open pits
Lettered with bones, charred gibberish, of those
Who dared to love or sing and fell to mobs.
Language has become volatile liquor,
Firewater, that lovers pour for prophets
Whom haul, from air, tongues of pentecostal fire –
Poetry come among us.

SELAH

Don't talk so violent, don't talk so loose.

SHELLEY   Were I a man, I'd take a butcher knife
and jack out Scratch's heart
right in front of the tavern
and leave it for the crows to chew on.

AMARANTHA   He shot him down like a dog, jes like a dog.
His eyes are black; they're just black,
and cold like an animal's.

         CORA weeps; she shatters a glass on the table.

CORA   My only son is lost! Now there's nothing.
There's nothing left but death insurance.
When I birthed him, I was sad he was born
Into this impurity, this diseased dream.
But I never feared he could so die first,
Before me, to concede me so alone.
If this is holy, then butcher my heart,
For I am already dead with his death.
Othello, Othello, where now are you,
My son, my splendid, sable Romeo?
I wanna soak your limbs in gold perfumes
Of myrrh and frankincense to erase death–
The dark earthen odour of moist dead leaves.
I want you to rise! I want you to rise!

AMARANTHA   Hush, Ma! Hush! Hush!

SELAH   Go with Am, Ma. Go with Am. We love you.

         SELAH hugs CORA, then AMARANTHA leads her from
         the kitchen.

SHELLEY   Look at what Mr. Justice Pious Cutthroat said when he let
Scratch out of prison on $10 bail, without cash or property
as security: "The background of the case indicates the victim had been an evil drunk." He called Othello "an evil
drunk"!

SELAH   There's no worse drunk than that Scratch Seville! And he's
claimin he shot Othello in self-defence.

SHELLEY   But the knife they found by O's body had no fingerprint on
it!

SELAH   And how did O crawl all that way over gravel, one hand
over his stomach and one hand on the knife?

SHELLEY   The trial's a carnival. Scratch's lawyer, Jack Thomson, hired
            him a jury of twelve rednecks. And the attorney-general,
            that white liar, crawled into the papers – just like a rat –
            and cursed us: He preferred letting an assassin piss on O's
            bones.

SELAH   He's gonna get off. They's gonna let him go.
            It's a white man's world. No justice for us.

            The two sisters embrace as the lights go down.

10. RIVERSIDE

*The chorus assembles down by the river – in early summer
sunlight. They begin to moan, mournfully, but with anger,
and a few, disconsolate wails. Also the sound of a sad organ
or a sobbing piano. O's coffin lies before them.*

CHORUS   (*singing*)
            There's a black wind howlin by Whylah Falls;
            There's a mad rain hammerin down the flowers;
            There's a shotgunned man moulderin in petals;
            There's a killer chucklin to himself;
            There's a mother keenin her posied son;
            There's a joker amblin over his bones.
            Go down to the Sixhiboux, hear it cry,
            "Othello Clemence is dead and his murderer's free!"

            There's a black wind snakin by Whylah Falls;
            There's a river of blood in Jarvis County;
            There's a government that don't know how to weep;
            There's a mother who can't get no sleep.
            Go down to the Sixhiboux, hear it moan
            Like a childless mother far, far, from home,
            "There's a change that's gonna have to come,
            I said, a change that's gonna have to come."

            *As the chorus finishes, its black-robed members comfort
            CORA, AMARANTHA, SHELLEY, and SELAH. REV.
            LANGFORD, X, and PABLO are also present.*

11. SPOTLIGHT

*Still dressed in black, AMARANTHA orates, as if in a
trance.*

AMARANTHA   I saw a black man who was half-fire.
I saw a white woman who was half-fog.
I remember Joseph Howe's secret bastard;
He wore long hair that dropped past his shoulders
and he Cunarded the seven seas.
Father Preston galloped through four-sided weather
when he come to baptize Whylah Falls.
His face was lightning and his hands were bronze.
He brought us black Bibles and blackberry jam.
His first wife, Leila, changed into a butterfly
because he was away in America too long.
This Spanish lady, Corinna, had gold teeth
and mice in her hair.
She cursed the Clear Grits and the Tories.
One winter, there was no summer.
One summer, the ground was matted with rotting fish.
The boughs of trees were draped with bodies
of decaying eels.
The old books open like moth wings.

I was born in Nictaux Falls.
I grew up surrounded by witnesses.
I brewed spring rain tea from the quick freshes.
I fell in love with a jug of red wine
on a table lit by candles and sunflowers.
Everyday I bring candles and sunflowers
to Othello's grave.
Once, we will pass to the dark side of the sea
beyond the waves.

The usual darkness falls.

12. CORA'S KITCHEN

SHELLEY and SELAH crackle the paper.

SHELLEY   The *Whylah Moon* is chock full of mistakes. Listen to this.

(*reciting*) Last week's recipe for Whylah Falls Apple Pie should have listed the ingredients as including seven peeled apples, not potatoes. The *Moon* regrets the typographical error.

SELAH   That idiot man, Jack Thomson, I heard this, went and tried to use the recipe. He baked this apple pie, usin black and rotten potatoes, sprinkled all this cinnamon on top, and tried to feed it to some children. Well, they damn near killed him!

SHELLEY	He got what he deserved.
SELAH	I don't feel sorry for Jack Thomson. I hope he dies with maggots droppin from his mouth an cockroaches crawlin up his ass.
SHELLEY	I'm just glad he was run out of Ottawa when he was caught stealin the loggin company pension funds.
SELAH	He should be dropped straight into Hell.
SHELLEY	Listen to this editorial, "No Prejudice Hair in Jarvis County" by Mo Verbiage.
	(*reciting*) A Toronto repeater was in town seasonally and raised severed questions about a ratio problem in the aria. His questions got only half antswered.
	I wonder if anyone told the man that our ton and money-cipal council are foolly elected. No membrane of any erase other than the caucus race has run for marsupial council.
	If only a few coloureds live in town, it is likely dew to a shortage of hymns or appointments or because, as one parson told me, "I prefer to love outside of town."
	As Christmas drawls near, I hop that we can all show coppassion, understating, and respeck to the Humus race.
SELAH	Ain't that a hellish bit of stupidness, Shell?
SHELLEY	What's even worse, Selah, is how you took up with X when my back was turned.
SELAH	Now, I'm glad you put it like that cos nothin woulda happened if you hadn't turned your back on him.
SHELLEY	You did me shame, Selah, you did me dirt. You didn't have to buse my trust like that.
SELAH	Everyone thought – even X – that you didn't care. So come right down off that high horse fore I make you come down.
SHELLEY	Now don't go gettin in my face either, Selah. You knew better than to do what you did; it was almost as evil as what Scratch did to Othello.
SELAH	Is your name Cleopatra, that you can judge me?

SHELLEY	You acted like I had no love; you turned X into a Sally-Ann Solomon, Schooled for a prodigal, immodest bed.
SELAH	Love loves to love; it hungers for itself. Me and X was a symptom of that need.
SHELLEY	Don't you feel any symptoms of guilt?
SELAH	You magine Othello'd want to see us fussin like this? Over a man?
SHELLEY	I'm just sayin, sister, that that's *my* man.
SELAH	You can have him. He'd be a good man if he weren't a man.

The lights darken.

13. WHYLAH FALLS AFRICAN BAPTIST CHURCH

PABLO enters the church and sits in one of the back pews. He addresses the audience.

PABLO The newspapers lie, but God never does, and His voice shivers the stained-glass in the church, the Whylah Falls African Baptist Church, where *Death* dies, or so Rev. F. R. Langford would claim. He once tried to fly to Heaven on wings he fashioned from sheepskin. He didn't make it, but he was a majestic preacher.

The church fills with other worshippers, including CORA, SHELLEY, AMARANTHA, and SELAH. REV. LANG-FORD steps into the pulpit as the choir members flank him in two gorgeous wings.

CHORUS (*singing*)
Wipe away your tears,
Set free your fears:
Everything is free.
Only the lonely
Need much money:
Everything is free.

The congregation shouts "Amen" and "Preach it" as LANGFORD delivers his poem, banging the podium for emphasis.

LANGFORD   Is the world now ending or beginning?
      The stars keep time; lovers still moan in beds,
      In questionable, Babylonian beds.
      But God is patient. You can't hurry Him –
      But Judgment is a-hurtin you anyways!
      Despair, children, despair is choking us!
      Death is all around us; Death's everywhere.
      We are mere, waving grass, momentary
      Lightning, the dead already forgotten.
      Doncha know that death overshadows you?
      Dirty your knees in the worship of the Lord!
      Confess, confess, confess! Love satisfies.
      Can you be redeemed without Love? No, No.
      Love is the only thing that can't be oppressed.
      If you try to deny love, why, the stones'll tear
      Free from their graves and howl, and howl, and howl,
      Howl *disgust* at all your implicit trusts.
      It's not enough to be in the right church:
      You gotta be in the right pew. Confess!

      We turn to love before turning to dust so that the grave
      will not compress our lives entirely to insects, humus, ash.

      Love is our single resistance against the dictatorship of
      death.

      And for the moment of its incarnation, we will worship
      God, we will make ourselves beautiful in the glinting of an
      eye.

      Can I get a witness? A witness, witness?

      LANGFORD ends with a flourish, mopping his brow; the
      church erupts in pandemonium.

CHORUS   (*singing*)
      Don't try to bind
      The love you find:
      Everyone is free.
      Your lover's yours –
      Surrender force:
      Everyone is free.

      The sun melts down,
      Spreads gold around:
      Everything is free.
      The rain is spent
      Lending flowers scent:
      Everything is free.

REV. LANGFORD returns to the pulpit.

LANGFORD　　I'm not blind to wrong. God's got mine eyes open! I know
the callousness of the Government of Nova Scotia. I spy its
white-washed criminality!

In this granite country, this home
Of hard rock and harder water,
Cattle trudge cold across hills, then slump
In snow – deep, dark, and constant like pain.
My one true love is a pension,
My messiah a bingo prize.
I own only muscle, wine, and wind.

Yet, in my heart's imagination,
I watch wild geese fly, fly,
To thatched colonies of refuge
Founded and fortressed in Tantramar marsh
Far from any possible hunters.
I lust for wings–
Grand impossibilities possible–
To inherit not earth, but *Heaven.*

　　　A welling up of music.

CHORUS　　　(*singing*)
The sun melts down,
Spreads gold around:
Everything is free.
The rain is spent
Lending flowers scent:
Everything is free.

　　　Lights out.

14. CORA'S LIVINGROOM

CORA sits and rocks in candled darkness.

CORA　　　(*singing*)
The snow-dissolving crocus,
The butterfly-trembled grass,
Don't seem to think about death.
But nothing that breathes can last.

Thello, you were night's fleshed-out fire;
You were dawn's star-drizzling frost.
No poet could tell your beauty;
Now, darling, all beauty's lost.

> *The ghost of OTHELLO appears. He begins to play the piano. He smiles at CORA so much that she begins to smile.*

CORA   That you, Thello? O, O, you've come back. My son, you've come back. I'm so happy, so happy. Othello!

OTHELLO   (*singing*)
Mother weep, mother wait;
Doncha worry:
God bless them that got their own.
Ope the pearly gates
And please hurry.
I'm close to home.
(beat) I love you, Mama.

> *As CORA reaches to touch OTHELLO, the lights fade as the song fades.*

15. SCRATCH'S KITCHEN

> *SCRATCH sinks down against a wall. He is a corrupt misérable. He drinks a half-empty bottle of white rum, then sets it aside.*

SCRATCH   Ma name is S. Scratch Seville. Call me "Fool."
I have made my own house my freezing hell.
After I slaughtered Othello, I learned
That evil drives this universe. I feel
As if I've been galled by ice. Understand –
No one's prettier than Angel, no one's
More poisonous. It wasn't Othello
Enthroned twixt her; no, it was Jack Thomson.
Call me "Clown." I slew Othello for false
Reason. My part in this drama is clear:
I'm just someone who cherished a shotgun
And played an ass, an assassin, a sin.

> *SCRATCH puts the end of the shotgun into his mouth and gropes for the trigger, tears belling his cheeks. The stage darkens. A shot is heard. When the light comes up again, SCRATCH is gone. The shotgun lies on the floor. A huge blood stain – like liquid roses – runs down the wall. The lights go down again.*

16. CORA'S KITCHEN

Sunlight. Apple blossoms waft across the room. PABLO gets up from the table and moves toward the door.

PABLO It was April again. A whole year had lapsed since X had come home from Paris. I saw Shelley navigating through the new grass, the bright, cool dew drenching her white cotton socks. She was carrying seeds in her pockets.

Self-exiled to States County, X was missing all of this Beauty. However, he remembered that Shelley's bones were fire and her skin the plush colour of crushed berries and cream and her scent a sweetness like earth, thistle, and hazelnut. He recalled Shelley, *There was a woman, beautiful as morning.* Listen:

Only once do we love:
Never is there another.
After the first love,
There is no other.

As PABLO exits, SHELLEY enters. He doffs his beret, but she ignores him because he is a figment of our imaginations.

SHELLEY ... snow on green branches–
April has come at last.
The earth is astonished,
maddened, by chlorophyll.
Purple and yellow crocuses
arc through snow:
watercolours rainbow
across white paper.
How beautiful!

SHELLEY unfolds a piece of paper and reads it aloud.

Dear X:

Maybe we just need the right words. We must think the same, trying to get them out to each other.

Understand that I'm slow to love. Too many hurt. Life's too full of all of these such things.

I've just written you a poem. I hope you like it:

The river's beauty
glints

and is lost

yet remains
beautiful.

    I'm never quite sure what to say. My pencil talks better
than my mouth.

    I want to see you smile soon. Yes.

    I'm waiting impatiently for your love
To come through to me.

Love,
Shelley.

As always and always will be.

    CORA bustles into the kitchen as SHELLEY refolds the
paper.

CORA   I know you're writin to X, Shelley. You can't hide nothin
from me. If you wanna be a well child, have some sense.
Hear me talkin to you. Can't do no harm to let some words
percolate in your love-heated head. Talkin bout love, learn
these facts:

Better two lovers in bed than two hypocrites in church.
Better two lovers than none.

    If love ain't a problem, you're too lucky. But even if your
bed is steady, your house can still shake. Know this gospel:

Indifference signals approval.
Beside a rosebush, shit smells sweet.

    Beware of people with empty hands, big stomachs, and
big mouths: They're politicians. In filthy times, they spring
up like mushrooms. When the water's low, the fish will be
big. Never dig a hole you can't fill. Remember: the road to
Hell is paved before elections.

    Never mind death. Nothing ends. Truth never ages, wis-
dom never dates, and love never goes out of style.

SHELLEY

Here's my proverb, Ma:
Rose petals must be crushed to give off their scent.
I feel I've been crushed into beauty.
I feel as if I've been cut – into a diamond.
We cannot live only for death.
What is sweeter than lover's breath?

17. SPOTLIGHT

X unfolds a letter and jigs with joy.

X

April, sweet April!
There's nothing I can do but chant my love,
African Baptist beauty, quart'ly queen,
Image of *Germinal* and *Floréal*.
I like to make poems, but let us make life:
Couch long in sweet sweat, rise husband and wife.

The moon twangs its silver strings;
The river swoons into town;
The wind beds down in the pines,
Covers itself with stars.

The light goes out.

18. WHYLAH TRAIN STATION

*SHELLEY approaches X as he exits from the station. The
train whistle fades.*

SHELLEY

You and me'll ramble in the wet
Then return home, smelling of rain.

I understand death and life now –
How Beauty honeys bitter pain.

X and SHELLEY embrace.

X

If you can forgive me, if you forgive,
I'll wrench poems from apple blossom branches,
Scribble your name in the waterfall's noise,
And make all Nature our rose-embroidered
Canticles, to give this dark-complected love
A hearing. *Them that have ears, they will hear.*
Je t'aime. Je t'embrasse de tout mon coeur.

SHELLEY   Your skin is dark sand or ochre.
            Your eyes are black as the Sixhiboux.

            Let us rise and go to Grand Pré
            and loll beneath apple blossoms
            and descant Longfellow's ballad
            about exiled *Évangéline*,
            the pastured scene of her mourning
            spread out lushly before our gaze.

            X, we are responsible
            for Beauty.

                    *X and SHELLEY kiss. They stroll away, hand-in-hand, into
                    light. Religious blues – with harmonica and acoustic guitar.*

19. A STREET IN PARIS

PABLO stands before the original café.

PABLO   After Shelley and X were reunited, Am and me decided to
            voyage the world. We lived a spell in Cuba, then we steam-
            ered to Sierra Leone in Africa (where some of the Coloured
            Loyalists of 1783 went to settle), and then we went back to
            Nova Scotia. We couldn't forget Whylah Falls. There was
            no place ever more beautiful – despite O's murder, despite
            the injustice system. I've come here to Paris to rediscover
            what I thought I had to flee. But, as X said, "We are our
            pasts. Nothing is forgotten." Am, hear my song of songs!
            After two weeks here, I'm coming home.

            I'm coming home, I'm coming home,
            Lonesome for Spanish and sunflowers
            And a love as complex and black
            As water poppling upon stones
            In Jarvis County.

                    *The players join PABLO on stage. The Chorus enters. All
                    sing the spiritual, "Coming Home."*

                    Curtain.

sistahs

by maxine bailey & sharon m. lewis

maxine bailey was born in England, manages to reside in Toronto, yet yearns to be a resident of Barbados. She writes, directs, and produces theatre in Toronto, in that order. Sometimes, rarely, and constantly. She works at being an attentive mother, sistah, daughter, and friend to all the wonderful folks in her life.

sharon mareeka lewis is a callaloo mix of Trinidadian and Jamaican heritage. She is a professional actor, published writer, producer, and director who was born and raised in Toronto, Canada. sharon graduated from the University of Toronto with an honours degree in political science. She combined her political activism with her penchant for drama and worked in political theatre. She then co-founded "Sugar 'n' Spice," a production company devoted to producing works by and for women of colour, and has continued her career in the entertainment field in Los Angeles.

HEALING IN THE KITCHEN: WOMEN'S PERFORMANCE AS RITUALS OF CHANGE

by Andrea Davis

sistahs by maxine bailey and sharon lewis is a powerful testimony of black women's potential to nurture, nourish, restore the self and the community through transforming rituals of healing. The play charts a cycle of women's suffering from West Africa to the Caribbean to Canada and confronts not only the betrayal of "New World" slavery and indentureship but the continuing racist and sexist realities that affect women's lives in the contemporary experience. The two writers assemble a cast of five women whose experiences are made distinct by differences of geography, ethnicity, class, age and sexuality. Yet, their shared experiences are powerful enough to provide the basis not only for individual regeneration but also for communal action. The women find that the power to heal and transform lie in their ability to harness each other's strength through seemingly everyday, ordinary rituals.

The play is structured in eighteen episodic scenes with the primary action taking place in a kitchen and organized around the female activity of cooking. The kitchen has always provided an important space for black women within the African diaspora. During slavery, some of the boldest acts of covert resistance were initiated by women who worked in the kitchens of plantation Great Houses. After slavery, the kitchen became an important female communal space where black women could nurture their own families for the first time, could exercise power and could articulate and express their own creative potential.

In this kitchen, five women are gathered to confront the cancer that has invaded the womb, the birth space, of their mother, lover, sistah, friend. Sandra, a Trinidadian Canadian, has invited the women closest to her to share in a communal act of cooking soup in an attempt to confront her own dying, make peace with the past and make arrangements for the future care of her teenage daughter. Her daughter, Assata, is forced into painful maturity in a too early confrontation with the reality of dying. She must also examine her mother's definition of the world in an attempt to reconcile the contradictions in a relationship that has been both nurturing and estranging. Sandra's lover, Dehlia, is a Jamaican Canadian exorcising her own middle-class past and exploring non-traditional meanings of family. Rea, Sandra's half-sister, confronts her own repressed sexuality even as she comes to terms with her sister's sexual choices. But Rea also has to confront her multiracial identity as both African and Indian. As she comes to accept, she is "history in the flesh" (p.319). Like Sandra and Dehlia, her difference is a necessary variation, not a mutation. For Cerise, Sandra's friend, the meeting in the kitchen has special significance because she is connected to Sandra not only through friendship but through the shared experience of her own mother's dying.

The soup they stir is broth, medicine, old world magic for new world ills. The cancer, itself, is an important symbol of a cycle of oppression that connects women of colour across the African diaspora – women like Sandra who carry the stories of their suffering in their wombs. Black women, after all, have been socialized to believe that strength—psychological and emotional—is their particular inheritance that they should wear with pride because only white women have the luxury of weakness. These women, then, learn how to internalize their pain and find innumerable ways to camouflage and mask their suffering until it's too late. This play is concerned with articulating and confronting the sources of that pain even as it challenges the myth of black women's strength.

But the play addresses not only the racist and sexist oppression women face but also the ways women must work out their relationships with each other. maxine bailey and sharon lewis carefully recognize the breadth of differences across which women must negotiate their relationships. What they attempt is, first of all, a critique of narrow, identities—national, ethnic, sexual—that create artificial boundaries. This will not be a Jamaican or Trinidadian soup, an Afro- or Indo-Caribbean soup, but a West Indian soup cooked in a Canadian kitchen from memories of back home and the bitter sweet of now. In the act of cooking the women begin to reconcile the past with the present by creating a radical definition of family. As Sandra explains, "When I say family, I mean it in the biggest sense. A complex, extended, non-traditional family with its own secret language, a recipe to survive genocide" (p.310). The suggestion is that only in this kind of family do women really have the potential to heal themselves. Sandra's secret language is shared by women who learn to accept difference as a necessary act of loving and forgiving.

The play is worked out importantly against the background of the mother/daughter relationship. The meeting in the kitchen is an important opportunity for Sandra and Assata to make peace. That this meeting takes place in the kitchen is, again, significant because the kitchen has traditionally provided an important generational connection between mothers and daughters. It is here that a large part of a girl's socialization takes place as she is taught how to become a woman. The play examines the extent to which Sandra, a "feminist mother," can move outside the traditional roles perfected by her own mother to offer her daughter survival strategies that can help her avoid the mistakes of the past.

In this play about living, loving and dying, maxine bailey and sharon lewis paint evocative scenes of women's lived realities. They explore possibility and loss, creativity and silence but insist that the moments of deepest loss can also provide the greatest opportunities for spiritual beginnings. The physical and psychological crises that women undergo are often emotionally releasing devices that can initiate processes of renewal – self-journeys into the past that can provide the roadmap for the present, if not for them, then, for the people they love.

Andrea Davis, is a Ph.D. Candidate and Course Director in the Division of Humanities, York University.

sistahs was first produced in Toronto, Canada, by Sugar 'n' Spice Productions at the Poor Alex Theatre, in October 1994.

SANDRA	Melanie Nicholls-King*
DEHLIA	Lisa Richardson
ASSATA	Carol Anderson
REA	Kim Roberts
CERISE	Shakura S'Aida

maxine bailey	Playwright/Producer/Costume Designer
sharon m. lewis	Playwright/Director
Bryan James	Set Designer
Christine Buckell	Lighting and Sound Designer
Diana Sookdeo	Stage Manager
Sonia Dhillon	Assistant Stage Manager
Fleurette S. Fernando	Choreographer

*Best Actress Dora Mavor Moore Award nomination, 1994.

Glossary
Ancestral time: slow, repetitive movements
Lecture mode: refers to Sandra
Real time: happening in the present

CHARACTERS

SANDRA	Mid-thirties, history professor
DEHLIA	Thirties, Sandra's lover, coordinator of a women's centre
ASSATA	Sixteen years old, Sandra's daughter, a student
REA	Early thirties, Sandra's half-sister, government bureaucrat
CERISE	Thirties, family friend, filmmaker

The Setting

A warm, bright, large apartment. The kitchen is centre stage, signified by a huge, old, wooden kitchen table with five wooden stools at varying heights. Worn shelving, with five huge ceramic bowls and five large wooden spoons resting inside the bowls, forms the backdrop. A large stand/stove for the soup. The living room is signified by an overstuffed loveseat and a beatbox. Other rooms/spaces are re-presentational.

Back left to right:
Sharon Lewis
Kim Roberts

Front left to right:
Melanie Nichols-King
Lisa Richardson

photo by Dawn Stephenson

PROLOGUE

DESSERT

SANDRA   Then came the sullen acceptance that their fate was to serve, bc born, work, and die under threat...?

ASSATA steps out of the shadows and joins her mother.

ASSATA   Kill the gravillicious... cells.

DEHLIA joins SANDRA and ASSATA.

DEHLIA   You never see cells on their own.

CERISE joins SANDRA, DEHLIA, and ASSATA.

CERISE   Provide? Yeah, I was busy providing... a martyr of a mother.

SANDRA   I carry my story in my womb. Most women do, but not all. How many of you are...?

REA joins SANDRA, DEHLIA, ASSATA, and CERISE.

REA   They know no boundaries.

CERISE   Even a mother's womb is not a safe home for her child.

ASSATA   (*giggling*) In one soup is the taste of all our mothers.

SANDRA   The end... signaled?

Lights down.

SCENE I

THE PREPARATION

Early morning. SANDRA has her head in the oven, cleaning it out.

SANDRA   Assata, (*pause*) Assata, ASSATTTTA!!

ASSATA enters the kitchen, sleepily.

ASSATA   I'm here, you don't have to yell.

>ASSATA *is not paying attention, has found her walkwoman, and is rapping along.*

SANDRA   We have people coming over you can't help clean up the house this one time. (*sucks her teeth*) I've been trying to wake you since seven o'clock.

ASSATA   I can't hear you, what areya saying?

>SANDRA *comes out of the oven.*

SANDRA   How are you ever going to learn–

>She notices the walkwoman, takes it off.

ASSATA   What?

>ASSATA *slouches at the table.*

SANDRA   (*pointing to walkwoman*) This is why I yell.

ASSATA   You don't have to yell, I know what you were saying.

SANDRA   How are you ever going to learn how to keep house if–

ASSATA   Mom, I'm shocked! You a *feminist* mother, *forcing* your daughter to learn how to keep house.

SANDRA   Very funny, you know very well you don't do a damn thing around this house.

>SANDRA *goes back to cleaning/preparing.*

ASSATA   I dusted.

>ASSATA *starts tinkering with her walkwoman.*

SANDRA   When?!

ASSATA   Last week. (*pause*) What are Auntie Rea and them bringing? I hope it's not that slimy, potatoey thing.

SANDRA   Who is them?

ASSATA   Cerise.

SANDRA   What happen to *Auntie* Cerise?

ASSATA   Cerise told me I could call her by her first name.

SANDRA   Not in my house.

ASSATA   I thought you said this is *our* house.

SANDRA   Go clean up the bathroom.

ASSATA   Done. Will me cleaning house make you better?

SANDRA   Assata, we've been through this.

ASSATA   I just wanna know how making a soup is going to make you better?

SANDRA   I never said it would make me bettah.

ASSATA   Well, why do it?

SANDRA   It can't hurt.

ASSATA   Well I don't know, it depends on who's doing the cooking.

SANDRA   Assata I am tir–

ASSATA   Well maybe you wouldn't be so tired if you would go back to the doctor and get that stupid cis-carb playtane.

SANDRA   Sounds like plantain. Carb-platin.

ASSATA   Why did you invite Auntie Rea, you don't even like her?

SANDRA   Time for things to change.

ASSATA   Obviously.

SANDRA   I told you before Assata it's time for me to make peace it's time for you too.

ASSATA   I don't have a problem with Auntie Re–

SANDRA   I mean peace with me, Assata.

SCENE II

THE PREPARATION

> *DEHLIA enters kitchen from living room with a bag of groceries, kisses SANDRA, and starts to unpack.*

DEHLIA   Girl, Kensington market was packed I've never seen it like that.

SANDRA   I love it when it's packed, it reminds me of back home.

DEHLIA   Back home again?

SANDRA   Yeah Dee-Dee.

ASSATA   (*to DEHLIA*) Yeah Goo-Goo.

DEHLIA   (*back to ASSATA*) Yeah Ass-Yass.

> *DEHLIA throws a small bag of mangoes to ASSATA.*

DEHLIA   These are yours. Catch.

> *ASSATA catches them, does some stylish moves.*

ASSATA   Stylin'!

DEHLIA   (*to ASSATA*) Careful with those mangoes, Nicey's told me they are fresh off the boat from Jamaica.

ASSATA   (*looks at the mangoes*) Oh yeah, how come the sticker says "Made in Mexico."

DEHLIA   What!

ASSATA   Foolie!

SANDRA   (*to ASSATA*) I nevah hear about mango in soup.

DEHLIA   I got plantain.

SANDRA   I nevah hear 'bout plantain in soup.

ASSATA   I like my plantain fried.

SANDRA   Well then you better learn how to fry it.

> *DEHLIA throws ASSATA the plantain.*

DEHLIA   In Jamaica, we have gungo pea soup, red pea soup, cowfoot soup... what kind of soup is "everybody bring something soup"?

SANDRA   It's Wes' Indian. (*gets up, gets the mop and pail ready, and starts mopping the kitchen floor*) What would you know about cooking? You had Molly.

DEHLIA   Esta, how many times I haf to tell you the 'ooman's name is Esta!

SANDRA   (*pushing the mop*) Look Esta here now.

DEHLIA   (*eyeing SANDRA as she's bent over*) Well you don't look like Esta from behind.

ASSATA   That's because Mom has no behind.

SANDRA   (*to ASSATA*) You must be mixing me up with your Auntie Rea.

    DEHLIA unpacks the sugar and throws it to ASSATA.

DEHLIA   Always put a little brown sugar at the bottom of the pot.

SANDRA   Only if it's a Dutch pot.

DEHLIA   Where we come from, its called a dutchie.

SANDRA   Yeah, well where I come from, we know how to call things proper, not like you *small* island people.

DEHLIA   Whoevah hear of Trinidad, is Jamaica everyone know about, right Assata?

    DEHLIA starts humming Rita Marley's "Pass the Dutchie," and ASSATA starts singing.

ASSATA   "Pass the dutchie pun the lef hand side, me say pass the dutchie pun the lef hand side it go burn."

SANDRA   (*laughing to DEHLIA and ASSATA*) Well I see you all do know something about cooking?

DEHLIA   About proper Jamaican cooking. (*pause*) It's that Trini food we caan deal with.

SANDRA   Yeah well you seem to enjoy Trini dining.

SANDRA kisses DEHLIA.

ASSATA   Mom... Natalie wants me to come over... after dinner

SANDRA   What do you think?

ASSATA   I was just asking. I've been inside helping you and I haven't seen Natalie *all* day.

SANDRA   You've been on the phone to her at least three different times today and its only ten o'clock.

ASSATA   Its not the same.

SANDRA   I'm not going to get into this, if you want to go, ask *your* Dehlia.

ASSATA   (*interjects*) But–!

SANDRA   No. (*pause*) You satisfied now. (*mutters under her breath, as she gets the mop and pail and moves towards the bathroom*) Bathroom not done right, I might as well do it.

> *Ancestral time. SANDRA moves in a circular mopping motion towards the space that represents the bathroom. She continues this circular motion, the movement becomes a larger dance movement, until the rhythm and movement brings her to the living room.*

SCENE III

THE PREPARATION

ASSATA and DEHLIA in the kitchen.

DEHLIA   So wha' happen? You said you did the bathroom.

ASSATA   I did.

> *SANDRA in the living room.*

SANDRA   She wants to help?! I'm the one mopping. No, all she wanna to do is stand up and ask me question, why I don't take the treatment, why I don't see this and that doctor? When I'm not here, then she goes and runs street.

> *SANDRA leans tiredly on the mop.*

DEHLIA   Now *I* know you did the bathroom, *you* know you did the bathroom. Is your mother going to go and find the bathroom done her way?

ASSATA   Well...

DEHLIA   It's a big day.

ASSATA   I know.

DEHLIA   It's an important day.

SANDRA   She don't see a doctor standing up in front of her?

ASSATA   I knooow!

SANDRA   She thinks she knows everything.

ASSATA   I know it's an important day.

DEHLIA   Now I know you know, but do you know that I know, that you know.

ASSATA   Yeah, I know that you know that I know that you know.

DEHLIA &
ASSATA   (*simultaneously*) You know! (*laugh*) Boom.

           Pause.

DEHLIA   She *doesn't* know that you know.

           DEHLIA and ASSATA place the plantain, mangoes, and sugar on the table. Ancestral time. They continue putting away groceries in a repetitive motion that complements each other until Scene IV. As SANDRA continues talking, her movements take her back to the kitchen.

SANDRA   She doesn't know I struggle everyday in this country. Sleet, snowstorms, blizzards, freezing rain, (*sucks her teeth*) nearly fall down on the ice carrying the child. Why can't she hear? I tried their way, this is for me.

DEHLIA   (*yelling from the kitchen*) Sandy you alright, you need some help?

SANDRA   No. (*sighs quietly*) Yes.

> *SANDRA slowly puts the mop and pail in the bathroom and then moves into the kitchen. Lights down and spotlight up on SANDRA as she begins her lecture.*

SANDRA   How many of you are African? In the beginning there was confusion, battle, and disbelief that their own people had turned against them. Something had come into their life unwanted. First sign: states could not carry out their normal functions. Greetings. This is HIS 101. I'm professor Sandra Grange-Mosaku. For the next eight months we are going to be rethinking World History. That's right not Third World, not Emerging World, but the part of the world that's been around, three trillion plus times and that's not including eclipses.

> *Spot comes down. SANDRA returns to her original position, starts washing the Dutch pot, drying it. She puts sugar in the pot.*

A halfa handful of sugar at the bottom of the Dutch pot, warm it until it dissolves. (*she fills pot with cold water and puts it on the stove to boil*) If the soup is for plenty people, add more water. (*DEHLIA and ASSATA help SANDRA add more water for the soup*) If you have a cold add some cayenne pepper. If you have a fever make the broth light and add lots of garlic. If you have–

> *CERISE yells from offstage.*

CERISE   If you have what?

SCENE IV

PEELING, CHOPPING, CUTTING

CERISE   (*off-stage*) If we have to have soup, put in lots of those dumplings.

> *CERISE enters the apartment, dumps her groceries in the living room, and continues into the kitchen.*

SANDRA   (*yelling to CERISE*) Cerise, what do you know about dumpling? You were born here.

> *CERISE enters kitchen, gives SANDRA a hug. SANDRA then moves away from the pot towards table, where fresh herbs await.*

ASSATA   Cerise!

SANDRA   Its Auntie Ce–

CERISE   Hey Assata, Dehlia.

DEHLIA   Only you could wear something like dat and get away with it.

CERISE   Honey close your mouth, I know I look good.

> *SANDRA starts to chop fresh herbs, such as thyme.*

SANDRA   But do you taste good?

CERISE   As fresh as that thyme you're chopping.

DEHLIA   Auntie Dotilda made dumplings once, but they never turn out like Esta's.

> *Pause. SANDRA knows it's just another Dehlia-ism*

SANDRA   Rea and I are making them today.

DEHLIA   Rea is going to get her hands dirty?

SANDRA   You know she makes dumplings.

CERISE   Good. As long as she makes me those long, long...

ASSATA   ...long...

SANDRA   ...dumplings.

CERISE   Assata come help me bring in my groceries.

SANDRA   Groceries? I thought you were only bringing sweet potato.

CERISE   I brought potato, I'm sweet enough.

> *CERISE exits to living room. DEHLIA gets up and helps SANDRA chop the thyme. ASSATA picks up her walkwoman and mangoes, then follows CERISE to the living room. She hides the mangoes by the already hidden bowl, knife, and spices.*

SCENE V

PEELING, CHOPPING, CUTTING

DEHLIA and SANDRA in the kitchen, chopping the thyme.

SANDRA   So what are you putting in the soup?

CERISE   So what are you doing over there?

> *ASSATA is hiding mangoes in the living room. CERISE gets her groceries.*

DEHLIA   I told you the plantain.

ASSATA   Never you mind.

> *ASSATA pulls out the recipe for "Mango Chow" and starts reading it.*

DEHLIA   But you've said you don't like plantain in soup so I'll–

SANDRA   No Dehlia, I told you to put in what you want to. Just add lots of...

CERISE   It's my job to mind.

> *CERISE moves towards ASSATA and starts reading over ASSATA's shoulder.*

SANDRA   ...pepper.

> *CERISE and ASSATA read the recipe out loud together once. Ancestral time. They quietly repeat it until SANDRA's lecture.*

CERISE &
ASSATA   Mango Chow:
green Julie mangoes
washed, peeled, and sliced in thin strips
add pipe water
add sea salt
vinegar
fresh lime
black pepper
and of course pepper sauce to taste
let sit
cover with a towel to keep the (*mumble*) away

DEHLIA   But if everyone puts in what they want how is it going to taste?

SANDRA   Just do it with love.

DEHLIA   I've got plenty of that.

> *She squeezes SANDRA's bum. SANDRA hands her the plantain to peel and chop.*

SANDRA   Good because the soup is for plenty people.

DEHLIA   It's only five of us.

SANDRA   That's enough.

> *SANDRA has a small, sharp pain.*

DEHLIA   Why are you breaking your back to make the soup in this way? (*sits SANDRA down to massage and wrap her head*) How come you don't let me wrap your head anymore?

SANDRA   Not enough time.

DEHLIA   I thought you were going to make time.

SANDRA   If I could *make* time I wouldn't have to make this soup.

DEHLIA   Let me help you.

SANDRA   Make the soup?

DEHLIA   Make time.

SANDRA   C'mon we have to get the soup started.

DEHLIA   We're making the time.

> *DEHLIA continues to massage and wrap SANDRA's head. SANDRA gets up, spotlight comes up, and she moves into lecture mode. DEHLIA continues massaging motion, ancestral time.*

SANDRA   Slavery does not develop on healthy sites. The cells must be stressed...

> *As CERISE and ASSATA are flipping through the recipe, words pop out.*

**CERISE &
ASSATA**   Add sea salt...

SANDRA   Slavery based on race is the only kind of slavery that crossed geographical/national/political state bound-aries...

**CERISE &
ASSATA**   ...let sit...

SANDRA   The second stage...

**CERISE &
ASSATA**   ...washed, peeled, and sliced...

SANDRA   Slavery was governed outside of the bodies that produced the slaves. Okay, the middle passage. How many of you can give me a definition of what that was...?

**CERISE &
ASSATA**   ...cover with a towel to keep the (*mumble*) away.

SANDRA   Too early huh?

> *Ancestral time. Spotlight comes down and SANDRA returns to her original position in the chair, with DEHLIA massaging her head.*

SCENE VI

PEELING, CHOPPING, CUTTING

> *ASSATA and CERISE finish looking at the Mango Chow recipe.*

CERISE   Does this go in the soup?

ASSATA   No.

CERISE   Green mango?

ASSATA   My granma told me this was Mom's favourite, especially when she was pregnant.

CERISE   Yeah, trying to score brownie points.

ASSATA   It fits the criteria.

CERISE   All natural?

ASSATA   Check. Mangoes fresh from Jamaica.

CERISE   Cultural relevance?

ASSATA   Strictly a Trinidadian recipe.

CERISE   Cheap too.

Knock at the door. CERISE goes to open the door. REA enters.

REA   Oh hello Cerise, I didn't know everybody was here already.

CERISE   If everybody means me, I guess we're all here.

REA   Hello Assata.

ASSATA   (*loud and formally*) Hello, Auntie Rea.

She kisses REA on the cheek, with a quick hug. REA puts the bags down.

REA   I haven't seen you since Christmas. You've grown.

ASSATA   I know it happens.

She gestures to ASSATA's afro.

REA   What's that? Afro? That's coming back now?

CERISE   Well in my time we called it a 'fro. Girl, I had me one to die for. Just like Angela Davis... I was so upset when I found out it was a wig.

ASSATA   She has dreads.

CERISE   In my time she had a 'fro. I got up two hours before school started to get the sleep dents out of my hair to have a perfectly rounded 'fro. This guy, what's his name... would just torture me. He'd mess it up with his fingers. He pushed me too far one time. I chased him with my afro pick... I had me one of those metal ones.

CERISE play-stabs ASSATA. ASSATA blocks it.

ASSATA   You don't look the type to be roughing people up.

CERISE   Baby, when it comes to black womens' hair, you know we don't mess. Do you let people touch up your hair?

ASSATA	Uh-uh. No way.
CERISE	I didn't think so.

CERISE &
ASSATA   (*in unison*) Hmhmmh!

> *CERISE, REA, and ASSATA laugh.*

REA   In school, PSYCH 101, I sat in front of Jack Becking. I kept feeling this tapping, and I'd turn around and Jack would be smiling, and I'd smile back. He was kind of cute too. Walking out of class, I heard these giggles, and when I turned around, I felt something on my neck. I ran my hand through my hair and ping... ping, two, three, about ten pencils fell out of my hair.

> *REA is laughing. CERISE and ASSATA are quiet.*

ASSATA   But Auntie Rea, your hair's so straight now.

REA   Well, your mom had an afro, and I had to have one too. Before I left Trinidad, Sandra helped me fluff it up, and work with my natural curl. She loved it when I followed her style.

CERISE   So how'd it get so straight?

REA   I'm not fighting it.

CERISE,
REA &
ASSATA   (*in unison*) Hmmmhmmmh.

> *SANDRA enters living room. DEHLIA takes out her jigsaw puzzle on a tray and puts it on the kitchen table. SANDRA enters, pauses, and moves to hug REA.*

SANDRA   Hello Rea.

REA   Sandra, I didn't realize I was late, I thought you said noon.

SANDRA   I did, Cerise just came over early.

REA   Oh? (*turns to get her bags*)

SANDRA   Assata, what did your Auntie Rea do to her hair?

REA   I haven't done anything to my hair.

SANDRA   It looks different from when I last saw you.

REA   It's the first time I've worn it out.

ASSATA   I think it looks good.

DEHLIA   (*yelling from the kitchen*) Sandy the water is boiling.

SANDRA   So.

    She starts to go towards the kitchen.

DEHLIA   So you not coming in to look at it.

CERISE   (*gathering her grocery bags*) I better take this stuff in there.

REA   Sandra you didn't tell me to bring anything.

SANDRA   Oh I thought we could make the dumplings. But I see you brought stuff anyway.

REA   Just a few things, some yam, daschene, pumpkin, sea salt, garlic press...

SANDRA   Well, lets bring it in the kitchen. Assata, come show your Auntie Rea your–

ASSATA   I will in a minute Mom I just gotta finish something out here.

SANDRA   Probably the phone.

SCENE VII

PEELING, CHOPPING, CUTTING

SANDRA, CERISE, and REA go into the kitchen. DEHLIA and REA smile politely at each other. Ancestral time, ASSATA stays in living room, playing with the mangoes.

CERISE enters the kitchen, dumps her groceries, and watches DEHLIA doing the puzzle. She tries to help but it's not her forte. SANDRA and REA start to unpack REA's bag on the kitchen table, crowding out DEHLIA.

DEHLIA   (*to REA*) Rea, we already went grocery shopping this morning.

REA   I see Sandy does the cooking and you do the–

DEHLIA	Nice of you to come, Rea.
REA	Thank you for inviting me.
DEHLIA	You'll have to thank your sister San–
SANDRA	She did.

        Pause.

REA	Well, I better start chopping up the provisions.
SANDRA	Yes we're all here now. (*pause*) Except for Assata.
DEHLIA	She'll be along.

        CERISE throws down a puzzle piece.

CERISE	Dehlia, what kind of puzzle is this? (*picks up puzzle-box cover*) Where's the picture?
DEHLIA	There is no picture.
CERISE	What do you mean no picture? That would drive me crazy.
DEHLIA	The fun is in doing it. Cerise maybe you need a hobby, one that doesn't involve lying down so much.
CERISE	What's the point in putting in all that hard work if you don't know how its going to turn out.
SANDRA	Just like the soup.
CERISE	Just like sex.

        REA starts washing the provisions.

REA	Depends on how long it takes. You taste it as you go along.
CERISE	How many have you tasted, Rea?
REA	Enough. I make *soup* quite often.
DEHLIA	You not putting any of that kuchi, kulchah stuff in the soup.
SANDRA	Kuchela. You leave us Trinis alone, don't you Jamaicans drink Irish Moss?
CERISE	Is that the thing you made for me Dehlia... with the seaweed?

DEHLIA   You said you wanted something to make it last.

CERISE   Make *him* last not me.

SANDRA   (*to DEHLIA*) What you know about cooking?

DEHLIA   Yeah, I know... I had Esta.

SANDRA   Rea, how did you find this stuff, its exactly what Mummy used to put in her soup.

REA   Well I wasn't even going to bring anything, since you didn't tell me everyone else was asked to bring something.

SANDRA   I want us to make the dumplings.

> *REA starts peeling, chopping, and cutting. SANDRA gets a knife and joins her. Spotlight up on SANDRA with knife in her hand. She's back in lecture mode. In ancestral time, REA continues chopping, ASSATA mango chowing, and DEHLIA and CERISE shuffle puzzle pieces.*

SANDRA   The middle passage... the surgical removal of female reproductive organs... I received some interesting papers on this topic. Women were kept at the bottom of the ship, as they fetched less of a price than a stud; a few were kept on-deck to cook for the captain, and some were used for... you see, a good doctor will tell you as many facts as possible about the... give you books to read, but a brilliant historian... Indian women...

REA   ...they can be your sistah...

SANDRA   ...single and widowed... whatever caste were...

> *REA, ASSATA, and DEHLIA speak together, but DEHLIA adds her own take on it.*

REA &
ASSATA   ...they can be your sistah.

DEHLIA   ...they can be your sistah-in-*law*.

SANDRA   ...whatever caste were forced to cross the Kala Pani and become indentured labourers or face death... (*pause*) many faced death no matter what they did.

> *Spotlight comes down, and SANDRA continues chopping, peeling, and cutting. CERISE and DEHLIA put away the puzzle and start chopping.*

SCENE VIII

PEELING, CHOPPING, CUTTING

ASSATA takes the bowl, ingredients, and knife from their hiding place and sits on the floor, playing with the knife. This character has now moved into real time.

All four of them are around the kitchen table, doing peeling, chopping, and cutting motions; DEHLIA doing the plantain, CERISE doing the potatoes, and REA and SANDRA doing the provisions REA brought. Throughout this scene everyone gives their sounds of testifying.

REA   Chop it thin.

SANDRA   Don't chop it, slice it.

ASSATA   (*in living room to herself*) I don't even want to be here.

DEHLIA   I can't peel the skin off of this.

ASSATA   (*in living room*) Cooking. A few years ago we were just fine. Cleaning. Now all of a sudden everything has to be just like it was in Trinidad. Cook with love.

REA &
SANDRA   If you can eat, you can cook.

ASSATA   (*in living room*) How about *buy* Mickey Dee's with love.

REA   Slowly, do it slowly, trust me it'll turn out better.

DEHLIA   We always do it slowly!

             Sounds of laughter.

ASSATA   We used to skin teeth, laugh... (*sounds of laughter from the kitchen*) Well we're not in Trinidad. Chopping. We didn't have Dehlia in Trinidad. Seriousness. I'd go to New York over Trinidad any day.

REA   Do we have to talk about that?

ASSATA   Beat. Mom said "Lets go to New York." Just like that. For the day. Stir. We drive to Buffalo, take the first plane to New York, take a bus to downtown Manhattan, and by five p.m. we had bought like nuff stuff and we're sitting in a restaurant talking. Like big women y'know. Melt. Next morning, Mom and I are sitting around the kitchen table. Toast. Dehlia asks us "What's up?" Mom just smiles. Didn't say anything. It was like it was our little secret. Flavour.

> *ASSATA starts peeling, cutting, and slicing the mangoes, adds the pepper, vinegar, salt, lime, and pepper sauce to the bowl of sliced mangoes, puts the bowl aside, and covers it with a tea towel. This action takes place throughout the scene.*

CERISE   I never understood in cookbooks, the difference between pare and peel.

SANDRA   Pare is when someone from the department cuts you down in a faculty meeting, and peel is when–

DEHLIA   Peel is when I tear the skin off the bus drivers that pull into the station, park the bus, and won't let us on. Jus' mek us stand up in the cold while he goes pee!

CERISE   I wanna crush those guys who yell out "Sweetie, gimme your number."

REA   That never happens to me.

CERISE   Oh! Your pussy's too pricey.

REA   I was spit on by this crazy old white man on my street.

DEHLIA   Where did it get you?

CERISE   Girl we in it now. We're cutting them up. Did you cook a lot back home?

SANDRA   I was too busy stirring up revolution.

CERISE   Hmmh. Black Power.

REA   Only no revolution took place.

SANDRA   Eric Williams as Prime Minister and no revolution.

REA   Eighties brought us oil and blue notes and French patisseries on a Caribbean mountaintop.

DEHLIA	Manley as a Reaganite.
CERISE	Jesse Jackson running for president.
DEHLIA	Chitlins *a la flambe*.
SANDRA	Feels good.
CERISE	Go on.
SANDRA	I'm going to chop up the next teacher that questions if I'm "cultivating an environment conducive to learning for my daughter."
REA	Mash them up–
CERISE	–with your Ph.D.
DEHLIA	Sandra you would never do that.
SANDRA	Time for things to change.
REA	What's changing?
CERISE	(*to SANDRA*) Let it out. This is the place.
SANDRA	That's what's changing.
CERISE	Some people never change. My mom wanted me to get a government job.
DEHLIA	But your mom hated her job.
CERISE	Yes, but "we don't have the luxuries they do, we have to work twice as hard as–"
REA	You know, maybe your mother had a point, Cerise. Filmmaking – that's what you do isn't it? – is supposed to be cutthroat.
CERISE	Where is it you work again?
REA	I'm a senior policy advisor in the Ministry of Culture and Communications.
CERISE	The government.
REA	Yes.

CERISE   How do you stand it in there?

REA   Well, I try not to blow–

CERISE   Really, I don't mind it at all.

REA   Blow, you know lose my cool. Just yesterday, Mr. McDuff said *you* people are good at blah, blah, blahblahblahblahaaaaaaaaah-blah...

> *REA continues under SANDRA's yelling with a government droning sound, until her next line is heard. CERISE and DEHLIA make blah-blah sounds.*

SANDRA   (*yelling*) Assata. Dehlia, what is that child doing in there?

REA   I told him that I didn't appreciate his comment and I would send a recommendation to... blah, blah, blahblahblahbla-haaaaaaaaahblah...

> *REA continues under SANDRA's yelling with a government droning sound, until her next line is heard. CERISE and DEHLIA make blah-blah sounds.*

SANDRA   (*yelling*) Assata. (*to DEHLIA*) Isn't she going to help with this soup?

REA   I presented it last week. He hasn't looked at it yet, but I've filed a complaint with human res– blah, blah, blahblahblahbla-haaaaaaaaahblah...

> *REA continues under SANDRA's yelling with a government droning sound, until end of scene. CERISE and DEHLIA make blah-blah sounds.*

SANDRA   Why can't she try more?

ASSATA   (*takes a leftover mango, caresses it*) Mmmm a ripe one... (*bites into it, then spits some out*) It's rotten. How can it look fine on the outside and be... (*smashes and pounds the mango with her fists*) Why can't she try more?

> *ASSATA gets up and takes the bowl of Mango Chow into the kitchen.*

DEHLIA   She does. Maybe it's not always your way–

SANDRA   (*yelling to ASSATA*) Can't you hear me?

SCENE IX

PEELING, CHOPPING, CUTTING

ASSATA enters kitchen from living room.

ASSATA   I'm right here, you don't have to ye–

SANDRA   Yell.

CERISE   (*to ASSATA*) So what are you up to?

ASSATA   I made Mom's favourite.

SANDRA   Really?

DEHLIA   You bettah than me.

REA   Good for you Assata.

SANDRA   I didn't see you by the pot.

ASSATA   Its ready, I made it out there by myself.

           ASSATA hands SANDRA the bowl of Mango Chow from behind her back. SANDRA is speechless.

DEHLIA   (*feigning surprise*) What's that? Green mango chopped up?

REA   Is that Mango Chow? (*takes bowl from SANDRA and tries a piece*) It's good, its almost like back home.

ASSATA   I know. I got Granma's recipe.

REA   But honey, Granma died just before you left Trinidad, you were only two.

ASSATA   I mean my daddy's granma.

SANDRA   When did you talk to her?

ASSATA   I called her in Trinidad. (*to her mother*) I'll pay for it.

REA   Sandy, I didn't know you still talk to them.

SANDRA   I don't. Nothing happened. But since Tony died, I just lost touch. No time...

ASSATA   Time. For. Things. To change.

SANDRA   Didn't I ask you to come help with the soup?

ASSATA   What's the difference, I made something. Besides, you said Mango Chow is your favourite.

SANDRA   But I wanted you to help with the soup, don't you have anything to add!!

DEHLIA   Sandy, she can still help.

SANDRA   I wanted her to be in here, chopping and ting with everyone else.

DEHLIA   There's still time.

SANDRA   The water is boiling.

REA   That's the best time.

SANDRA   (*to ASSATA*) Don't cut your eye at me Assata, you know what you were supposed to do and you didn't do it. You would rather sit in the living room and chat on the phone than–

ASSATA   I wasn't on the phone, I was chopping the mango – forget it.

ASSATA storms into the living room and puts on her walkwoman. Pause.

CERISE   Girl, when you let it out, you let it out hard.

CERISE exits to living room and watches ASSATA. Pause.

DEHLIA   (*to SANDRA*) What are you really mad at Sandy?

DEHLIA follows CERISE to the living room and remains hidden, watching CERISE and ASSATA. REA is rooted to the spot, spotlight up, as SANDRA does her lecture.

SANDRA   There has been a change in the syllabus, oral stories will not be allowed as a valid historical document. It's beyond my control.

Spotlight down. SANDRA is with REA in the kitchen.

SCENE X

PEELING, CHOPPING, CUTTING

DEHLIA, CERISE, and ASSATA in the living room, while REA continues chopping.

SANDRA   Here let me help.

REA   Food doesn't taste right from an angry cook.

SANDRA sits down and REA continues chopping.

REA   Wait until you simmer down.

Gradually SANDRA starts to rock back and forth in sync with REA's chopping motion, in ancestral time. ASSATA is listening to her walkwoman. CERISE approaches ASSATA.

CERISE   Your mom's probably had these up-and-down moods for awhile.

ASSATA doesn't acknowledge that she heard CERISE, but keeps listening to her music.

CERISE   You heard me, I know you did.

ASSATA   (*doesn't take off the walkwoman*) Does she have to talk to me like that in front of everyone.

CERISE   Mothers talk, sometimes you just don't want to hear what they have to say.

ASSATA   Do *they* listen?

CERISE   Sometimes they don't want to hear what we have to say.

DEHLIA enters, takes the walkwoman from ASSATA. ASSATA glares at DEHLIA as DEHLIA puts the walkwoman on and starts to dance. Both CERISE and ASSATA start laughing. DEHLIA stops and puts down walkwoman. ASSATA grabs it but doesn't put it on; she fiddles with it.

ASSATA   I made her favourite thing... from Trinidad.

CERISE   (*to ASSATA*) She knows.

DEHLIA   She wants the soup.

ASSATA   I don't. I want things the way they were.

DEHLIA   We all do. I need to remember the first time I met the two of you. It was cold and you were all bundled up in this pink snowsuit.

CERISE   And let me guess, she was this big.

> *CERISE gestures how small ASSATA must have been, exaggerating.*

ASSATA   I was ten. I was this big. (*shows them*)

DEHLIA   You know this country is cold. Esta warned me... Esta gave me a sweater somebody had sent her from foreign.

ASSATA   ...a sweater.

CERISE   (*to DEHLIA*) Who is taking the drugs you or Sandra?

DEHLIA   Neither of us. Sandra stopped chemo last year.

CERISE   I didn't know.

ASSATA   I knew it.

DEHLIA   She is trying other things, Assata.

ASSATA   Like what?

DEHLIA   Eating good food.

ASSATA   Like that will cure her.

CERISE   (*to ASSATA*) You can try to stop it from eating at you.

ASSATA   How?

CERISE   My mom never even tried.

DEHLIA   Your mom took everything they gave her.

CERISE   Yeah, everything... the shit they dished out, the long hours with little pay...

ASSATA   That's not her fault.

DEHLIA   Sandy lets things eat at her.

ASSATA   Am I eating at her?

> *Ancestral time. CERISE and DEHLIA comfort ASSATA in silence, rocking back and forth. SANDRA and REA are rocking in the kitchen.*

SCENE XI

BOILING!

CERISE, DEHLIA, and ASSATA in the living room.

CERISE   (*quietly*) It's serious.

> *ASSATA goes into the kitchen. DEHLIA and CERISE follow to find SANDRA moving in sync with REA, who is continuing the chopping motion. SANDRA turns to see ASSATA. ASSA-TA picks up the plate of chopped provisions – the edoe, daschene, etc. – to put some in the soup. No plantain or dumplings are added at this time. SANDRA helps ASSATA. She takes some provisions and drops them in the soup, and then stirs it.*

SANDRA   Old and...

> *ASSATA puts some spice in the soup.*

ASSATA   New.

> *On each of their lines, DEHLIA, REA, and CERISE also drop the chopped vegetables into the soup. They are all around the pot, making stirring motions. DEHLIA takes some provisions and drops them into the pot.*

DEHLIA   Me and you.

> *REA takes some provisions and drops them into the pot.*

REA   Kuchala with...

ASSATA   Kool-aid made from...

> *CERISE takes some provisions and drops them into the pot.*

CERISE   Kool-aid?

ASSATA   Kool-aid in mango flavour.

SANDRA   Why not?

REA   Free enterprise.

SANDRA   Recipe of the century.

REA   An historical lime.

ASSATA   With the essence of time.

CERISE   T-I-M-E.

DEHLIA   T-H-Y-M-E.

SANDRA   Tarragon. (*starts to add some to the soup*)

REA   And... curry powder. (*adds some to the soup*)

ASSATA   Ground up fine.

DEHLIA   Like sands in an hour glass.

SANDRA   When you cut a cucumber, (*she demonstrates*) slice the ends off and then take those pieces and rub each end of the cucumber. This takes the bitterness from it.

REA   If I rub my sistah, from her head to her toes will that take away the bitterness from her?

DEHLIA   Is it an English cucumber or a hybrid?

           Pause.

REA   A hybrid.

SANDRA   What about the plantain?

DEHLIA   Put it in later or it'll get soft 'n' mushy.

CERISE   It don't feel right in your mouth when it's soft 'n' mushy.

SANDRA   (*to CERISE*) Whatchya know about plantain? (*to DEHLIA*) Molly recipe that.

DEHLIA   Esta.

           Spotlight on SANDRA as she does her lecture. DEHLIA, ASSATA, REA, and CERISE continue stirring the soup in ancestral time.

SANDRA   When I say family, I mean it in the biggest sense. A complex,
           extended, non-traditional family, with its own secret language,
           a recipe to survive genocide. Nourish the good cells. Prepare
           the baby cell.

           Spotlight comes down. SANDRA continues stirring the soup.

SANDRA   (*to ASSATA*) I hope you're writing this recipe down.

           *REA moves towards the table, starts wiping it down, mumbles
           under her breath:*

REA   Plantain in soup?

           *DEHLIA moves towards table, joins REA, and "helps" wipe it
           down.*

DEHLIA   You start relaxing your hair now?

REA   We went through this in the living room. *No.*

CERISE   I've permed my hair at one time or the other. (*swings her hair
           to and fro*)

SANDRA   Cerise, do you have to play with your hair over the soup, you
           can tell you ain't Wes' Indian.

           *SANDRA shoos CERISE in the direction of the table, where she
           sits and watches REA and DEHLIA clean around her. SAN-
           DRA and ASSATA continue stirring the soup.*

CERISE   My hair is clean, I just got the braids put in.

DEHLIA   We had to take off our school hats when we were inside the
           house. Mama nevah let us wear them inside.

REA   Dehlia, we're not talking about "hats" the topics are soup and
           hair.

SANDRA   It all makes sense in Dehlia's mind. (*tastes the soup*) Rea, pass
           the salt.

CERISE   Sexual positions are the only things in Dehlia's mind.

ASSATA   (*to CERISE*) I don't want to think about it!

CERISE   Think about what...?

REA   Oh you mean your mother and Dehlia!

ASSATA   *Yes!* No! I mean *parents* having sex!

CERISE   Why? They make noise?

DEHLIA   Sunday afternoon, Esta had gone to country. Me, Mommy, and Daddy sat down on the verandah, with three bowls of grapenut ice-cream, no I lie, Daddy had rum 'n' raisin, him always like him rum. Anyway, we laugh till we drop.

CERISE   So?

DEHLIA   That's how I found out!

               Pause.

CERISE   How did I find out?

ASSATA   When will I find out?

REA   Not now.

SANDRA   (*to ASSATA*) Well honey, at least you and I had a talk, our mommy (*indicates to REA*) never told us anything, I had to learn with your father.

REA   Don't tell a lie Sandy.

SANDRA   We never had sex.

DEHLIA   Who?

REA   So what did you do up on Maracas beach whole night?

SANDRA   Talk.

ASSATA   That's what I told you, Mom, when I–

DEHLIA   Who?

REA   Octopus.

DEHLIA   Octopus?

SANDRA   Reggie Alleyne... he was...

REA   A Belmont boy...

SANDRA   ...he was going to teach me how to drive standard, so we went up to...

CERISE   So what did he use as the stick shift?

REA   Exactly.

SANDRA   He drove. We parked. He put my hand on the stick shift...

CERISE   ...it was bigger than you thought...

SANDRA   ...I put it in reverse and walked home.

REA   I wish you'd told me.

DEHLIA   Kissing is sex.

ASSATA   Well then, I've had sex.

REA   What?

ASSATA   Well Dehlia said–

SANDRA   You *are* talking about kissing, not sex.

DEHLIA   It depends on what kind of kissing.

CERISE   I never allow the "tongue" in on the first date.

REA   I don't like it at all.

DEHLIA   Poor James.

CERISE   (*to REA*) Girl, you don't know what you're missing. If they
             have a nice size tongue and know how to work it... hmmh...
             hmmh... hmmh!

REA   No... (*she mumbles*)

CERISE   Why?

REA   He has a rough tongue.

CERISE   Oh! That must hurt when he goes... (*gestures downwards*)

ASSATA   That's rude. (*looks towards her mom for approval*)

SANDRA   Assata, come help me with the soup... (*mumbles as she moves
             towards the pot*)

ASSATA   (*whispers to CERISE*) So anyway, if the tongue is–

REA   Look, go help your mother... (*to CERISE*) So. You mean the tongue should be smooth–

DEHLIA   (*interrupts*) No. A rough tongue can feel good, it just has to...

REA   How do you know... (*realizes, looking at SANDRA*) Oh! You need help, Sandra?

> *REA gets up and rushes towards SANDRA and ASSATA by the stove. CERISE winks at DEHLIA, who is bringing out her puzzle. CERISE groans but starts doing it anyways. REA, SANDRA, and ASSATA are stirring the soup.*

SCENE XII

BOILING!

SANDRA   (*to REA*) So how is James?

REA   Well if you had invited him... because it's family isn't it?

SANDRA   *You and I* are what I wanted to deal with.

> *SANDRA gives the stirring spoon to ASSATA, and moves to dust off the kitchen table. Satisfied, she moves to get broom to sweep the kitchen.*

DEHLIA   You know my family didn't get invited either Rea!

CERISE   Well I'm glad they're not coming... (*gets up from doing puzzle and ends up doing nothing*) ...not enough room (*looking around*) or soup for *both* sides of the family.

ASSATA   Natalie didn't get to come, and she's my best friend.

REA   They... they are not family.

SANDRA   It's *my* definition of family.

ASSATA   (*stirring soup*) Uh... uh... soup's heating up.

REA   And that's that. Right Sandra?

DEHLIA   (*to ASSATA*) Put the peppah in.

SANDRA   Wait!

ASSATA   What? (*stops*)

REA   (*thinking SANDRA means her*) I said, you always have the last word.

> *SANDRA puts the broom down, rinses her hands, and moves towards the stove to check the soup.*

SANDRA   Rea. I was talking to Assata, I don't want the peppah in yet. (*stirs the soup*) It smells good, just a bit more...

ASSATA   Pepper.

SANDRA   Yes.

> *ASSATA puts in some bonnet pepper.*

REA   I just want to know why some people were invited and–

SANDRA   My house.

DEHLIA   Our house... (*looks at SANDRA*) ...hon.

REA   Anyway Sandra I'm glad to be here, I just think that it's really important that you surround yourself with people, like, well like James and myself.

SANDRA   I think it's important that I have the people I want around me.

REA   Well, Assata's future is... and she is *my* niece.

DEHLIA   Assata's future is right here with me... and her mother.

CERISE   ...and me...

SANDRA   Her future is exactly why we're here.

ASSATA   What? What are you talking about?

REA   I'm pleased that it's finally out in the open.

DEHLIA   We're doing fine.

CERISE   Let's hear what Sandra has to say.

REA   (*looks at CERISE*) Do you think this is the time and place to discuss it Sandy?

SANDRA   This is exactly the time and the place. I need to know what everyone here can and will do to support Assata *and* Dehlia...

ASSATA   Are you giving up?

REA   The last time we talked Sandy, I thought you were trying alternative methods, now it seems you're not trying anything. One of James' clients is an onco-logist. I can get the number so you can call. But I also think we should prepare for the worst. (*pause*) You know... the insurance... a college fund for the child. James' daddy has invited us to come home and we'd like to take Assata to Trinidad.

SANDRA   So Dehlia, you going Trinidad?

DEHLIA   Auntie Dotilda and dem have a sixteen-year-old boy child.

REA   So?

DEHLIA   So she... Assata won't be alone when we all go down next summer.

SANDRA   It's not confirmed yet Dehlia. I am not talking just about summer, I'm talking about what we all can do together...

REA   I want Assata to be raised like I was in a proper Trini home.

SANDRA   So, if Dehlia was a Trini it would be okay?

DEHLIA   Most of the raising has been done. By me... (*she takes her time*) ...and Sandra.

SANDRA   Rea, pass the salt.

REA   No, I'll do it... your hand was always too heavy.

SANDRA   Do it with love.

   REA sucks her teeth, puts down the salt.

ASSATA   Is anyone interested in what I think?

CERISE   I'm listening.

REA   I'm her family... what if anything... was to ever happen.

DEHLIA   Nothing is going to happen.

SCENE XIII

BOILING!

ASSATA moves to go into the living room.

SANDRA   Where are you going?

DEHLIA pulls her back down in the chair.

DEHLIA   Relax Sandy.

SANDRA   I just want her here, she's always running.

ASSATA reluctantly stays.

DEHLIA   Maybe she needs time-out.

REA   I think Sandy knows her own child.

DEHLIA   Rea, for the last time she is our child.

CERISE   Is anyone listening to Assata?

REA   What's the matter you worried she might turn out too Indian, she might like men.

DEHLIA   Why don't you and your man go have a child?

SANDRA   That is not the point.

REA   We can't.

SANDRA   I want the soup to be like it was back home. Dumplings – cornmeal and flour – no plantain, ground provisions, no mango. Taste exactly like back home. A real Wes' Indian family. No fighting.

REA   We fought.

CERISE   I'm not West Indian, I don't know the ground rules.

DEHLIA   We're here now. We are a Wes' Indian family. It's going to taste like us.

CERISE   I do know how to support Assata and Dehlia.

REA   What about me? I'm *the* family.

SANDRA   This is my family.

REA   Sandy, I don't know why you carrying on? This isn't like any soup I know back home.

SANDRA   But it could be Rea, we have all the same ingredients.

REA   No, we don't. Things change. The food doesn't even come from the same place. You've romanticized this back home, back home. What hasn't changed is the way a child should be brought up – with James and I.

SANDRA   We were raised by one woman.

DEHLIA   Yes, Rea things change. Families change.

REA   You and Dehlia... it's a lot to handle.

SANDRA   You couldn't make an effort to get along this one time? A lot to handle? I wanted a dinner, one dinner with the people that I care about. Try waking up each morning, deciding whether or not to be drugged up, or sit with the pain all day. Getting needles stuck in you. It took me three hours to get off the bed this morning. A lot to handle? Fuckery! Pure fuckery running through my blood.

ASSATA moves beside SANDRA.

ASSATA   Am I a lot to handle?

SANDRA turns and slaps ASSATA.

SANDRA   This not about you!

ASSATA is stunned and runs into the living room. CERISE follows, and calls after her.

CERISE   Baby, are you all right?

DEHLIA   Sandy! You caan rule everybody. It's one thing the way you treat me and everyone else, but Assata. You want to stop surgery okay, you want to stop chemo, you want some Trini diet, okay. You want your sister okay. But Assata. No!

DEHLIA storms out into the living room. CERISE and DEHLIA comfort ASSATA. SANDRA's in the kitchen, crying and holding herself, while REA sits in silence. Silence all around.

SANDRA I lost my temper. I lost control. Casualties. I lost control of the situation... I've *lost!* This war. Fighting, and trying to control my child. I've hit her. Fighting. This gift from my womb, and... this thing in my womb. I have done something terrible. My daughter. Where do you have time to learn. (*a piece of pain hits SANDRA in the womb; she looks down and sees blood running between her legs*) Blood.

> *REA comes and helps her change her skirt. Ashamed, SANDRA unwraps her skirt and hides the bloodstained wrap in the corner. SANDRA now sits with her hand rubbing her belly, almost like she's pregnant. REA comforts SANDRA. CERISE, DEHLIA and ASSATA are in the living room.*

SCENE XIV

SIMMERING

> *Convergence of ancestral and real time. SANDRA and REA get up and go to the kitchen table, and start to prepare the dumplings, measuring the flour, salt, cornmeal, and water, mixing it in a large, beige, ceramic bowl, making these repeated motions/movements together.*

REA A Long Time.

SANDRA A Lifetime.

REA Yes.

> *REA starts looking for a board to roll out the dumplings on. SANDRA takes out a battered, wooden bread board and hands it to REA.*

SANDRA Use this.

> *REA holds it in astonishment and presses it towards herself.*

REA How?

SANDRA It arrived just in time.

REA It was my daddy's. Mine.

SANDRA All yours Re. Not my daddy.

REA I'm Indian.

SANDRA   Half Re–

REA   My daddy is a whole man, was a whole man.

SANDRA   Our mama was a whole woman.

REA   All black and... all Indian.

SANDRA   History in the flesh.

REA   A mutation?

SANDRA   Variation.

REA   Unique.

SANDRA   Ten percent of the population is...?

Pause.

REA   Dougla. Half black half Indian...

SANDRA   Gay. (*pause*) A mutation?

REA   No. A variation.

They both return to rolling out the dumplings.

SCENE XV

SIMMERING

ASSATA, DEHLIA, and CERISE in the living room.

CERISE   My mother died of cancer.

ASSATA   What kind?

CERISE   Not in her womb.

ASSATA   Breast?

CERISE   It ate away both her breasts and started to feed on... she died a bag of bones, screaming at me.

ASSATA   My mom was just screaming.

CERISE   I know. Your mom needs to scream, my mom needed to listen.

ASSATA   Why?

CERISE   Your mom never lets it out.

ASSATA   I mean why did your mom need to listen?

CERISE   I don't want to have cancer. I don't want to be like my mother. She was miserable.

ASSATA   What made her miserable?

CERISE   Until today, I thought it was me.

ASSATA   What was it?

CERISE   Nothing and everything, her supervisor, the loans officer... and nothing.

ASSATA   What?

CERISE   My mother never saw the joy in anything, nothing was ever right.

     SANDRA and REA finish the dumplings. SANDRA sends REA out.

SANDRA   Go call Assata. (*puts the dumplings in the soup, then decides to put the plantain in the soup*) Plantain.

     REA enters the living room and watches from the back. Ancestral time. Lights dim on SANDRA as she grabs her womb and does a rocking motion, maybe humming, crying sounds come from her.

CERISE   Years later, just after we found out she had cancer, her and me and my aunt were sitting around talking about my cousin being a boy child and my aunt having to do "The Talk." My mom offered that there were lots of good books nowadays. Again. Fuck. In front of me. Talking about a book! She's seen more shit than I can even imagine... I wonder, if we never went through slavery if we would still have all this shit.

ASSATA   I wonder...

     REA moves closer.

REA	...if we never went through slavery...
DEHLIA	...if she would have this shit.

ASSATA moves into CERISE's arms, and they rock.

ASSATA	It's alright Cerise.
REA	(*to CERISE*) It seems *we* all share similar stories.
DEHLIA	When I used to get headache, my mom would tell me to stop thinking about boys.
CERISE	(*to DEHLIA*) Everytime you can't deal with some-thing you go and space out.
DEHLIA	I used to get a headache when "Granma from Redhill came to visit."
ASSATA	"Granma from Redhill"?
REA	We used to call it the "curse."
ASSATA	We call it my "thing" at school, but Mom says she's "flowing."
CERISE	I like that "flooowing."
ASSATA	My mom still rubs my belly with almond oil and tells me to let it out. So we...
DEHLIA	They groan together.
ASSATA	You love it Dehlia, you're right in there too.
DEHLIA	Yeah but my groan is melodic.
REA	Our mother used to do that for us.
ASSATA	Your groan is...

ASSATA starts to let out a groan, DEHLIA starts to riff on it.

REA	No, no you're supposed to do it from your diaphragm.

She demonstrates.

ASSATA	Any sound will do. C'mon Auntie Cerise.

CERISE starts to let out a low growl.

DEHLIA   It's not sex Cerise, it's womb pain.

REA   Sometimes it's the same thing.

> *CERISE continues with her growl. ASSATA joins her,*
> *DEHLIA follows, and finally REA. They all start to do a*
> *soundscape of womb pain that continues under SANDRA's*
> *rocking movement.*

REA   (*to ASSATA*) Your mom wants to see you.

SCENE XVI

BOILING!

> *ASSATA goes into the kitchen. CERISE, DEHLIA, and REA*
> *sit in the living room, continuing their soundscape.*

ASSATA   What?

> *Silence.*

SANDRA   I'm sorry, I had no right to... I know I shouldn't have hit you. Nobody deserves to be hit. I'm old enough and big enough to rationalize my feelings.

ASSATA   Don't.

SANDRA   Assa...

ASSATA   No.

SANDRA   Do you know how hard I have worked to...

ASSATA   Why?

SANDRA   I... I lost control.

ASSATA   Control? What do you think I am...? Some pet?

SANDRA   I'm tired.

ASSATA   I don't care.

SANDRA   I'm your mother and you–

ASSATA   No. You listen to me now. I'm not you. I hate you. You're ugly.

SANDRA   You are such a selfish, self-centred... you always turn it back to yourself.

ASSATA   No. You hate that you won't be here to shape me, mold me, pick on me. Well you know what, Mom? Dehlia, Cerise, Auntie Re, and I will be just fine.

SANDRA   You want me to die?

ASSATA   Umm... Mom, I'm not saying I want you to die, but you treat me like a fool.

SANDRA   There are things you learn as you get older...

ASSATA   You never let me talk. All you want to talk about is what you want. You walk away whenever I talk to you. You shut me up when I talk about my... you never stop lecturing. You stop... me.

SANDRA   I told you I made a mistake, one mistake can be forgiven.

ASSATA   What about my mistakes? You never forget. You don't trust me. Always on me, about my friends.

SANDRA   I just want to spend time with you.

ASSATA   Well that's what I want Mom... more time.

SANDRA   Me too.

ASSATA   You've been mean, you haven't liked me, the one that's not you, but a part of you. Am I going to get sick? Is this how it's going to be for me? How come everyone close to me in my life has died? My granma, my father, and... I'm eating at you. It's me, isn't it... I'm scared. I...

SANDRA   Cancer. Some parasite feeding on my womb. The nerve.

ASSATA   Uncontrollable.

SANDRA   Invisible.

ASSATA   Blood?

SANDRA   Maybe.

ASSATA   When?

SANDRA   Soon.

ASSATA   Why?

SANDRA   It's time... it's time to serve the Mango Chow.

ASSATA   Why are you giving up?

SANDRA   I'm not Assata. I'm fighting with everything I have left. Cutting and more cutting until there is nothing left of my womb. Three years of cutting and slicing, and pricking and burning. Cursing myself each day for not being more careful. It didn't feel like *my* body anymore. So many things in my life have been beyond my control. I'm doing the... cutting, chopping, and slicing. With help from my daughter.

        Pause.

ASSATA   I want you to rub my belly, who will? I wish you didn't have to feel pain. I wish...

SANDRA   You need to make peace... peace with me Assata.

ASSATA   I'm not at war with you. You need to make peace with yourself.

SANDRA   Something burning?

ASSATA   Only candles.

        DEHLIA enters the kitchen with a candle. She sets it down. CERISE and REA stay in the living room. Silence.

REA   I hope they'll be okay.

DEHLIA   You okay hon?

CERISE   They will.

        CERISE puts some soul music on the boom box. CERISE and REA light candles and incense.

ASSATA   Yeah.

SANDRA   Mmmmh.

DEHLIA   Mmmmmh.

        CERISE and REA enter kitchen with candles and incense, and set them down.

SCENE XVII

DISHING

SANDRA   Dehlia bring down those bowls.

> *DEHLIA gestures for CERISE to get them and rubs*
> *SANDRA's back. CERISE goes to get the small soup bowls*
> *and REA stirs the soup.*

DEHLIA   Cerise, West Indian soup.

CERISE   Uhuh.

DEHLIA   Big bowls.

> *CERISE brings down five huge bowls for the soup.*

ASSATA   I'll get the spoons.

CERISE   I guess they're big too.

REA   We have big appetites, it takes a lot to feed us.

SANDRA   Are you hungry?

REA   Yes.

CERISE   Uhuh.

DEHLIA   Always.

> *SANDRA gets up and starts to dish out the soup. CERISE*
> *rushes up with her bowl, then ASSATA, DEHLIA, and REA.*
> *They all sit down at the table and eat their soup.*

SCENE XVIII

NYAMMING

REA   Plantain in soup, taste good.

DEHLIA   Thank you.

CERISE   Which one is the plantain?

ASSATA   It looks like the banana.

SANDRA   It taste good. Sweet.

CERISE   The dumplings taste sweet too.

REA   I made them the Bajan way, I put some sugar in them.

DEHLIA   Sugar in dumplings? We put sugar in stew-chicken, sugar in–

SANDRA   But that's not how we made them back home.

REA   Things change.

CERISE   I like them.

SANDRA   Me too.

> *ASSATA eats some soup, makes a face.*

ASSATA   Ugh... daschene.

REA   That face reminds me of your mother's when she had to eat daschene.

ASSATA   Mom hates it too?

REA   Yes, and with our mother you never had a choice. (*imitating an older mother*) "I walked barefoot to school, food is scarce, money doesn't grow on trees..."

ASSATA   (*to REA*) It runs in the family, right Mom?

SANDRA   It's a good thing I used to give you my daschene. Maga skinny but could eat, and (*to the others*) would eat anything.

REA   Still do.

DEHLIA   My mother would take me to the hospice by Half-Way Tree and we would give out money to the old women who were left there. We couldn't tell Daddy. She didn't take Neville or Janice.

REA   Sandy, remember I got nuff buffs from Tony for being skinny. "You nah know woman supposed to be fat and nice like me wife Sandy?"

ASSATA   So my daddy liked his women plump.

CERISE   (*to ASSATA*) How do your men like you?

ASSATA   Most men are cads.

SANDRA   What would you know?

ASSATA   They rub up on you, crank down your neck while you busting a slow song, they can't sing and they have stinky breath.

CERISE   Some things never change. Remember "These Eyes the Place to Socialize"?

SANDRA   Oh gawd yes, we went there Rea.

REA   Oh yes. It had that flocked-velvet wall paper, disco globe in the ceiling, and you're praying, hoping that no man with drip-drip head is going to ask you to dance.

CERISE   I had to do this whole espionage business, just to get out. I was in a party. My mother, with her housecoat underneath her trench coat, came inside looking for me. My mother didn't have a loud voice. But I could hear her softly calling, "Cerise? Do you know Cerise? Have you seen Cerise?" I ran out that back door so fast.

ASSATA   I wouldn't know nothing about that.

SANDRA   You bettah not.

CERISE   When I got home my uncle beat me so hard I couldn't even think about party or boys.

SANDRA   Respect! Respect!

REA   Respect. It wasn't Aretha who taught me how to spell that, it was our mother.

DEHLIA   "R-E-S-P-E-C-T, that is what love means to me." What does the song say again?

SANDRA   Is it "love"? That doesn't even sound right.

CERISE   (*singing*) "Sock it to me, sock it to me, sock it to me."

DEHLIA   You would remember that part.

ASSATA   "Sock it to me"! I can't believe the stuff you all put in your music.

REA   What's in you music?

ASSATA   Deep stuff.

           SANDRA starts making fun of rapping, DEHLIA joins, then
           CERISE, and then REA.

REA   I knew that.

ASSATA   When did this big pot of water, spices, and stuff start to taste
           like soup.

DEHLIA   It's alchemy.

REA   It's magic.

DEHLIA   Alchemy is magic.

CERISE   It's Voodoo.

ASSATA   It's Obeah.

SANDRA   Sistahs.

DEHLIA   It's soup.

           SANDRA doubles over in pain. Lights come down onstage.

Come Good Rain

by George Seremba

Originally from Uganda, George Seremba began acting and writing at Makerere University, Kampala, Uganda. His first full-length play, *The Grave Will Decide*, was written in 1985, a year after his arrival in Canada. With *Come Good Rain*, Mr. Seremba has discovered his own and authentic dramatic voice. He has recently completed a new play, *Napoleon of the Nile*.

THE NEED TO TELL THIS STORY: GEORGE SEREMBA'S NARRATIVE DRAMA, COME GOOD RAIN

by Modupe Olaogun

George Seremba's *Come Good Rain* opens on a dark stage. From the audi-torium the narrator, George, approaches the stage, bearing a lit candle and singing a song. The song is that of Nsimb'egwire, a young girl in a Ugandan legend who is buried alive by her stepmother.[1] Nsimb'egwire's song is a pro-leptic disclosure by the narrator of the despair that the girl will experience as she confronts the fate engineered by her stepmother. After singing Nsimb'egwire's song, George takes the story to the beginning: how Nsimb'egwire, the daughter of the hunter Mbaire from an earlier marriage, provokes the murderous envy of her stepmother. The stepmother's problem is that her biological daughter is plain, while Nsimb'egwire is beautiful. On one occasion when Mbaire is away from home hunting, the stepmother decides to bury Nsimb'egwire up to the neck in a forest. At the point that a famished and bushed Nsimb'egwire loses hope of a timely rescue, George stops his narration, but only temporarily. He will resume the tale of Nsimb'egwire spliced adroitly with his own story, both stories serving as parallels in a taut, gripping drama. When Nsimb'egwire sings again (through George) she has moved away from a lugubrious farewell "My friends play me the ceremonial drum" to a testimonial of her struggle: "You who happen to pass by the Passion tree / Let it be known that it harbours Nsimb'egwire." Will Nsimb'egwire's song reach the hunter Mbaire who can help the young girl? At the end of the song, the lights come on, and George shifts to his own story, becoming both narrator and character.

The transition to George's story makes Nsimb'egwire's tale seem like a recollection of one of the many tales that George heard as a child. But the tale is a clever trope used by Seremba thematically and structurally to frame his own story, the extraordinary experience of an execution that he survived. The tale becomes a device for Seremba to interpret his experience and to validate himself. The tale is also a means through which Seremba elicits a critical dia-logue between his past life in Uganda and his present life in exile; and between the Ugandan society he had known and the cosmopolitan audience to which he is narrating his story.[2] The transformation and expansion of the folk tale and the personal story into a scripted play result in a narrative drama with a heightened sociality whose purview includes a hearth, where one or several people may read the play, and a stage, where several people may experience it in performance. Seremba's narrative drama traverses a wider spatiality and temporality.

The story of George, the undisguised persona of author Seremba, is his miraculous survival of his torture and execution by a group of soldiers in Kampala on the 10th of December, 1980.[3] On that day, Seremba and other Ugandans had gone out to vote in what they thought were democratic elections for a government that should protect their freedoms. Seremba, whose surname was Bwanika up till his execution, was twenty-two years old and an undergraduate at the University of Makerere. In a bizarre turn of events, some of the country's soldiers took over the election process and proclaimed their chosen man, Milton Obote, president. The soldiers accomplished their task through a campaign of intimidation in which they abducted, tortured and murdered huge numbers of people. In his five-year rule from 1980 to 1985, daubed as his "second coming," having been the country's head of government from 1962 to 1971, but sacked from that office by Major General Idi Amin who had been his ally, Obote would ruthlessly suppress opposition. Obote would precipitate a civil war in Uganda that would claim the lives of several thousands of people, as he spurned the democratic aspirations of his people. In the height of his power, Obote would make some Ugandans longingly remember the catastrophic rule of Idi Amin from 1971-1979 (Bwenge; Karugire; Kasozi; Ingham).

Seremba's version of the political history of Uganda in the period covered by Amin's rule and Obote's rule suggests a close correspondence in the attitudes of the two rulers to power. Desperate for total political control, Amin and Obote resorted to brute force. Seremba powerfully captures the brutality of the Amin-Obote era through his depiction of his experience in *Come Good Rain*. The soldiers who abducted Seremba drove him into Namanve forest in the outskirts of Kampala and hailed bullets on him. The assassins abandoned Seremba's body to a drizzle. As it turned out, the bullets did considerable damage to, but didn't kill, their target. The drizzle became a "good rain" that began Seremba's healing process presumably by holding a fever in check. In the first moments of his recovery from shock, Seremba pledged to tell his story. Seremba's narrative of his survival, his defiance of a death-dealing dictatorship, constitutes a challenge to the certitude of the stark reality of Namanve forest.

Uganda's possibly darkest moment in the postcolonial period engenders in Seremba's hands a particularly remarkable play. *Come Good Rain*, while it forcefully evokes the sad rule of Amin and Obote in Uganda, is ultimately not about these tyrants. The novelty of Seremba's treatment of the political era may be grasped when *Come Good Rain* is compared to two earlier, also powerful plays that focus on that era: Francis Imbuga's *Man of Kafira* (1984); and Wole Soyinka's *A Play of Giants* (1984). Imbuga in *Man of Kafira*, as playwright/literary critic John Ruganda has observed, seems overly fascinated "by the psychological effects of exile on a deposed head of state and on those with whom he comes in contact" (xix). The "deposed head of state"/the "man of Kafira" (and the anagram should be obvious), addressed as "Boss," is an unconcealed Idi Amin who is being frantically entertained in the state of Abiara (Arabia?) where he has fled. The "giants" in Soyinka's play are the megalomaniacs, Kamini, Kasco, Gunema and Tuboum – transparent anagrams for Amin and three other dictators: Jean-Bedel Bokassa (of Central African Republic), Nguema Mbasogo (of Equatorial Guinea) and Mobutu Sese Seko (of Zaire). In his play, Seremba invests his energy not on these infamous engineers of misery but on the human community and tenacity that challenge them.

Seremba sets up the story of his execution through his reminiscences of his growing up in Uganda in the early 1960s. The young Seremba and his generation were subjected to a neo-colonial education that frequently but not wholly consisted of obedience drills, lashes and anglophonisation. That form of education anticipated the later events in Uganda.

An inspiration for the composite drama-narrative form employed in *Come Good Rain* is the oral storytelling tradition. But Seremba is also a trained actor, beginning his career at Makerere in Uganda and developing it in Canada, where he took refuge following his rescue. Storytelling was a tradition in Seremba's household in Uganda. When the family came together in the evenings, they explored proverbs, puns and riddles. The peak of the evenings was usually the story that George's mother told. Young George and his siblings yearned for the spotlight of the storyteller, and perhaps of the hero, too. But the spotlight, as the older George would realise from his experience in Namanve forest, was not fun for the victim of a grisly event. Seremba was in the spotlight in the macabre drama of the gunmen of Obote's Uganda.

If Seremba's story recalls that of Nsimb'egwire, it perhaps also recalls that of Lazarus whose death is reversed through the miraculous intervention of his friend, Jesus.[4] The specific circumstances of the stories will, however, indicate different trajectories of significance. Nine years after Seremba's escape from death and from Obote's Uganda, his mother tells him about the people who found and rescued him from Namanve forest: "They kept tabs on you over the years. You are their most prized son. No one had ever come out of Namanve alive. You are the first one they ever saw".[5] But the defiance of death *per se* is not what is being celebrated here; Seremba is no ordinary Lazarus. Seremba owes his survival only partially to the soldiers' misfiring of their bullets. He owes his life also to his own resilience. Above all, he owes his life to the compassion and the community of the people of Bweyogerere village (near where he had been executed) and the members of his family who organized an extraordinary rescue for him. The community's quick action and efficient organization beat Obote's formidable but ultimately imperfect surveillance system.

Come Good Rain underscores the transformational potential of certain communal acts. Seremba's earliest storyteller, his mother, recognizes that power when she describes his special bond with the people of Bweyogerere village: "You are their most prized son." A similar celebration of community comes across in a poem by the Nigerian writer, Niyi Osundare, "Dialogue of the Drums." In this poem, an anthropomorphic drum tells his rival who is in complete awe of authoritarian rule:

Listen, palace singer, listen royally–
The day is coming, coming fast
When your drum will be mute
Like a royal statue
For if you listen properly
To the dying echoes of your drum
You will hear this resounding fact:
The people always outlast the palace (8).

Ugandans finally overthrew Obote and they have been rebuilding their society. Seremba got to tell his story, and in doing so uses and generates other enabling tales. Nsimb'egwire's song does reach her father and she is rescued even though some irreversible damages have been done to the buried parts of her body. *Come Good Rain*, the narrative drama into which Seremba has distilled his experience is a testimonial of one person who has defied the destruction engineered for him by a powerful political apparatus. Seremba's narrative drama is also a "therapeutic voyage"; it is a means by which the author-actor finds his own voice, wills himself into being through his imaginative faculties. On his completion of the manuscript of *Come Good Rain* in 1991, Seremba expressed his desire to tour the play in various parts of the world. He mentioned Nigeria among the places where he would like to perform. Shortly after, Nigeria became the arena of a very repressive dictatorship under General Sani Abacha. Would a touring of *Come Good Rain* in Nigeria have made a difference? That Seremba's imaginative retelling and dramatization of his story raises a question like this one testifies to his creative and critical contributions to the important dialogues of our time.

NOTES

[1] For another version of the Nsimb'egwire motif, see "The story of Nambi and Nvuma," in Taban lo Liyong, ed., *Popular Culture of East Africa: Oral Literature*.
[2] *Come Good Rain* had its debut in Toronto in February 1992 with Seremba in the role of all the characters. In May of the following year an adaptation of the play was aired on the Canadian national radio medium, CBC Radio. Between 1992 and 1997, Seremba performed *Come Good Rain* in the following cities: Ottawa, Kingston (Ontario), Montreal, Los Angeles, London (England), Cork, Galway, Limerick, Dublin, Belfast, and Jerusalem. Seremba has expressed the desire to tour the play in South Africa, Nigeria and Scotland – perhaps places to which he thinks he can gain easy access. Of course, he expects the play to "continue its life in the hands of another actor," as any playwright would expect of his or her play.
[3] A recorded account of a torture that is similar to that of Seremba's is by Bakulu-Mpagi Wamala, formerly a lecturer at Makerere University, and a prominent member of the opposition party at Obote's inauguration. See the "Epilogue" in Kasozi's *The Social Origins of Violence in Uganda, 1964-1985*.
[4] John 11: 1-45.
[5] Seremba, George. *Come Good Rain*. Winnipeg: Blizzard Publishing, 1993. P. 10.

REFERENCES

Bwengye, Francis. *The Agony of Uganda: From Idi Amin to Obote*, London; New York: Regency Press, 1985.

Imbuga, Francis. *Man of Kafira*. Nairobi: Heinemann, 1984.

Ingham, Kenneth. *Obote: A Political Biography*. London; New York: Routledge, 1994.

John, 11: 1-45.

Karugire, Samwiri. *The Roots of Instability in Uganda* Kampala: The New Vision Printing and Publishing Corporation, 1988.

Kasozi, A. B. K. *The Social Origins of Violence in Uganda*, 1964-1985, Montreal; Kingston: McGill-Queen's University Press, 1994.

Lo Liyong, Taban. *Popular Culture of East Africa: Oral Literature*. Nairobi: Longman, 1972.

Osundare, Niyi. *Village Voices: Poems*. Ibadan: Evans Brothers, 1984.

Ruganda, John. *Telling the Truth Laughingly: The Politics of Francis Imbuga's Drama*. Nairobi: East African Educational Publishers, 1992.

Seremba, George. *Come Good Rain*. Winnipeg: Blizzard Publishing, 1993.

Soyinka, Wole. *A Play of Giants*. London: Methuen, 1984.

Modupe Olaogun, Ph.D., presently teaches in the Communications Department at Humber College, and in New College, University of Toronto.

George Seremba

photo by Michael Cooper Photographic

Come Good Rain had its debut at Toronto's Factory Theatre's Studio Cafe in February, 1992, funded by the Ontario Arts Council. It was produced by Jim Millan and Crow's Theatre as part of the Flying Solo series. George Seremba played himself and all the other characters.

Dramaturge/Director	Sue Miner
Musician	Emmanuel Mugerwa
Stage Manager	George Athans
Lighting Design	Peter Cochron
Production Assistants	Kathleen Lantos, Paula Lind

The playwright would also like to gratefully acknowledge financial assistance from the Toronto Arts Council and the Canada Council for the Arts, as well as the following individuals for dramaturgical and other help: Michael Miller, Robert Rooney, Alex Mackenzie Gray, Rita Davies, Stephanie Bennett and Christine Seremba.

CHARACTERS

GEORGE BWANIKA SEREMBA
FATHER
TEACHER
ANNOUNCER
VOICE
STUDENT
IDI AMIN
SOMEONE
NALONGO
CUSTOMER
CUSTODIAN
STUDENT
CROWD
JOHN
WIFE
SOLDIERS
OFFICER
FEMALE VOICE
BOY
CHIEF
MOTHER
UNCLE GEORGE
DR. WALUGEMBE
MARY
DOCTOR
AUNTIE GLADYS
BROTHER STEVEN
GRANDMOTHER
IMMIGRATION OFFICER
DAVID RUBADIRI
WELSH VOICE

A musician/percussionist can perform music and sounds on stage.

ACT I

*The stage is dark. A flute plays a haunting melody that will
become a recurring theme throughout the play. A solitary
figure makes his way through the auditorium. He holding a
candle and singing a song – or is it an invocation? Once on
stage almost ritualistically, he finds a convenient spot. He
tells the story with the infectiousness of a seasoned raconteur.*

ANNOUNCER

GEORGE   (*singing*)
Abe Mbuutu
N'abe ngalabi
Banange munkubire ngenda
Mbaire yagenda nga alidda
Aligenda okudda
Nga luwedde okwaba
Mbaire yagenda nga alidda
Aligenda okudda
Nga luwedde ngenze.

[My friends play me the ceremonial drums
Come bid me goodbye
My father Mbaire went as though he would return
By the time he does
it will be too late.
My father Mbaire went as though he would return
By the time he does
I will be long gone.]

This is a story that the old people tell. Once upon a time, a
long time ago, there lived a man called Mbaire. Mbaire had
a wife and two daughters. One was from an earlier marriage. Her name was Nsimb'egwire. Mbaire was also a
good hunter, his expeditions sometimes took him away for
many a day and many a night.

Nsimb'egwire was a humble teen. She was the talk and
pride of the village not only because of her breath-takingly
good looks but also due to her remarkably good manners.
This did not sit well with her stepmother. Her own daughter did not have much to cheer by way of any of these
attributes.

It so happened once that Mbaire set off for another one of his expeditions. Both girls were promptly summoned by the wife. The next day was market day. There would be a lot of people to and from the nalubabwe [marketplace]. She shaved Nsimb'egwire's head with a vengeance then smeared her with soot and ashes and made sure her own daughter was clean and smart. That done, the girls were paraded by the roadside.

Unfortunately for the mother, even long before the sun set at the end of the day, each and every passer-by she asked who of the two was more beautiful pointed at Nsimb'egwire in spite of all the soot and ash.

She couldn't take it any more! So she dragged the girl off into the wilderness. There she found a secluded spot deep in the jungle where even the herdsmen seldom ventured with their cattle. Behind the armour of thick foliage and branches, she found a spot in the heart of an old passion tree. There she dug a shallow grave in which half the girl's body was buried under the sticky earth. Secure in the knowledge that the only likely company would be dreaded tropical snakes and animals, and that there would be no chance of human encounter, she abandoned her under the cover of darkness.

Condemned alive to solitary death, Nsimb'egwire waged a stubborn struggle to come out of her grave. For days and nights, come rain or steaming heat, she continued to struggle. But her energy was dissipating. Hunger and thirst made matters even worse. Now more than ever she wished her father would come home – death would obviously rear its ugly head. Sooner or later it would certainly knock on her door.

And yet she sang.

He sings.

Ani oyo
Ani oyo
Ani oyo ayita ku mutunda
Ku mutunda kuliko Nsimb'egwire
Nsimb'egwire muwala wa Mbaire
Mbaire yagenda nga anadda
Aligenda okudda nga luwedde okwaba
Mbaire yagenda nga alidda
Aligenda okudda
Nga luwedde ngenze...

[Who is that?
Who is that?
You who happen to pass by the Passion tree
Let it be known that it harbours Nsimb'egwire.
Nsimb'egwire is Mbaire's daughter.
Mbaire left as though he would return in good time
But by the time he returns it will be too late.
By the time he returns
I will be long gone.]

Lights come on. George blows out his candle. He gets on his feet and plunges into his sea of memories with childish excitement and innocence.

Strange how it all comes back. Yes, with Mother at the centre. My sisters and I would form a semi-circle on the opposite side. We would start with a few proverbs, trade some puns and riddles.

Koyi Koyi
(*in response*) Lya!
Question: I have a wife whose house has no door. Who am I?
Answer: An egg.

Koyi Koyi
(*in response*) Lya!
Question: Gobo ne gobo?
Answer: That's what the cow's hoof says to the rock.

We would get into little ditties, tongue twisters and song...

Question: Kiiso kya mbuzi!
Answer: Kabaka

Question: Mbulira ensozi
Answer: Mengo

At the climax of the evening Mother would always tell a story. Soon we too would try our luck centre stage. It was always a heady and enrapturing experience. But then, I must have been eight years or so when... it happened.

Dad had talked about a boarding school. One morning I heard him call, "Bwanika! Bwanika!" The first thing I thought was, not me! What have I done this time? "Rise and shine George. Rise and shine tall George." (*heaves a sigh of relief*) I liked that. It usually meant there was nothing to explain or atone for. Even if something was amiss and somebody swore, "George did it."

FATHER   Did you fill the forms? What do they teach you at the local
          school? (*benign laughter*) The letter said in triplicate
          remember. Province? Buganda. Country? Uganda. The
          two may sound alike but the Kingdom of Buganda is only
          one province in the entire country! Date of Birth?
          November 28th, 1957. Sorry, son. Change that to 1956.
          This way you'll be able to start next year rather than wait-
          ing till January 1966. We will correct the mistake once you
          are admitted. You're tall enough anyway. No one will
          bother cross-checking your age. The interview is next
          week.

          *A flute is heard: the haunting and solitary theme we heard at
          the beginning.*

GEORGE   (*to audience*) After the interview, we stopped at Rubaga for
          a quick visit with grandmother. I couldn't wait to show her
          my brand new pair of "Back to school with Bata shoes."
          I loved everything about her place. From the incense that
          hit your nostrils at the door, to the spiced tea and the water
          from the ancient clay pot in the corner. The pictures, too, all
          over the wall: one of Auntie Gladys in her nurse's uniform
          at school in England. Good old Brother Stephen, with most
          of us when he came to visit last Christmas. One of me a
          few years ago... fully dressed in my Adam's attire; and an
          eight-by-ten of Jesus Christ – complete with dark blue eyes
          and straight long blonde hair.

          I loved the people too. It was always full of people, like a
          school. You watched, learned and did. "As long as the
          good Lord provides, there's always enough" was her motto.

          We got back into the car, branched off at Nabunya off past
          the tiny "Kabaka's Lake." To our immediate left stood the
          enormous red brick wall that went all the way around the
          palace.

FATHER   You should ask your grandmother to take you for a visit
          next time she goes to the king's court. That's her lineage.
          Your great-grandmother's father was King of Buganda.
          Sekaba Kalema he was called. His daughter would later
          marry Semei Kakungulu. Your grandmother would be
          Kakungulu's eldest daughter, she too would marry a
          famous man from across the Nile, Yekoniya Zirabamuzale.
          They would give birth to two beautiful daughters. Your
          Auntie Gladys and your mother.

GEORGE   (*to audience*) We stopped the car. I edged closer. Finally touched and stroked the ancient wall. My ancestors were no longer just names. They began to throb in my bones. I could touch and feel the country as if it had flesh and blood. Unlike those lifeless maps of mountains, lakes and rivers that hung in the back of the classrooms at the local elementary school at home.

Drums are heard.

FATHER   It's getting late my son. Can't you hear the drums in the palace?

GEORGE   (*to audience*) At home that night on a distant hill, I could see the faint lights of Mugwanya Preparatory School. It all looked so far away. (*as a boy*) Moreover, it's still a whole year away. Assuming I get in. Besides, there's something else on my mind. Tonight I promised Mother I'd tell my first story. Something simple like "Nsanji and the Ogre"... I'm sure nobody will laugh at me... even if they do it's only a beginning. Their turn will come. There is still a whole year of practising. Humiliation, make a fool of myself. Then one day I'll stand up and recite...

A drum roll is heard.

Once upon a time, there lived a man called Mbaire. Mbaire had a wife and two daughters. One was from an earlier marriage. Her name was Nsimb'egwire. It so happened once... yes. Death would certainly rear it's ugly head. It would certainly knock on her door! And yet she sang. She sang about her beloved father, his absence, the trip, her rapidly deteriorating condition, her plight. Her voice like a magical flute rode the back of the wind that brushed through her confines.

A loud and relentless bell is heard. The school teacher takes a few steps across the length and breadth of the class, like an army instructor meeting the recruits in boot camp.

TEACHER   My name is Pius Mulindwa. For those of you who do not know me, I'll be in charge of English Language and Mathematics. You are welcome to Mugwanya Preparatory School, Kabojja. "Many are called but few are chosen." So you should all feel proud of yourselves and once again welcome. Please be seated.

He turns to the register and starts the roll call.

John Bosco Baguma, George Bwanika, please don't stand just say, "Present, sir." Peter Luzige... good. Joseph Mary Odongo, Stephen Ruhinda... Paul Semazzi, David Tamale. Is there anyone whose name is missing?

Being the class master of Primary 3B, it's my responsibility to supervise the elections for the Class Monitor and one Junior Prefect. (*beat*) Silence. As tomorrow's leaders and responsible citizens, remember it's your birthright to exercise your vote. Feel free to nominate anyone. Once they are seconded, we shall proceed with a show of hands.

Before we do that, each of the candidates will come forward and address the class. No big promises... you just tell the class in a minute or two, why they should vote for you.

Very well then. (*walks to the black board*) Fred Ma-Ku-Mbi seconded? Amoti Ruhun... wait a minute what happened to your Christian name my boy? Good, very good John A. Ruhundwa, no more nominations, volunteers?

Hmm! (*aside*) I hate to see any youngsters toy with "popular consensus." That is for socialists and the birds, I shouldn't worry though. They are all under thirteen. All ours to shape and mould.

(*back to the class*) John and Fred, please come forward. I'm pleased to announce that the pupils of Standard 3B now have a School Prefect and a Class Monitor. A round of applause for your new leaders. Very well. Please be seated.

You have now become the eyes and ears of the school. Remember to always serve by setting a good example. Only then can you make sure the rule of law is maintained. No one is above the law, not even the Prefects. Repeat after me, not even the... yes we don't care whether you are the son of the President of the United States or even the Queen of England!

> Gleefully, he parades his stick.

Just don't put us to the test. Believe me we shall pass it with flying colours. At Mugwanya Preparatory School, we have more punishments than all the rules put together.

There are a lot of people who put money in this school. Some from as far away as Canada and even the United States of America. However bright you are, if you prove too unruly we'll ask you to put on your Sunday uniform and tell your parents that we'd be more than happy to recommend you to the reformatory school at Kampiringisa.

I have seen mothers drop on their knees and threaten to shed tears of blood.

He brandishes and strokes his cane.

Now, lateness. Some of you actually sauntered into class like little gazelles! From now on late-comers eat bones. No more African time! Punctuality is a must. Punctuality is a what?

Beat. The class responds.

There are some of you who are still "speaking vernacular"! Save that for your grandmothers during the holidays. From now on you must speak English. Eat English, sleep English, and dream English. You must...

A chorus of children's voices is heard.

Good. Any questions? Wait a minute George Bwanika...

He gestures with his hand for George to come forward.

Your father tells me you might need extra help in mathematics. Make sure you report to the Staff Room after lunch. Are you related to Brother Stefano Bwanika? Then I must watch you with extra care. The children of the religious are the worst behaved.

He turns to the class.

Very well then. Do you all remember the song we learned this morning? Look at it and take your friends through. Are we all ready? No sissies this time. One, two, three...

(*he sings*) Hey diddle diddle
The cat and the fiddle
The cow jumped over the moon
The little dog laughed
To see such fun
The dish ran away with the spoon

A school-bell rings.

GEORGE   (*to audience*) Having gone through an entire year, I felt
                immensely glad that at least I was no longer a newcomer.

                One Saturday afternoon I stood outside the classroom... I
                did not feel like "Batman and Robin," or taking a "French
                leave" to buy Coca Cola or Pepsi. What should I do, I said
                to myself?

                Mr. Mulindwa always told us that "an idle mind is a devil's
                workshop." I had to keep myself busy. So I sat down and
                looked at the sky. All of a sudden I saw a rainbow. Its
                trunk huge and long: full of colour. I instantly found
                myself on my feet, as if in conspiracy with a gentle creature
                beyond the horizon.

                (*he sings*) Enkuba etonya
                Omusana gwaka
                Engo ezala
                Ezalira ku Iwazi

                [The rain is falling
                The sun is shining
                The leopard is giving birth
                It's giving birth down on a rock.]

                A school-bell rings. George is oblivious to it.

                Ka nemu kanabiri
                Kafumba mwanyi
                Kata konkome
                Kalangaja ka nakwale
                Ofumba otya ku lugyo

                *The school-bell rings again. Mr. Mulindwa arrives; he
                strikes one of his favourite poses.*

TEACHER   Five of the best my boy. Thou shalt neither speak nor sing
                in vernacular.

GEORGE   But sir, there is no translation for that song.

TEACHER   One more stroke for every excuse you make. What's that
                word you used? Translation... (*exasperated*) Stubborn boy.
                If you make any more excuses, I'll multiply the strokes and
                put your name in the black book. Unless... when you go
                back to the dormitory tonight, you make me a list of all the
                vernacular speakers. Even the walls have ears, remember.

You have two full days for the list.

Organ music.

GEORGE   (*on his knees*) Our Father who art in Heaven. Please let me not betray anyone.

The school-bell rings.

For the Kingdom, the Power and the Glory is yours, forever and ever. Amen.

(*to audience*) Nothing short of a miracle would alter my fate. Those strokes and the big horrendous Black Book kept my eyes open all through the night. Suddenly I heard bursts of gunfire in the distance. Could this be a dream?

Rapid gunfire is heard.

The whole school saw it the next morning. A cloud of thick black smoke billowing out of the Kabaka's Palace at Mengo. The Palace! More guns and mortars. A bit of a lull. Then it resumed until the rain fell that afternoon.

In the Staff Room the teachers were huddled together around the radio.

Martial music is heard.

ANNOUNCER This is a special announcement. The recent "conflict" between the Government of Buganda and the Federal Government has finally been resolved. His Excellency, Dr. Milton Obote has now become the President of Uganda. None of the changes he has made can be questioned in a Court of Law. The old Federal Constitution as well as the monarchy is now null and void. Soon a new Republican Constitution will be in place. There will be a curfew and a state of emergency in Buganda until further notice. This is not a military coup.

Martial music is heard again.

TEACHER   (*addressing GEORGE*) Have you got the list of vernacular speakers? No? You are forgiven. Go.

Wait. There is something to be said for your loyalty to your friends. Courage for a good cause is a good thing. Even when one has to be punished for it. (*a characteristic laugh*) Which brings me to the heart of the matter.

Just like the Brothers, all of you are my children, even if one sheep strays from the herd, why I pick up the cane and abandon the ninety-nine.

He looks around; takes a deep breath.

I'm telling you this because listening to the radio this afternoon I found myself asking deep and painful questions.

(*pause*) Why should I flog you for speaking your mother tongue, which I have the audacity to call "vernacular," when the same language or your name alone is enough to ruffle the soldiers' feathers at a roadblock? They are all over the province. Just like locusts, even in the villages from Luwero to Lwabenge, Kalisizo and beyond. See the one at the junction, some of our own staff have already been victimized at it.

All I see is a long monstrous tunnel. At the end of it strange and merciless beings that would have made Julius Caesar wail like a child. At their head, the new Headmaster Milton Obote wielding a large whip.

At least my days of flogging are over. The rest is up to you. (*barely audible*) When you grow up remember... you have a right to disagree... (*his tone changes; he laughs*) and maybe even make mistakes. (*more deep and painful laughter*) You are a free man my boy.

Three shots are fired in the vicinity. He goes down on his knees.

(*pause*) It's far from over. The real tragedy is we are all Africans. All Ugandans and all just as human as those men in uniform! The landscape has changed.

GEORGE (*to audience*) This was all too much for my little head. I looked at the teacher walk away as the rain began to fall... and then I thought about Nsimb'egwire, the little girl in the proverb all by her lonely self in the wilderness. One-eyed death staring her in the eye. And yet she sang (*the haunting flute theme is heard*) with the hope that by chance a well-meaning human soul would come to her rescue. If the worst came to the worst, at least they would know who she was, then the Mbuutu and Ngalabi drums would be played, the way they always do during the last funeral rites. Unwilling to quit, she almost stubbornly continued to reach out beyond the periphery of the branches...

(*he sings*) Ani oyo
Ani oyo
Ani oyo ayita ku mutunda
Ku mutunda kuliko Nsimb'egwire

> *Addressing the audience, slowly, he ticks off the years on his fingers.*

One, two, three! Another year went. Another year came and went.

> *Drums.*

As for Obote and his UPC Party Loyalists, they now spoke about being in power for ninety-nine years. "I am the only African leader who is not scared of a military coup." Outside the country Obote had become a big hero for "poetizing" the masses; whatever that means. In January 1971 another opportunity availed itself for the dynamic "Prince of Progressive Africa" to roast the British at the Commonwealth Conference in Singapore.

> *Martial music is heard. A voice comes on the radio.*

VOICE This is a special announcement. My name is Captain Aswa. We the officers and men of the Uganda Armed Forces...

GEORGE We couldn't wait. We all struggled for a place around the current affairs notice-board. Both the BBC and Voice of America confirmed it: A bloodless coup.

> *More martial music.*

VOICE And there will be a curfew in Akokoro District. From dawn to dusk...

GEORGE (*to audience*) "Dawn to dusk" could have been a slip of the tongue. After all, the man himself was choking with emotion. So were we. Down at the Kampala-Masaka Highway people had gathered; singing, dancing and drinking, they thronged both sides of the road. Motorists moved at a snail's pace. Some dragging and flogging Dr. Obote's effigy. Someone pulled me aside. A fellow student from Senior 2C.

STUDENT It could be a hoax, you know.

GEORGE What?

STUDENT	African presidents do it sometimes. Then arrest everybody that comes out to celebrate the fake coup.
GEORGE	So why are you here? I couldn't tell where he stood on this. But it was clear he hated military coups. At least for now, I remembered 1966, Obote's pillages, rapes, murders and could not help but join the celebration.
	Back at St. Henry's College it was standing room only in the tiny old hall where we usually gathered for "bull dances" on Sunday afternoons. The television was on. The gates of Luzira Maximum Security Prison were open. The five M.P.s, dubbed the "Bantu Five," were free at last. Rumour had it some of them would become Cabinet Ministers in a matter of hours. Thousands of other detainees were out too. The cameras were now focused on one man.
	More martial music.
IDI AMIN	I, Idi Amin Dada, do solemnly swear...
GEORGE	(*to audience*) For some reason he spoke next to no English but we were ready to accept this gentle giant.
IDI AMIN	I am... not... a politician. I am... a... professional Sodya.
GEORGE	(*to audience*) We loved the noble savage. He played the accordion and the bagpipes. He was a smash hit in England itself. After a sumptuous dinner by no less a person than his ex-Commander in Chief, Africa's big Daddy articulately stood up to express his gratitude: "I would like to completely... and... also, undress the Queen. When you come to Uganda we shall... do it again. Thank you..."
	We applauded his sincerity in those early days and laughed, not at him but with him. As a gesture of his magnanimity, the remains of King Freddie, Sir Edward Mutesa, would be returned from exile for the kind of funeral he deserved.
	The royal drum is played. George sings the first stanza of the Ugandan National Anthem.
	Oh Uganda, may God uphold thee, Lay our future in thy hands, United, free, for liberty Together we'll always stand.

Amin had another appointment with magnanimity. It came
in the form of a decree that God air-mailed to him by way
of a dream. Accused of milking the economic cow of the
country "without feeding it," the Asian community was
given ninety days to leave the country, their pockets empty
as their ancestors had been when they built the railway.

Now to the next phase. Operation Mafutamingi. In droves,
people came, cued up; their ethnic and religious stripes
clearly displayed. It all happened too quickly, some people
found themselves propelled from house boys to pharma-
ceutical tycoons.

Then the shortages set in and prices quadrupled. Amin
said: "Where is the Governor of the National Bank? Print
more money or you're dead!" (*beat*) And he died.

The good old watering holes for the illicit Enguli or Nubian
gin really began to flourish. Every once in awhile I too
would walk in and take my place among the customers for
the cheap and lethal drink.

SOMEONE   Did you hear about so-and-so?

GEORGE   Yes. How sad.

(*to audience*) Byron Kawadwa was his name, a playwright.
Only recently he'd returned from a Festival in Nigeria.
Members of the "State Research Bureau" arrived at the
National Theatre; in broad daylight. For every scene he
wrote, another tooth was knocked out of his gums. At the
end of the exercise, his body was soaked in acid.

He turns to NALONGO, the proprietor.

Nalongo, give us another drink. Life is too short.

(*to audience*) News of the latest victims would be exchanged
on "Radio Katwe," the grapevine telegraph, through which
people got the news behind the news.

SOMEONE   (*repeating the refrain*) Did you hear about so and so?

GEORGE surveys the place.

GEORGE   (*to audience*) Yes. How sad. It had become the refrain; the
new riddle. Did you hear about so and so?

(*to NALONGO*) Nalongo. One more please, for the road.
The road of life. Truth is we might as well celebrate.
Otherwise we'll die long before the trigger is pulled.

(*to audience, exceptionally candid*) Think about it, friends.
Especially those of you lucky enough to have been spared
the luxury of growing up in countries where no one should.

Did you hear?... yes...

In the early days, the sight of a dead body on your way to
school was something you talked about for a long time to
come. Time passed. Things changed. We found ourselves
haunted by images of people shot and abandoned for the
vultures. Men with their genitals stuffed into their mouths
like Cuban cigars. Others burnt with acid. Pregnant
women with their bellies ripped apart by bayonets. Alleged
foes, naked and chained, paraded on national television
before facing a firing squad.

Eh... did you hear about so and so?

Pause. He stands and walks away.

Yes?... how sad indeed.

My watering hole visits were reduced now because of my
obligations – studies at the university and rehearsals for a
play. But last time I had been, Nalongo the bartender told
me about her daughter. The daughter was dating a soldier.
The soldier had money and she wanted him to take her
shopping.

The daughter got her wish.

NALONGO   The soldier said she'd bugged him too much so he drove
her to Namanve Forest.

SOLDIER   You said you wanted to shop. Let's go.

NALONGO   It was already dark so he flashed a torch and led her deeper
into the forest. They arrived and there they were, piles of
dead bodies all over, newly unloaded, some only dead for a
matter of hours. She had her pick from handbags to shoes,
watches and necklaces. He forced her to load the trunk
with valuables and he dropped her home.

GEORGE   At least she's alive...

NALONGO   But, she's joined the living dead.

GEORGE   (*to audience*) We all kept quiet except for one gentleman who stood up and said:

CUSTOMER   Today it's me, tomorrow it's you! They can't go on killing us yesterday and mounting our daughters tomorrow. When my turn comes I'll tell them you can take my body but not my spirit.

GEORGE   (*to audience*) A few months later our play, "The Fire Spreads," had opened at the National Theatre. A different kind of fire was spreading. During the second act I was putting my costume on when we heard a thunder-like sound... the theatre was instantly half empty. More deafening sounds. (*makes the sound of mortar shells exploding*) The Tanzanian Army and the Ugandan Exiles were closing in on both Kampala and Entebbe.

Eight years and five hundred thousand deaths later, Idi Amin had finally fallen. A new provisional government was in power. The nightmare was over.

(*he sings*) Bewayo abaana bebazibwa
Ku lwaffe bawayo obulamu
N'ebyona

Babasulaamu amabomu
Babakuba na amasasi
Babatemamu
Obufififi bona ...

[Our selfless children who sacrificed themselves are hereby applauded.
For us they gave their lives
And all.

The were showered with bombs
Drilled with bullets
Hacked
Into pieces...]

Ninety days later Professor Lule, the first provisional president, was put under house arrest and sent into exile. Milton Obote's stalwarts now appeared in prominent government posts. The honeymoon was over.

For us it was a time to scream if that's the only way we
could be heard. Men, women and children with the women
at the forefront, some with babies strapped to their backs,
all took to the streets singing:

Ffe twagla Lule
Oba tuffa tuffe
Atamwagala agende.

[We love Lule,
We love him to death.
Those that hate him should leave the country.]

The soldiers gathered around them all over the city from
Nile Mansions to City Square and Entebbe Road. Their
guns did the talking.

The sound of gunfire.

But the massacres did not stop us. All around the city, bar-
ricades were mounted and fires lit. My friend Richard and
I were at the forefront of the demonstrations and against
the return of Obote. There was no turning back. We both
knew it. We gathered a few friends and at night littered the
city with pamphlets to keep the voice of protest alive.

Campus politics, too, was now fully revived. Lumumba
Hall was our first experiment. Through some kind of
alliance all our candidates came to power in a resounding
victory. The Guild Presidency was next. Me, who had
never held a single office in my school years, had all of a
sudden been propelled into a spokesperson for the voices of
dissent.

If Obote ever returned to power, it would be time for me to
become a "Sandinista."

One afternoon I get into Lumumba and a custodian friend
hastily beckons me to the desk.

CUSTODIAN   (*whispers*) The Bad Boys were here... Intelligence Officers.
Probably from Impala House. Asked for your name and
room number. Actually went up and waited a long while.

GEORGE   Hmm. (*laughs*) Didn't know I was that important to them.
Keep it to yourself. I'll lie low for awhile. Make myself
more scarce.

(*to audience*) Then came news that Gasta Nsubuga, a prominent businessman who funded a great deal of our Guild
Presidency Campaign, was shot. Rushed to hospital by the
family, they shot him again in his hospital bed but he still
defied death. His family finally smuggled him across the
border to a Kenyan hospital. Obote's well-oiled machine
was getting stronger and more vicious by the day. Lameck
Ntambi, another popular politician, was the next target, I
helped him escape. (*pause*) Who would the next target be?

Obote himself had finally landed on Ugandan soil. It was
time for me to lie low in self-imposed exile across the border in Nairobi.

In Nairobi I saw Robert Serumaga. The Ugandan playwright, actor and director turned freedom fighter, was one
of those that were exiled only ninety days after they overthrew Amin. Noble, humorous, generous almost to a fault.
I remember asking him once: "How about another play?"
He replies, "I'm in a play now, except that in this one the
main characters must die."

And he died a brutal and tragic death that raised questions
about foul play and betrayal. Through his friend, David
Rubadiri, I started teaching school in Kilungu.

    A bell rings.

My name is George Bwanika. I'll be in charge of English
Language as well as Literature and Drama.

    Bell rings again.

(*to audience*) Although I did take to Kilungu like a fish to
water I found myself homesick within no time. On the
twenty-eighth of November I would be twenty-two. The
prospect of having my first Christmas away from home and
family was far from endearing.

The elections in Uganda were hardly a fortnight away.
"Take advantage of the confusion," I said to myself, "soon
the elections will be over and should Obote be firmly
entrenched it's going to be far more difficult to enter, let
alone leave the country!" I decided to go home for
Christmas.

As the bus approached the border before the crack of dawn
on the fifth of December, I began to have serious doubts
about my decision.

There were rumours of lists and pictures on the Ugandan end. My heart was throbbing like a drum as I whispered my last prayer before going through Ugandan customs and immigration... and... bingo! I had gone through both in record time. I was standing firmly on Ugandan soil.

The haunting flute theme is heard.

A few days later we drove towards Kampala. The closer we got, the more tense I felt. This was election day. Minutes after my arrival at the campus, Paulo Muwanga, one of Obote's stalwarts, issued a disturbing proclamation.

ANNOUNCER (*As if over the airwaves*) Nobody is allowed to release the election results except me... if you are caught doing so you will either pay a fine of half-a-million shillings or go to prison for five years, or both.

GEORGE   That evening as I walked towards Lumumba Hall, a student I once considered a friend confronted me with great hostility.

STUDENT   Why didn't you stay and vote in Moi's Kenya?

GEORGE   (*to audience*) I was with two undergraduate friends of mine who remained quiet. Their party, the DP, had already won seventy percent of the seats, unofficially.

STUDENT   Why didn't you stay and vote in Moi's Kenya?

GEORGE   (*annoyed*) I do not bandy words with fools. I don't even have the time to waste. (*to audience*) There was a ferociousness in his tone and eyes. He walked away accompanied by a chorus of derisive laughter. (*slight pause*) As we approached Lumumba Hall...

He starts to walk. Stops. Addresses the two friends.

Do you see what I see? Two military jeeps. Hmm. Under cover of darkness they won't know who we are. Wait here.

He walks ahead.

(*to himself*) They are empty. But there are a lot of soldiers right at the main gate to the Hall.

He looks through a window.

They seem to be splitting into little groups, traversing the corridors and... knocking on doors! Who are they looking for? I'll make just one more stop to see John and his wife and then out of the campus... (*to his friends*) I'll see you tomorrow.

(*to audience*) I turned right... before I got to the mango tree in John's courtyard I could hear voices of celebration. Pronouncement or no pronouncement, nobody would rob them of their victory.

John worked on the switchboard in the main hall, and ran a watering hole on the side. He and his wife were friends to a great many of us. Despite his blindness, he knew most of us almost by sight.

> *In the distance drums, victorious chanting, clinking glasses, ululation, etc., is heard; the volume rises as George approaches.*

GEORGE   (*knocks at the door*) John, it's...

JOHN   Don't tell me it's you, George. Come in... come in. We are so glad to see you.

GEORGE   (*to audience*) I had never seen him that happy. Except for a head-bowed medical student in a corner it was so wild and euphoric you would think Idi Amin had just fallen.

> *The crowd swells even more.*

CROWD   Welcome back. (*he ululates*) Welcome back from exile.

GEORGE   (*to audience*) Some of them had always been intimate friends. Some had even nicknamed me "Okigbo." A name I would never have escaped if my fellow "Penguins," as the Literature students were called, got wind of it.

CROWD   (*chanting*) Umuofia Kwenu... Uganda Kwenu... DP, hoye... hoye, UPM, hoye hoye. CP, hoye... UPC... chini... chini, Obote zii... zi zaidi...

GEORGE   (*to audience*) Not a glass or a single bottle was idle. They were also rubbing it in; but as if on a mission, the man in the corner appeared unruffled and determined to stay. I also had my say, appropriately quoting from Achebe's "Things Fall Apart": "We do not wish to hurt anybody but if anybody wishes to hurt us, may he break his neck."

(*sits and looks at his watch*) I have to leave for Kasubi in the next five minutes.

(*to audience*) I reluctantly accept John's drink although for some reason I just haven't felt like drinking at all. Nine o'clock. It's time to say goodbye.

(*looks at his watch again*) I have to leave.

    A menacingly loud knock on the door.

(*to audience*) Silence. Before John opens it two people walk in; one is an armed soldier, the other a student in UPC party colours.

**FIRST
SOLDIER**   Who here is George Bwanika?

GEORGE   (*to audience*) Everybody has instantly sobered up. You can almost hear the silence. A round of silence.

    His inner voice takes over.

How long do you think they will manage without revealing your identity? Look as normal as they are, George... whatever that means... (*to audience*) The man in the corner is no longer head bowed. He looks very calm and unthreatened. (*inner voice; cold and calculated instinct*) Grab him, he is within easy reach. You have the speed and the power to hurl him in front of the soldier. Remember there is a seldom-used door to your immediate left. Don't be afraid. Grab him by surprise, he will give you cover, then jump as soon as you open the door... what if it's locked, though?!

(*to audience; still glued to his seat*) A second soldier walks in and I abandon the option.

(*reverts to his thoughts*) Sooner than later someone is going to point me out. True they did welcome me back from exile but, there is a limit to a lot of things... then there is this pretentiously quiet man to my left in the corner. If nobody points me out, he will.

**SECOND
SOLDIER**   All of you produce your identity cards.

Pregnant pause. Through a quick light change, there is a spotlight on George as he pulls his card from his shirt pocket. He drops it on the floor, steps on it, and then slides it downstage as if underneath a bench. He pulls out his diary, flips through it. Satisfied, he slides it under the bench with his left leg. It's now his turn.

GEORGE Sorry. I inadvertently forgot to carry mine. Didn't know it was a necessary prerequisite within the confines of the campus.

(*to audience*) This was a bit of a loop. None of them could identify George Bwanika. To make matters worse they expected him to simply stand up and say: Present Sir, just like we used to do at school. They turned to John and his wife.

SECOND SOLDIER Ako wapi? Where is he?

JOHN I am afraid it would be very hard for me to...

GEORGE (*to audience*) He's slapped across the face.

SECOND SOLDER Who here is George Bwanika?

GEORGE (*to soldier; quickly retrieving his card*) Here. It's me. I quickly retrieved my card.

FIRST SOLDIER What have you come back to do here?

GEORGE (*aside; to audience*) This is ridiculous. Isn't Uganda my country too?! (*to soldier*) I came back just like any other Ugandan would... especially so because of the elections. I thought it was time to chip in and do my part in the enormous task of rehabilitation. Regardless of whoever came to power, after the free and fair elections. If you have any doubts about what I say, ask the Department of Literature or Music, Dance and Drama, they will fill you in.

SECOND SOLDIER Sumama!

GEORGE flings himself to his feet.

FIRST SOLDIER Face the wall.

SECOND SOLDIER	He wants to somersault!
FIRST SOLDIER	Walk to the corner.

> *GEORGE does so.*

There. Sit down! Do you deny that we have seen you in Nairobi? Do you deny that we have seen you in Nairobi with certain exiles?

GEORGE I have lots of friends and relatives in Nairobi... but if you... expect more answers, take me to whoever... your boss is, so at least I know that...

FIRST SOLDIER You really want to meet the boss?

GEORGE (*to audience*) What else could I say? With my blood slowly trickling down to the floor; the best I could do was buy a little more time. Better going to prison anyway. Word gets around. My friends will try getting me out before my family gets the news.

I turned to the rest for one last look.

Outside, another medical student was standing guard. He nodded to confirm that they had the right man, then raised his left hand and six more soldiers emerged. They had made an extended line outside the house.

My hands were up. All around me a spectacular ring of gun muzzles. As we turned towards Lumumba Hall...

STUDENT Who is that?

GEORGE I knew the voice. It was Mr. "Why-didn't-you-vote-in-Moi's-Kenya?" himself.

STUDENT Agh. That one. You just kill.

ACT II

A few minutes later.

FIRST
SOLDIER (*thick north Ugandan accent*) Sasa we lia kama mbugi.

GEORGE bleats like a goat.

Stop. Now you laugh.

GEORGE laughs wildly.

Stop. Now you cry like a cow.

GEORGE ends up bellowing like a bull.

Stop. Now, bark like a dog.

GEORGE barks.

Now cry... stop.

GEORGE continues moaning.

Stop!!

GEORGE (*to audience*) I stopped. So too did my hopes of striking a human chord.

With me spread-eagled on the floor of one of the military vehicles, we made our way through the speedbumps and potholes that filled the streets. I was a doormat to their thick boots.

He tries to absorb the hits in a spread-eagled stance. A position he takes and discards as occasion demands it.

Sometimes the butts of their guns would have a little dialogue with my ribs. The first soldier who was the leader, issued orders quietly and his pistol kept my wrists busy.

A blinding flood of lights hit my face. This was Nile Mansions; the five star hotel where the top brass lived and worked, indulged themselves and felt more secure than living among the real people.

FIRST SOLDIER	Toa viatu. [Take your shoes off]
GEORGE	(*takes his shoes off*) The walk into the building was an interesting display; you should have seen it, a soldier at the back and one at the front as well. All around us imaginary foes that kept them busy.
FIRST & SECOND SOLDIERS	He wants to somersault. He wants to somersault. He wants...
GEORGE	Me in the middle. Encaged in the now familiar and spectacular island of steel and human hands. Definitely more protected than any Life President.
SECOND SOLDIER	Have you been to Israel?
GEORGE	The voice sounded almost friendly.
SECOND SOLDIER	Have you been to Israel?
GEORGE	(*not answering the soldier*) I couldn't help but smile looking at him... were they more afraid than I? One doesn't have to go to Tel Aviv to fight this rag-tag bunch. Still, I would neither confirm nor deny.
	We finish the final flight of stairs, pass through a door into what looks like the outer chamber of a bigger office. Less than a year ago someone was killed in this building, I recall. A teenage girl. Her father, a Cabinet Minister, was at work down the street. They said it was a stray bullet that did it. There tends to be a lot of those when certain governments are changing... in Africa.
	The office is full of gadgets. A uniformed figure sits behind a huge desk.
FIRST SOLDIER	(*clicks his heels, then executes a quick salute*) We have brought him. The man who had come to cause chaos at Makerere.
GEORGE	(*to audience*) I had finally met the boss. No less a man than Brigadier David Oyite Ojok. His name alone made the blood of many a Ugandan freeze.

"Sir..." I struggled through bleeding lips. His eyes were so small they looked like little slits... so red, more red than they used to look on television. He looked tired. Ruthlessly cold. Insensitive.

(*to Brigadier Ojok*) Sir... some of my friends and relatives fought alongside you in the struggle against Amin.

No response.

FIRST SOLDIER	Do you deny that you escaped from prison?
GEORGE	Sir, I have never been to prison. Which prison?
FIRST SOLDIER	You were supposed to be in prison anyway. We have it in your file.
GEORGE	(*to audience*) The boss gestured to him to move this "walking blasphemy" out of his office. I was shoved onto a small balcony.
FIRST SOLDIER	Talk! Talk! Talk you bloody bandit! Do you deny that we have seen you in Nairobi? Do you deny that we have seen you in Nairobi with certain exiles? Talk. Talk. Name them.
GEORGE	(*to audience*) I knew which name they wanted most. Robert Serumaga; the playwright, buried in a foreign land. Cause of death: dubious. Even in his death I couldn't betray him. All I could say was "(*mutters*) ...let his soul rest in peace."

I could have dropped a few names of prominent exiles who were still alive. Every silent response earned me another blow, the pain was more and more distant. I reduced my body to an empty husk. Now I was a little bird perched on a little branch witnessing perhaps what mankind enjoys most.

After a few more blows, he resolves to say something.

(*facing the soldiers*) Thank you... thank you... thank you.

FIRST SOLDIER	(*disturbed*) Why are you thanking us? Why are you...?
GEORGE	Because you know what you are doing.

> *There is a beat. Soldier laughs menacingly.*

(*to audience*) His friend had returned with an ashtray full of burning cigarette butts.

FIRST SOLDIER Bend forward. Put your chin under your knees.

GEORGE They were stuffed into my shirt. All over my back. I remembered a story about a Greek Cypriot mercenary on the eve of his execution somewhere in Africa. His sister who'd visited him in prison, couldn't bear to say goodbye. She broke down and wept. All he would say was: "Never let them see you cry, remember you are a Greek." A youthful officer approached the scene.

OFFICER What has he done?

> *Silence.*

GEORGE (*turns to him*) Sir, among other things they are accusing me of having escaped from lawful custody... but I have never been to jail.

OFFICER (*cautious reprimand*) You should not take such drastic steps if you don't have enough evidence.

FIRST SOLDIER Chacha hi mkubwa nasema nini? [What the hell is this boss saying?]

GEORGE (*to audience*) It was as though this was the stupidest statement they'd ever heard. They were enraged. They dragged me back to the inner chamber. Promptly explained everything in their mother tongue. The "almighty" Ojok issued some rapid orders and took a good long look at me.

Back at the waiting vehicle the soldier with the friendly tone leaned over to brief the one in the driver's seat.

SECOND SOLDIER He says kill!

GEORGE Lord, now lettest thou thy servant depart in peace.

> *GEORGE assumes the spread-eagled position once again.*

(*to soldiers*) Gentlemen, since I do not have that much time left, can you please allow me a final look at the moon and stars? (*sits and begs for a little more*) And please don't hit me as hard. All you'll do is deprive me of the pain at the end. If you don't mind, I'll say my last prayers.

Head tilted skyward, arms together, he begins secret prayers.

Two things, good Lord. One, these men have humiliated me a great deal, when the moment comes let me not go like a coward. If nobody else sees my body at least let my mother see it, so she does not spend the rest of her life thinking I'll one day show up. Do shorten the family's grief, Lord, and give them as long and as safe a life as possible.

FIRST SOLDIER   Lie down.

GEORGE   I could tell we had reached the major roadblock at Ntinda.

SECOND SOLDIER   (*at the checkpoint*) We are members of the G Branch. We are on a mission and we shall be back soon. Thank you.

GEORGE   (*to audience*) And so we went through Banda, Kireka, Bweyogerere and finally stopped in the middle of the road. This was the famous Namanve Forest, the place where lots of Ugandans had met their deaths. The place where Nalongo's daughter went shopping.

The soldier with the friendly tone pulled me aside. He was a bit of a giant and reminded me of the noble savage in Swift's voyage to Brobdignag.

SECOND SOLDIER   You refused to talk so now... you will talk when it is too...

GEORGE   When the bullets begin to flower.

SECOND SOLDER   Take off your watch. What about the money... is this all you have?

GEORGE   I wish you had told me before... I would have given you more but I left it at John's place, tucked in my little diary.

SECOND SOLDIER   Where?

GEORGE   In a corner below the bench I was on.

SECOND
SOLDIER   You have a diary... anyway, we have to go back and pick up
                two students who were seen in your company.

GEORGE   (*to himself*) Thank God they weren't with me at John's.
                Thank God the soldiers are going back there though, now at
                least people will know and spread the news of my tragedy.

                (*to audience*) For a moment I thought about Dora Block, the
                elderly Israeli woman who was dragged from Mulago
                Hospital as soon as the Israelis rescued their hostages at
                Entebbe. What were her last thoughts? Her remains were
                finally discovered not too far from here. "Do not let them
                see your tears... remember you are a Greek."

                It was getting dark. The front door opened for the mean lit-
                tle boss who'd called the shots all the way from Makerere.
                He stuck his pistol in my lower ribs.

FIRST
SOLDIER   Escort me.

GEORGE   Excuse me, could you please not shoot me through the
                back? I would prefer to look at you while you shoot. (*takes
                a few short backwards steps*) Is this okay?

                (*internal*) Goodbye Mum, I owe you an apology for over-
                staying this night on the campus. Goodbye Dad... goodbye
                my lovely sisters, Abby, little Tony, every single one of you.
                Remember he loved you all and loved his country.

                (*to soldiers*) Please give me a minute or two to say my last
                words. Now that you have come to power through the bal-
                lot box and not the barrel of a gun, even if I had committed
                a treasonable offence you should at least have taken me to
                prison or a court of law. I know it's too late for me to live
                but whoever will continue to live in your country will find
                it hard to forgive, let alone forget. I am ready.

                (*to audience*) So were they, except for the "noble savage."

SECOND
SOLDIER   No I'm not shooting, but you can use my gun.

GEORGE   (*internal*) Oh, Robert Serumaga, what would you have
                done...? Give me strength to go through this.

A gun goes off.

(*to audience*) The first bullet had hit the right leg. I was down on my knees... I actually squatted. Before I knew it the left arm was grazed.

Another shot is heard.

The body now contorted as another got a bit of skin just above the forehead. But this time the body moved back and forth, never still and unwilling to give them a clean shot at the chest or the stomach.

Yet another shot is let go.

The next one found my right hand at an angle just over my heart.

Bang.

It felt big compared to the tiny needle-like sensations, as though it entered with a vengeance. Then another through the right thigh.

A fifth shot is fired.

There was a brief lull. Someone picked up "my friend's" gun. It was a rocket propelled grenade. There was a grin on his face as he put the gun over his shoulder. I stared at him in disbelief. Oh, God there goes the rest of the body.

The deafening sound of a small rocket-propelled grenade is heard.

A big bolt-like cluster of sharp little machetes had drilled through my thigh... I was on my back, the feet were burning, there were a few flames and a pungent smell. I rolled backwards. I could see a little thicket and some undergrowth to my immediate left, a bit of a ditch as well.

The familiar and by now comparatively tame sound of another bullet is heard.

A solid bullet went through my left ankle as I rolled over.

An instantaneous barrage of bullets is heard.

The AK 47s were now on rapid fire. There was lead all around me... sort of like popcorn. The AK 47s were quite clearly on rapid fire.

Another stomach-churning barrage.

I had landed in a shallow stream or marsh. I could smell the clay. Except for the head I had practically sunk. There was still one crucial bullet. The one I wouldn't see. The one that would end it all. The one that would enter through the back of my head.

Shooting ends as suddenly as it had begun.

It is quiet. Frighteningly quiet!

(*internal and very quiet*) Be still, George, still as a stone. What are they up to ... God, let it not be that they are planning to cut the head off the corpse to show their boss! Or simply dump it in the lake or the Nile: the "Poet's Corner" of Idi Amin's Uganda. After the longest five minutes of my life, they turned and drove towards Kampala... God save my two friends...

Grant me enough strength to come out of the marsh and save my body so my mother can see it. It's dark. The abduction was around nine. The latest it can be is eleven-thirty. By dawn I will finally leave the world.

(*to audience*) I turned towards the east; a few metres in that direction was the foundation stone for a monument that was never built, "To the Memory of all that had died in Idi Amin's Uganda."

He summons incredible energy and drags himself out of the marsh.

I stumbled eastwards. Got to the road. Turned towards the highway. (*pause, then his inner voice takes over*) Zig zag on the edge of the tarmac, George. Avoid leaving a blood trail.

Points to the other side after a few more steps.

(*to himself*) That's the spot where the shooting was. The sky is getting even darker. Around me is a misty grey colour. The pain throbs like unrelenting high-pitched drums. Tears are welling in my eyes. The earth feels like a rag slowly pulled away under my elephantine feet. (*pause, then to audience*) Still I "walked," supporting myself by leaning against a tree or holding onto a branch.

My entire family, relatives, friends, places too, were rolling over the screen of my mind. All the faces looked shocked. Lord let this Government not last, at least let them not kill too many people.

> *Soft throbbing drums.*

The images kept rolling. My entire life... its landmarks from primary school... the best years. Short, intense...

(*internal*) God if there is a way of coming back to this earth... make me a little bird, a spirit of the woods and custodian of Namanve Forest. I will always come back to my nest at sunset and sometimes disrupt the foul murders... enable the victims to escape.

You my ancestors, all of you from Kabaka Kalema whose remains lie in Mende, Kakungulu and Mugujula the two valiant warriors. My grandparents back in Masaka. My grandmother, Bulaliya Nakiwala, you who always danced agile as a duiker without touching a drink in your entire life. Yekoniya Zirabamuzale, you who lost your sight and never your wisdom and legendary charity. My stillborn brothers, you who never left the void, please pave my way and ease my transition.

(*to himself*) I see distant flares cut through the dark hide of night... (*thunder is heard*) and feel a few drizzles drop on my body. It's raining.

(*internal*) This is a good resting place. The Ministry of Works Labour Camp is close, someone will see the body and "Radio Katwe," the grapevine telegraph will do the rest. I also have an uncle not too far from here, if he is home he will save the body and deliver the news.

(*to audience*) The right arm is already swollen by more than half its size.

> *He removes his shirt and folds it into a pillow.*

The trees and the undergrowth swirls at an incredible pace. Their shapes begin to change, taking on the threatening ones of the gnomic creatures and spirits that inhabit my folklore.

I have made my peace and put my borrowed time to good use. I'm a bird flapping my wings and gazing at the husk that was my body. Maybe I'll be like Christopher Okigbo, the Nigerian poet.

They say he was sent back to earth after his death. Condemned to sing his lines eternally, at a village well. To this day when the little children are sent to the well, they sometimes hear a pair of little birds singing:

So let us sing tongue tied
without name or audience
and make harmony
among the branches.

I don't recall anything else.

> *The drums stop. More thunder and lightning. A tropical downpour is heard. It stops. Dawn: birds and other forest sounds. A determined tropical sun makes its way through the foliage. George opens his eyes. Slight pause.*

(*to himself*) Am I in Heaven or Hell? (*another pause*) It must have taken about five long frightening minutes to come to terms with the discovery that I was still alive. That was far more shocking than the previous night's events. There was a long pregnant moment of silence. As if body and spirit were getting into sync. (*pause, then very muffled agony*) The pain is enormous. The earth is wet and soggy. I can hear occasional trucks in the distance... Obote has finally returned to power.

You know how much I love life, Lord. Why tantalize me with another glimpse of it? (*pause*) If I had my way, my request would be to live long enough to tell this tale. But even if you allowed me to live long enough just to see my mother, I wouldn't complain. But home is Jinja and Jinja is almost fifty miles away. And between here and Kampala the military roadblocks are manned by Obote's henchmen who will ask me to identify myself and explain my wounds.

Will the forest be my perpetual prison? Perhaps all I can do is sing like Nsimb'egwire, the little girl in the proverb.

Flute.

Yes I feel a certain kinship with her. Understand her in a
way I have never done. Her voice clear as a bell:

A female voice is heard singing the solitary lyrics.

FEMALE
VOICE   (*singing*) Ani oyo
                     Ani oyo ayita
                     Ku mutunda...

GEORGE   (*picks up story from where it stopped*) She was not ready to
                     quit yet. Unknown to her neither was her father who had
                     recently returned from the hunting expedition. Something
                     told him not to believe anything her stepmother said. So he
                     put a search party together.

                     One day they heard a familiar voice.

                     Singing continues.

FEMALE
VOICE   (*singing*) Ku mutunda
                     Kuliko Nsimb'egwire
                     Nsimb' – Egwire
                     muwala wa Mbaire...

GEORGE   She'd finally been found. Half rotten and famished, they
                     unearthed her and headed home. As for me, Obote has
                     finally returned to–

                     (*interrupting himself*) Who's that? A little boy. Must be
                     about twelve.

                     He beckons to the boy.

                     Tontya. Who sent you?

BOY   They sent me to check and see whether the village lost one
                     of our own. Whenever we hear the bullets at night we
                     come to check in the morning.

GEORGE   Go check across the road. My two friends might be there...
                     no. Thank God. Then please, go back and tell them I'm the
                     only one.

                     (*to audience*) Soon they arrived. Headed by an elder, a chief
                     of some sort.

(*to the villagers*) No, they took all my papers... but believe me, there is nothing sinister about this. Thank you. Thank you all so very much for the risk you're taking. The little boy should go ahead as a scout. At a sign from him simply dump my body by the side; should worst come to worst... well at least you will have done your best.

> *The villagers load their "delicate cargo" onto their backs.*
> *They walk for a while, unload without any incident.*

(*to audience*) As soon as we got to the village, I was placed on the floor of a tiny concrete grey store. We were right next to the highway and more and more people were milling around. No one had ever come out of Namanve alive. Then said the chief...

CHIEF   What would you like us to do?

GEORGE   I have an uncle around here. His name is George Kakaire.

(*to audience*) We wasted no time after his arrival. Kampala was so near and yet so far. Our best bet was Jinja. The roadblocks were fewer and except for the one at the Owen Falls Dam practically all of them were entirely manned by Tanzanian troops.

The first roadblock was Mukono. We stopped. We soon got to Lugazi. Mabira Forest. Bulumagi, and finally reached the road block at the Nile, the one stop we feared most. Will our story work? (*slight pause*) "He had an accident between here and the last roadblock. We've been referred to such and such a hospital."

SOLDIERS   Pole sana! Mumuharakishe. [How sad! Rush him.]

GEORGE   (*to audience*) It worked. We had crossed the "Mighty Nile." The next stop was home.

Mother had just come out of the bathtub when Uncle George walked in. Before he said anything she asked:

MOTHER   What brings you here so early... is he dead?

UNCLE   Not yet. No. Dress up. He's in the van. We have to get him to hospital.

GEORGE   (*to audience*) At first my sister Mary and my mother just looked at me through the window. With tears streaming down my mother's face they edged closer. The blanket was lifted. There was a little relief. At least the chest and stomach seemed intact.

At the hospital, it was as if all our friends had conspired to be on duty at the same time.

Looking at the X-rays.

FRIEND   You're lucky. Doesn't seem to be any bone injuries. Two bullets have to be dislodged. One from the right thigh, the other from the right arm.

GEORGE   (*to audience*) All along there were no questions asked. Down in my warm and cosy bed I looked at the ceiling, highly impressed... tried to sum it all up for myself. There was a knock at the door. Dr. Walugembe walked in.

WALUGEMBE   (*very calmly*) The surgeon in charge is already pacing up and down... asking leading questions. I'm not saying it is true, but given his political stripes there is no guarantee that if he got wind of your story, he may not leave you on the table.

GEORGE   (*to audience*) He didn't have to say anymore. Outside a different car was waiting and ready to go. Destination: twenty-eight miles away, in the famous town of Iganga.

My sister Mary got to work.

MARY   See this?

GEORGE   (*to audience*) It was the bullet in the right thigh.

MARY   You have to tell the Doctor it's come out. Lest they start drilling and fishing for it where it's not. It's also left another wound. Remind them about it.

GEORGE   (*to audience*) There was something else on my mind this afternoon. Anybody with bullet wounds had to have a certificate of some sort from the police before getting any treatment. Dr. Walugembe would vouch for us. For my part all I had to do was remember a story we had gone through in the car. Inside the operating theatre the story is subjected to a severe test.

(*to doctor*) My name is Paulo Nyende, Doctor. I was over-speeding along the Jinja-Kamuli Highway... it all happened too quickly and it's entirely my fault. Before I knew it, I was passing a roadblock manned by our esteemed army. Realizing my mistake I'm sure they never shot to kill. If you ask me, they were extremely kind in the execution of their duty... to say the least.

DOCTOR   How can you say you hadn't anticipated the roadblock?

GEORGE   I don't live here. In fact I am a Student at the University of Nairobi.

DOCTOR   (*literally pouncing on him*) You can't say Kamuli in one breath and then Nairobi in the other.

GEORGE   (*to the doctors*) With due respect to all of you. There is a difference between the hippocratic oath and the Spanish Inquisition. My pain is unbearable. With the last ounce of my physical and psychic energy, I put it to you sirs, with all my heart, that I made a mistake. It's none but me to blame. Please don't turn this operating table into an abattoir. If I have committed any crimes against the state... believe me, I will be more than happy to face a firing squad. I'll answer any other questions after the surgery.

DOCTOR   Count one, two, three.

GEORGE   (*to audience*) Late in the afternoon, the next day, I opened my eyes for the first time. What's this? There is drip hanging over my head. Here behind a partial screen in an open hospital ward... why does it look so familiar? Their positions as well: Mary, Mother, my grandmother...

          But oh... the pain is a lot worse, unparalleled by anything I've gone through before the operation.

          They have begun to arrive. Soon this corner of the ward will be full to the brim with relatives, friends just like my grandmother's house at Rubaga. One of the first ones to arrive is my Auntie Gladys.

AUNTIE   You look too anemic my son.

MOTHER   For some reason they refused to give him even a single drop of blood.

AUNTIE   (*angry and sad*) I'm not surprised.

Methodically, she circles around pointing to the wounds.

Look. Look. Look at this...

Pulls Mother aside.

Can I tell you something my dear sister... of all the years of training and practise both at Mulago and the hospitals in London... I have never seen the like! Did you have a good look at those sutures? God, I hate it when people put my Christianity to the test. They stitched our son up like a gunny bag. Only post mortem surgeons do that. It's for dead bodies.

GEORGE	(*to audience*) Uncle Paulo Kasekende was the next one to arrive. Right next to him was my great uncle, good old Brother Stephen. Now in his sixties. Still far from frail. I had no doubt he would gladly have traded places with me or any other victim in the family. He reminded me of Mark Antony on seeing Caesar's body.
BROTHER STEPHEN	(*vents his spleen, quoting Shakespeare, a flourish of trumpets is heard*) "Oh judgement, thou art fled to brutish beasts, And men have lost their reason... You blocks, you stones, you worse than senseless things!" *Removes his glasses. Pulls out a handkerchief.* "Oh you hard hearts, you cruel men... These dogs. These shameless, Godless... beasts." Forgive me. (*pause*) You know Brother Andrew... yes, the Canadian. He goes to Nairobi from time to time. He's promised to help. Once your condition improves, he'll have to get you across the border. God willing.
GEORGE	(*to audience*) Three weeks later we celebrated a rather sunken eyed but warm Christmas. We had moved to an anonymous little house next to the District Prison in Iganga. Auntie Gladys headed the underground medical team that included my cousin Betty and a male nurse. Except for the right arm, all other wounds were healing fast. Now I could sit and stand. But I couldn't stand the bedpan any longer! (*tries walking*) By hook or crook I had to get to the toilet.

He toddles his way across the stage.

I stood under the mid-afternoon Boxing Day sun, pleased as punch.

Half-way between the toilet and stairs, I stopped. First I heard the sudden curious sound, then right in front of me a military jeep. They've finally caught up with me... they will take my body but not my spirit. The door opens. Brother Stephen steps out.

BROTHER
STEPHEN   Sorry for the lack of warning. These are Tanzanian officers. I talked to the commander himself and he graciously offered to help. Go in and say goodbye. We'll say a little prayer. Then we'll leave as soon as your grandmother is ready to board.

GEORGE   (*to audience*) Soon, I was having my last look at the mighty Nile. Then came Mukono, Namanve, Bweyogerere. I thought about all those people that rescued me. Uncle George, the pilot, the gentleman who offered his car and drove us on the morning after. Forgive me, I would like to pay tribute to the so called African extended family. Then and in the days that followed the stream of relatives that poured in to reaffirm their love, support and best wishes, uplifted my spirits, hope, faith and accelerated the healing process... their presence alone gave me something to live for. They will always be etched in my memory.

We finally arrived in Kampala. I even had a glimpse of the famous Nile Mansions from my front seat. After the round-about at Kibuye, we stop to let Grandma off.

For a person in her late sixties, she's tall and erect. The lines on her face more pronounced than ever before. But no amount of oppression will remove the inner dignity and proverbial wisdom of Semei Kakungulu's daughter and granddaughter of a noble King of Buganda.

GRAND-
MOTHER   You come from a line of brave and courageous people. I need not say much. You've seen it all. You know! Just one favour: When we die, even when you hear we are all dead and gone... I beseech you, never come back to the land of your ancestors. Let us pray for one another.

GEORGE   (*to audience*) We embraced again. Scared of attracting too much attention at this busy intersection, I get back into the vehicle nursing a lump in my throat. We drove towards Kisubi.

Photographs are taken. A new identity card is issued and stamped. For the first time I use the name Seremba, a name I had never used before officially. I'm also listed as a postulant, a Brother in the making so to speak. The card also calls for a brand new story: I had gone to visit some friends at the senior seminary in Masaka Diocese... all of a sudden the car swerved off the road... you should see the condition it's in! But God is great. If all goes well I could be back in two weeks... just as soon as a few more experts examine me. God knows I love Uganda.

Brother Andrew and Brother Aidan, were both flying on the twenty-eighth. My name had been attached to the Travel Permit Clearance form, signed and stamped by no less a man than the Honourable Minister for Internal Affairs.

The next afternoon Dad came to say hello and goodbye. We shook hands. Embraced. Shook hands again. I knew at least in his eyes I was a hero.

That evening Auntie Gladys arrived. Offered me a sling.

AUNTIE   You have now become a seasoned patient... from time to time you may have to dress the wounds yourself. I hope they get to look at that arm again. Son, always remember to thank God and the rain. Without that and your will, this would be a different story. So remember to get down on those knees. Don't forget to say: "Come good rain. For none but I will bear my cross."

GEORGE   (*to audience*) As we drove to the airport the next morning it was my mother's turn to bid me goodbye.

MOTHER   God alone knows how many of us you'll ever meet if things change. You know the rest as you have yourself witnessed. I beseech you though, do us one favour, please do not write that story. Wait.

GEORGE   (*to audience*) It is Sunday, December 28th. Obote the second was sworn in last night. There is not much staff at the airport because of the big victory celebration the night before. Brother Stephen leaves us at the check-in counter and goes to the waving bay where Mary, Mum and the rest are.

Brother Andrew has already started chatting with some acquaintances. They let Brother Aidan pass. After a few casual explanations I pass through too. With Brother Aidan at the front and Andrew at the back we proceed to board.

Panting and nervous, he stumbles across the tarmac.

Halfway up the stairs I take one last look.

Inside the plane, a flight attendant's voice comes on.

FLIGHT
ATTENDANT Mabibi na mabwana, tuna wakaribisha ndani ya Kenya Airways... [Ladies and Gentlemen, we welcome you on board Kenya Airways...]

GEORGE (*to audience*) We were up in the clouds.

(*closes his eyes, then internal*) Thank you Lord. Goodbye Uganda.

(*to audience*) Soon we would be getting into Kenyan airspace. Lake Victoria would be behind us, over the Rift Valley... finally we'd landed at Jomo Kenyatta International Airport.

It was my turn to go through Customs and Immigration.

OFFICER Wapi kitambulisho?

GEORGE It must have dropped on my seat or the toilet.

OFFICER This is a country not a toilet. That plane is leaving for Mombasa. You'll have to go back to Entebbe.

GEORGE Not with all these wounds. Look sir... besides niko mwalimu [I am a teacher] ...here in your country. (*beat*) Yes. Kilungu Day High School, in Ukamban, they call it Kwa Mwanza.

OFFICER You're lucky. That's my home area. No Immigration Officer is allowed to do this. But because you teach our children I'll let you go but next time... next...

GEORGE (*to audience*) Next time. Hmm... when would that be?

With my arm firmly in the sling, I limp through a corridor and behind a door for my first pee on Kenyan soil. (*brief pause*) Here is to freedom. That evening we knock on the door of the Rubadiri's at Hurlingham. (*to them*) Lazarus has come to see you.

(*to audience*) The whole family gathers. All sure glad to see me. David too was short of words.

DAVID My son, you are larger than life. Do you feel sorry for yourself, my son?

GEORGE No.

DAVID Here. This is more important than the medicines.

> *GEORGE relights the candle with which he first entered.*

GEORGE (*to audience*) He opened a bottle of brandy. He places something on the turntable. A Welsh voice booms its way through the African night.

VOICE "Do not go gentle into that good night, Old age should burn and rave at close of day; Rage, rage against the dying of the light."

GEORGE (*to audience*) If there was rain that night, I didn't hear it. Two little birds stood guard outside my window. Their sweet song cut my dream short; I remember seeing a stepmother hastily pack and desert her home after an abominable act, to live like a pariah for the rest of her life. Then I saw a beautiful young figure. Her song sounded familiar:

(*he sings*) Abe mbuutu
N'abe ngalabi
Banange munkubire ngenda
Mbaire yagenda naa alidda...

> *GEORGE picks up his candle and returns to the place on stage where he first began. There is a slow fade to black. He blows out his candle and exits.*

When He Was Free And Young And He Used To Wear Silks

by Austin Clarke

Austin Chesterfield Clarke was born in Barbados in 1934 and emigrated to Canada to attend University of Toronto in 1955. He quickly became a leader of the civil rights movement in Toronto. He worked from 1965-73 as a journalist and broadcaster covering social issues. Between 1968-74 Clarke served as visiting professor at Yale, Brandeis, Williams, Wellesley, Duke, and the universities of Texas and Indiana. He assisted in setting up Black Studies programmes at Yale and Harvard. He was also involved in the establishment of black intellectual publications such as *Black Lines*. In 1974 Clarke became cultural attache of the Barbadian Embassy in Washington, and from 1975-77 he served as general manager of the Caribbean Broadcasting Corporation in Barbados. From 1973-76 he served as advisor to the Prime Minister of Barbados. From 1989-94 he was a member of the controversial Immigration and Refugee Board, among many other boards on which he has served. Last year he became the host of the TV book show "Literati", where he interviews leading writers from around the world.

SEARCHING FOR SILKS

by Djanet Sears with Amela Simic

Austin Clarke is one of Canada's most significant literary figures. His extensive body of work includes nine novels, three books of non-fiction, several volumes of short stories and over a thousand columns and articles for a wide selection of magazines, newspapers and journals. The entire collection of Austin Clarke's writing, including his unpublished work, is housed in the William Ready Division of Archives and Research Collection of the Mills Memorial Library at McMaster University. After nearly two decades, Clarke's play, *When He Was Free And Young And He Used To Wear Silks*, will finally take its rightful place among the other works.

When He Was Free And Young And He Used To Wear Silks, the stage play, was first conceived by Ardon Bess, a Toronto-based actor and director, widely known for his appearances as the Nestor, the postman in the popular "King Of Kensington" television series. Bess was thoroughly enthralled with the book of short stories, (Anansi, 1971), and spoke with friend and colleague Jeff Henry about the idea. At the time Jeff Henry was a professor at York University, and he was also the founder and artistic director of Theatre Fountainhead, which along with Black Theatre Canada, was a leading force in African Canadian theatre in Toronto. Jeff Henry and Ardon Bess approached Austin Clarke about dramatizing the short stories, and he agreed.

In the early eighties, after graduating from university, I became involved with Theatre Fountainhead, doing everything from PR assistant to Stage Management. I was asked to be an actor in a reading of Austin Clarke's new play, commonly referred to as *Silks* – and that's how I first got my hands on the script. Theatre Fountainhead had planned to produce the play as part of the following season, unfortunately the arts agencies did not find the wherewithal to support the season and the project was put on hold. The final blows to the project took place several years later when funding cutbacks forced the company to close, and then water damage from a major flood destroyed most of Theatre Fountainhead's archives and what was thought to be the only remaining copy of Austin Clarke's play manuscript.

Almost twenty years later, while contemplating the plays that I wanted to include in this collection, Clarke's script kept coming to mind. Although the play has yet to be produced, I recalled the work as an important examination of the Caribbean immigrant experience of the mid-sixties and early seventies. With poignancy and an enormous dose of humour, *Silks* attempts to expose issues of both Canadian racism and Caribbean immigrant racial hypocrisy. Yet Clarke compassionately portrays the immigrants desire to establish a presence as equal and respected citizens of their adopted country. However, it is in the use of language that Clarke's brilliance soars. His uses of authentic Caribbean dialogue against the backdrop of Toronto transforms the Canadian sound. Clarke's characterizations are remarkably subtle and brutally authentic. I had to find this play.

My countless attempts to obtain a copy of the play through the regular channels were fruitless. It was written before the personal computer revolution and no hard copy could be found, even at the McMaster archives. I don't usually discard scripts that I've worked on—I have a collection of scripts that go all the way back to university—but *Silks* was not among them. Then, as coincidence would have it, I received a phone call from my mother who was attempting to clear out the garage and unload herself of decades of books, papers, photographs, memorabilia and clothes stored there by her several daughters. When I arrived at my parent's home to sort and throw away the things that were taking up so much space in their garage, there was *Silks* lying under a sea of personal affects.

In the intervening years since I first read the play, Austin Clarke has fully established his presence in Canadian literature and his substantial contribution has been acknowledged many times. He is the recipient of the 1999 W.O. Mitchell Prize, awarded each year to a Canadian writer who has produced an outstanding body of work and served as a caring mentor for other writers. His novel *The Origin of Waves* won the Rogers Communications Writers' Development Trust Prize for Fiction. In 1992 Clarke was honoured with a Toronto Arts Award for Lifetime Achievement in Literature. Frontier College in Toronto also granted him a Lifetime Achievement Award in 1997. In 1998 he was invested with the Order of Canada and received an honorary doctorate from Brock University. On January 30, 1999, in Montreal, he received the Martin Luther King Junior Award for Excellence in Writing.

There already exists a modest collection of literary criticisms and biographical information on Clarke and his work that can be used as a starting point for further examination. For a complete selection of Clarke's work, please refer to the Mills Memorial Library at McMaster University.

Djanet Sears is the editor of *Testifyin': Contemporary African Canadian Drama*, Vol. I. She is the Barker Fairley visiting professor at University College, university of Toronto. She is also an award-winning playwright, director and actor.

Amela Simic is a translator and writer who immigrated to Canada in 1996 after living through the war in Sarajevo, Bosnia. Her most recent translation is a book of poetry by a Bosnian poet published in the USA by White Pine Press. She has made Toronto her home.

CHARACTERS

AGATHA
THEO
BOYSIE
SAGABOY
ESTELLE
DOTS
HENRY
THEOPHILUS
POLICEMAN

As noted in Djanet Sears introduction, *Silks* is the only play in the collection not to have had a professional production. Hence, the lack of a production history.

ACT I

It's the back porch of a ground floor apartment. Steps stage right descend to the back garden. Up-stage right a glass-door opens into the party room. The wall separating the back porch from the inner room is transparent enough to allow the action inside to be visible. The wedding reception party is going on inside. On the porch and in the garden are a few stragglers "cooling off". Whenever the door right is opened the music escapes loud and clear. The impression inside is of a lot of people having a good time. AGATHA, the white Canadian bride of HENRY, is sitting visibly just inside the door while the party, hers and HENRY's, is happening around her. Outside the door and to one side of it is Theophilus sitting in tails and top hat with cane. On the other side of the porch HENRY is dancing slowly and tightly with a slim sexy black girl. AGATHA looks bored and alone. Next to HENRY is a wide window inside of which is the new stereo BOYSIE bought for the party. AGATHA gets up and opens the door and steps outside. She stands uncertainly next to THEOPHILUS. She notices HENRY and turns away accidentally facing THEOPHILUS.

AGATHA   (*to THEO*) Hello.

THEO   Oh hi.

AGATHA   I'm Agatha.

THEO   I know that. (*pause*) Congratulations.

AGATHA   Thank you. Very much.

THEO   You welcome.

AGATHA   That's alright.

THEO   You come out for some fresh air?

AGATHA   Well, it certainly is crowded in there.

THEO   (*forcing a joke*) Body heat.

AGATHA   Pardon?

THEO   Body heat. They is a very hot people.

AGATHA   (*laughs*) Oh. Yes. They really know how to enjoy themselves.

THEO	For that.
AGATHA	I beg your pardon?
THEO	I say for that, you know, for that.
AGATHA	(*not understanding*) Yes. (*pause*) You have a very peculiar idiom.
THEO	What?
AGATHA	You know, a twist of phrase. A picturesque style. Nothing wrong with it, mind you. Unique.
THEO	For that.
AGATHA	You see? There you go again.
THEO	Yeh?
AGATHA	For that.

> *THEOPHILUS catches on. They both laugh.*

THEO	(*rising*) Oh, sorry. You want to sit down?
AGATHA	Well, OK. (*she sits down*) Why don't you take off your hat?
THEO	(*leaning on his cane*) Oh, the dew, you know. At this hour the dew does fall.
AGATHA	Dew?
THEO	Dew falling. An' I does catch cold very easy.
AGATHA	Prevention better than cure, eh? There is rather a chill in the air. Are you a friend of Henry's?
THEO	Oh excuse me, please. I forget to introduce myself.
AGATHA	You're excused. But any friend of Henry's is a friend of mine. I'm interested in meeting all his friends. Even on the island one day.

> *BOYSIE opens the door. The music blasts. He steps outside and closes the door.*

BOYSIE   Mrs. Agatha Barbara Sellman-White. I see you just meet up with none other than his highness the Bajan High Commissioner to Canada, the Honourable Jefferson Theophilus hyphenated Belle.

AGATHA   Boysie again. Indulging his inimitable sense of humour.

BOYSIE   Humour? What happen to you, madam? Henry don't have joke friends in this party. They might look like joke friends, but this is people of quality, child. What you say, your honour?

> *THEOPHILUS cracks a small smile but does not answer. SAGABOY, outside on the lawn, begins to cough.*

Ay, Sagaboy, don't full up my yard with a whole set o' Trinidad spit. Eh.

SAGABOY   Ay Boysie boy, you have any Kleenex, man?

BOYSIE   Kleenex for what, man? I hope all you guys not doing' no rudeness in my backyard, you.

AGATHA   (*reaching in her purse*) I've got some.

BOYSIE   (*takes it and throws it to SAGABOY*) Here. Alright folks, time to stop the music.

> *The window is opened. There is a terrible scratch as someone removes the record. BOYSIE rushes to the window.*

(*yelling*) Jesus effin' Christ man! That is a diamond needle on that stereo head, man. And I didn't ask nobody to take the record off for me, man. Only I touchin' that set.

> *ESTELLE and DOTS come out from inside. ESTELLE goes to SAGABOY, DOTS to her husband, BOYSIE.*

ESTELLE   You alright?

SAGABOY   Yeh, man.

ESTELLE   I keep tellin' you to stay out of the cold air. At least sit down on the step.

DOTS   What happen to the set? Boysie? Now look how the fete spoil.

BOYSIE   It not spoil. Ay, who touch something here, man?

BOYSIE fiddles around with the knobs.

DOTS   Be-Jesus Christ! The damn thing hardly half-day from Eaton's and it done spoil already.

BOYSIE   I telling you it not spoil, woman. Is one o' these knobs here somebody turn by mistake or something.

HENRY   Listen, but look at knobs on that bloody set, boy.

DOTS   Fifty-five dollars and twenty-five cents a month, and I really don't know where the money comin' from to pay for it. But dat set there is high-fidelity and stereophonic too, so nothing don't better go wrong with it now.

HENRY   Knobs like hell, boy.

DOTS   And what happen to you, you can't dance with your wife?

HENRY   What?

DOTS   I say you should be dancing with your wife, Henry.

BOYSIE   Yes. What kind o' thing you getting on with, man?

HENRY   So what, man? This is my last night to be free, honey.

DOTS   Honey? Is only one honey-pot you have now, brother-man. So you better careful where you dipping your finger. And besides, you not free no more. The knot do tie for better *and* for worse. (*BOYSIE cracks an extended high-pitched laugh*) So you better give the girl a good time for her wedding. And what you laughing about?

BOYSIE   Me? Nutten.

DOTS   A person can only get married one time. Even if we divorce and marry a second time, the second time don't seem to be like the first time! So the first time is the time. And that is my philosophy. So all you get that ting fix, and you dance with you wife. (*She moves over to ESTELLE and SAGABOY*) You alright, Sagaboy? He OK, Estelle?

ESTELLE   He has a slight fresh cold, tha's all. I even tell him he should have stay home, you know.

THEO   That look like consumption.

DOTS   (*Not paying attention to the comment*) Well bring him inside. The chill is not too good for him.

ESTELLE   You will come inside, Sagaboy? Dots say you should come inside, you know.

SAGABOY   Nah, man. Is OK. (*he coughs again and spits*)

THEO   That spit look too red for just a ordinary fresh cold.

ESTELLE   (*Turning on THEOPHILUS*) And who ask you, Doctor Theophilus?

THEO   (*turning to AGATHA*) I have a lot of friends who is doctors. You know back home a doctor is a lord and king and you can't even say good morning or good evening to them without fraiding.

AGATHA   Really?

THEO   Yes. Really in truth.

AGATHA   Well I guess it's because there are so few of them. But I don't see any reason to fear a doctor.

THEO   But look at here now in this country. I have no fear of any doctors. For that matter a lot of them come to my parties when I invite them. Even some who I don't invite comes with other friends.

SAGABOY   You know I never even as much had a blasted headache before I come to this damn god-forsaken Canada.

THEO   And from what I learn listening to my doctor friends, that what we have there ain't no ordinary fresh cold. That is sure consumption. That is death he playing with.

AGATHA   Well I suppose he ought to have it checked out, yes. But then *he* ought to know how serious it is.

THEO   Maybe he is afraid.

AGATHA   Of what?

THEO   Maybe he still fraid the doctor.

SAGABOY   (*halfway up the stairs, he turns and says quietly*) Theophilus, why you don't shut up your arse?

Pause. Then SAGABOY continues inside.

AGATHA   (*embarrassed*) Well I suppose you were only trying to help.

THEO   I was only trying to help. These people don't understand when somebody trying to help them out.

AGATHA   Maybe he *is* afraid of the doctor.

THEO   That all I saying.

BOYSIE   Hear me nuh, Sagaboy. You have a little experience in this kind of thing, man. Come and check it out, man.

ESTELLE   But in truth! And you say you used to be a electrician in Trinidad? He should know something about stereo and that sort of thing.

SAGABOY   I only have a little experience in this you know, man. But I will see. What is the power of this amp, man?

BOYSIE   What you asking me, man?

SAGABOY   Well that is a forty watt, making it twenty per channel. And them speakers looking about twenty to twenty-five. So you can't have blown a speaker. Jesus, Boysie man!

BOYSIE   What happen?

SAGABOY   How much thing you have plug in this one plug, man?

BOYSIE   How you mean?

SAGABOY   You overloading the circuit, man. You could start a fire.

BOYSIE   You think we was playing it too loud?

SAGABOY   You could blow a weaker speaker that way. But a fuse could blow in the amp if you plug too overloaded. You have any extra fuse?

BOYSIE   I don't think so. Dots, we have any extra fuse?

DOTS   Me? How I must know?

SAGABOY   Wait. (*he begins to check behind the amplifier*) And try and get a screwdriver for me.

BOYSIE   Dots.

DOTS   (*as she looks*) These man and them never know where anything is.

HENRY   But Sagaboy, you is a boss, man!

DOTS returns with a screwdriver.

AGATHA   It's an old colonial fear that still lingers on.

THEO   Sorry, what you say?

AGATHA   I imagine the doctors in your country are all white?

THEO   Not all.

AGATHA   Well, at the beginning anyway. And the deep awe and respect you developed for the white man in authority because of his power and also his misuse of power is something that is very difficult to eradicate in the native. Wouldn't you say?

THEO   Well, yes, in a way.

AGATHA   Have you read Fanon?

THEO   What?

AGATHA   Fanon. Have you read Fanon.

THEO   Yes, I think so. Who write that?

AGATHA   Well, Fanon was a psychiatrist who was working with the French army in Algeria, and he wrote a number of studies on colonialism as he experienced it in Africa and the Caribbean. He was born in Martinique. He died of cancer.

THEO   Yes, now take cancer. That is a very serious disease. And it does kill people a lot of times. You know anybody who had that?

AGATHA   No. Not really.

THEO   Well mostly people who have it don't live.

AGATHA   I know. And in this...

THEO   That is why my doctor friend was telling me that is important that people don't 'fraid to go to the doctor when they feel some pain anywhere in any part of their body.

AGATHA   So Fanon wrote about the way French doctors treated the
          native Algerian patients. And he observed that they instilled
          and perpetuated in their patients a distinct childlike response
          which always developed into acute inferiority complexes. So
          much so that these patients were often convinced that they
          could do nothing on their own.

THEO   Yes, I see.

AGATHA   And in this helplessness, created and perpetuated by the
          white man, they would develop a childlike dependence
          which was both taken advantage of and scoffed at by the
          European. And the white man became a dreaded father-fig-
          ure. A surrogate to be respected and feared.

SAGABOY   You blow a fuse, man.

BOYSIE   It goin' to be alright?

SAGABOY   Yes. You have extra fuse in the back.

BOYSIE   It will work?

SAGABOY   Yeh, man. No problem.

BOYSIE   (*shouting*) Oh, Goooooawd! Awright, awright, awright!

AGATHA   Oh, I guess the set's OK now.

THEO   I know nothing serious was wrong. These tings is under a
          guarantee, you now.

AGATHA   Oh, sure.

THEO   It has a form to fill out and send back.

AGATHA   Henry!

HENRY   Yes. What happen?

AGATHA   Did Boysie fill out his guarantee form? It's safe to do that
          right away.

BOYSIE   What is that?

HENRY   She want to know if you fill out a guarantee form.

BOYSIE   For what? And we have Sagaboy right here? Man, look, let we play the damn thing for today and enjoy it, you hear, and then see what happen. We don't have no time to think 'bout guarantee now. Is fete!

AGATHA   Still, you know. He should.

HENRY   You have something to drink?

AGATHA   Let's dance.

HENRY   What?

AGATHA   Can't we dance?

HENRY   Boysie was going to make another speech.

BOYSIE   Tha's alright, man. Ay, Sagaboy, play out a whole tune to make sure the damn thing workin', man. I could wait.

> *SAGABOY puts on a fast calypso beat. BOYSIE begins a wild gyration by himself. AGATHA holds on to HENRY and tries the dance with middling but slightly ridiculous results. The tune plays for a minute until HENRY detaches himself from AGATHA and turns to BOYSIE.*

AGATHA   What's the matter?

HENRY   Nothing ain't wrong. You see something wrong? (*shouting*) Ay Boysie! You can't put on something soft and slow, man?

BOYSIE   Stop the music, stop the music! (*SAGABOY takes off the record*) What it is you say, man?

HENRY   A nice cosy tune, man. Quiet and loving.

BOYSIE   Quiet and loving for quiet lovers, ladies and gentlemen. Sagaboy know just the tune for that. Sagaboy, you heard the request, fulfill it for the newlyweds.

HENRY   (*to AGATHA*) Come inside dear.

> *The tune starts and HENRY and AGATHA dance inside. They do a slow one-two step.*

DOTS   After all it's the girl wedding and she should have a good time like everybody else.

ESTELLE   But you know, she make a really stunning bride as they say.

DOTS	Girl, I really couldn't bear the thought that she would have to sit down all by she lonesome self on the she side of the church. You would think that even if her friends wouldn't come at least her blasted mother or father would at least show their face through a window even.
ESTELLE	I mean, even if they was so vex, at least they could come and sit down their vex self, just to be there.
DOTS	Estelle girl, you new in this country, and you have a lot to learn if you see you immigration come through. What you seeing here and witnessing is the way o' white people. They would kill their flesh and blood just to prove a blasted point.
ESTELLE	It is sad, though.
THEO	Everybody entitled to his own opinion.
DOTS	What he say?
ESTELLE	He just want to enter the conversation.
DOTS	What you said there, Theophilus?
THEO	They is two people who have to live their own life. And if their parents choose not to come to the wedding, that not suppose to change things.
DOTS	Yes? You think that girl feel good that not a single one of her people didn't even turn up to bless this union?
THEO	It bless by God. You want more than that?
DOTS	Well you probably living in this place too long to remember that you have any mother and father at all; but that is one thing I will always have sticking in this craw o' mine. I will never forsake my children, if you see God see it right to bless me with any. And I will never forget the mother and father who bring me into this world and give me life. Never.
THEO	I didn't say nothing about to forget your parents.
DOTS	You will tell me it's not a shame, a great burning shame that that bastard, Agatha's father, thinks he is too great and too proud to come and witness his own daughter on her wedding day? Eh? A person does only have one wedding day in her life and that bastard didn't even come. *He did not come.*

ESTELLE   They love one another, though, Henry and Agatha. And they won't be living at the parents anyway.

BOYSIE   Not Henry, man. Not he. I know Henry, and if it's one thing, Henry won't low-rate himself to go and live in somebody else house, even if they is his own in-laws.

THEO   If it come to that, I don't see why he can't put away his false pride and live there for a while.

SAGABOY   False pride! You call that false pride? What you know about pride, dress up in you damn stupid monkey suit looking like a red-arse 'rangutan?

BOYSIE   Hey, all you take it easy, man! We makin' love tonight, brother man, not war!

THEO   Is OK, I know jealousy when I see it.

SAGABOY   What jealousy? I Jealous o' you? I don't want no blasted house in Rosedale and big shiny Cadillac and up to my arse-hole eyebrow in debt. You think 'is that I want from this country?

THEO   I work hard and save my money to buy what I have.

DOTS   And what it get you? When last you ever think of writing even a little postcard to you mother home?

BOYSIE   Dots, that is not your business, man.

DOTS   How you reach here tonight, anyway? I didn't know you to be hanging out with the likes of people like us anymore since you move up to a sophisticated property owner in high-class district. Eh? (*THEO does not respond*) One thing I will never do is sell my soul to gain the world. You think I will ever take my old father or mother and put them away in some old people home for other people to clean their shit and curse them under their breath? Just because I decide that they getting in my way in the house and coming a nuisance? When my parents could ever become a nuisance to me? (*to ESTELLE*) Ay, girl, you well perspiring. It running down you arm and dress.

ESTELLE   Yeh? Oh shucks, you right. Lend me your deodorant, please.

DOTS   Wipe it off first with you kerchief. Boysie, hand me my purse from under the stereo nuh boy. Give me the Ban deodorant.

ESTELLE   So what happen? 'Is only under my arm, you know. I don't
                 know for the rest.

BOYSIE   (*adopting a stance as in a T.V. ad*) If it could work for a nigger,
                 think what it could do for *you*. (*turning his head in THEO's
                 direction*) What you say, your honour?

                         They laugh. THEO remains unmoved.

ESTELLE   (*spraying herself*) Anybody watching? It's the heat in there
                 you know, girl.

BOYSIE   While you at it, put some down there too, man.

DOTS   What happen to you? You want to see free show? Boy, look,
                 shut you rude mouth, eh.

BOYSIE   Is nothing I never see before.

DOTS   Boy, get lost please.

                         *BOYSIE spins around a couple of times to the music making
                         some mildly obscene gestures with his hips. THEO sighs in dis-
                         gust. The music stops.*

BOYSIE   OK! Alright! Sagaboy, just gently remove the disc from that
                 turntable and switch she off. How the lovers doin'?

SAGABOY   (*with a slight cough*) Them doin' real fine, man.

                         *HENRY and AGATHA can be seen separating inside.
                         AGATHA resumes her seat inside the glass door and HENRY
                         walks in the opposite direction toward the record player. He
                         doesn't take her to her seat. He just disengages himself and
                         walks off.*

BOYSIE   (*to HENRY*) Everything OK, bossman?

HENRY   Yeh.

BOYSIE   OK, brethren, speech time and toast time! Dots, pass out the
                 glasses and Henry, open the bottle. (*to someone inside*) Listen
                 man, how you expect to drink a toast with a big fat chicken
                 leg in your blasted mouth, man?

DOTS   (*going toward the kitchen*) I will put all the glasses on a waiter,
                 full them up, and then just pass around so everybody could
                 take a full glass.

BOYSIE	Start opening the bottles, Henry!
DOTS	Who eating already?
THEO	I think that is a better idea.
ESTELLE	What you say?
THEO	It's a good idea to pass the full glasses around.
ESTELLE	Well, that is what Dots say, the very thing she just say. You don't hear?
THEO	I just agree, that is all.
DOTS	(*yelling*) Who tell people to eat, man? Who give anybody permission to eat yet?
BOYSIE	What happen?
DOTS	Somebody already stick their stinkin' hand inside the pot o' food. A' mean, people can't wait, man? I don't like this blasted niggerishness, man!
BOYSIE	Well, OK, alright, Dots.
DOTS	How you mean. "OK. Alright Dots"? It not OK alright! Somebody dying of starvation in this fete? Everybody suppose to eat at the same time. People don't have a little bit o' trainin' even? That is all the conduct they learn to conduct theyself in the people country? And it look like they didn't even use a spoon even. An' leave the damn pot open and all.

> *HENRY pops the cork. It strikes the ceiling and the froth flows over. A joyous commotion. DOTS continues to grumble while she lays out the glasses. BOYSIE is trying to calm her. Now and then she raises her voice at him. She enjoys this expression of decorum. BOYSIE enjoys calming her. They pour out the drinks.*

THEO	You take a pig from out the mud, you bathes it clean, you powder it and perfumes it under it four arms, you dress it up, put lipstick and rouge on it and then let it go. You know what it do? (*ESTELLE looks at him with a serious face and he looks away*) It will run straight back in the mud. (*he pauses*) You could take the pig from out the mud. But you could never take the mud from out the pig.

DOTS   The next ting you know them niggers eat out all the meat and
            leave bare rice in the damn pot!

ESTELLE   You is a philosopher, too?

THEO   (*begins to lose his affected accent*) You and Sagaboy lookin'
            thick.

ESTELLE   Yeh?

THEO   I fin' so.

ESTELLE   And what is that to you?

THEO   I just observing.

ESTELLE   So observe.

THEO   You know what you doin'?

ESTELLE   Since when you so concerned?

THEO   You know I always concerned 'bout you.

ESTELLE   Tha's why you come here tonight?

THEO   In a sense, yes.

ESTELLE   Oh.

THEO   You deserve better, a woman like you.

ESTELLE   What you mean? Better than what?

THEO   You know what I mean.

ESTELLE   No, I don't know what you mean. What you mean?

THEO   You well know.

ESTELLE   You mean a big house in Rosedale and fancy car?

THEO   (*sitting beside her on the steps*) Why you don't come with me,
            Estie?

ESTELLE   (*taking a quick glance toward SAGABOY*) Estie? What is this
            Estie all about?

BOYSIE   (*inside*) Open a next bottle. Sagaboy, you take the first tray 'round. And no coughing over them glass. Go to the bride first. You have that honour, for fixing the stereo.

THEO   (*a little anxious*) I have my immigrant status. You don't have to go and beg no immigration officer for nothing. You don't have to low-rate youself in front o' them for nutten. Sagaboy is not no immigrant. Even if he tell you so, he lyin' to you. And that T.B. or consumption that he have, how long you think he will last with that in this cold country? He don't have nothing to offer you, darling.

ESTELLE   Be-Jesus Christ! What I all on a sudden deserve to get all this darling talk, lord?

THEO   Don't mock me like the rest o' dem, Estelle.

ESTELLE   Mock you? Mr. Theophilus, when I first come to this country with the little bit o' money in my pocket and you tell me you was catching your royal, I didn't find it outa my place to spend the little scratch I had so we could have a little good time together. Everybody here know what happen to dat. Everybody! From then on I learn never to trust a Wessindian man further than where you could always keep a eye on his drawers.

THEO   All dat change now. You have to forgive and forget.

ESTELLE   And all this time you savin' up your money without tellin' me a single word. Forget? When I was beginning to catch my tail and I couldn't even land a stinking little domestic job to redeem my soul, which I still fighting to get, that time you did well know how to forget. You out of all the people I know is a expert on how to forget. So you could tell me. Well I forget now, you see. I damn well forget.

THEO   And what make Sagaboy so different?

ESTELLE   You just don't allow Sagaboy to worry your soul, you hear?

THEO   I need you, Estelle.

ESTELLE   Need me? Sure you need me. You need me to full up you empty house in Rosedale. To cook you food and be *your* domestic.

So why you don't do that in truth?

THEO   Do what?

ESTELLE   Employ me as a domestic if you is this big Canadian immi-
              grant, and pay me minimum wage even. I will do the same
              job.

THEO   That is not what I want Estelle.

ESTELLE   What you want any black monkey could get on Yonge Street
              or in any old disco club downtown.

              *Another cork pops. Commotion. THEOPHILUS takes advan-
              tage of the distraction. He gets close to ESTELLE and places
              his hand on her leg.*

THEO   Estelle, I really love you bad bad.

              *Estelle takes a quick look around. Then she looks him in the
              eyes. A brief contact. She can almost yield to his honesty.
              SAGABOY appears behind them with a tray of drinks. He
              stops, looking at them, himself unseen, ESTELLE breaks the
              contact with a short laugh.*

ESTELLE   Look man, Theophilus man, behave yourself, you hear.

              *SAGABOY clears his throat and advances. Without looking
              around THEOPHILUS gets up and resumes his previous stand-
              ing position. SAGABOY approaches him with the drinks.*

SAGABOY   To toast the newlyweds. (*THEOPHILUS takes a glass*) Well
              take one for the lady too, Mr. Gentleman.

              *THEO takes a glass and hands it to ESTELLE. She takes it
              over her shoulder, smiling. SAGABOY waits, looking at
              THEO. THEO looks questioningly at SAGABOY.*

              Well. Sample it. See if it good enough for you.

THEO   (*sips the drink*) Very good.

SAGABOY   What year?

THEO   What?

SAGABOY   Is it a good year?

THEO   A very good year.

SAGABOY   You sure about that? We don't want to displease your well-
              cultured taste, you know.

THEO	It is fine for the occasion.
SAGABOY	What brand would you say it was? Ah mean is it compara- ble, as they say, to the type you would serve at your little soirées in Rosedale?
THEO	Champagne is champagne.
SAGABOY	Well that might be so, your honour. But what you have in your hand there is none other than well brewed, long-stand- ing *ginger ale*, you jackass! (*SAGABOY turns to leave*)
THEO	You think–
SAGABOY	(*turning back*) What?
THEO	You think I don't know ginger ale from champagne. Eh? What you take me for?
SAGABOY	I just tell you. Or you deaf too?
THEO	You think 'is right to treat some things light? You think everything is a big joke?
SAGABOY	*You* is the big joke, Jefferson Theophilus Belle, *you!*
THEO	A man wedding is a holy and sacred thing. You don't joke around with ginger ale.
SAGABOY	So what you want?
THEO	You think it is a big thing for me to bring a bottle of cham- pagne to do things in a proper way?
BOYSIE	(*approaching*) What goin' on here, man? All you holdin' up the ceremonies, man.
SAGABOY	This man think you should have real champagne to do thing proper. He find it tastin' like ginger ale.
BOYSIE	What does go wrong with black people sometime, man? Look, we in Canada at a Canadian wedding, one of the party is a full-fledge Canadian and 'is a Canadian ceremony bless in a full-fledge Canadian church. So, 'is only right and proper to use genuine Canadian champagne. So what else you want? You want to toast the bride and bridegroom with more ol' stinkin' Barbados Mount Gay run? You ever hear people does toast a ceremony with rum?

THEO   I didn't say anything man.

BOYSIE   And how the man tell me you say the champagne tastin' like
                 ginger ale? You didn't hear the bottle pop? (*THEO does not
                 respond*) What happen now? You drunk? Jesus, man!
                 (*BOYSIE goes back to the kitchen window*) Everybody have a
                 glass? We could begin?

DOTS   What happen with Theophilus?

BOYSIE   How I must know what happen with he, man? The blasted
                 cork pop like a damn cannon and nearly lick off the kiss me
                 ass ceiling of the apartment; the bottle froth over and nearly
                 drown every body in the bloody kitchen. What else you want
                 after all that?

DOTS   (*goes to ESTELLE*) You alright, girl?

ESTELLE   You hear a bell ringing?

DOTS   Bell? What kind of bell?

ESTELLE   You know. Like a big bell?

DOTS   I didn't hear no bell.

THEO   I think it's getting late for me.

DOTS   You leaving, Theophilus Belle?

THEO   I think 'is better for me to go.

DOTS   Somebody chasing you away?

                 THEO does not answer.

ESTELLE   Nobody asking you to leave.

THEO   I know that.

DOTS   So why you leaving?

THEO   I think 'is better.

DOTS   You think 'is better. Better than what? You do something
                 wrong?

THEO   I don't think so.

DOTS   Somebody do you something? Or you missing your big-shot friends?

THEO   (*quietly*) Big-shot friends!

DOTS   You know it's not a good sign to hear bell ringing just like that.

AGATHA   (*who has come through the door*) You don't want to leave now, do you?

THEO   Well, I sorry, but you know how it is.

DOTS   Nobody di'n askin' him to go, you know.

AGATHA   Come on, the fun is only just beginning. You can't leave now.

ESTELLE   'Is probably nothing, you know.

DOTS   But nobody else didn't hear nothing. (*to the others*) Anybody hear any bell ringing?

SAGABOY   What?

DOTS   All you hear any bell ringing?

SAGABOY   Bell? Nah, Nobody hear any bell out here. Is must be the music.

ESTELLE   No music was playing at the time. You know, it was like it come from the sky, from high up.

SAGABOY   Who hear bell?

DOTS   Estelle.

SAGABOY   You know Estelle, she crazy like hell.

ESTELLE   You shut your mouth, Sagaboy.

SAGABOY   (*in good humour*) I know. she was sitting down so close to his majesty there, she probably hear Theophilus Belle ringing.

Laughter in the back.

THEO   You see what I mean?

AGATHA	Come on Theophilus, they are just having some good fun. They don't mean any harm. What's this thing about bells, anyway?
THEO	You don't know we people and the way we behave.
DOTS	Estelle say she hear bells ringing and nobody else hear anything.
AGATHA	Is it supposed to mean something?
BOYSIE	(*inside*) Look, if all you prefer, all you could spread out on the balcony.
THEO	Superstition.
DOTS	Call it what you want, but when you see people dead, some gifted people does get signs.
ESTELLE	Look here, chile, don't say things like that, nuh. You get me frighten right away, I would want to go and make a long distance call to the West Indies now now self.
BOYSIE	I could talk from right here so if people still inside they could hear me as well as the ones outside.
SAGABOY	(*who is now listening to DOTS and others*) Huh! Since when all you have telephone in all you house too?
ESTELLE	What happen to you, boy? Don't take people as they look in this country, nuh. Because all you see me desperate trying to get my status and land a job, don't feel I didn't come from a comfortable family at home.
SAGABOY	I only joke, Estelle.
DOTS	Well, some other people around here I know think them is the only one with some class. So you have to make it clear to them.
ESTELLE	And for their information, you might see me trying to get a job servanting after people who don't know how to treat you as a human being, but I know when I was home I always had a maid to bring me a cup o' tea when I want any time o' day or night.
THEO	So why you don't return back then?

ESTELLE	Because I have ambition and I wouldn't step on other people to climb and satisfy myself alone.
THEO	That didn't answer the question.
SAGABOY	And who is you that she must answer your questions?
THEO	Goodbye, Agatha... I mean Mrs. White, good luck.
AGATHA	Look, it's only a friendly discussion. You take these people too seriously for your own good.
DOTS	He looking for somebody to beg him to stay.
BOYSIE	Ok? Where Henry? Henry, sit next to your bride, and we shall begin. Theophilus, you not goin' anywhere now, so just sit your backside down and listen and sip you ginger ale like a gentleman.
	The guests arrange themselves conveniently while BOYSIE begins his speech. HENRY sits beside AGATHA. THEO is on one side of her.
BOYSIE	OK OK ladies and gentlemen to use the phraseology in a general loose manner! Ladies and gentlemen too! Greetings and salutations, because on this most auspicious of evenings, on the aurora of long and felicitous matrimony, I say to you, ladies and gentlemen, I say *ecce homo*, behold the man! *Ecce homo*, here I stand! *(there is general acknowledgment, laughter, and compliments while AGATHA laughs with a growing intoxication)* I say to you, ladies and gentlemen. *(laughter and talk)* I say to you! I say, I say to you!
DOTS	People have some manners please. The man still talking. Quiet! Quiet!
	The noise dies down.
BOYSIE	I say to you, ladies and gentlemen I say to you, I say...
SAGABOY	Oh God, man, how you takin' so long?
DOTS	Because he is a man like that.
SAGABOY	Henry, take note!
AGATHA	Oh, I have nothing to fear in that department, you can rest assured. *(laughter)* By, I could have another wedding reception like this tomorrow.

HENRY	Don't tempt Fate!
BOYSIE	I say *ecce homo,* behold the man! *Ecce homo,* here I stand!
AGATHA	(*to HENRY*) What did you mean by that, darling?
HENRY	Listen to the man, nuh!
BOYSIE	Here I stand, ladies and gentlemen, with a glass–
SAGABOY	Ay, Dots is a lucky woman, you know. How Boysie like to stand so!?

Laughter.

ESTELLE	All you don't have no appreciation for language at all?
BOYSIE	Alright! Alright! Here I stand with a glass of drink in my hand, wherewithal, I say, wherewithal for to mitigate the aridity of my thirst. (*appreciative sounds*) and as I have arisen from my esteemed seat this fifth time, and as I have quoth to you, *bon swarr* my dear Agatha, good evening Henry, yu lucky old Bajan bastard you! (*loud appreciation*) Ladies and gentlemen, a toast to the meeting of the continents! (*laughter and toasting*) To the virginal, so it speak, angelic Agatha, and to Henry with his specially prepared for the occasion Afro hairdo!
AGATHA	I'll drink to that! (*to THEO*) Don't you think he looks Afro-Canadian! He looks Afro-Canadian!
HENRY	Carry on you speech, man, Boysie.
AGATHA	Come on, I can say something too.
BOYSIE	You have my gracious permission, ma'am!
AGATHA	A toast to my loving husband, the most handsome African! (*noise, raised glasses*) The man with the inimitable grace of a Watusi warrior!

Uproar.

HENRY	(*protesting as he rises*) Look, come now! I ain't no blasted Watusi warrior!
ALL	Watusi! Watusi! Henry the Watusi!
AGATHA	(*raising her glass, slightly tipsy*) Watusi! Watusi!

HENRY grabs her hand with the glass, spilling her drink.

HENRY   (*yelling*) Stop this shit man! I ain't making no joke! I ain't no bloody Watusi! I don't even know what a bloody Watusi is!

The crowd settles suddenly into an embarrassed silence.

AGATHA   Henry, dear, don't spoil a fine evening!

BOYSIE   Come on, Henry, take it easy, man, have a drink!

HENRY   I didn't come from Africa! I ain't no damn African!

THEO   You don't despite your roots, man!

HENRY   If anything I am a damn Canadian for whatever that worth. What is that, Theophilus, sir?

THEO   Your roots is African.

HENRY   Look, you might come from some tribe in some jungle, and you might just have some kind o'long tail roll up and hidin' in that fancy pants you wearing, but not me, you hear, I sure as hell don't come from *there*!

THEO   And what so wrong with *there*?

AGATHA   Please Henry, why do you always have to take it as an insult when people call you an African?

HENRY   (*yelling*) Because I is not a African, I am a blasted Bajan! You don't understand that?

DOTS   Estelle, see if you get a old piece o' cloth to mop up the drink. Come Agatha, let me see if you dress get wet. The girl wearing such a nice dress, Henry, the least you should have is a little respect for people clothes, man. (*she takes AGATHA aside*)

BOYSIE   You too damn sensitive you know Henry. A mean you is me good pardner and everything, but don't be so serious tonight, man, not tonight of all nights, man.

ESTELLE   (*who has returned to mop the floor*) You lucky to married a good, educated girl like Agatha, Henry, so treat the woman good, for goodness sake. And don't get on like some uncivilized animal and let people down.

HENRY   Uncivilized animal! You know that woman does call me a beast, a black fuckin' beast and swear to God is a compliment she payin' me?

ESTELLE   The woman love you, Henry. Look at all the trouble she going' through just for you. All the embarrassment in the church and everything just for you. You will tell me that is not love?

HENRY   I ain't questioning that.

ESTELLE   So that is how man does express their love? By humiliating people like that?

BOYSIE   (*in good humour*) So Agatha call you a beast, Henry?

ESTELLE   She have a right! Look at the kind of language he using as well.

HENRY   The woman say she actually love me because of that.

BOYSIE   Because you is a beast!

HENRY   Because I am a big black beautiful black beast! You don't see something wrong with this woman?

BOYSIE   But Henry, how you so stupid man! That is good!

HENRY   She love you for what you are, Henry.

HENRY   She even say that if I was lighter in complexion, like Harry Belafonte, she wouldn't love me so much.

ESTELLE   The truth of the matter is that the poor girl love you. What else you want?

BOYSIE   (*enjoying all this*) Henry the Watusi! You know that have a nice sound to it.

HENRY   Come on, man, Boysie, man!

BOYSIE   You could open up a soul food restaurant and out in front in lights big "WATUSI"! And you is the usher, Henry, in leopard-skin loin cloth and a necklace o' teeth and you big lip and thick thick Afro.

HENRY   That's exactly what she tell me too, man.

BOYSIE   What? To open a restaurant?

HENRY   No, man. That she love me because of my thick woolly hair and me thick purple lips. You see my lip purple, man?

BOYSIE   You could get purple lipstick, man; and you stand up there and welcome you guests with a big Colgate or Crest smile! And you could have a floor show on Saturday night. But even so, people not comin' to eat or to see you show as they want to tell their friends, 'I goin' to Watusi tonight, man!" If you want to know wha' tuh see go to the WATUSI!

HENRY   I have fuckin' purple lip!

BOYSIE   You will make a killing, man! Bring your beauty to the Watusi! Take your beauty to the beast! Jesus Christ, Henry!

ESTELLE   (*leaving*) Anyway, watch your language young man. Sagaboy, go and start some music instead of sitting down there and grinning. And Henry, you better go and tell your wife you sorry.

HENRY   Why I must be sorry? I does ever call she a damn Jew or Hebrew? Dots ever call you a damn black beautiful black beast?

BOYSIE   But Dots black like me, Henry you beast.

HENRY   You is a beast too, man. If I is a beast, you is a beast too.

BOYSIE   Man, Henry, you is one first, man! Your wife call you one first! Come on, man, go and kiss and make up. You can't sit down here and sulk, man.

     SAGABOY has started the music.

HENRY   Yeh, awright, but gimme a li'l break first.

BOYSIE   Go on now, man. You killin' the fete. We need a beast in there.

HENRY   I suppose you right.

BOYSIE   I ever wrong, man?

HENRY   Anyway, what about the little German thing, man? You still screwin' it?

BOYSIE   You ain't the only beautiful black beast in this bloody place you know! Come on.

They go inside. HENRY goes to AGATHA and holds her close to dance. Applause.

Ladies and gentlemen, a toast to Beauty and the Beast!

Applause. Glasses emptied. Music.

BOYSIE   OK, folks. Fete down the line! Dots, close the window and let us get *cosy*, man!

DOTS closes the window and then comes to close the door stage right. She notices Theophilus still outside.

DOTS   What is wrong with you? The party not good enough for you?

THEO   I didn't say so.

DOTS   You don't have to say so. What you still doing outside?

THEO   Don't worry about me.

DOTS   Well it don't look too proper, everybody inside and you alone like a jumbie keepin' guard. You want a drink?

THEO   I have a drink, thank you.

DOTS   You welcome. (*she waits a couple of seconds*) Well you comin' in or not?

A policeman appears to the right of the garden.

THEO   In a few minutes.

DOTS   Well, suit yourself.

She goes in and closes the door. THEO takes a couple of steps down to the garden then brushing the step carefully with this hands, he takes out a handkerchief, spreads it out on the steps and is about to sit when the policeman approaches. Surprised, THEO jumps up.

THEO   Wha' you want?

POLICE-MAN   Are you the occupant?

THEO   Wha'?

POLICE-MAN	Are you the occupant, sir?
THEO	I name Jefferson Theophilius Belle, sir.
POLICE-MAN	Do you live here?
THEO	I live in Rosedale, sir. I have a card with my address on it right here. (*he reaches in his pocket*)
POLICE-MAN	Don't reach in your pocket!
THEO	What, sir?
POLICE-MAN	(*shouting*) I said don't reach in your pocket!
THEO	Yes, sir. I was only goin' to show you my–
POLICE-MAN	Never mind that! I can get what I want if I want to. I didn't ask you for anything. Now did I?
THEO	No, sir.
POLICE-MAN	All right! Now let's start again, shall we?
THEO	I don't live here, sir.
POLICE-MAN	Who does?
THEO	I beg your pardon, sir?
POLICE-MAN	Do you belong to the party going on inside there?
THEO	Well, in a sense–
POLICE-MAN	Answer the question please!
THEO	Sir?
POLICE-MAN	Are you with that party going on inside?

THEO	Not really, sir.
POLICE-MAN	And you said you don't live here?
THEO	No, sir.
POLICE-MAN	You just told me you live in Rosedale.
THEO	Yes, sir.
POLICE-MAN	So what are you doing here at this time of the night?
THEO	Well, in fact sir–
POLICE-MAN	You are a prowler!
THEO	In fact, sir–
POLICE-MAN	Take off your jacket!
THEO	Sir?
POLICE-MAN	(*shouting*) Take off your jacket! And your hat!
THEO	Yes, sir.
POLICE-MAN	Slowly!
THEO	Yes, sir. (*he begins to take off his jacket*) I is not a criminal, sir. I have not done nothing to nobody.
POLICE-MAN	Shut up! Empty the pockets on the steps! Your pants too!
THEO	Take if off, sir?
POLICE-MAN	(*looks at him briefly with arrogance*) Don't be stupid. Just empty the pockets. OK, turn around!
THEO	Sir?

POLICE-MAN	Are you dumb? Turn! (*the policeman roughly spread eagles THEO against the banister, frisks him and then begins to check his wallet*) Stay there! You own a car?
THEO	Yes, sir, the new car that park up next–
POLICE-MAN	So you really live in Rosedale?
THEO	Yes, sir.
POLICE-MAN	What is your occupation?
THEO	Engineer, sir.
POLICE-MAN	Yes? Where do you "engineer"?
THEO	City engineer, sir.
POLICE-MAN	Who do you work for?
THEO	The city, sir
POLICE-MAN	You haven't told me what you are in fact doing here.
THEO	I really with the party, sir.
POLICE-MAN	You sure about that?
THEO	I sure about that, sir.
POLICE-MAN	OK, relax.
THEO	What, sir?
POLICE-MAN	You could turn around now and put back on your jacket.
THEO	(*turning and taking his jacket*) Thank you sir.
POLICE-MAN	So who is the occupant?

THEO   Sir?

**POLICE-
MAN**   (*shouting*) Who lives here?

THEO   Boysie and Dots, sir

**POLICE-
MAN**   Boysie and Dots?

THEO   Yes, sir. You know them, sir? Is nice people. Well, they never do me nothing, sir.

**POLICE-
MAN**   Who is Dots?

THEO   That is Boysie wife, sir.

**POLICE-
MAN**   OK – what you say your name was?

THEO   Jefferson Theophi–

**POLICE-
MAN**   OK, Theophilus. I want you to go in there and tell Mr. Boysie that I would like to have a word with him. (*THEO turns to go*) And you come back with him, you hear?

THEO   Yes, sir.

> THEO goes in and comes out immediately followed by BOYSIE.

BOYSIE   Hey, man, take a shot before you leave! Get it? Take a shot! (*He laughs*)

**POLICE-
MAN**   (*he is not amused*) You Boysie?

BOYSIE   Always been and ever will be! So what you say, boss?

**POLICE-
MAN**   You know why I'm here. So don't try to be a wiseguy, OK? (*yelling*) Cut it!

> BOYSIE's expression changes to a grim stare. He stands at the top of the steps quietly and looks at the police officer.

This Mr. Theophilus Belle here belong to your party?
(*BOYSIE nods assent*) OK. Well, break it up soon, all right,
buddy? It's past midnight. We have complaints about the
noise.

BOYSIE   (*almost expressionless, quietly*) We'll turn the music down.

**POLICE-
MAN**   Good boy.

BOYSIE   I ain't a boy.

**POLICE-
MAN**   Pardon me?

BOYSIE   I said I am a big man, I ain't a boy.

**POLICE-
MAN**   Good, then behave like a man, OK?

> *BOYSIE remains quiet. The POLICEMAN turns to go.
> DOTS comes through the door, stage right.*

BOYSIE   You forgetting something.

**POLICE-
MAN**   (*stopping*) What is that?

BOYSIE   Target practice.

**POLICE-
MAN**   Look, I didn't come here for trouble, so I don't want any, OK?
I came to the front and knocked and nobody would answer
the door. Your music is too loud. And besides, the neighbours are complaining that you are keeping them up with
your talking on this back balcony.

BOYSIE   You forget to check, man. I got two arms with me. I even
pointing them at you. (*he extends his arms*) So shoot. Go
ahead and shoot.

**POLICE-
MAN**   Just remember what I said, OK, buddy? If I have to come
back, I'll have to empty your apartment. And you, (*to THEO*)
I'm going to check on you next week.

> *He goes. DOTS, who had entered through the doors had been
> standing just outside them, climbs toward BOYSIE.*

DOTS   And the poor girl just beginning to enjoy herself so much!
                And on her wedding day, man? Jesus Christ, these people is
                savages, man. They damn uncivilized! You mean to tell me
                on the girl's wedding day?

BOYSIE   (*putting his arms around her*) Don't worry. We going to party
                till that son of a bitch come back.

DOTS   But Boysie, how you could do that?

BOYSIE   Well how the hell we could tell people the party done now?
                How we could ask people to leave? Ah mean, how you think
                Agatha would feel? How you think Henry would feel, on his
                wedding night to boot?

DOTS   I know all that, Boysie. But we only just move here and we is
                the one have to face the people when everybody gone.

BOYSIE   So you want me to kick people out?

DOTS   I not saying that. You alone will eat all that food that cook in
                the kitchen there?

BOYSIE   So what you saying then?

DOTS   Turn down the music, Boysie.

BOYSIE   I not goin' to turn down the music, Dots.

DOTS   You don't have a choice. You have to.

BOYSIE   I don't *have to* do anything because some little hunky police
                come and tell me something. You want me to throw on some
                kind o' ovskipovski symphony and have people rockin' to
                sonata in black o' blue o' some kind o' shit so? Not me, man!
                This is a wedding, not any old damn party with beatnik an'
                hippie stick up in dark corner smoking all kind o' shit and
                catching' fits. So I goin' to play my music on my stereo and I
                goin' to play it so I could damn well hear it. Let that hunky
                police come and stop me.

DOTS   At least we could hold up a little bit, Boysie. And we could
                make people sit down and eat, and then start again.

BOYSIE   I don't care what you do now, but I goin' to show them neigh-
                bours something tonight! (*he begins to descend the steps*)

DOTS   (*shouting*) Boysie!

BOYSIE   (*he focuses upstairs, shouting*) All you hear me?

DOTS   (*she follows him quickly, embracing him to keep him quiet*) Come on, Boysie, behave yourself for God sake. You not drunk!

BOYSIE   (*shouting*) I know what it is! Is Saturday night, and some old bitch upstairs can't sleep because she can't find a man. Well watch down here, you ol' bitch. You want man? Look man! Come and get man, you frustrated ol' bitch!

DOTS embraces him closer to keep him quiet. Blackout.

ACT II

An hour later in the morning. The scene is the same except that there is an impression of fewer people. DOTS is moving around collecting used paper plates and glasses. ESTELLE is helping her. BOYSIE is sitting on a chair on the verandah stage left with his feet up on the landing—the picture of contentment after his meal. He plays with his partially bare stomach, but is a bit ruminative. Behind him standing in semi-darkness is the tall dark girl who was dancing with HENRY at the beginning of Act I.

DOTS   All nigger waiting for is food and then they gone. (*to BOYSIE*) What happen to you? You too heavy to raise you tail and help?

HENRY   (*entering hastily from S.R. to BOYSIE*) How Agatha know, man?

BOYSIE   How *you* know?

HENRY   Agatha tell me, man.

BOYSIE   I didn't want *no*body to know in the first place.

HENRY   So how she know, man?

BOYSIE   So what she saying?

HENRY   She want to go home.

BOYSIE   She want to go home?

HENRY   How I could go home now, man? 'Is only two o'clock.

DOTS   The poor girl probably tired you know, Henry. After all it was a long exhausting day for her.

HENRY   You asking me to leave?

DOTS   Don't be stupid now.

BOYSIE   She could take a rest inside if she want.

HENRY   Is not that, man.

BOYSIE (*rising suddenly*) If was some other blasted district in Toronto, no fuckin' cop, rookie or no rookie, woulda' be so stupid as to break up a wedding party because some jackass complain about the noise. That some goddam hunkie cop would think twice, three times even, before he knock on them rich people door.

DOTS Well we is not no rich people, you see. That is life, and we have to see it as life.

AGATHA (*who has entered during DOTS' line*) Let's go home, Henry.

Pause. Nobody speaks. Then.

HENRY Nah, man. I can't do that!

AGATHA And why not?

HENRY How you mean, "and why not?'

AGATHA Let's go home please, dear. (*HENRY sucks his teeth at her*) This is no time for a fight.

HENRY (*turning on her*) Fight? Who fighting, man? I fighting? If I was fighting you won't be standing up there in front of me talking, man. I not fighting.

AGATHA So are you or aren't you?

HENRY What?

AGATHA (*yelling*) Are you or aren't you coming home?

HENRY Hey, look! Let's get one thing straight right here and now please God. Before things go too far in the wrong direction. OK? You are not, I repeat, *not* raising your voice at me in front of my friends, or for that matter, *ever*.

AGATHA OK. I'm sorry, Henry. And I'm truly sorry, Boysie and Dots and others.

DOTS Tha's awright, chile.

AGATHA But I'm tired and we've got a long drive tomorrow, so I'm asking you please to excuse us.

HENRY Who us, man? Who us is being excused?

BOYSIE Henry–

HENRY	No, wait a second, man–
DOTS	Henry, if the girl–
HENRY	No, *wait*! Just give she a little break to reply. Who us?
AGATHA	I already said I refuse to have a fight, Henry.
HENRY	(*shouting*) Who fighting, man? We having a bloody argument! Nobody fighting. How in hell you could call a plain blasted argument fighting?
AGATHA	Alright, it's not a fight, I'm sorry. I'm merely asking you to come home.
HENRY	Why?
AGATHA	I already said why.
HENRY	Say it again for everybody here. Go on, say it again.
AGATHA	Come on, Henry.
HENRY	Say it!
AGATHA	Now you are asking me to play games. I'm too tired for that, Henry.
HENRY	It ain't no games, man!
AGATHA	Boysie, Dots, thanks a lot. You know how we feel about you but we've–
HENRY	Say it, dammit!
DOTS	(*yelling*) Henry!
HENRY	No, Dots, 'is awright. But you know what she say to me, man?
AGATHA	Please, Henry.
HENRY	She wait to go because she too embarrassed to stay, man. She too embarrassed! She fraid the policeman come back here and have to put out *she*, she, a solid, educated, upstanding Canadian girl having to hustle out of a black apartment like a common prostitute at two o'clock in the morning. That is why she want to go now!

BOYSIE   Look, I sorry, man Henry man.

HENRY   Nah! You don't have to be sorry, man. If anybody have to sorry, let *she* be sorry. I not sorry. I stayin' right here and I will finish this party when I feel like it. You don't have to be sorry. Sorry because some damn policeman was playin' fresh at twelve o'clock in the night? Nah! Sorry for that? So you just give me a drink and play some music, man.

AGATHA   Please, Henry.

HENRY   (*shouting*) Please me backside! You want to go. You go! I stayin' right here with my friends!

BOYSIE   Henry, look, maybe you should really consider the girl tired and you should take she home.

HENRY   You putting me out you apartment?

BOYSIE   No, man, how I could do a think like that? You self!

HENRY   No, you tell me plain and simple if you don't want me anymore in your place and I shall be most willing to leave right away. I have plenty place I could go. You just say the word, brother.

BOYSIE   C'mon, don't really talk shit now, Henry.

HENRY   Awright, OK. So I stayin' until you put me out.

BOYSIE   You know I will never put you out, man.

HENRY   OK. So what is the worry?

DOTS   (*going over to AGATHA*) Look, darling, if you like I could–

HENRY   No, Dots! No, man! Leave she alone. She don't need no sympathy. Let she find she tail home if–

DOTS   (*shouting*) You didn't say enough, Mr. Big Stuff! Come on Henry! What the blasted hell wrong with you tonight? Enough is enough! The poor girl on the point of tears because of your damn inconsiderateness! So you give *me* a break, you hear? (*HENRY is quiet as DOTS goes to AGATHA*) Come on, dearie. We could talk it over inside. Estelle.

ESTELLE follows her and AGATHA inside.

HENRY   Play some music. Boysie. This place too dead, man.

BOYSIE   Music? Have a drink, Henry.

HENRY   Something soft and sexy. Something to grind to, man. I want to grind. (*he walks over to the black girl*) Lewwe grind, sexy. (*she walks past him and goes through the door stage left*) What happen to she now?

BOYSIE   Las' lap done, sweetheart. You married now.

HENRY   So what about the little German thing you still screwing? You ain't married?

BOYSIE   Black woman different. Here, take a shot and sit down, man. Once you married, pardner, black woman done with you. You have to go all white now, man. Now take me. I still have Dots. And I could still check out a white chick when I feel the urge. But you have a good educated woman there.

HENRY   Too damn educated, if you ask me. Man, Boysie, man, if you see books this woman done full up in my apartment already. And that ain't even the half of it yet.

BOYSIE   Man, you could start reading and educate yourself. You lucky.

HENRY   Boysie, as a old man, I am too fucking old to start worrying about books and education. And in any case, all them books write in a language I can't understand or talk in anyhow. Zoology this, sociology that, anthropology language! I don't know why *one* person—and a woman at that!—have to read so many kiss-me-arse books just to be a human being and live in this blasted twentieth-century world.

BOYSIE   Agatha is a highly educated woman. And she is your wife. Sometime I wish my wife was more learned. But Dots is only a domestic.

HENRY   Highly educated! My wife who talk so much shit about if our wedding reception was held in another place, in a better community, the police won't have interfered, the police interfered mainly because in this district, a periphery slum district – as she does call it in she language – there are many police calls?

BOYSIE   She say all that, boy?

HENRY   Jesus Christ, you and I know that they come here only because it is a fucking black man's party. She know that too. She *have* to know, after having so much books. And most of them, Boysie, almost *all* of them is about black people.

BOYSIE   Shut up, man. Who go write books about black people?

HENRY   I telling' you, man. Books about black people. Books everywhere. Books in the bathroom up there, books under the bed. Books about black people stifling me in the little two-by-two apartment. I can't breathe. I tell you, Boysie, we might be trying to make a little screw and you never could tell where a fucking book will end up. Don't laugh, man.

BOYSIE   You just jealous of the damn woman, man, Henry man. Tha's why you married she. Eh? Why you married she, then?

HENRY   You think I making joke, Boysie. 'Is no joke. And I married that same woman, man. And a same white policeman like she coming to talk to people like we is some kind of savage with no understanding.

BOYSIE   Man, Henry, you self say that is why the woman say she love you.

HENRY   Why?

BOYSIE   Because you is a damn black ugly beast. A savage, man.

HENRY   You makin' light o' the matter, Boysie. But this thing does really gripe me, man.

THEO   (*entering from door*) She left.

BOYSIE   Who?

THEO   The Fulani princess.

BOYSIE   Who?

HENRY   (*rising*) What shite you talking, mister?

THEO   She say that you frightened her.

> *A bell sounds faintly.*

HENRY   You is some kind o' self-appointed messenger-boy? Who give you a message to carry for Agatha?

THEO   I am not talking about Mrs. Agatha White.

HENRY   (*approaching THEO*) Madam Agatha Barbara Sellman hyphenated White to you, sir. Who give you a blasted message for she?

THEO   The black girl has departed.

HENRY   I don't want to hear about no black girl, man. You tell Agatha that the police was here?

THEO   I did feel it my duty to inform she.

HENRY   You know what kind o' trouble you cause, man? Eh? You know?

BOYSIE   Awright, that pass now, Henry.

HENRY   (*jerking THEO forward by the collar which comes off*) Answer me, man! (*THEO remains quiet taking the punishment*) You blasted dunce! You monkey! You ape! (*with every exclamation HENRY pushes THEO to another part of the back gallery*) Who the hell you think you is?

THEO   The princess–

HENRY   Princess? Princess who, man? You is the princess, man. Queen, not princess, man, queen. Queen monkey! (*THEO takes the pushing with a strange pathetic dignity*)

BOYSIE   (*trying unsuccessfully to stop HENRY*) Henry, now you giving the police a real reason to come back, man.

HENRY   (*turning to BOYSIE*) What happen, man? You so fraid the damn police?

BOYSIE   When I in my rights, they can' do me one shite man.

THEO   You, man. The princess say you is the ape, sir.

HENRY   (*turning back on THEO violently*) I is the ape!? You is the white man? (*HENRY grabs his arm and throws him down the steps to the ground, then runs down after him*) Mr. Man-with-the-big-house!

    DOTS, ESTELLE and SAGABOY have come out.

ESTELLE   But Henry!

DOTS   Boysie, how you let this damn ting happen and you stand up right there?

SAGABOY   Le' Henry break he arse good for him.

> BOYSIE *is coaxing* HENRY *back from* THEO *who sits on the ground with his head bowed.*

DOTS   And let the police come and lock up every jackass here?

THEO   (*raises his head slightly*) Evening classes.

ESTELLE   Why somebody don't go and see if the man alright?

SAGABOY   You is the rightest one. Why you don' go?

THEO   I takin' evening classes now, mammy. I have to save up for that.

ESTELLE   Come on, Sagaboy.

DOTS   (*following* BOYSIE *and* HENRY *stage right*) All you people is something else when all you ready, yes.

BOYSIE   Sit down here and cool it, Henry.

HENRY   Where Agatha?

DOTS   Sleepin. If all the noise you make didn't wake her.

> ESTELLE *and* SAGABOY *approach* THEO.

THEO   Five years, mamma, five years I come to this country with one pair o'shoes.

ESTELLE   (*kneeling while* SAGABOY *stands*) You alright, Theophilus?

DOTS   (*going in to check on* AGATHA) And all you please ah beggin' not to dirty up the white people Sunday morning with a set o'cussin and fightin. (*she goes*)

SAGABOY   Nutten ain't happen to he.

THEO   Jew people do it. Eyetalian people down a whole part o' the city, mammy. Greeks do it an' Indian people do it, mammy.

ESTELLE   Theophilus?

THEO   So tell me what wrong with me, mammy. I know you sick. I know dat. After all I is your own flesh and blood. I must know you sick. But hold out a li'l bit longer. It won't take long.

ESTELLE   Theo?

BOYSIE   Ay, Sagaboy. You sleepin' on youself or what?

SAGABOY   Me? Nah!

BOYSIE   Well bring you tail over here, nuh. Romy for Theophilus' jacket. (*laughs*)

ESTELLE   (*to SAGABOY*) Where you goin'?

SAGABOY   You want me to stand up here and listen to he?

ESTELLE   Well go out the dew then.

SAGABOY   (*going*) He only talkin' a set o' shit, man.

THEO   Dear Mamma, I have register in the university. I went and speak personal to the head in the university and he told me I have plenty of ambition. He say in fact that he never meet anybody so ambitious as me with my qualification. Other people make me out to be as if I don't know two and two is four.

BOYSIE   Estelle makin' a breakthrough or what?

SAGABOY   He talkin' away to heself.

BOYSIE   He have plenty practice living' in that big maco house all by heself.

SAGABOY   Like a obeah man. Deal.

THEO   Like if I don't know, Mamma, that the world round, that Columbus discover it in 1492, that that bastard sailed down in my islands and come back and called the people Indian... eh? If it was me that make that mistake, my boss would fire me tomorrow.

BOYSIE   Queen to you. Hearts. Bounce.

SAGABOY   No hearts, boss. I goin' to pack.

THEO   So next time you write, put down my full name on the envelope, and just to see what it look like, Mamma, as a favour write down behind it BA, and PhD, MA, MLitt, DLitt, just put down that. No, don't worry what it mean. The postman will know.

BOYSIE   Ace! Spaces!

SAGABOY   Jack for jackass. Like 'is all fours?

ESTELLE   Theophilus, who you talking to?

THEO   Is that damn policeman, Mammy. He cause everything. How they could come just like that and grab me? I was only looking over the house and wishing it was up for sale. And tellin' me where I get nine hundred dollars from in my pocket. You know how helpless I feel when they start to beat me up. I tell them I have to work just to save up to buy a house and they start to laugh at me. In Rosedale? You goin' to buy house in Rosedale? So I show them as soon as that house gone up for sale I was the first to make a offer. That is why I didn't send no money for you operation, Mammy. But the house still there. And the car. Bells. They say they hear bells. How they could hear bells, Mammy? And you know what?
I burn that letter. Maybe I shoulda jest tear it up. But I burn it, Mammy. And de Bible. And de Bible too.

ESTELLE   Theophilus.

THEO   (*rising and going toward the steps*) No! Leggo me. All you blasted bastard policeman! Kick me? Never again! Never never! What I do? Who I is? Me Theophilus say so. Theophilus! Jefferson Theophilus Belle, BA, to be! I burn God very words that he spake to mankind. And my own mother letter. But she dead. Why the telephone must ring? Why? Tell me why? (*yelling*) Just tell me why? Why they can' just let the damn postman bring the damn telegram, they have to ring, they have to... are you alone sir?... are you prepared for this news, sir... are you quite sure, sir... are you standing or sitting, sir... maybe you should sit... yes, sir, sit... get a drink... no damn drink in the house... next room... sit... sit? On what? Sit on what? Well, tell me straight! I could take it.

> Pause. The others have approached him by now. He stands stock still like a tired animal.

ESTELLE   (*going to SAGABOY*) His mother dead?

BOYSIE   It look so.

THEO   From room to room? No. Not from room to room. Empty. Go to the reception. They have a reception. Everybody there. They don' talk to you. Non o' them. They jealous you house. And you car. Go to the reception. Everybody there. Everybody.

DOTS   (*at the door*) What happen with he? You tell him something, Estelle?

ESTELLE   I think his mother dead.

DOTS   Oh me God! When?

ESTELLE   Bells. And I tell you I hear bells?

DOTS   The girl really say she hear bells for true.

BOYSIE   Have a drink and sit down, Theophilus. Come on, man.

THEO   (*impulsively*) No! I must put on some clothes. (*he moves to where his hat, coat and umbrella are outside the door stage right, and begins to frenziedly put on his coat*) Put on some clothes! Put on some clothes! Sit down. Sit down! (*he sits*)

BOYSIE   (*handing him a drink*) Drink, something, boss, you will feel better.

THEO   (*stiffly, taking the glass*) Thank you. What is it, if I may ask?

         SAGABOY chuckles.

BOYSIE   Sorry, man. You know niggers and drinks. All we have is some dry wine.

SAGABOY   Nothing wrong wid dat. The worse it could taste like is vinegar.

THEO   'Is alright. I will take the cup, and I will sit here.

BOYSIE   You want a cup instead?

DOTS   Well give him a cup, Boysie. He might break the glass.

BOYSIE   You want a cup?

THEO   You don't have to watch wid me.

BOYSIE   Eh?

THEO   I sure you all will go to sleep. Well, go to sleep.

ESTELLE   We won't go to sleep and leave you here. Theophilus.

THEO   You will. I am alright. I am not alone.

DOTS   Just leave him alone, Boysie. All you, just leave him by his-self.

ESTELLE   (*walking back to HENRY who has not moved*) Awright. You playin' solitaire, sweet man?

HENRY   How I should know de man mother dead?

BOYSIE   Don' blame youself for anything, man.

ESTELLE   (*suddenly*) And I tell you I hear bells ringing?

SAGABOY   What?

ESTELLE   Bells! (*she pulls him down the steps*) Dots, come and hear it, girl!

DOTS   What happen to this one now?

ESTELLE   (*she is excited*) Come down here and listen. I tellin' you 'is like it descending straight down from the sky.

              Bells sound very faintly.

DOTS   (*coming down*) I can't hear nutten.

ESTELLE   Shh! (*they listen together*) Like the mornin' breakin' wid music. 'Is heavenly music, Dots. I never hear music so. O my Lord!

DOTS   What happen, Estelle?

ESTELLE   You mean you can' hear de bells? They actually playin' a hymn, Dots.

SAGABOY   (*breaking the spell and sitting*) O Jesus, you know what she hearing?

DOTS   Oh Gosh, girl, I could hear it now. (*she starts to laugh*) 'Is the church bells you hearing.

              Bells are clear now but not obtrusive.

ESTELLE   Church bells?

SAGABOY   So what you think it was? 'Is a man up there playing them bells.

ESTELLE   (*still amazed*) In truth, Dots?

DOTS   A man sit down up there and playin' the bells like was some kinda piano.

ESTELLE   Oh shucks! Girl, I could of swear... but it sound so beautiful. You mean 'is a man, girl... I wouldna think... bells playin' hymns! God bless my eyesight! Girl, sometimes I does can't help to think that this Canada is a damn great country, in truth!

SAGABOY   Great because you hear hymns playing on some bell up there? (*he coughs*)

ESTELLE   How I could just up and say goodbye to something like this, Dots?

DOTS   Things will work out, chile. Don't worry.

ESTELLE   No problem, man, as long as Dots working for Immigration.

DOTS   Don't harrass the poor girl, Sagaboy.

ESTELLE   I could just sit down here, right here on this piece o' grass and listen to that man up there in the skies playing them bells.

SAGABOY   It don't have nothing like this back in them islands, sweetheart, so listen good.

ESTELLE   I remember, girl, I barely had time to swallow a mouthful o' hot-water tea back home, before, bram! I wasn't in a different place.

DOTS   Aeroplane is something else, girl.

ESTELLE   And now, look me! I am now in this big-able Canada! Dots, from a little little village somewhere behind God back, I come up here, and now enjoyin' a little goodness of life, listenin' to God own music playin' on a bell in the pureness of the mornin'.

SAGABOY   A little goodness that only the white people and the rich black people back home does enjoy.

DOTS   This is the way every black people should live if you ask me.

ESTELLE   Look, I putting my hand pon a blade of grass... look, Sagaboy, this blade of grass is the selfsame grass as what I leave back in the West Indies. The said grass that I sitting down upon, the same grass, dots.

DOTS	But only different, chile.
ESTELLE	Different only because it situated in a different place. A different place. Different, but a more better place. A more advance place.
SAGABOY	It ain't have no fairness in this damn world, you know that?
DOTS	What you goin' to do, girl?
ESTELLE	Do?
DOTS	About the immigration
SAGABOY	Four weeks goin' on five, I waiting' on them bastards. And you think they would give me a chance?
ESTELLE	Christ Almighty, girl, if I could just get one little chance, one little opportunity to work as a domestic servant in this place...
BOYSIE	(*at the back with HENRY*) O Jesus, man, Henry, man, you pass three jack and now you pass a next one. You takin' *me* for the jackass now. What you want me to do? Bray or sing?
HENRY	Anything you want to do. You win?
BOYSIE	Why I won' win? I ain' gettin' no competition from you. You blasted mind somewhere else or you sleepin'.
HENRY	I not sleepin, man.
BOYSIE	So go inside and check you damn wife then.
HENRY	She sleepin'.
BOYSIE	Then go and sleep wid she.
HENRY	Haul she arse, man!
ESTELLE	Jesus, girl, just listen to the sweetness in them bells. It have a sweetness like a sadness to make you cry... you know what ah mean? Sometime I does think it is the wonders of God that bless me with this opportunity.
SAGABOY	(*suddenly*) It ain't no wonders of no blasted God, woman!
ESTELLE	Sagaboy, you don't appreciate the way that–

SAGABOY   So why you don't married to Theophilus, then. You will be Mistress Belle and anyhow you turn you go be hearing bell, bell, bell in you arse all the time.

DOTS   Sagaboy!

SAGABOY   It ain't no damn wonders, man! We just get a pissin' tail tiny taste of the way we should be livin' from the blasted day we born! You *(to ESTELLE)* spending your lifetime in the West Indies waiting for a piece o' the pie that all the big shots eating, rich black pie, man, pitch lake pie and petroleum pie, money flowing more than water in some o' them island, but you living' the same way as you forefathers and foremothers, in the kiss-me-arse cane field and in slavery. Why you think everybody turnin' "rasta". Because if you can't get a chance to make some o' the money, you might as well make a living out o' poverty.

ESTELLE   Is true, Sagaboy, but it never too late to get some education.

SAGABOY   Education what? Down there *education* even is run by the big shot and them, and all they does ever teach people children is to come out of school after five or six years and say yes yes yes to everything they say.

DOTS   Sagaboy, 'is early in the morning. Keep you voice down.

BOYSIE   Nah. Let 'im wake up Henry here, man. He gettin' so much licks in this game he beginnin' to think 'is a nightmare.

THEO   They couldn't wait one hour with me.

ESTELLE   Theophilus say something?

SAGABOY   Then one morning you get up, bright and early, and Satan get in you arse, and you look around you, and bram! What you see? You eyes see the topsy-turvy world around you down there, and you turn round and look at yourself, and you don't see nothing but a bust-up shirt and a ragged gym-boots and a one-room shack and over-population and employment of flying cockroach. Who they building big maco highway for? You ever see me shooting down a dual carriageway, hell bent for leather in my dirty gym-boots? Man, when I could buy a tricycle for less a motor-car? But it have motor-car down there wider than the road and them. *(he coughs)*

ESTELLE   It getting chilly.

DOTS   You should go inside, you know, Sagaboy.

SAGABOY   And what happen? You will up you stakes and run overseas. Brisk, brisk, is pulling out for so! Setting sail! Jumping on jumbo jet! Pawning things that we never even own or possess even, borrowing and thiefing, and bam! We end up here in Canada! And what happen?

DOTS moves to go inside. AGATHA is at the door.

DOTS   Lewwe go inside, Estelle.

SAGABOY   You come here in a more progressive country, a more advance country, and you still goin' to exist in a worser life than what you was accustom to back home.

ESTELLE   (*as DOTS waits for her*) Come inside, Sagaboy.

SAGABOY   Look, everyone owe, you, me, Henry can't even married a white woman in peace an quiet. Boysie and Dots, we get so damn tired, man, we get so damn vex...

ESTELLE   So awright, nuh, Sagaboy.

SAGABOY   The only think I ever succeed in getting in this country is a blasted bad consumption.

DOTS   (*seeing AGATHA*) Ay ay, you wake up?

ESTELLE   Come out o' the dew, Sagaboy.

SAGABOY   Is awright.

DOTS   But Henry, 'is the girl wedding night, and how she still looking like a beautiful virgin so.

HENRY   Which part o' she?

ESTELLE   (*joining DOTS*) What does happen to these man an them?

THEO   (*rising*) So glad you could come.

AGATHA   Pardon me?

THEO   Evening class not necessary.

AGATHA   Henry?

BOYSIE   Henry over here.

AGATHA begins to move towards stage left.

SAGABOY   Like I was talking to myself.

THEO   Madame.

AGATHA   What time is it?

THEO   Time? We have time. Plenty time. Time is not a problem. Time for everything.

AGATHA   (*she stops, concerned*) Theophilus?

THEO   Jefferson Theophilus-Belle Esquire.

DOTS   'Is awright, Agatha. He catchin' a kind of fit.

AGATHA   Fits?

DOTS   Kind of fits of the mind. You know?

HENRY   She won' understand.

AGATHA   Henry darling, it's the first morning of our married life.

THEO   Good evening!

AGATHA   Good evening.

THEO   Thank you... a lovely party. Oh, I do beg your pardon... did you meet... but then, of course... how can I be so forgetful... but thank you...

BOYSIE   (*approaching*) Dots, what happen to the blasted man now?

DOTS   Shut you mouth nuh Boysie.

THEO   Ah! My esteemed friend from the West African territories.

BOYSIE   What de arse he talking about now?

THEO   Laluba!

BOYSIE   What?

THEO   I was discussing... ha ha ha... I was having cocktails with the Russian Embassy... I discussed the possibility of granting nuclear weapons to Tobago... and other Caribbean powers like Dominica, Grenada.

ESTELLE   Theophilus.

THEO	Belle Esquire. Miss... haw haw... do forgive me... I forget your... but then there is so many... but of course I will take care of it. The foreign secretary left only months... minutes ago. I already speak to him about your problem. No problem, my dear. Lady Hawgh Hawgh, the name is Theophilus-Belle, engineer, structural and retired... (*to BOYSIE*) But what a surprise... well, not really... I expected you! So the postman di'n disappoint we after all. You did receive my invite. Registered, you know. Must make sure.
BOYSIE	I receive you invite, Theophilus. But why de...
DOTS	Boysie...
THEO	And you lovely wife... so charming, also from Africa? I don't keep furniture in the house. So people could move around lots. Mix. Black and white and blue.
ESTELLE	Dots, why somebody don't do something?
THEO	Do something? No need. Mr. Sagaboy, why not change that name? No bother. Haw haw! But I myself will Christen you.
DOTS	Do something? About what?
	Blackout.

dark diaspora...
in dub

by ahdri zhina mandiela

dubb artist ahdri zhina mandiela has been working on the toronto theatre scene since the late 70's. from black theatre canada to theatre fountainhead, canadian stage to young peoples theatre, company of sirens to theatre in the rough; mandiela has directed numerous productions on mainstages and for school tours. founder & artistic producer of b current, mandiela has worked in all aspects of theatre and been involved in all kinds of creative jaunts... often with a specific focus on black women's art aesthetics & arts/ed material for young people. mandiela is hailed as a poignant renaissance artist, with acclaimed works ranging from poetry books—including *dark diaspora... in dub*—audio recordings, film & video, dance, theatre, and varying media anthologies. her film "on/black'stage/women" premiered on BRAVO! tv network in 1998, and had been sold internationally. she is currently working on new poetry stylings, a followup performance doc, "black stage II" and the 5-minute short, "moments...". mandiela is also scripting a new stage work, while developing other theatre works, including nourbese m. philip's *harriet's daughter*, a hip hop *twelfth night*, and a performance repertory company for b current.

Redemption Dub: *ahdri zhina mandiela and the Dark Diaspora*

by Afua Cooper

dark diaspora in dub offers a stunning discourse on Black woman's creativity, Black womanhood, Black feminism, and presents a solution for Black female emancipation *dark diaspora* as tangible text is comprised of poems; but to say that dark diaspora constitutes only poems is to do a disservice to this text. Because *dark diaspora* is also a stage play and performance.[1]

Diaspora means an involuntary scattering or migration of people. In this instance it is used to describe the scattering of Africans all over the world. For the purpose of the dark diaspora, this world is the "New World" – especially North America and the Caribbean. One reading that I wish to put forth of mandiela's use of the word dark as opposed to Black, is that for the poet, since our forced removal from African over 400 years ago to the New World, we have been wandering in the dark valley of white racism and other forms of spirit-crushing isms. But we trod the diaspora guided by dub: our poetry, our music, our art. Dub: a specific African Caribbean/New World poetic genre premised upon Reggae music, Nyahbinghi traditions, and nation languages. mandiela is declaring that dub offers a viable vehicle, if not for our collective redemption, then for hers. I now wish to divide my discussion on *dark diaspora in dub* in two parts. First, discuss it as a book of poems, and second, as a stage performance.

Dark Diaspora in Dub as Poetry

The poems in *dark diaspora* chart the journeys of Black women (and Black people) from their uprootedness from Africa, across the dreaded and feared Middle Passage, to the So-called New World, this sorrow land called America.[2] This journey parallels the inner journey these diasporic women's experience. This inner journey is constantly punctuated by periods of psychic torture, despair, rage, anger, silencing, and death. However, Black women, and by extension Black people, through an engagement with their own creativity can find their "balm in Gilead" and come into peace.

Dragged from Africa by capitalistic racists, we were taken to New World lands where we endured captivity and slavery for several centuries. Yet even after slavery ended, we could not lay claim to the land we fed with our breath, our blood, and our bodies. The European captors ushered in a new kind of domination called neocolonialism; its twin brother was imperialism. One manifestation of this new kind of tyranny was the rise of American, Canadian, and British multinational corporations. They exercised almost total control of the land and its resources. In their control and domination of land and people, they compromised the ecology of the landspace. One example is the Bauxite companies operating in the Caribbean. Through their mining operations, they polluted the earth and water. mandiela testifies about this:

in my country there are aluminum forests...
in my country once called xamaica
land of wood and water
now your aluminum forests (p.451)

mandiela invokes the presence of Jamaica's (Xamaica) original population, the Tainos, to bear witness to the destruction of the land they named
"land of wood and water." But the Tainos, or Arawaks are dead, killed by the
genocidal war of conquests. Yet mandiela knows their spirits live. In fact,
they live in her, and through her mouth, springing from her entrails the
Tainos speak in thundertones. One could well say that it is Atabeyra, Mother
Goddess of the Caribbean Tainos, who is speaking through mandiela.
Atabeyra angrily roams the Caribbean region and laments the aluminum
forests.

One of the most poignant and stirring poems in the book "in the canefields" narrates the story of our aunt vida who flew north to Canada where
she slaved for white people until she drop down dead "sugar [diabetes] filled
the blood in her her head." A familiar story. But its familiarity does not take
away its horror. mandiela makes a parallel between the sugar in aunt vida's
blood with the sugar produced in the Caribbean by aunt vida's people. The
sugar cane fields and sugar itself had spelled death for our people for centuries. It was because of sugar cane production that Africans were kidnapped
and taken to America. For Caribbean people sugar equalled tyranny. And
when sugar was no longer a viable crop—it was not making enough money
for whites as it used to—and the aluminum forests began to proliferate in the
Caribbean, Black people were forced to migrate to places like Canada "seeking a better life." But as aunt vida's story shows, a better life (for women) was
not found. What was found was a new kind of slavery: working in white
people's home for starvation wages, being vulnerable to all kinds of exploita-
tion, including the sexual, and experiencing racism.

So sugar (incidentally, it is in northern countries like Canada that brown
or "raw" sugar is "refined" into white sugar), a metaphor for white people
and their racism, kills aunt vida, and she is sent back to be buried in the sweet
acid earth of the canefields. We lament with mandiela as she chants in
graphic (almost macabre) language of aunt vida (p.453):

unpacked her luggage
in the canefields
buried her baggage
in the canefields: fell
dead, sugar they said
filled the blood in her head

And if we don't die like aunt vida, some of us descend into madness
(which surely is a form of death) as we ride the "blues bus" on a "snow white
morning" in Toronto. But *dark diaspora in dub* is not simply interested in narrating our grief and loss. mandiela as woman and poet, does not suppress
her rage. She lets it out, confronts it, wrestles with it, dances with it, engages
it, and finally transforms it into positive action. Though *dark diaspora* is a

story of sorrow, it is ultimately a story of love. Because the Black woman, though dead, resurrects herself. The poem "mandiela", one of the opening poems in the book, signals that the poet would not leave us bereaved. For she was "born of an ancient dance... as time slithers on." (p.447) Like the primordial snake, that ancient symbol of powerful womanhood, the poet through her art would transform, resurrect, and recreate herself time and time again.

Love is realized in "a kiss in the dark" and maternal love is celebrated by mandiela in "jahjube" a poem about her daughter. Finally, in the title piece, "dark diaspora" mandiela commemorates Black art and culture, her Blackness, Black heroes, whose struggles for worldwide Black emancipation continue to resound, her Black woman's sensibility and sexuality, the migratory journeys of Black people, and closes the text with the firm knowledge, that we will continue to fight like rass as long as forces that oppress us and seek to silence us continue to do so. mandiela posits two models of liberation for Black people. The first involves a reclamation of our art, and the embracing of our artistic self. The second model suggests the use of arms. Revealing her Rasta consciousness, mandiela invokes, in "dark diaspora," Jah Rastafari. By calling on Jah, mandiela lays claim to our culture of resistance, and reconnects us in the diaspora to our African homeland.

> & rub-a-dub tracks
> replay the rumbling revellers
> chanting arms
> viva! mandela/chanting arms
> garvey forever/chanting arms
> and say it/say it/say it
> say it loud/I'm black
> & I'm proud/say it loud
> black black black
> black/gay gay gay/hey
> say it loud/come what may
> we're here to stay/
> rally round/jah! rastafari
> a luta continua... (p.470)

Dark Diaspora in Dub as Performance

I saw *dark diaspora in dub* performed at Toronto's Poor Alex a few years ago. The concept that mandiela had for *dark diaspora* was realized in the mounting of it as a stage performance. Her vision in creating this *dark diaspora* "was to expand the literary tradition of dub poetry—by producing an integrated script composed entirely of dub poems—as well as to present a totally new experience: dub theatre." (*dark diaspora*, p.x)

Dub Poetry is unapologetically *rebel* poetry. It is oppositional in nature. It functions as the people poetry *par excellence*.[3] This could account for mandiela first presenting *dark diaspora* in oral form as a performance piece, before issuing it in book form. As performance, it was more immediate, more accessible, and definitely more visceral. In creating dub theatre, mandiela used sound, riddims, movement, dance, the spoken word, and textile art. Truly an integrated script.

With a team of six dancers and "chanters"—Deborah Castello, Charmaine Headley, Vernita de Lis Leece, Junia Mason, Kim Roberts, and Vivine Scarlett—mandiela presented *dark diaspora in dub*. It was remarkable. As the lead character and poet maestra, mandiela took the audience through a journey of sounds and dance. Her journey became our journey because by utilising the technique of call and answer, she lead us into the world of African theatre: a space where the audience and performers are one. The dance, the drumming, the worn textile, gave multiple meanings to the word sounds that the mouths and bodies of seven dark women uttered. We, as audience, became the women on the "blues bus," and we cried for our sister "whose/heart broke against a poem." We could not resist mandiela's words, she forced us to feel, to feel our own longings and sorrow as she "de-iced" our collective heart.

I believe mandiela broke new grounds in the Canadian art scene, and certainly in the dub poetry world with *dark diaspora in dub*, whether as book or performance. Her dub theatre is truly innovative. It harked back to mandiela's earlier "page-to-stage" productions at A Space Art Gallery in Toronto. Dub theatre puts mandiela at the cutting edge of theatre production in this country.

As mentioned, Dub Poetry is by its nature resistance poetry. Dub theatre as presented by mandiela postulates an oppositional discourse with Black woman emancipation as its intention.

[1] ahdri zhina mandiela, *dark diaspora in dub*, a dub theatre piece (Toronto: Sister Vision Press, 1991).
[2] By "America" I mean all the Americas-South and North America, and the islands in between.
[3] Afua Cooper, *Utterances and Incantations: Women, Poetry, and Dub*, (Toronto: Sister Vision, 1999)

Toronto poet Afua Cooper has published four books of poetry. This includes *Utterances and Incantations: Women, Poetry and Dub* . Her poetic tribute to Bob Marley, "Stepping to Da Muse/sic" is featured on the buses, trains, and streetcars of the Toronto Transit Commission. Afua has also contributed to the growing field of African Canadian history by publishing critical works on Black women's history. She is completing the requirements for a Ph.D., degree in African Diasporic History at the University of Toronto.

dark diaspora... in dub had its first workshop production in 1991 at the Toronto Fringe Festival with the following cast:

Produced by b current
Sponsored by Nightwood Theatre
Associate Producer   KJ
Co-Directors   Ahdri Zhina Mandiela & Djanet Sears
Collective Choreography   Mandiela & the dancers

Cast   Deborah Castello
                                     Charmaine Headley
                                     Vernita de lis Leece
                                     Mandiela
                                     Junia Mason
                                     Kim Roberts
                                     Vivine Scarlett

Stage Manager   Akhaji
Set/Lighting Design   Veronica MacDonald
Costume Design   Winsom & Evelyn Bastien
Poster Design   Denise Maxwell
Photographer   Liz Kain

CHARACTERS

1 woman   *a voice (internal)*
3-5 dancers/female   *shape/sound*
3-5 actors/singers/female   *voice/shape/sound*

or

15-50 woman   *voice/shape/sound*

The text's imagery unravels onstage with bodies and voices only; minimal set; lights only for atmospheric changes if desired.

Costuming: close to bareness, with anything from a splash to a simple steak of colour.

The imageries unfold through a specific combination of sounds and musical styles, tailored vocal delivery, and a unique dance language, based on a combination of traditional, pop, and contemporary movement.

Left to right: ahdri zhina mandiela, Kim Roberts

photo by Dawn Stephenson

this claimer

>not
>a commentary.
>presumed socially significant/except
>a channel/my
>creative/pipe to
>let out/blocked hopes.
>
>these words are/for/ever/
>more/just fossilled:
>language
>
>& this: one
>of many/million
>dark tales

mandiela (sacred dancing)

>born of an ancient dance
>not by chance: a first child
>to ease the pain.
>for when the steely blades
>clipped/my life-
>line broke with the skies: chanting
>chanting/red/rain
>
>come come come come: dance
>mandiela
>come: dance
>mandiela
>
>i remember the initial rite
>on that moonless night
>2/bodies/trapped
>in a storm/solar
>thunder claps/sing in newborn
>lights brimming
>from a broken sky.
>and time slithers on
>by
>
>come come come come: dance
>mandiela
>come: dance
>mandiela

my mother's hollowed womb
sighed, i began to cry: the rhythm
missed beat
as a chantrel voice took height
in the drum chamber,
a steady breath
raised/in praise: repeat

come come come come: dance
mandiela
come: dance
mandiela

time
slithers on
by/time
slithers on/by
/mandiela

time.

who is my lover? now

this flower/bloomed to pollen pus
borne of back
-lashing and unconstructed
promises
trapped in the dew of twilight
passion
who is my lover? now

when my body/black/comes often
wrapped in fab-factory print
on british wax
who is my lover? now
when tie-dye & batik streak my womb
& slinky/*essence*/stalk
my motherly nape
who is your lover? now

i hear a rasping voice, (gasp)
a brother maps my bed/my child
calls his name, and pre-
sent memories swim/still
in my river's head
he is your lover? now

i hear a sister's voice,
moan in the recess of my desires
peaking obsessions
in the basal drops of dark sticky tones
this sister sounds/
slide past my throat
onto the lifesongs i peal
she is your lover? now

you lay me down to sleep
wrapped in fertile dreams
pulsing eclipse
now be sheeted in my black/
my 3K bonfire dust
my pre-frost/bush body
lush-copper-coloured
passion/spike
now be conscious who i be/
the blackness/beauty that you see
and ask: not who

you be my lover. now

black/woman/i/be

sugar & spice & parboiled rice

what is your life made of
made of: sugar &
spice &
parboiled rice? sprinkle in
some sun-
dried blood or fish/preserved
in sweat/
dehydrated: pepper pepper pepper
pepper pepper pepper pepper pepper
pepper pepper pepper pepper to taste.
mix it up
stir it in the one-
pot/creole slot/you put your right
foot in: blood gut
& rhythm

thank you
for the world so dark:
(diasporic talk)
thank you less often &
(not for the enfalac
or chicken back
or white "sweet & low" packs)
never for a big-son-of-a—
mac-attack.

thank you for iron vultures/
fly south/swoop down
on my backyard/have beach/bum
fun-in-the-sun &
tongue-tied-calypso-rum.
thank you for/never knees in limbo/
pounding sands: inside
my blood gut
& rhythm

for all these i am grateful
for all things borrowed and never
returned/like great burial grounds:
my future now squirting small towns
& newly-vacuumed office towers
& all things dungeon-
covered/dust-to-dust: blood gut
& rhythm

all things considered: i remember
sugar & spice & parboiled rice
that's what life is made of
made of

aluminum forests

in my country
there are aluminum forests

in these rusted spaces
where my navel string was once/
planted
when a tree falls
i hear the sound
the sound
the sound of cranes, long-
neck/noisy/cousins to
the jan cruh/vulture race.
it's not local birds
calling me home again
but ex/ca ex/ca
excavating/men in hats
industrial lead toes
turned-red
from the carbon flesh of my ancestors
bleeding: masked museums/

arawak tombs
ex/hu ex/hu
exhumed in the light – of day
left over-
night: exposed & oxidized

become the mass of marinated clay
you now/
once called bauxite

in my country
once called xamaica:
land of wood and water
now your aluminum forests

when a tree falls
the noise
the noise
the noise becomes foil-
ed wrapped around my tongue

when a tree falls
in my country
do you hear
the sound
the sound
the sound
the sound
the sound
the sound
the sound

in the canefields

her mind has
become my mouth... her
eyes & ears/my
teeth/my tongue
her feet now planted
in the ground
our stories unsung
except
in the canefields

no more messages in letters
home/no more
sleeping on sultry subways
no more chillblain-boned winter days
only sweet rest in the canefields.

my/aunt vida: lithe
bird of youth
took off to canada/surfaced
on a river called don, circled
under dundas bridge: docked
on an edge, lived on a ledge
like the pigeons

no news/papers caught the landing
no taxman demanding
a cut of her nearly unpaid/earning
bread, cooking &
cleaning, making beds
morning & evenings
tending kids she couldn't care about

shopped at *zellers*
woolco & *biway*
shipping a barrel home each holiday
time/pass/new season
spring/summer/finding new
reasons to stick around
no matter that it's underground

she was young, willing &
able/learning french
from food labels
polishing well her accent
for special events/a game
show or lottery winnings:
really only a dream,
in the beginning

& the frayed hopes end
caught her with the same
dream/spent/her bags stamped-
sent home by air/
presents
wrapped in gauze.

unpacked her luggage
in the canefields
buried her baggage
in the canefields: fell
dead/sugar/they said
filled the blood in her head

her mind
has become
my mouth/her
hands & foot & teeth
& tongue/
her tendrils
clinging under-
ground
our story now sung
in the canefields

change in season

> once upon a time/in
> fall, a wolf stood
> on its hind legs to kiss a bird.
> they swayed in this unreason-
> able – unlikely – embrace
> through winter. come spring,
> the little bird still stiff
> from cold, watched with glassy eyes:
> the wolf
> off to find a summer pack.

blues bus

> she feels blue
> today. brown
> skin poured into
> paris cloth: cruel legacy.
>
> shrouded (migrant) ice-
> dancer
> melting in the
> pungent mosaic
> of coloured faces/racing
> thru wind-drawn subways
> and handwarming malls: "city hall
> next stop" he calls
> "exit centre door"
>
> enter: wide-eyed shopper
> spits/indignance
> easing onto the front
> seat reserved for paid
> passengers: "fuckin slave"
>
> some do
> on a melancholy morn
> forget the etiquette
> of justice
>
> mooning for familiar cultures/&
> cheap merchandise: "penny-wise/pound
> of opportunity".

gold
-en beams dropping
from a moody sky
often colour her state/
of/mind/bring
images of last night's rage/
today: "just a peaceful ride home
please",
blues bus/uniformed in salt
can't hide feelings of in-
equality:

"shut up you two"
does he know
she feels blue
today?

in a city where the sun
doesn't melt/snow
no one sees *black*
in the rainbow.

a snow white morning

got up this morning
saw a white man
in white shirt & tie
standing: off white walls
in his white/office
blowing his white nose
in some white/tissue.
i
reached for some white/
paper to record the white/
words i knew could not describe
the colour of my disgust.

for my sister whose/heart/
broke against a poem

>it's easy to fall in: love
>holds like a grave
>our bodies/mesh: wire
>& lace/from dust/to dawn.
>i know you must leave
>you, tied to the paper
>often balled in a fist: jus-
>tice leads me down the path of need
>by night my fridge: a moon
>my days a furtive stroll/greeting
>a demo/or blocko in the middle
>of a song. kisses flower from a snap-
>ped nail as my mind swims
>in the sweat of your fingers/even
>then the musk of rhymes seep on-
>to my tongue/i spit blood
>thinking again it's just: ink
>residue from your pen
>but this time my heart is a well.

>and your pen is dry

a kiss in the dark

>a kiss
>in your voice
>turned my head.

>ole talk/in between/new
>masks unveil the soca
>seed now blooming.

>blood/pumping/music seething/takes
>my mind into slow/song: young
>gifted & black.

>my heart strolls past
>your tongue. our memories
>spread/deep/dark
>violet scents
>below
>our feet:

dry tides splash
rain on my cheeks.
your eyes
speak my name.
(my name)

i taste tomorrow.

on my way home

pack only what yuh need
she said.
so i crammed my past/life/present
foreign/future
into fresh fake leather/used up
every crevice of storage space

left/with 3 suit-
cases full/with 5 kinds
of baggage: blouse & skirts
and undergear...
headtie-kerchief-bellyband
& two pairs of socks
folded/tight/rolled into bank bills.
no cuffs or collar hanging/loose
to derail a zipper
nothing darned/not one bare thread
to unravel this dream/no entangle-
ments or wire hanger:
sharp objects don't travel
well, she said. old trinkets
become cow bells
in this mousey trail
on my way home

when you arrive, she said
don't unpack
because yuh can't
unfold/four seasons in a month
or three... just

run run free
into beckoning hill country
then step each step
slowly... no!
sink yuh feet deep
into rivers where crayfish hide
in silted-
sands, where hands fear
where prawn minds retreat

if, she said
(then when instead)
when you return, only
you 1: suitcase loose/light
dark/deep/empty spaces
(no more gaps in yuh head)
don't... shake the dust
from your feet
dirt proves home is/
not a fig-
ment of your dreams
& too, customs will dig.

declare all: duty-
free & chained junk/transformed
by sun-
culture
flash the pearly beach: smile,
fix your eyes on the sky-
line of your shadow in front
& behind yuh/step
yuh step in confidence
show your tag/1 last time
then drag your bag-
gage from home.

home again

barefoot & black

take a tour
through
my home-
land

take a trip
into
my bantu-
stan

take a seat
inside
my simple
shack

see me/one/two/thirty billion
masked.
barefoot & black

de-icing

dis dis dis dis dis
disrupt/
disprove/displease/
dismiss/disown/disapprove/
displace/disarm/disturb
dismantle/distort/
disgust/dispel/
dis dis dis
dis the myth

black is not a state of mind
it's the color of my skin
the places i've been
struggles i've seen
it's the trance i dance into
when you try to lock into
my control
& hey my point ain't new
this be the dark/
continental view

dis dis dis dis dis

i don't appreciate
you trying to tell me

you're a bonafide homey
b-bopping-
with my brother *x*/medal-
lioned/t/ed on your chest/
dressed in your best
high top/b-boy dap
cameo slicked/side cap
saying you got a right to rap
i say it's just
another appropriation mishap

dis dis dis dis dis

i don't give a damn
what you understand
greeting/hi-
fiving/slapping hands
in private
i be your enemy/public-
ly deferring me
with policing & policies & u
b/busy/busy/
busy doing the black thing
i don't b/down with it
that's why i'm de-icing

dis dis dis dis dis

this be a dis
check it: now
i'm *chillin*

ice culture

sugar & spice & rhythm
on ice
spell resistance.
in a zip
take a trip
in a triangle route
slip in-
to pure resistance

ships at sea
transporting me: crew
& cargo
fodder & feed/trans
planting me: cane
& cotton
these seeds have/not/
forgotten home
though/ice is the coldness that i breathe

mirror image
on the wall/do you listen when i speak?
my accent glued to my teeth.
at this tea for 2
beer for you/by the jug
no face/no black mug/
plug/on your tv

no/nothing for me: just/ice.
the coldness that i breathe

blue/light/blustery breeze
singing: through my teeth.
like a comb/rasping my mind
as the spears from my nostrils drip
onto my chapped lips/my frozen
finger tips jingling
dust/pennies
from your streets fountain/flow: milk
& honey & ice.
the coldness that i breathe

take me home/poor ass
to a banana walk or sugar piece
a pebble swing from the river

far from montreal/standing
tall/prepping
for erections
of pleasure palace retreats/on/ice.
the coldness that i breathe
and a new golf course

take me home
to the far—the—st place of all.

take me home!

before madness comes

today was a vow.

with the last clean dress/donned
backward
from day before
yesterday
i pack: the shine
of patent leather round my eyes
throw out all shoes
that fit
but/one/so
they would not see my soles
begging the pavement
to come home

rub stale-
nut extract into each pore
the stench familiar from last year's cooking.
wrap my womb in new-
born/bought/lost &
found swabs
to keep the life from running out
when the pain of nine-
month's conviction
should come/would come

scrape the salt-
drenched smile from my tongue
and speak no more
to the one stone pillow/
purse my lips shut/no more
milk & honey/no more
ice/no more
caged/eyes wide: bare/
breasts/flat/no more
my head a staircase
outside guts twisting:
no more/dreams/no more
/this voice
no more: this
no more

before madness comes

it nuh sweet

it nuh sweet
dih sugar & spice
all dat is nice
in life
it nuh sweet
when some/one/nex door/
cross dih hall
ah sleep pan floor
nuh have nutten
fih eat

it nuh sweet
if one room batten
her feet/from
movin cross dih street
so her dreams in private
places may cover
in the dark/under
separate sheet
from dih pickney dem
low calcium teet
threatening exiled
cavities.

it nuh sweet
when your sun is a bokkle
of bitters/nuh sweet
sleeping on a winter's grate
or summer-stained
concrete/jus
fih ketch likkle heat
yet some/native/ex/north/
american/chiefly/indian
people ah dweet
it nuh sweet

pack up your life
in a briefcase
spread out your mind
on a little desk space/
oneway course in the rat race
adrift
on a 9 to 5 shift-
ing other people's
bread like a thief
ketching corporate heat!
no matter which way
you're bound to get beat/
everytime/

no time/off/on-
time/sometime/more time/this
time/anytime/last time/now
your time & my time: anytime
is the time
for a change/time
to make it sweet.

jajube

come dance: mandiela

jah!
send some sun/
shining
thru
on this: one
talawa
another sacred dancer

catch a rhythm: a new
beginning/mixing
morning/noon/evening light
run come/before night
celebrate with me/see
sun-
shine.
continually

jah!
send some sun/
shining
thru
on this: one
forever.
another sacred dancer

afrikan by instinct

yo!
this is a diasporic rap

afrikan/by instinct
afrikan/by instinct
afrikan/by instinct:
you & me

splash-
ing/*new*-waves in *boo york*/*u. s.*
moon/dark/nite: rave in *london*
tune/old/world/beat on *paris* streets
wailing/in walled in/*berlin*
double/dutch-date/in *amsterdam*
you & me:
original *australians*
diasporic black *canadians*
money makers/city council shakers
from *rio* to *belize*/
street musicians/politicians
strait/talkin/hippin-hoppin
thespians/gays & lesbians
shape identity;
in *mo'town*/*watts*/yo'town/any downtown
d.c./*l.a.*/*green bay*/*north bay*/*vancouver*/*calgary*
live/walking graffiti: you & me

never seen the motherland
still afrikan
our memory/ourstory
makes me:

afrikan/
by instinct/
afrikan

enter: the caribbean/see/we
afrikan/by instinct/here
l'overture roam free/here/
against poverty/here
shackles without keys/here:
a different slavery? here/check
here/check/check/check
by air/by boat
fidel's big "c"
then *mobay/ja.*/visit my auntie
/cousin/dead grannie/rise *nanny*:
afrikan spirit in *garvey*
one god/one aim/one ancestry

afrikan/
by instinct/
afrikan

one stop! *port-o-spain!*
gimme bastard rum
gimme my own tongue
lemme state me name: afrikan.../
bajan/kittisian/st. lucian
i from *martinique*/
he say he not *dutch* but *aruban*
an hear this *guyanese*:
she great/great/great/
granfather from *china*,
mother's *surinamese*
she like kaiso, hi-life, r&b,
zouk, & dance hall stylee
curry... *miss lou*, dub poetry
jamming in the streets (karamba)
kente, kwanza, *nkrumah*
c.l.r., cesaire, ngugi
sanchez, shange... even *cosby*
& she still mourns the killing
of *walter rodney*
this woman just like me...

afrikan/
by instinct
afrikan

taste earth & grass
and desert sand / *congo*
mountain wave *nairobi* sun
point me now new nile
up / thru the frontlines
from the red / golden / dusty / dusk
of apartheid's horrorzone
see: *liberia* / roughing
algeria / puffing
uganda & *sudan*: dutty / tuffing
afrikan... /

angola: still proving
libya: unmoving
rhodesia's gone / *namibia* stands /
steve b's inheritance / forever:
afrikan / *nelson* & *winnie* /
sheilas / *anc* / *pan afrikan* /
mali / *akan* / *mau mau*
masaii / *baka* / *swapo* /
on our psyche: distinct

afrikan /
by instinct
afrikan

(slaves do have beginnings)
struggles / end / when won:
our stories can't be forgotten /
memories / dispensed.
see a woman / i / mother / daughter / auntie /
sister: come closer
glimpse a nation / man / son / brother /
father / many / generations
never seen the motherland
still afrikan
our memory / ourstory
makes me:

afrikan /
by instinct /
afrikan

these pages

>at the end/near the begin-
>ning/from the centre
>of this passage
>thru collective consciousness
>
>/i dream/i wake/i look/
>i see
>
>these pages
>mirror a black-
>print

dark diaspora

>check
>the blues dance affair
>passing
>in brown paper
>bottles, tarnished by a 100
>militant skank: rub-a-dub
>rumbling revellers
>in red hot civilian fatigue
>chanting arms
>in the dark diaspora
>
>welcome broke bookmakers
>as they close shop/tune in
>to the midnite parade: hear
>airwaved pirated blues/no
>commerce news of flatfoot marketeers
>jingling pound weight/
>sensi: legal trade
>in the dark diaspora
>
>listen to lyrical lectures/
>hurry-come-bring
>linguistic reflections: reality/
>chucksing style

in tight-roped poster panache
in the dark diaspora
finger the free-formed
cultural remnants, etched
on immaculate sheets of black
while/plain-painted stages
stand accused/piping
solo versions
of memories bubbling resistance
in the dark diaspora

  follow the northwest detour: south
parade down soca-
lined streets
in search of carnival sceptres:
madwomen & hustlers
born of infected morning rain
echoing the pain
of pans
beating our distant
suns/and
daughters thirst forever
drinking 30 years
of immigrant legacy
in the dark diaspora

in the dark diaspora
here cameras work on gear/shift
without reverse/into
tomorrow's resolution
moving rhythms
of yesteryear's birthing
to expose the martyred skulls
of forgotten victory

& rub-a-dub tracks
replay the rumbling of revellers
chanting arms
viva! *mandela*/chanting arms
garvey forever/chanting arms
say it/say it/say it
say it loud/i m black
& i'm proud/say it loud
black black black
black/gay gay gay/hey
say it loud/come what may
we're here to stay/
rally round/*jah! rastafari*
a luta continua...
sanctions now/sanctions now/
by any means necessary/we shall overcome/
our will be done today/
after 50 eons of black tracks/
better mus come!

chanting arms
chanting arms
chanting arms
chanting

Tightrope Time: Ain't Nuthin' More Than Some Itty Bitty Madness Between Twilight & Dawn

by Walter M. Borden

Walter M. Borden has been called the dean of Nova Scotian actors by the critics in that province, and the father of the artistic and cultural renaissance which is sweeping through the Africadian community. He considers himself simply a teacher, and hopefully a worthy "bearer of the torch."

WALTER BORDEN'S *TIGHTROPE TIME,* OR
VOICING THE POLYPHONOUS CONSCIOUSNESS

by George Elliott Clarke

Even if Walter Marven Borden had never written *Tightrope Time: Ain't Nuthin' More Than Some Bitty Madness Between Twilight & Dawn* (1986), he would be crucial to any conception of African-Nova Scotian—or, to use my neologism, *Africadian*—art and its *Renaissance.* After the preternaturally gifted contralto Portia White (1911-68) withdrew from the concert stage in the late 1940s, a generation passed before another Africadian artist—namely Borden—achieved notice. Born in New Glasgow, N.S., in 1942, Borden was fourteen when then-premier Robert Stanfield abolished racial segregation in Nova Scotian schools, thus catalyzing the expansion of the Africadian intelligentsia. An exemplar of that heroic generation that primed Africadian consciousness in the 1960s, Borden attended Acadia University and the Nova Scotia Teachers College, graduating in 1964. After teaching in black community schools for a few years, he exiled himself—dramatically—to New York City to become a thespian. Returning home to Halifax, in 1970, he tested himself—boldly, incessantly—in acting, activism, poetry, journalism, and oratory, becoming a model and mentor for many aspiring Africadian writers, actors, artists, singers, and musicians. His acting won accolades, and his poetry attracted a provincial prize in 1976. In 1986, Borden starred in Moliere's *Tartuffe* at Halifax's Neptune Theatre, garnering lush ovations – and an Outstanding Theatre Achievement Award. Later, he composed and took *Tightrope Time*—his one-man show—-to St. John's, Vancouver, and Amsterdam, where he represented Canada at the 1987 World Multicultural Drama Festival. As of 2000, Borden has played in more than sixty productions, organized the Nova Scotia Mass Choir, and even brought the Broadway musical, *The Gospel at Colonnus,* to Halifax—in 1998—to absolute acclaim. Although Borden has done grandly enough in theatre to ensure his reputation, I need to add that, in 1986, he published *Tightrope Time.*

I still remember the day that he loped by my bachelor apartment in proletarian North End Halifax in September, just after having signed up to play Tartuffe, to hand me his newborn play. Frankly, it looked *louche.* It was printed in an issue of *Callboard* (the quarterly of the Nova Scotia Drama League), typed on an IBM Selectric, and issued on squalid, dingy newsprint. Despite the play's humble—shabby—birth, a grey—but now festive—Haligonian light saturated my room as Borden lit a cigarette and dreamt, rightly, that *Tightrope Time* would enjoy a delicious, rapturous reception. That afternoon, he seemed transported, elegant, an intellectual insurgent justified, with his visage—in the guise of Ethiopia the Drag Queen—peering sassily at us from *Callboard's* fuchsia-coloured cover. Why not? The play summed up, I knew, at least a decade's worth of trial and thought. It was theology read as political economy but scored as psychology. It was autobiography, but autobiography written in the way that Africadians—and all African Canadians—

must write it, I mean, as communal memory *and* as the kaleidoscopic mirror of a multiply-divided soul.

In *The Souls of Black Folk* (1903), the profound scholar W.E.B. Du Bois (1865-1963) judges that Negro American intellectuals exhibit a "double consciousness." Both Negro *and* American their dual identity, fractured by white racism, engenders in them psychological conflicts. Though compelling, Du Bois's formulation doesn't fit African Canadians. I think we possess a multiple—or "poly"—consciousness, one that recognizes our Afro and Canadian identities, but also our allegiances to various ethnicities, regions, languages, religions, and cultural heritages. For this reason, Borden's *Tightrope Time* was prophetic for African-Canadian drama. Before Andrew Moodie's *Riot* (1995) and maxine bailey and sharon lewis's *sistahs* (1996), it demonstrated that the Black Canuck psyche stages an opera of identities. Yes, *Tightrope Time* dramatizes multifarious perspectives of blackness by touring one black man's polyphonous consciousness. Thus, Borden's dozen characters, all aspects of his principal narrator, the Host, field several registers of speech—including Africadian Vernacular English, Queen's English, and French—as well as rhetoric encompassing biblical prose and bureaucratese, narrative poetry and syncopated *vers libre*, blues and spirituals, street slang and Hollywoodish glam-speak. Importantly, Borden presents male, female, cross-gendered, and—irrepressibly—Queer voices. In making this gesture, Borden is radically *avant-garde*, for, in African-Canadian literature, male homosexuality receives, rarely, any consummate dramatic and lyrical annunciation.

Borden conducts his polyphonous text by subtly chorusing in borrowings from signal African-American writers like Lorraine Hansberry (1930-65), James Weldon Johnson (1871-1938), Langston Hughes (1902-67), and the *spirit* of James Baldwin (1924-87) – that beautiful, Gay essayist whose words have been wine and manna for Borden for nigh fifty years. In my article, "Must All Blackness Be American?: Locating Canada in Borden's 'Tightrope Time'..." (*Canadian Ethnic Studies*, 28.3, 1996, 56-71), I show that Borden domesticates these influences, especially that of Hansberry, to produce a fierily original meditation on *time* and *value* – his themes in *Tightrope Time*. Hansberry's finest play, *Raisin in the Sun* (1959), stages the integrationist move of the Younger family from the "ghetto" to the suburbs, but Borden's version focuses on the "many mansions/In the complex of my mind." Hansberry explores sociology, Borden sounds psychology. His Host reveals the "many chambers"—of identity—"In the mansions of my mind." Borden relates a phantasmagoric rendering of the African-Canadian consciousness.

Tightrope Time maps a taut knife-edge of existence, where "Boundaries and labels/Are debilitating limitations." Countering the slavery of orthodoxy, the Host endorses only natural, organic, ideational liberty:

I am Nature's love-child,
And Freedom is my father;
I have been called by many names–
I am called by many still;
But restless is the name they gave me,
And I am fashioned from the wind.

The Host strives to articulate—and struggles to uphold—these emancipatory precepts. Thus, when he remembers that, as a mixed-race child, "i watched my living room become/an auction block" where an "honoured guest.../bought the goods–/and called my blue eyes,/honey hair and/mellow/yellow presence/ *A WONDERMENT!*," he also castigates "the way that compliments/could flower from contempt." The Host rejects the idea that space meant for "living" should become an "auction block" where the body of even the pseudo-white black child may be defined as "goods." The play attacks all forms of false e/valuation, for this sin reduces human life to "*CHEAP GOODS.*" Vitally then, in II.i, Adie the Hooker insists that she'll fix her own value. A beautiful realism inspires her declaration that "I... rid myself of charitable persuasions,/and sell a little pussy on the side." She appreciates that "necessity does kick choice in the ass/twenty-five times a week,/and you have to be able to make adjustments." Like the Host, she knows that she must assess a situation and determine what will bring freedom – I mean, a life without other people's "prices" being affixed to one's own. Thus, in II.v, the Old Man warns that

> It's a lonely, troubled journey
> From the cradle to the grave,
> Tread softly,
> Too many wait with bated breath
> To snuff the tiny flame
> That lights our way.
> Scarcely recognizable,
> Such action lurks behind the guise
> Of many labels,
> And I have heard it called concern
> and guidance.

In II.vii, the Minister of Justice, responding to the "accidental" shooting death of a black boy, tells of his mother, who, insisting on a positive valuation of her son's life, demands, "How come a life/Weren't worth no more/Than a stupid little bullet?" Yet, the mother devalues herself by thinking that Rose Kennedy is worthier of being named "the Mother of the Year.../Because of all her suffering." In II.iii, Chuck the Hustler, rejecting other people's labels, chooses to value his Gay body, declaring,

> I don't fuck for I.O.U.'s
> for Master Charge
> or Visa
> Just hard old cash...
> and services delivered
> to the buyers
> or to those I choose
> to sleep with
> cuz
> I want to...

All discussions of value and time in the play protest against our alienation from a true understanding of our own worth and being. Even the loss of time—of life—is equated with living according to false e/valuations of our own worth. In *Tightrope Time*, one man's quest for satisfactory identity becomes emblematic of every man or woman's search for this salvation.

Borden's vision is generous. He sings enough African United Baptist Association of Nova Scotia theology to recognize that some folks believe human beings descend from "dust and dirt." But he also knows that all God's children got wings.

George Elliott Clarke is a professor of English at the University of Toronto, and is the author of *Whylah Falls: The Play* and *Whylah Falls* the book of poetry.

Tightrope Time was first produced in July 1987 at Centaur Theatre, Montreal with the following cast:

Walter Borden played all roles:
      THE HOST
      THE OLD MAN
      THE MINISTER OF JUSTICE
      THE MINISTER OF HEALTH AND WELFARE
      THE CHILD
      THE OLD WOMAN
      THE PASTOR
      THE MINISTER OF DEFENCE
      THE MINISTER OF THE INTERIOR

      ADIE THE HOOKER
      ETHIOPIA THE DRAG QUEEN
      CHUCK THE HUSTLER

Director	Frederick Edell
Stage Manager	Alice Green
Lighting Designer	Robert Elliott
Set Designer	Eva Moore
Musicians	Sandy Moore
	Lorca Moore
Music by	Sandy Moore
Co-Producers	Acadia University Drama Dept.
	Nova Scotia Drama League

Walter Borden

photo by Norval Balch

<u>**CHARACTERS**</u>

THE HOST
THE OLD MAN
THE MINISTER OF JUSTICE
THE MINISTER OF HEALTH AND WELFARE
THE CHILD
THE OLD WOMAN
THE PASTOR
THE MINISTER OF DEFENCE
THE MINISTER OF THE INTERIOR

ADIE THE HOOKER
ETHIOPIA THE DRAG QUEEN
CHUCK THE HUSTLER

NOTE

During the half hour prior to the beginning of the play, the following musical selections are to be played in the order indicated below. The timing of
the selections should be such that the final piece ends thirty (30) seconds
before the house lights begin to fade, thus signalling the commencement of
ACT I.

ARTIST	SELECTION
Leontyne Price	Summertime
Billie Holiday	God Bless The Child
Lena Horne	Stormy Weather
Cleo Laine	Send In The Clowns
Edith Piaf	C'est L'Amour
Judy Garland	Over The Rainbow
Nina Simone	Something Wonderfull

ACT I

SCENE I

*The stage is black. As the house lights begin to dim, the sound
of a heartbeat is heard, faintly at first, then gradually rising in
crescendo. Simultaneously, the lights fade up and out on each
of the stage areas allotted to the individual characters during the
play. The areas are to be lit once and at random selection, with
the exception of the HOST area, which will not be lit until the
HOST first appears. During the lighting of the various stage
areas, the song "Many Rains Ago" by Letta Umbulu is played
softly. The stage goes to black; music continues; HOST enters.
Lights fade up on the HOST, seated on a stool at downstage
centre, listening to the last strains of the music.*

HOST   Well, mum, I said, I'm forty now,
And I feel... old.
The kitchen had that old time feelin'–
You know what I mean,
The closest thing to a womb
Outside the real thing.
I felt safe.

My head was pressed against my arm
Which was propped onto the warming closet
Of an oil-burner stove,
And I thought,
They couldn't – quite make – the transition;
But that's alright–
It makes me feel... safe.

My mother smoothed the doily
Half finished on her lap,
Expertly, casually looped the slender threads
Over just the right fingers,
And then quickly established
An enviable rapport
With her crochet hook.
Old, she said,
*Oh no, no, no, no, no dear,
You're still just a child!*
And she punctuated that remark
With a double chain.

My half cooked egg looked up at me
With its large, yellow and uncaring eye,
Then spat some fat on my clean new shirt.
I hissed: *Oh shit!*
My mother croched faster.
The egg stared;
The bacon sizzled
And snuggled close to the egg–
And I felt... safe.

The sun will rise, I thought,
And it will set;
And in between
I have no delusions
About who I am.

I read the other day
That, on the open market,
I'm worth about five ninety
Allowing for inflation.
But that's alright–
I'd hate to think
That I was priced beyond accessibility.
A second glance, however,
Reveals a flaw in pigmentation,
So, regretfully you must look for me
In the *reduced for clearance* section.

But if, by chance, it happens
That you amble by my way,
Stop and have a look.
There are many mansions
In the complex of my mind;
And if it were not so,
I'd be the first to tell you.
If I say you're welcome,
Take me at my word;
But once inside, please recognize
Who is keeper of my castle.

My mother and the crochet hook rested.
The egg impersonally indicated
That it knew what I was thinking–
And didn't care.
A curious fly winged in
For a landing on my shoulder,
Thought about the meal in the pan,
And decided to avoid a closer scrutiny.

There are many chambers
In the mansions of my mind;
And those that I have visited
Aren't so hard to find again.
But there are doors unjarred, unnamed,
So – I have work to do.
If you'd like to come along–
I'd be pleased to have the company.

My mother dozed–
The hook relaxed–
The egg stared–
The bacon sighed–
The fly performed a manicure–
And I felt... safe.
And not so old...

The HOST rises and gestures to the audience.

Come with me
Into the mansions of my mind,
Where I sing of songs
That are written in a minor key,
But that does not mean,
Necessarily,
That I am the singer of sad songs.

Boundaries and labels
Are debilitating limitations
Which at best serve only to lock us
Within the convenience of others.
Yet, conveniently put–

I am Nature's love-child,
And Freedom is my father;
I have been called by many names–
I am called by many still;
But Restless is the name they gave me,
And I am fashioned from the wind.

Born on some forgotten *FRY*day,
That's *FRY*day with a 'y',
Not *FRI*day with an 'i',
At half past discontent,
Mama sat down on life's sidewalk,
Spread her legs
And pushed one ain't-no-problem time;
And spewed me there
Where *MAYBE-YOU-WILL-CHILE BOULEVARD*

Cuts across *MAYBE-YOU-WON'T-CHILE AVENUE,*
And Indifference sauntered by
To serve as midwife,
To wrap me in my soul and say:
You are Nature's love-chile–
And Freedom is your father.
You'll be called by many names...
I *am* called by many, still,
But Restless is the name they gave me,
And I am fashioned from the wind...
From the wind... from the wind...

*Lights fade on the HOST as the sound of wind rises and mixes
with the music of Cotton Head Joe played on the accordion or
harmonica.*

SCENE II

*Lights fade up on THE OLD MAN. He looks out at the audi-
ence, wanders about for several minutes trying to find his bear-
ings and at last sits, his back largely to the audience. He
removes a hard-boiled egg from his pocket, cracks it, salts it and
is about to bite when suddenly he turns.*

OLD MAN   You might as well know that you do not frighten me. I shall
eat my breakfast and be content whether you stay or go. And
when you recover your tongues, I will accept your directions.
I should like with your consideration, to reach some outpost
of, if you will forgive the reference, civilization by nightfall.
(he turns his back to eat, then is suddenly struck with the thought)
I wonder if you might tell an old man something. If only I
might persuade you quite what it would mean to me. You
see, I should very much like to know– *(deep pause)* –what
TIME it is. You think that's silly, don't you; I rather thought
you would. That a chap might go off and hide himself in the
woods for twenty years and then come out and ask: What
time is it? *(he laughs)* But you see, one of the reasons I left is
because I could no longer stand the dominion of time in the
lives of men and the things they did with it and to it and,
indeed, that they let it do to them. And so, to escape time, I
threw my watch away. I even made a ceremony of it. I was
on a train over a bridge... and I held it out the door and
dropped it. Quite like– *(he gestures, remembering)* –this. But
do you know the very first thing I absolutely had a compul-
sion to know once I got into the forest? I wanted to know
what time it was. Certainly I had no appointments to keep –
but I *longed* to know the hour of the day.

Of course, there is no such thing as an hour, it is merely some-thing that men have labelled so – but I longed to have that label at my command.

I never did achieve that. Ultimately, I gave up minutes, hours, too; ah! But I kept up with the days! It got to be a matter of rejoicing that the seasons came when I knew they would. Or, at least that's how it was for the first fifteen years. Because, naturally, I lost track. I accumulated a backlog of slipped days which, apparently, ran into months because one year, quite suddenly, it began to snow when I expected the trees to bud. Somewhere I had mislaid a warm autumn for a chilly spring... I almost died that year; I had lost a season.

Consequently, among other things, I no longer know how old I am. I was fifty-eight when I went into the woods. And now I am either seventy-eight or perhaps more than eighty years old. That's why I have come out of the woods. I am afraid men invent time*PIECES*; they do not invent time. We may give time its dimensions and meaning; we may make it worthless or important or absurd or crucial. But, ultimately, I am afraid it has a value of its own.

It is time for me to die, and I have come out to see what men have been doing; and now that I am back, more than anything else just now, you see, I should very much like to know: what time it is...

Lights fade on OLD MAN. The sound of a clock is heard tick-ing. "The Old Folk" by Jacques Brel is played. The clock should tick in syncopation with the music.

SCENE III

As the music and clock fade, the lights rise on the MINISTER OF JUSTICE who is seated upstage centre.

MINISTER OF JUSTICE And well you might ask, old man, what time is it? On numerous occasions I have been moved to make that same inquiry. It disturbs me, however, that the motivation for your asking that question is fuelled by nothing more than a pathet-ic desire to tally up a few million minutes. For what purpose may I ask? It isn't as if you were cheated out of them. You clearly stated that you simply did not know whether you were seventy-eight years of age, or older. Regardless of the age that you attribute to yourself, those lost minutes, as you seem compelled to consider them, are not, in fact, lost at all.

Not accounted for, perhaps; behind you, most assuredly; but certainly not lost. I should think that you would be more concerned with what you did with them when you had them. If you squandered them, you may say they have been wasted. If you put them to good use, I see no reason for your remorse.

You did capture my attention, however, when you stated that you had come out to see what men have been doing. In my capacity as Minister of Justice, and in a position, therefore, to have observed most closely *what men have been doing*, with all due respect for your age, sir, seventy-eight, eighty or whatever it might be, I strongly suggest that you remain unenlightened about that.

Interestingly enough, though, you have stumbled upon an example of what some people are doing. It is, so I have been led to believe, a celebration of some sort, commemorating the arrival of *Black people* to Nova Scotia some two hundred years ago. Given the endless series of – how shall I put this delicately– (*pauses, thinking*) – unhappy circumstances which have been visited upon these people during their sojourn in the promised land, I fail to see the purpose of the event. Nevertheless, our Host (*gestures toward the HOST area*) has assured me that there is a valid reason for our being so assembled. (*directing his full attention to the HOST area*) But I would caution our Host to remember that Justice has been an observer of, if not always a welcome participant in, all matters dealing with those people from the moment they first set foot on the shores of Nova Scotia and for a considerable length of time preceding that. I shall consider it my duty, at any appropriate moment, to inject into these proceedings the necessary objectivity which might be required to prevent our being swallowed up by a tidal wave of mindless, subjective revelry. In anticipation of such an event, perhaps I had better provide you with a bit of background information which hopefully you will find useful. I can do that best by answering the question you posed earlier – what time is it?

> the small electric clock
> > perched on the night stand
> is humming
> > that it's
> way past tightrope time/
> and the illuminated amber face
> is not unlike the illuminated amber *ANGER*
> that beats a steady throbbing rhythm
> > along the highways &
> > > biways of my mind/

and i long for joplin fingers
       rippling solace
       over frayed & battered heartstrings
       that could perhaps provide
       a touch of soothing comfort
for some neglected instrument
              lying
          on a dusty corner shelf
in the universal pawnshop/
and i know
       that i am drowning
           in the panic
           that devours
               reason/
i have dialled my own number
& found i wasn't home...

i take my shadow
           by the hand
           & side by side
we walk
a quiet midnight mile
           together/moonlighting
           with a teardrop/
& silence conspires with night
to make light
of my sense of helplessness/
       so
in my desolation/just before the dawn/
       i cry &
       i tell my friend
           the shadow
that i'll never let the sun trap me
           defenceless
& then reflect some mockery in my tears
by casting rainbows/
       i nestle close
           to mother night's
           protective bosom
& i am wrapped in raven's wings
to soar above life's ritual
that ceaselessly demands a sacrifice...

red   black
      white   &   yellow
      PLAYTIME SPECTRES/
prancing
            on my sanity
dancing
            on my dignity
leering
jeering
sneering mother fuckers

CATCH ME IF YOU CAN... follow
                              me
                  and
                    i
            will
      show
   you
moving
   fingers
            that
                  etch
                  a
                  story
                        on
                  graffiti
            laden
      walls
      that
   speak
of
   loneliness
            and
            always
                  of
                  submission...
do you wonder why i don't submit?
i-have-crawled-through-days-as-long-as-pain-
&-twice-as-piercing
never stopped to croon laments in
                        secret
            places

i'll still trumpet
I AM HERE
            & life will find in me
NO EASY VICTIM...

trudge
      with
           me
on
  well-worn
          sidewalks
that
    bear
        the
          sounds
of
    many
       hooves
hoofing
        nowhere
        because
the
    traffic
        lights
are
    constant
         red
and
    every
      weary
          traveller
who
    yields
       to
        sheer
          exhaustion
is/trampled/by/the programmed/herd/
that/grinds/his/blood/and/bones/on/
well-worn
        sidewalks
that
    bear
        the
         sounds
of
  many
     hooves
hoofing . . . . nowhere...
      I'VE BEEN THERE!

do you wonder why i run from smiling faces
that stop smiling when i don't come bearing gifts
gaily wrapped in shredded bits & pieces
of my soul?

sons of night/
        festooned in peacock splendour
        or costumed in some other guise/
debase themselves as timid whores
& speak of passion &
      of love
in trembling notes
that they have written in the blood
        of lesser kin/
& delivered/with a serpentine finesse/
to the keepers of the veil...

daughters of darkness
          cradle heavy burdens
          in sorrow's mantle
& wonder
why their sacrifice is called
      emasculation/&
why they sometimes wish
that every womb become a bed of death/
& every sperm be beckoned there
to seek a final rest...

BUT nature seems
intent upon the right
to play the game
with just a single stack of
JOKERS.

    Lights fade on the MINISTER OF JUSTICE.

SCENE IV

    While the stage is black, the MINISTER OF HEALTH AND
    WELFARE begins to sing.

**MINISTER
OF HEALTH
AND
WELFARE**   Sometimes I feel like a motherless child,
Sometimes I feel like a motherless child,
Sometimes I feel like a motherless child,
A long ways from–
A long ways from home.

    Lights rise on the MINISTER OF HEALTH AND WELFARE
    stage left, as he sings the second verse.

Sometimes I feel like I'm almost gone,
Sometimes I feel like I'm almost gone,
Sometimes I feel like I'm almost gone,
A long ways from home–
A long ways from home.

Celebrations are usually embellished with joyous songs, so it might seem strange to you, Mr. Justice included, that I as Minister of Health and Welfare, should greet you with a selection which is not particularly conducive to having you dancing in the streets. As a matter of fact, I rather suspect that Mr. Justice would have preferred that I had greeted you with a more festive piece, if for no other reason than to accommodate his insistence that we are about to indulge ourselves in mindless, subjective revelry.

Well, this celebration is not so much an historical documentation of the quest by a people for a place in the Nova Scotian or indeed the Canadian mosaic, as it is an illumination of the resiliency of the human spirit. Now in order to appreciate that fact, it is necessary that first we get our spirits in sync, as they say.

Surely there is not one person here who has not felt, at one time or other, like a motherless child. And surely there is not one person here who has not felt, at one time or other, that he or she was gone a long, long ways from home. You see, the human spirit has no special resting place. It will find a lodging wherever it is received. So welcome to a celebration that was nearly met with cancellation due to human error. The reason was simple enough – Langston Hughes explained it best when he pondered:

> *What happens to a dream deferred?*
> *Does it dry up*
> *Like a raisin in the sun?*
> *Or fester like a sore–*
> *And then run?*
> *Does it stink like rotten meat?*
> *Or crust and sugar over–*
> *Like a syrupy sweet?*
>
> *Maybe it just sags*
> *Like a heavy load.*

OR DOES IT EXPLODE?

I had a dream. It was a simple dream. It had something to do with my trying, in quite a humble way, to make this world a better place in which to work – and play. But you would be amazed at how dangerous that little dream seemed to a great number of people. And they took appropriate action.

So my dream dried up, just like that raisin in the sun until, in spite of all my resolve, I had to stop and say, I do not care any more. I cannot care any more. It seemed as if desertion was working overtime and I was placed on round-the-clock surveillance. On more than one occasion I remember thinking:
There's always a hush
waiting at home,
so eager to greet me.
As I open the door,
it creeps down the hall
and slips into my mind.
Well I guess that it feels
that I am in need of a friend now;
and although that is true,
it's one kind of friend
I don't want to find.
There's no getting used to the silence
that says there is no one
to ask how I feel
or offer to fill
a moment or two of my day–
so painful thoughts rummage through
the few last pieces of my heart,
take what they want,
discard the rest,
and go on their way.

Sometimes I could swear
there's laughter again
out in the kitchen,
and with hope I rush in
expecting to find someone in a chair.
But I am met by haunting echoes
of yestersounds
that brought me comfort,
and I watch a leaking faucet
sadly shed a lonely tear.
The fireplace flame gives a flicker
and dies
in the parlour;
the dining room glow has decided
it should do the same;
and the emptiness that I see

makes it very clear to me that
the living room has dropped the living
from its name.

And every room has a pain of its own.
There is heartache, precious heartache,
behind every door...
yet I feel the need to step inside
and search the sorrow that they hide,
for bits and pieces of love
that I have known.
But when the truth that they contain,
Touches my soul like gentle rain,
I know that memories,
wrapped up in teardrops,
are all that remain.

So no, I said, I cannot care anymore. But as hard as I tried not
to care, I knew that the truth of my situation lay in the words
of the gifted, Black writer Lorraine Hansberry, who eloquently
stated:

I care. I care about it all. It takes too much energy not to care.
Yesterday I counted twenty-six gray hairs on the top of my head
all from trying not to care... the why of why we are here is an
intrigue for adolescents; the how is what must command the
living. Which is why I have lately become an insurgent again.

So I gently placed my bruised and battered psyche securely
under my arm, riffled through my catalogue of songs for all
occasions, and started the long trip back home.

Lights fade on the MINISTER OF HEALTH AND WELFARE.
Music begins "No Ways Tired" by the Barrett Sisters.

SCENE V

As the music ends, lights rise on the HOST seated downstage
centre.

HOST   Summer Saturday afternoons are special
to children...
I know they were for me.
No matter what the weekly crime,
the verdict always seemed to be
Saturday afternoon at the movies...
my joy, my escape.

Ten cents bought a lot back then,
and ever faithful Saturday
put a dime into my right hand
and a nickle in my left,
for treats,
and life was complete.

> *The HOST begins to assume the character of the CHILD by*
> *putting on a baseball cap, a jacket, and removing a yo-yo from*
> *his pocket. He begins to play with the yo-yo.*

They say that children see everything
out of perspective;
in a way I guess that's true.
I can't remember many summer days
that were not 90 in the shade...
and yet,
in many conversations now,
I still am moved to ask:
What's happened to all those thunderstorms?
When I was small... I always say,
And so on... and so on...
You know the rest,
You've said it too.

> *The CHILD sits, cross-legged, in front of the stool on which the*
> *HOST has been sitting. Music is heard faintly "London Bridge*
> *is Falling Down" and recurs at various moments during the*
> *CHILD's monologue.*

CHILD   Death came riding
over the hill by my house
on one such Saturday afternoon.

I sat on Granddad's step
that faced toward the road,
holding my nickel
and clutching on my dime,
and waited for my cousin
to gather up his treasure.

I watched a frantic, little ant
search diligently for hers
and naughtily,
but never with malice,
I frequently blocked her path
and watched her flee
in many directions–
exasperated.

The ant and I were playing
on each other's frazzled wits
when a happy little boy
with pleasure on his mind,
heard death give out a greeting,
and a machine gone wild
showed the power it had
over man, its creator.

   Discordant strains of "London Bridge."

My golden, private Saturday
dissolved
into a grotesque circus
of broken limbs
and blood
and dust
and shouting, screaming mobs
and neighbourhood gossips
who, like maggots
seem, forever, to be drawn
toward the kill,
and then devour in equal measure,
the tragedy
and tidbits of the latest news–
stopping now and then to sob a *MY!*
MY! MY! MY! MY!

I watched the grieving mother
throw herself upon the ground
and wondered why
she laughed
so high
so loud
so long!

The driver of the car just sat
and sobbed
and shook
as I recall,
and that disturbed me.
I had never seen a grown up man in tears.
His friend just thought of other things;
I could tell by how she stared
and frowned–
and I recall attempting to locate
the object of her interest
that seemed suspended somewhere
off in space...

I've heard it said
she stared like that
for many, many years...

And deep inside,
with sadness all around,
I felt that I should sense
a little sadness too;
and don't you know, I really did.
But somehow it was plain to me
that no one there would understand
my passion for the movies.
I turned from all that misery.

My mother unpacked groceries
when I arrived back home–
they were part of Saturday afternoon–
and as she knelt
among a jungle of paper bags and boxes,
I saw her wipe a tear away
with the corner of her apron.
Something told me I should cry,
so I pressed and rubbed my eyes
until one tiny little drop
escaped...
and trickled down my cheek.
I tried so hard to make it last
but all too soon it dried away–
I couldn't summon anymore,
and really wondered why I should.

I took an empty bottle
and headed for the berry field
across the way,
not far from home,
leaving at a distance, though,
the wailing,
the gossiping,
one confused ant,
Saturday groceries
and the movies...
A grasshopper and I
decided on a mutual understanding
and settled down
to explore a berry-laden patch
together.

Children always seem to know
the reason
for the cycle!

*Lights fade on the CHILD. "London Bridge is Falling Down"
is heard in very discordant strains.*

SCENE VI

*Lights fade up on the MINISTER OF HEALTH AND WEL-
FARE.*

**MINISTER
OF HEALTH
AND
WELFARE**   The streaming sidewalk
seems to know your mission,
little one.
Not one raised look is made
to interrupt your flight;
as if that downward glance,
those deep-thrust hands
and stooping back
that carries burdens
far too great for all your tender years,
have joined in some conspiracy.

But did I see you
quickly halt my gaze
with almond questions?
Perhaps...
I could almost swear
I saw... a panic... then... passivity.

Yet, long enough for me to see
a simple plea for understanding
why the world of giants is so strange!
Why it is that you must try to hate
with all you can;
And how by doing all we do you'll grow
to be a man–

Yet, we change our faces
everyday...

Why it's said so easily
that bad times are your plight;
and why your mama works so hard
and cries alone at night–

And who are you to blame?

You hurry on your journey
little one,
so you don't see
my puzzlement.
Did you really say all that?
It's hard for me to know–
Maybe... I should ask.

Lights fade on the MINISTER OF HEALTH AND WELFARE.
Reprise of "I Don't Feel No Ways Tired."

SCENE VII

Lights rise on the HOST downstage centre.

HOST (*To MINISTER OF HEALTH AND WELFARE*) Maybe you
should... but you won't. We rarely do because the answers
we are apt to receive are often those which we least wish to
hear. Ultimately, therefore, it becomes an individual responsibility to rid ourselves of the excess baggage which, more often
out of ignorance than lack of love, is placed upon our shoulders by those who likewise have been victimized.

To understand where we are at a given point in time, it is frequently necessary to properly appreciate where we have been.
Achieving that might entail our having to relive scenes long
since discarded somewhere on life's dumpheap; open old
wounds that time has encrusted with temporary scars; or
wander down a hazardous pathway which we thought, or at
least hoped, we would never have to walk again. On one
such journey, as I ripped away some obstructive mental
underbrush, it was suddenly clear to me that

i knew that there was something wrong
the day i watched my living room become
an auction block;
and heard the gentle voices
which had always seemed protective,
suddenly with urgency
and ill-concealed pride,
command me to perform and

earn the admiration
of our poised and honoured guest
who, with due consideration,
and unmitigated awe,
bought the goods–
and called my blue eyes,
      honey hair and
          mellow/yellow presence
A WONDERMENT!
i knew that there was something wrong;
and ran – and hid beneath the steps
'til she had gone;
then took my box of crayons
and filled with calm... and hate,
threw the brown into my dresser drawer,
the white into the fire...
POOR LITTLE SICK BOY.

i knew that there was something wrong
when after i had passed an easy boyhood day
and shared a hundred secrets and
      an apple with my friends,
i was told
i could not go to their house.
it doesn't matter;
you don't need them;
that's what people said – but
yes it did and
yes i did and
any child can tell you
i was right.

still, somehow i walked on, although
i knew that there was something wrong,
and loathed the way that compliments
could flower from contempt...
so i became well-schooled
in such gardening,
and weeded out a method
of survival.

i knew that there was something wrong
each time i sat uneasy
in a restaurant
and thought about the laws of equal justice
      that with eloquence
        and pomp,
      allowed that i could get
      a coke

but could not rule an
attitude.
and there was surely something wrong
when i was asked to overlook such indiscretions,
and then provoked a blazing wrath
when i refused to take the place
you offered me,
and rather chose to seek
and find my own.

if god is white,
well that's his plight,
not mine;
it would perhaps explain
why there are fringe groups.
if not, then may i say that
yesterday i heard it said
that jesus was a faggot
with twelve lovers
and slept with whores...
sounds like their opinion
of the average black man
who is always thought to start his life
with a spoon
around his neck.

may i humbly recommend
another box of crayons!

*Lights fade on the HOST and discordant music of "London
Bridge is Falling Down" is heard again.*

SCENE VIII

Lights rise on the MINISTER OF JUSTICE upstage centre.

**MINISTER
OF JUSTICE** (*addressing the HOST*) While you're contemplating that box of
crayons, think deeply about the yellow ones and remember
that someone made it possible for the master and his minions
to pay a little visit to all of our villages. It is my considered
opinion that

god was in the playground
frolicking, at midnight,
making out rejection slips
and chocolate ripple sundaes

for super special stepchild time
and treats at carnival crossroads;

and watched the mounting fury
of the ones who have no place
      the ones who have no face
and listened, as they raged;

     ring around a misfit,
     cannot get a little bit of action–
     the *ACTION*–
     so all fall down!

     the blacker the berry
     the sweeter the juice,
     so give 'em a nigger
     and turn 'em loose;
     yah! white boy,
     you made an *IT*.

     I cry to play on either team,
     skip-a-rope; skip-a-rope;
     I try to please
     so I might seem
     to be accepted;
     SKIP-A-ROPE!... bruised chiquita.

     black and white both stake a claim
          play a game
          hurt and maim;
     they don't even know my name–
          folly
          folly
          folly

The MINISTER OF JUSTICE begins to sing mournfully.

Go in and out the window,
Go in and out the window,
Go in and out the window,
Till the iron gates are locked.

*The MINISTER OF JUSTICE rises end sings the next two
verses as he moves through the various areas of each of the characters. He will finish the second verse as he enters the
PASTOR's area.*

Go in and out the window,
Go in and out the window,
Go in and out the window,
Till the iron gates are locked.

Go round and round the valley,
Go round and round the valley,
Go round and round the valley,
Till the iron gates are locked.

> *Standing in the PASTOR's area, the MINISTER OF JUSTICE raises his arms and sings as if he were addressing the HOST kneeling before him.*

Why do you kneel before me,
Why do you kneel before me,
Why do you kneel before me,
Till the iron gates are locked.

> *The MINISTER OF JUSTICE assumes the kneeling position of the HOST and sings.*

I kneel because I love you,
I kneel because I love you,
I kneel because I love you,
Till the iron gates are locked.

> *The MINISTER OF JUSTICE rises and sings the last verse as he makes his way back into his original position upstage centre.*

Go in and out the window,
Go in and out the window,
Go in and out the window,
Till the iron gates are locked.

> god is bored now,
> playtime's over;
> time to build some castles in the air.
> he'll come again
> when he's not so busy,
> and talk about the special band of angels
> he's going to form...
>
> being god requires
> a great deal
> of
> sensitivity!

Lights fade on the MINISTER OF JUSTICE.

SCENE IX

The MINISTER OF HEALTH AND WELFARE is heard
singing "Sometimes I Feel Like A Motherless Child." Lights
rise on him as he finishes singing.

**MINISTER
OF HEALTH
AND
WELFARE**   Often we have heard it said that sometimes, the cure can be
worse than the disease itself. Certainly there was little room
for argument against that somewhat controversial conclusion
as I set about the arduous task of gettin' it all together.

While speaking, he has lit a joint – now he tokes languidly and
says slowly:

I sang a song
of hungry, sweaty summer afternoons,
of burning seaside sands
and asphalt anger
that parched their way
to after-hour cool, when
pacified,
I watched the neon ripple,
the pavement rise and fall,
and grotesque images
dine on macaroni
and each other
then... drift...
and even as I wondered
why we take the fall
without a parachute,

helplessly
           I watched the struggles all around me;
           I heard the hollow words of hope pour on
                       a million times spoken
                       a million times carried
                                   on the wind
                                           and
                       all too soon

forgotten
while glazed or glaring glances
groped across a room and locked
                    and lied...
as the solitary sentinel launched
                    a last offensive and
                    dropped some of Death's currency
                         on the counter of our soul;
CHEAP GOODS,
it was heard to say
and rush us to fulfillment,
so we thought;
as misty mountains melted into victory
and hazy opportunities were claimed,
vision after vision filtered by
                    and vanished
in those places where reality holds its court.

but even then
the steel servant was let to bow its head
and drip destruction
which etched across the eye of time
a picture, carved in loneliness,
of children in a lost, abandoned kindergarten,
trying to spell *help*
with the wrong alphabet blocks!

Lights fade on the MINISTER OF HEALTH AND WELFARE.

SCENE X

In the black the HOST begins to sing "Oh, Sinner Man."
Lights rise on the HOST as he sings the second verse. He sings
the first line of the chorus again and continues.

HOST   I guess you run wherever you can and if you're very lucky,
you'll find a hand that's eagerly outstretched to greet you.

The HOST looks toward the downstage right area reserved for
the OLD WOMAN. Lights rise dimly to reveal a rocking chair
on which is placed a partly completed patch-work quilt. Next to
the rocking chair there is a wooden box on which there is placed
thread, patches, and a pitcher of lemonade.

the dusty brown afternoon drily said
it had nothing new to offer;
            and the pale blue cyclops seemed content
to beat some heat upon my head
with unrelenting anger...
and so
i scuffed along,
stopping for a moment
to pry one obstinate little pebble
from between my toes,
where it had seen fit to lodge itself
after finding easy passageway
through my battered old sneakers.

the feet and i had varying opinions
about what was and was not character,
but until my pockets could jingle
                  a somewhat merrier tune,
character would take preference over comfort;
that's how the conversation always ended–
and that's how it ended once more.

The HOST begins to move toward the OLD WOMAN's area.
Lights fade on the HOST area and rise on the OLD WOMAN's
area.

            i spied her then,
as i brought myself to an upright position,
and couldn't quite contain the laughter
            which leapt spontaneously
            from deep inside me.
a little dark head crowned with silver,
peeped over a mountain
            of multi-coloured threads and patches
while, nattily slippered
            in white and ginger fur,
her tiny feet
                  which dangled several inches
                  above the ancient rotting floor
                  of a rickety dark gray porch,
                  whenever she remained
                  in a motionless position,
periodically tugged on her spindly bowed legs
which stretched until
they allowed her toes
to meet a firm resistance,
and then infused with much momentum
sprung her reeling up and back
in the wicker rocking chair

that framed the precious sight.
        i also glimpsed a jar of lemonade
which cast a tantalizing stare
in my direction
as it perched itself on an apple crate
and demurely tried
to convey a sense
of minimized importance;
and as it played beguiling tricks
        on my parched and eager throat,
i ambled very casually
toward the front porch steps.

        two beady piercing eyes
locked in on me
but the nimble knurled fingers
        didn't miss a stitch.
i quickly smiled my warmest greeting
and tossed the usual opening
        in her direction:
        beautiful day, isn't it?

        hot as the hinges of hell, she croaked,
        but yes, i guess it beautiful enuf for
        them what got sense to see it.

        now that, i thought, is one cagey little come-on but i
summoned my resolve and stumbled on:
        looks like quite a heavy job;
        what exactly are you doing?

        puttin' the pieces together, she answered slyly,
        be surprised what you come up with.

the tone revealed a meaning
only hinted by those words,
and before i interjected
an appropriate response,
she rather calmly added:

        you lookin' like you all dragged out;
        go on and help yourself.

before too long a tangy cool
was coursing through my body,
and i felt content
to heave a sigh
cock an eyebrow
and vacantly stare around at... nothing, really–

but the keen old lady sized me up,
pursed her lips and said:

> *where you from, boy? – you from here?*

> *from over town,* i answered gently,
> *it's peaceful way out here*
> *and i thought i'd do some thinking.*

> *then what?* she asked.

> *well then... i... really couldn't say,*
i stammered.
> *i haven't thought that much about it.*

> *you got some nerve to call that thinkin',*
she snapped with great contempt.

that stung – but i pretended that it hadn't!

> *i've got some problems,* i continued...

> *who don't?* she quipped again.

i thought the conversation should be halted
      at that point.
but my pride stepped in
      about that time
and demanded that i get the upper hand.

> *everyone must find his way,* i started philosophically...

> *don't see how you gonna do it,*
> *when you can't but read the road signs;*
> *and don't go gittin' uppity with me!*
> *i seen a lot of mornin's,*
> *and i seen a lot of nights—*
> *so you jes lissen here...*

> *seems like everywhere i turn these days,*
> *the young folks always tryin' hard*
> *to find out who they is.*
> *mos' of 'em already knows;*
> *they wastin' all that precious time*
> *at tryin' to be what other folkses want.*
> *and that don't make sense to me—*
> *don't make no sense no how, no way!*

take Bessie Ann, live down the road;
pretty little thing;
from the day that chile come in this world,
her mother sayin', all puffed up,
Bessie this and Bessie that
and i got plans for Bessie Ann:
the chile could never say her thoughts.
and 'fore too long her mother tellin' me:
don't want to see my Bessie Ann
with trash that's livin' here;
soon she git her schoolin' done,
she hittin' out this town.
and you can take that to the bank!
she'll git herself some fine new friends
and be someone important in this town;

she stood right there a year ago,
her hands stuck on her hips,
and said to me:
well thank the lord, i got my wish
and Bessie's on her way;
now mark my words, i see it plain,
Bessie sure will come back big.

and that she did, without a doubt;
eight months big...
and din't know
what heppened to the daddy.

well her mother come a-hootin' and
                           a-bawlin' and
                           a-cryin'
and i jes said you git on out my face!
and 'pon my soul, 'fore a week went by,
she beat that chile all black and blue.

one day i'm sittin' on this porch
and hears the racket over yonder;
i says Suzie girl git off this chair,
                git down that road
                and set them people straight;
and don't you waste no time.

well it must have been a sight, my boy,
for anyone who seen me,
cause my dress was torn,
my head not combed
and my feet was workin' overtime!

and be the time i got down to the house,
i had to sit and catch my bress.
oh, lawd, lawd, lawd, lawd, lawd my boy
old Suzie was all done in;
but by and by i got some wind
and hollered for to wake the nations:
Lottie Mae—
Lottie Mae—
Lottie Mae, girl, where you at?

was nuthin' stirrin', chile,
round that house,
but the crickets and the bees,
so i hobbles up, and looks about,
and drags myself inside.
there's Bessie Ann against a wall,
holdin' on herself,
lookin' like she tryin' to hide a watermelon;
and Lottie Mae's upstairs somewhere
a-snifflin' and a-snortin'.
so up i goes
and there she is;
all laid up
and tryin' hard
to look like she be dead.

oh mama, mama, mama...

i said: don't you dare to mama me,
you overgrown heifer;
and git your ass up off that bed
'fore i slap you round this room!

but mama, mama, all my plans;
i had so many dreams;
yes, i said, i know you did;
but you never dreamed to tell that chile
about u word called no.

remember the simple things, boy.
jes keep it simple!

and Doodle Boy, jes seventeen,
he come to me and say:
i'm gonna be a lady's man—
a cool dude, like daddy.

that right, says i,
well you won't be much
and you won't be one for long.
and don't go blabbin' about your father;
he was walkin' in the devil's shoes
before he left his mama's tit,
and be the time that he was twelve years old,
every girl in this here country
knowed the colour of his drawers.

and that same old fool come in my face
and had the nerve to say:
my boy will be a real man;
yeah – steady, fast and deadly;
and true's i'm sittin' in this chair,
a chill went through my bones—

well Doodle Boy roared down that road
and drove hisself to hell;
he wrapped hisself around that tree
and took some young folks with him.
but that what come from heedin' unto others
before you pay a little lissen to yoself!

i understand exactly what you're saying, i ventured
unconvincingly,
but i...

boy, she said while looping several stitches,
if understandin' bought you up that field over there,
i guess you could afford... a blade of grass.

i was absolutely shocked.

so think on this a little bit
while you headin' back to town;

ain't no use in cryin', chile,
'bout things that you can't change;
jes stand up straight,
clear your eyes
and grab that gravy train
that's goin' somewhere;
there's always one awaitin'
at some station.

an' don't tell that man
that you can't say
your point of destination,
jes speak right up
an' say it clear—
determination pays my fare
an' sweet success will greet me
by an' by...
but don't go lookin' mean.
do your thing
but do it clean.

now after you've achieved your goal
an' things are lookin' fine,
don't go an' blow the whole damn scene
by sayin', what is mine is mine,
an' actin' like you had it all the time.
an' one more thing—
jes because your way was rough,
with some ole thing or other,
ain't no reason why you can't improve it
for your brother.

i got the message and she knew it,
so I turned and took my leave;

jes a minute, boy, she said.

i stopped and turned around.

you'll do okay; i know these things;
but there's something on my mind.
i don't expect you'll come back here
like poor dear Bessie Ann,
an' seem to me you won't be seein'
much of Doodle Boy;
i'm jes a simple lady
an' i probably got no sense,
but still an' all it is a fact
i gotta fill my stomach.
that welfare cheque they givin' me
won't hardly feed a flea;
now, i writ 'em several letters, dear,
an' no one's said a word,
ain't no big surprise, i guess,
cause the last one i done send 'em chile,
it didn't need no stamp—
it could sail right through the mail
all by itself...

but if you heppen to see those big boys
anywhere along the way,
remind 'em 'bout this little coloured lady
you was talkin' to...

her high pitched laughter followed me
a long, long distance
down the way.

Lights fade on the OLD WOMAN. A shaft of light in the form
of a cross falls across the PASTOR's area stage right centre.
The HOST sings three lines of "Oh, Sinner Man" and says:

HOST   You run wherever you can.

The HOST is standing at the edge of the shaft of light as the
song "Highway To Heaven" begins. The HOST moves up the
shaft of light until he is standing behind the pulpit and puts on
the PASTOR's vestments.

SCENE XI

As the song finishes, the PASTOR begins.

PASTOR   You know – it amazes me! It amazes me when I hear the
young folks talkin' about the confusion that's in their heads.
It amazes me. And I'm mindful of the many ways that somehow we seem to have failed them. I'm mindful of the fact
that we haven't always lit the candles that they need to find
their way. I'm mindful of the fact that we haven't always led
them before the throne of God – that same great God in
whom we find no chancey hit or miss, 'cause with my God
you hit your mark; there ain't no miss in God. God is the
bull's eye of the universe! And I want to say to you here
tonight, though billows roll, he keeps my soul; my Heavenly
Father watches over me.

And he watches over you. And you too, way on down there
in the back. Oh yes! He knows where you are; He sees what
you do; 'cause my God is watchin' all the time. He keepin'
his eye on you so He'll always be there when you need Him.

Now I know that some of you be sittin' out there right now
sayin': *Well He ain't always there when I want Him.* But you better heed me when I tell you, my God might not always be
there when you want Him; but my God is always there *on*
time.

I know that there are times when we are taxed past all understandin'; times when we don't know what to do; times when
we don't know which way to turn. But I want to tell this old
town tonight, when the storms of life are raging, I turn to
Jesus, my hope in my life; He'll deliver my soul out of trouble
and strife; yes from His blood I see and believe, the love of
God will ever keep me; and I'll cry holy, holy, holy, *HOLY*, I
found Jesus was the place to turn.

Now I'm talkin' to that young woman out there who thinks
she can go out into the world and do whatever she wants to
do, and no one's goin' to do a thing about it. I'm talking to
that young man out there tonight who thinks that he can hurt
whoever he wants to hurt and no one's goin' to raise a hand
to stop him. But you hear me when I tell you; God will stand
you toe to toe. And
    Young man–
    Young man–
    Your arm's too short to box with God.

But Jesus spake in a parable, and he said:
A certain man had two sons.
Jesus didn't give this man a name,
But his name is God Almighty.
And Jesus didn't call those sons by name,
But every young man,
Everywhere,
Is one of those two sons.

And the younger son said to his father,
He said: Father, divide up the property,
And give me my portion now.
And the father with tears in his eyes said, Son
Don't leave your father's house.
But the boy was stubborn in his head,
And haughty in his heart.
And he took his share of his father's goods,
And went into a far-off country.

There comes a time,
There comes a time
When ev'ry young man looks out from his father's house,
Longing for that far-off country.

And the young man journeyed on his way,
And he said to himself as he travelled along:
This sure is an easy road,
Nothing like the rough furrows behind my father's plow.

Young man–
Young man–
Smooth and easy is the road
That leads to hell and destruction.
Down grade all the way,
The further you travel, the faster you go.
No need to trudge and sweat and toil,
Just slip and slide and slip and slide
Till you bang up against hell's iron gate.

And the younger son kept travelling along,
Till at night-time he came to a city.
And the city was bright in the night-time like day,
The streets all crowded with people,
Brass bands and string bands a-playing,
And ev'rywhere the young man turned
There was laughing and singing and dancing.
And he passed a passer-by and he said:
Tell me what city is this?
And the passer-by laughed and said: Don't you know?
This is Babylon, Babylon,
That great, great city of Babylon.
Come on, my friend, and go along with me.
And the young man joined the crowd.

Young man–
Young man–
You're never lonesome in Babylon,
You can always join a crowd in Babylon.

Young man–
Young man–
You can never be alone in Babylon,
Alone with your Jesus in Babylon.
You can never find a place, a lonesome place,
A lonesome place to go down on your knees,
And talk with your God, in Babylon.
You're always in a crowd in Babylon.

And the young man went with his new-found friend,
And he bought himself some brand new clothes,
And he spent his days in the drinking dens,
Swallowing the fires of hell.
And he spent his nights in the gambling dens,
Throwing dice with the devil for his soul.
And he met up with the women of Babylon.
Oh, the women of Babylon!

Dressed in yellow and purple and scarlet,
Loaded with rings and earrings and bracelets,
Their lips like a honeycomb dripping with honey,
Perfumed and sweet-smelling like a jasmine flower;
And the jasmine smell of the Babylon women
Got into his nostrils and went to his head.
And he wasted his substance in riotous living,
In the evening, in the black of the night,
With the sweet-sinning women of Babylon.
And they stripped him of his money,
And they stripped him of his clothes,
And they left him broke and ragged
In the streets of Babylon.

Then the young man joined another crowd–
The beggars and lepers of Babylon.
And he went down to feeding swine,
And he was hungrier than the hogs;
He got down on his belly in the mire and the mud
And ate the husks with the hogs.
And not a hog was too low to turn up his nose
At the man in the mire of Babylon.

Then the young man came to himself–
He came to himself and said:
In my father's house are many mansions;
Ev'ry servant in his house has bread to eat;
Ev'ry servant in his house has a place to sleep;
I will arise and go to my father.

And his father saw him from afar off,
And he ran up the road to meet him.
He put clean clothes upon his back,
And a golden chain around his neck,
He made a feast and killed a fatted calf,
And invited the neighbours in.

Oh-o-oh, sinner,
When you're mingling with the crowd in Babylon,
Drinking the wine of Babylon,
Running with the women of Babylon,
You forget about God, and you laugh at Death.
Today you got the strength of a bull in your neck
And the strength of a bear in your arms,
But some o' these days, some o' these days,
You'll have a hand-to-hand struggle with bony Death,
And Death is bound to win,
Make no mistake about it;
Old bony Death is bound to win.

Young man, come away from Babylon,
That hell border city of Babylon,
Leave the dancing and gambling of Babylon,
The wine and the whiskey of Babylon,
The hot-mouthed women of Babylon;
Fall down on your knees,
And say in your heart:
I will arise and go to my father.

Lights fade on the PASTOR. Reprise of "Highway To Heaven."

SCENE XII

Lights up quickly on the MINISTER OF JUSTICE upstage centre.

MINISTER OF JUSTICE (*he speaks directly to the PASTOR*) It amazes me that you people, ever armed with your sanctimonious contrivances and legends, your fiction and your fables, could expect any sane, rational individual to believe in this God of yours who, from all indication, has perpetrated or aided and abetted the most glaring examples of incompetence it has been my misfortune to have witnessed.

I have seen your kind both ridicule and condemn man's attempt to fashion base metals into gold, yet you piously purport that this God of yours made the first of the human creatures from a lump of dust and dirt.

This first man Adam, I think you call him, was given a woman, Eve, who incidentally has Adam's extra rib to thank for her beginnings. But in spite of all my searching I have failed to find some legal proof of the exchanging of marriage vows and therefore must conclude that they entered co-habitation under some special, sanctified live-in arrangement.

Be that as it may, enter – Cain and Abel? Cain and Abel! Now I don't have to recall for you the name that is given to those people who make their entrance in this world preceded by salacious indiscretion, do I? Well, enter Cain and Abel – enter sibling rivalry. Cain slew Abel – hardly sibling rivalry; murder I think they call it and for that little show of temper he was given the holy equivalent of the slap upon the wrist – a special little mark upon his forehead. And wafting over the Garden of Eden, that heavenly Shangra-la, we heard the great stentorian harmonies of *So Long, It's Been Good To Know You* but *The Party's Over.*

And that's how things continued right down through the ages
until the Hebrew children
    Unionized
    Under Moses,
    Then sat down
    On the job
    And told old Pharaoh
    To fuck himself
    And build
    His own monuments!

    Then God stopped
    Gabbing
    With the angels
    Long enough to promise
    Seven plagues for Egypt
    If negotiations halted
    At the bargaining table...

    And He delivered!

    Ham's descendants
    Shouted *HALLELUJAH,*
    Caught a train
    And travelled
    To the Warden of the North
    Who counted heads,
    Heaved a sigh,
    And told them:
    Go, and make potatoes
    Out of rocks!

Then God stopped
Gabbing
With the Angels
Long enough to promise
Deep investigation into
Segregated schools,
And land titles,
And housing,
And equal opportunity
In general;
And threatened
Every kind of social action...

    Last I heard,
    God was at
    The Lieutenant Governor's
    Garden Party

Telling people
It was nice
To see the coloured population
Represented,
And yes, He was preparing
A paper on
Discrimination!

Can I hear an *AMEN*?

> *Lights out quickly. Music in: "The Boys From the Old Brigade."*

SCENE XIII

Lights fade up on the MINISTER OF DEFENCE seated at a table downstage left. He is finishing his meal at a banquet and as the song finishes he rises with much pomp and ceremony.

MINISTER OF DEFENCE   As Minister of Defence I have been takin' copious... (*rifles through his papers*) copious and strategic notes, and I say to you from the depths of my heart: *BURN THE CRAYONS!* Burn 'em all – the black ones and the white ones; the red ones and the yellow ones; burn 'em, I say, burn 'em! We are at battle stations and I say to you: we cannot maneuver in romper-rooms. Neither can we pitch camps in playgrounds. We must climb every mountain; we must ford every stream! I am prepared to lead the troops, yea, to the very gates of heaven; and
When I get to heaven
I'm gonna sing: I'm gonna shout;
And nobody there gonna put me out
Till I lay some heavy rap,
Till I mess some holy heads;
Can't do no more burnin'
Than I'm doin' here and now,
And gold ain't goin' to move me–
'Cause if the state of our economy
Is any indication,
I'll be standin' like a beggard
In a great big bargain basement.

And I'm gonna talk about hatin'–
Yes hatin';
'Cause there ain't no percentage
In my lovin' some fucked-up honkey
Who cannot stand the thought

That I'm alive
To make him know
He up and went and died
A long, long time ago!

Shoved his passion up fate's cunt
And got a dose of grief;
Now he looks at me
With steel gray eyes
And calls me nigger faggot,
And doesn't even know
The only thing he got worth blowin'
Is his mind;
And I do that
Just because
I am!

I'm gonna say
He butchered me
A thousand times
'Cause he couldn't find
His manhood
Jackin' off a stick shift:
Corvette lover... zombie...
He went and up and lost it
Suckin' at some mammy's tit,
While his old man got a little bit
Of some skinny pick-a-ninny
In some cotton field
Out back!
And made another bastard
To be another sacrifice,
When the master's boy done slithered
Into the sacred state of puberty.

Yeah, I gonna talk of hatin',
'Cause I know damn well
The master's precious son
Will always love his father's sins
More than he could love me.

I'm gonna talk about
A game was played–
And played for laughs
When heaven found
There was nothin' else
To laugh about...
Watch the black man lose his balls–
Ten points...

Watch him lose his manhood–
Fifty points!
Watch him lose his life–
Game over!
Funny – Very funny!

I'm gonna say
I've no regrets
For tactics I was forced to use
To aid in my survival;
Don't want to see but no one
Lookin' stern and calm and pious
And dealin' out them bullshit cards
And tellin' me
To turn my other cheek;
'Cause I only got but two,
And they was damned near jelly
'Fore I learned
If you can't walk on water, too,
You best get ready for the battle!

Gonna say:
I do not want
To hear my life reread,
When I know damned well
The parts that tell the real truth
Was jotted down in disappearin' ink–
'Cause heaven's got some fine old jive
About leavin' scars unopened!

And I will say this standin' tall,
And never on my knees.
The universe will crack and crumble–
The walls again will tumble,
And the bellow of Jerico
Will be a kitten's purr
When likened to the sound
Of my defiance.

No! Never on my knees!

He sits, lights a cigar, leans back and continues.

I recalls how just the other day this white man had the nerve
to say to me: sir, he says, life is a banquet; enjoy yourself.
Well, I looks this fool right into his eye and I says: sir, how
many times have we been led to the banquet table only to be
told that we could get our victuals in the kitchen?

How many times have we watched you wrap your lips around the giblets of sweet contentment while we have been asked to gnaw upon the drumstick of despair? How many times, I said, are we to be forced to accept the chocolate and not the mousse?

Well that same idiot looked at me with this Simple Simon grin across his face and said: My goodness, sir, I could be wrong, but you seem somewhat perplexed. What possibly could be the matter?

You can take your matters and you can shove your matters right on up your ass, I said. We will no longer be deceived. It is the eleventh hour – and the heat is on! We are ready to do whatever is necessary to redeem our right to sit down at the banquet of life with the rest of the human family. We are prepared to fight, and fight we will!
    We will fight you on the street corners,
    And in the pool halls.
    We will fight you on the dance floors,
    And at the back of the bus.
    We will fight you on the football fields,
    And at Bingo–
    We will fight–
    We will fight you at the welfare office,
    And in the taverns.
    We will fight you at the poker tables
    And on the basketball courts.
    WE WILL NEVER SURRENDER!

> *Lights fade on the MINISTER OF DEFENCE. Reprise of "The Boys From the Old Brigade." Music of "English Country Garden" fades in.*

SCENE XIV

> *Lights rise on the MINISTER OF THE INTERIOR seated down right in a high-backed wicker chair. He is staring incredulously in the direction of the MINISTER OF DEFENCE.*

MINISTER OF THE INTERIOR (*in a state of shock*) Did you hear that? Did you hear what he said? Did you hear what that man said? (*speaking to a woman in the audience*) Honey, I know you heard it; I know you did. I can tell by the look on your face. You as pale as a ghost, dear. You are, you are. (*to the rest of the audience*) She is; look at her. I was sittin' here, sayin' to myself: she's goin' to faint;

she's goin' to faint; my God, the poor thing is goin' to faint.
I was. I was sayin' it to myself. Oh, excuse me. (*to the
woman*) Do you need some water, honey? (*calling backstage*)
We got some water back there? (*to the woman*) Can I get you
a glass of water, dear? And maybe a little bit of Scotch... to
wash it down? No? You okay? Good. (*calling backstage*)
Forget it; she pulled herself together! (*to the woman*) But I
know how you feel, dear, I do... I do. My poor little heart just
goin' pitter-patter-pitter-patter-pitter-patter-pitter-patter! (*to
the audience*) Excusez-moi, s'il vous plait. Je desire une cigarette. That's a little bit of French.

> *He puts a red cigarette into a holder. Lights it. It is a folding
> cigarette holder, so he puts it to its full extension, drags deeply
> and continues.*

I am a-twitter; and palpitatin', honey, just palpitatin'. And the
last thing in this world I need is high blood pressure. Now
sweet things, you might not know it, but blacks and high
blood pressure go together just like white on rice; oh yes they
do; and ain't nothin' we can seem to do about it.

I recalls how just the other night I was sittin' down to have a
midnight snack before I went to bed. So I was puttin' a little
bit of salt on my pork chops and my ribs. And bless my soul,
as true's I'm in this chair, one of them chops looks up at me –
looks me dead into the eye and says to me as bold as piss:
"you next!"

Is that right, says l; we will see who's next. I'm here to tell
you, honey, that poor thing went to pork chop heaven in a
first class garbage can, and I been eatin' you guy's food from
that day on. Oh yes, I have. Makin' just like a rabbit, honey.
Hoppin' from salad to salad, and quickenin' wherever I can.
Yes dear, throw me in a croissant too. So I don't want to hear
nothin' about what that man's talkin'. I done took my little
chill pill so I don't need no stress and I don't want no mess.
I want to sit in my parlour and rock and fan; feather fan this
Lord's chile and sip on my little mint julep. I can't tell you
the last time I heard words like that. Well I think I was at the
Fleet Club or listenin' to "This Week in Parliament." If I'm
lyin' I'm flyin'!

I heard that. I heard that right over there. Now you all better
keep your smart remarks to yourself. You don't know me.
You have never met me. I can be lethal. I know you don't
want me to come down there and slap you up side your head
so you better watch your mouth.

Where was I? Oh yes. Talkin' about that man over there carryin' on with his *we will never surrender. We will never surrender!* There are times when I don't surrender. And there are
times when... surrender can be fun. You all know what I
mean?

(*to the same woman*) I know you know what I mean, girl.
'Cause I can tell from the look in your eye. Yes I can – you
can't fool me; I done wrote the book. I know that you done
waved your little white flag more than once. Gwan, yes you
did! You can tell me – look, you can't tell me, you can't tell
nobody. But that's alright, dear, don't you pay it no never
mind. You just keep right on truckin'. No, no – calm yourself
down honey. I said truckin'; *T* as in Tom, *R* as in Robert –
uckin. But I know where you comin' from. I bet you into aerobics, too, ain't you? Well you hold on to what you got, sweet
apples; and if you can't do that, you get someone to... hold on
to it for you. Ain't she cute?

Now, I know you all wonderin' who I am. Well let me put
your little old minds at ease. We must not let your minds
wander; they too small to be out on their own. Seriously
though, I am the Minister of the Interior. My professional
callin' in life was an interior decorator until I was pressed into
service... for the cause.

It is interestin' how that came about. Now it all started with
Leroy, my... room-mate. Laugh all you want, you don't know
my room-mate. Well anyway, it all started with Leroy.

I was just sittin' home mindin' my own business waitin' for
my welfare cheque to come in. I was between jobs. Well
chile, Leroy come charging through the door with his big ugly
self and he says to me: you better get your head together.

I said: you better settle down, Leroy. Don't you be comin' in
here actin' bad and sad and talkin' about my head. 'Cause
ain't nothin' wrong with my head. I just done put a brand
new S-curl in these locks so what you seein' is a world of
curls. So back off!

He said: I ain't talkin' about that. I'm talkin' about you findin' out who you are.

I said: Leroy, you must a-done took leave of your senses.
I happen to know who I am. And if you spent a few more
nights at home, you would know who I was too.

So he says: Don't you get smart with me. Everybody is needed right now to help our people. Everybody is needed. And
you gotta have your head together if you gonna be any help.

Well, I said, I can't promise you nothin' – *but* I will do the best
that I can.

Chile, I do not have to tell you, there was turmoil in the village from that day on. I was sittin' there at home, mindin' my
own business, waitin' for my welfare cheque to come in. I
told you I was between jobs. Well, chile, the only thing that
come in that day was Leroy. I say: Hi Leroy; Don't you be
callin' me that, he said. Say what? Oh pul-lease, I said, you
look like Leroy; you talk like Leroy; and God knows you act
like Leroy, so I don't know who the fuck you think you are.

He said: Look, we done got rid of all them slave names and I
ain't no Leroy, no more. My name is Abdul Muhammad.

Well you know me, dear, I just lets sleepin' dogs lie. I said:
Leroy, you can be Abdul or any other fool, it is no skin of my
ass. But I want you to understand one thing, a leopard do not
change its spots.

Before I know what's happenin' he was bro-in and he was sisterin' all over the place. And come to think of it, he was doin'
a hell of a lot more bro-in' than sisterin'. But like I said, dear,
a leopard do not change its spots.

Well everything came to a head the day I walked into my
apartment while Leroy was in the middle of his back to Africa
phase. I opened my door, honey, and there was spears on my
walls, shields over my windows, drums in my corners; there
was elephant tusk chairs, elephant stools, elephant tusk has-
socks – chile, I sat down to catch my breath and got the thrill
of a lifetime. But the best was yet to come. I goes into my
bedroom. The walls was black, the floor was black, the ceiling was black; the bed was black; the pillows was black,
honey, the bedspread was black. Leroy comes in the room
and turns off the light – it took me three hours to find him.
And that's when I said: I got to do something about this situation.

Well Lord I said what am I goin' to do. The first thing I got to
do is get me some power, and everybody knows that the
power is in the government. So I goes out and I calls a
meetin' of every black person in this province who works for
the federal government. And don't you know that every single one of them came to that first meetin'. Everyone of 'em.

And when the ten of us got together, we got right down to business. Now I was made the Minister of the Interior because it was felt that I was fully qualified to decorate the interior of your minds.

But it has come to my attention while I have been workin' to decorate the interior of the minds of my people, that we have a severe shortage of significant others. You all know what I'm talkin' about when I say significant others? Well – them are the folks you supposed to look up to so you can feel like you can do somethin'. You know – like when some poor little old chile be lookin' up at you and sayin': *I can't do nothin'.* Significant other say: *yes you can. – No I can't. – Yes you can. – No I can't. – YES YOU CAN! You think so? Hum! Well, okay; I'll give it a try.* That's a significant other.

Well everytime I went lookin' for one of your significant others, I found that you folks of the lighter persuasion done stole them all away. O yes you did dear. You fellows been commitin' larceny on a horrendous scale. You done damn near closed out our account. So I regret to have to tell you that some of your funds are about to be transferred.

Our lesson for this evening is called, *SKELETONS IN YOUR CLOSET.* Now I don't think you'll have a problem with the word *skeleton.* And I think that everybody here happens to know what a closet is. I heard that – I done told you to watch your mouth. Now you fellas has borrowed our skeletons for a mighty long time and we are takin' them back. I want to remind you here and now they was not out on permanent assignment. And for motor-mouth who's callin' me a congo queen, let us talk a bit about Queen Charlotte Sophia. Got you there, didn't I. Well Charlotte happened to be the wife of George III of England. That makes Charlotte the great, great, great grandmother of your present ruling monarch; and it is my duty to tell you that Charlotte was a lady of colour. So we are goin' to take from you skeleton number one.

And what about the Queen of Sheba? I ain't talkin' about no Gina Lollobrigida. I am speakin' of the authentic Ethiopian sister that had old Solomon climbin' up and down the walls. Chile, she nearly drove them other wives and concubines right around the bend. They be sittin' in they harem room brushin' out they hair; colourin' up they nails; rubbin' themselves with sweet-smellin' oils. All of a sudden they see Sheba, and they all be sayin': *Shhh, shhh, shhh – here come Sheba. Hi Sheba – Hi Sheba – Hi Sheba,* and skinnin' up they gums! And soon as Sheba turned away, they be sayin': *Black bitch –* and a-grinnin' and teeheeheein' and carryin' on.

One day Sheba had enough of that shit, honey, and she just up and said: *Look-a-here, I am tired of seein' the way you all be actin' up every time I drop in this place. I am sorry that I have to come all the way from Ethiopia to take care of your man just because none o' you all got whatever it is he needs. It ain't no fun bouncin' up and down on the back of some damn camel. And furthermore, though I know that no one here can dig the situation, the simple truth is – and git it clear – I am black but comely, you... daughters of Jerusalem.* We will take skeleton number two.

And I'll tell you something else, too. I don't care how many Liz Taylors play Cleopatra; if the sister was walkin' around today, she'd have a hell of a time gettin' a job with the Public Service Commission. And there goes skeleton number three. Can you spell – fun?

You got me wound up now. What about Beethoven? That's right, Beethoven. Da-da-da-dum. Yeh, him! Frau Fischer, an intimate acquaintance of the brother, has described him like this: short, stocky, broad nose (Lord, chile, the nose always gives us away) and blackish-brown complexion. Now she were not talkin' about Frosty the Snowman, dear. So I don't know where you fellas done got that picture you all keep plasterin' on his record albums. God knows what Lionel Ritchie be lookin' like in two hundred years. And another thing. Lord Haydn, who done taught Beethoven everything he knew, was also black and was referred to by the members of the Royal court as the Blackamoor. Regretfully I'll snatch from you skeletons four and five.

Then there was John VI of Portugal; Pedro I of Brazil; Charles XIV of Sweden. There was that Three Musketeers man, Alexandre Dumas, and that big Russian writer, Alexander Pushkin, and chile I could go on. But modesty do forbid and I don't know how much more your hearts could take. But I take five more skeletons out your closet.

Now as I draw our little lesson to a close, I would like to leave you with this bit of information. The first slaves held in the United States were not black; they were white. They were Europeans, mostly British. And did you know that in Virginia, white servitude was for a limited period of time, but sometimes it was extended for life? In the West Indies, particularly with the Irish, it was for life... White people were sold in the United States up to 1826 and Andrew Johnson, President of the United States, was a runaway and was advertised for in the newspapers. There were white children, dear, who were bootlegged and sold to blacks.

So remember, the next time you get an uncanny urge to stuff a watermelon in your purse; or you wake up from sleepwalkin' and find you be doin' the moonwalk; or you get a strange desire to kiss your T.V. set while you be watchin' "Roots", chances are you're being spooked by some skeletons in your closet. You all know what I mean. Of course you do!

The MINISTER OF THE INTERIOR exits laughing.

ACT II

SCENE I

The house lights begin to dim. Lights fade up on the HOST area and on a street sign which indicates where Maybe-You-Will-Chile-Boulevard cuts across Maybe-You-Won't-Chile-Avenue, while the song "Walk A Mile In My Shoes" is heard. ADIE enters from the rear of the house, dressed for work and carrying a bottle of champagne and a wineglass. She addresses the HOST area.

ADIE   Hey!... sweet thing... listen!
I hear you got a party goin' on.
(*pouring a glass of champagne*)
Well Adie Day is in a party mood
   'cause thirty years ago tonight,
(*she holds up the glass as if making a toast*)
   I entered the profession.
Chile, I stood across the street right there
   tryin' to make out like I was a virgin
   with a purpose,
   if not a meaning,
   like a rhinestone whore at Tiffany's;
Well, I thought, I'll come as close
   to lookin' like the real thing,
   until
   I know what I am doing in the store.

Well, chile, this car comes driving up;
   an' hon, it wasn't like it is today–
   you know, where some poor cock...
   (excuse my language, dear,
   but as they say, express yo'self)
   and you know how it is today,
   a poor old cock just wants to have some fun
       and gotta drag some stupid psycho
       everywhere it goes.

It wasn't like that in them days...
    you made your choice
    and did your thing;
    you paid your fee
    and went about your business–
    everything was copasetic!

Anyway this car drives up,
and this fine young thing
starts givin' me the sign.
Well I gets in a panic!
    I'm lookin' all around, my dear,
        for someplace else to go;
    I'm diggin' in my purse
    and I'm jus' actin' like a lunatic.

Will you get in this car, he said, I haven't got all night.
Well honey, I'm so scared, I jumped into that car,
    'cause I was thinkin',
    before I know what hits me,
    That man'll have me all laid out right here.
So I'm scrunched all up beside the door,
    and the poor man don't know what to do;
    he's tryin' hard to be so nice...
Dear, I'm clutchin' on that purse for all I'm worth,
    my old white coat is twisted all around me
    so I'm lookin' like a mummy,
    an' I sit there just a-starin' straight ahead.
Next thing I know, this hand is on my knee
    an' crawlin' up my thigh;
    now the only way it got there
    was because of all the shakin'
            and the shiverin'
            I was doin';
    an' chile, his timin' had to be like somethin' else,
    'cause he slipped right in between
            one of them shivers an' them shakes,
    an' found that Adie Day was on the case.
    I clamped them legs of mine so close together,
    I damn near fractured all of his intentions.

But that was my mistake, my dear.
Johnny Cake slammed on the brakes
    and flipped me in the air–
    I thought I was elastic woman...
    legs were flyin' everywhere;
    up across the seat,
    wrapped around the steerin' wheel–
Chile, it was enough to make a Negro woman blush!

So there I am
   sprawled out
   in all directions,
an' one ball Joe is huffin' and a-moanin',
an' you know what I'm thinkin'...
   if it wasn't for that dried up bag
   that wouldn't give me welfare
   when I needed some assistance
        for my baby and myself,
   I wouldn't have to cope with all *this* mess!
No, she sat there with her drippy self
   as old as God's great-grandmother,
   and said I was a strumpet...
   and then she said most coloured gals
        are a burden on the system
        because they're lackin' in integrity
        and instead of doing something useful–
        they would rather be a whore.
Well look, Miss Cunt, I said to her,
   since a whore is just a ho
   with a weakness for philanthropy,
I just rid myself of charitable persuasions,
   and sell a little pussy on the side.
And that should help to keep me off your back!
Well the bitch had made me mad
   and I didn't have much couth back then–
   couldn't fit it in my budget, dear–
But necessity does kick choice in the ass
   twenty-five times a week,
   and you have to make adjustments.
And a six inch heel from a platform shoe,
   adjusted very nicely
   to the side of Johnny's skull...
Well, in the end, he bitched a bit,
   but he gave me thirty dollars–
   probably didn't want to see some crazy woman
        rippin' up his car–
   and thirty bucks was money in them days;
   then he said I was a lousy fuck
        and threw my ass politely out the door.

His viewpoint was, undoubtedly,
   a minority opinion
   expressed while undergoing great duress...
A claim that quite a number of respected male citizens
   can support;
But Johnny Cakes had caught me
   while the flower was still bloomin',

And I hadn't learned the sayin':
   You must be a connoisseur at what you do.
I read that once when I was at my shrink;
    –all the girls was on that run–
    and what a lovely man but like I had to tell him,
    it's once around the track, my love,
          so run the race to win.
    see, he had this wife that nearly drove him crazy,
         and it took ages till I got that scene worked out.
        for a while I had to see him every day;
   well, I'd take him for a walk,
   then I'd help him go an' buy her little presents;
   a diamond here – a fur coat there–
   a little bit of sculpture–
   and I'd spend a little time with him
       to get him loosened up
        'cause the poor thing thought he couldn't function;
   but there was nuthin' wrong with him
       a dead wife wouldn't fix;
well anyway, the last time that I saw him,
   I was pleased to see that he had come so far.
and then he moved away
and I ain't heard a word of him in years;
Chile, I hope he's in some bed somewhere
   just fuckin' out his brains–

just like this man I had to see
   about my taxes.
Oh yes, my love,
I always gave the government its share.
   then they started gettin' greedy!
Now I done told them I was self employed
   and specialized in workin' with the public;
–I thought it best to be a little vague–
which gave me certain benefits;
and as a single mother I was makin' every claim
   that I could find;
which was my right.
well chile, they got their asses out of joint,
   and yelled about deductions disallowed.

Adie takes herself right to their office,
And they showed me to this boy
   who looked just like a computer–
   so he rambles on and on about they didn't make mistakes
   and he clicked and clacked and fooled
       with some contraption on his desk
       which apparently was all that he could talk to–
   this chile ain't even looked in my direction,
   and hadn't heard a single word I said.

Well he leaned all back and he shook his head
     and he started in to say: The apple says–
Now hold on there, I told this boy, control yo'self.
     I do not need computereze
     to understand the problem's not your apple,
     the problem is your wang!
     Let's do a little printout on frustration.
Twenty minutes later, dear,
   the government's back in swing,
   and settled down to represent the people.
It's just like raisin' children, hon–
   explain the do's and dont's;
   enforce the will's and wont's
   and life goes rollin' on!
God knows that it can be a trip, my dear,
And I suppose I have my ups and downs
   like everybody else;
   But I give a little nod to the rigours of the job,
     then I laugh an' go on easin' down the road.
   Capitulation really is accommodation
     with suicidal tendencies–
     now you can stop and drink your fill,
     but remember what your limit is.

Whoo – tonight I'm feelin' happy
like the woman I was meant to be
and knew I always was;
Chile, I might be fightin' fifty
and the legs don't climb the stairs
   the way they used to;
but the stuff is still in place...
so there's nuthin' much
   that's blurrin' up my technicolor outlook!

Oh – there's poor Harry comin' now.
   just regular as clockwork
   with his forty-seven fifty;
   two tens
   a five
   two two's and a one,
   roll o' quarters
   roll o' dimes
   roll o' nickels
   and one o' pennies
   and the other two bucks fifty in regrets;
don't ask me why – and come to think,
I wouldn't want to know,
'cause knowin' would destroy the satisfaction

that you get
from realizin' logic has
a few old warts and blemishes
            and then besides
you got to have consistencies in life.

Harry, what you doin' up this late?
Hah! You got your batteries recharge?
Well, honey, get out here and open up this door,
    like you got class,
        you talkin' to a lady who got standards to maintain.
Now, you might be forced to drop some other virtues,
    but never lose the art of being gracious.
Thank you, Harry.
Hey – here's to... style and elegance
    from the old, established school!
Yah! there's goin' to be some sweet sound
    comin' down,
    on the nightshift.

   Houselights down. Stage to pre set. Lights out.

SCENE II

*Lights rise on the centre stage area which becomes a club.
Lighting should simulate the garishness of the typical gay club,
a sign with La Mirage etc. Music is played loudly, "Git It Out
Your System" by Millie Jackson. The voice of a Master of
Ceremonies is heard.*

**RECORDED
VOICE**
COME ON NOW GIRLS, SETTLE YOUR TITS AND LET'S GET ON WITH THE
SHOW. YES, RAMONA DEAR, WE SEE YOU OVER THERE! IT'S IMPOSSI-
BLE TO MISS YOU. DIDN'T ANYONE TELL YOU HALLOWEEN WAS YES-
TERDAY? AND THERE'S MISS KITTY! YOU LOOK ABSOLUTELY DIVINE.
WHAT DO YOU CALL THAT, DEAR? VINTAGE SALLY ANN? OOOOOH,
TACKY!

WELL, NOW WHAT YOU'VE ALL BEEN WAITING FOR. THE QUEEN OF
TRAGEDY: THE EMPRESS OF REMORSE: THE HIGH PRIESTESS PATHOS:
LADIES AND... FIGURATIVELY SPEAKING... GENTLEMEN, THE PIECE OF
RESISTANCE OF THE EVENING... MISS ETHIOPIA!

*ETHIOPIA enters amid wild cheering and the beginning
strains of "All By Myself." When the noise has subsided, she
seats herself close to the audience, microphone in hand, and
begins to sing "All By Myself." ETHIOPIA will be seen in full
light until she begins her monologue. She will then be lit with a
single spot.*

ETHIOPIA   An image / passing as a human being / contorts a frown into a
smile / & telegraphs a message of HOW ARE YOU to my mind /

An image / pretending to be me / confuses fact & fiction
by responding with some
BULLSHIT
saying / EVERYTHING'S JUST GREAT-GREAT
GR-ea-t
graaate
graaaate /
that's the sound of a heart / draggin' into overtime / the sound
of the song / some ancient mattress sings / while whiskey-
flavoured promises are pledged / with panting slur / & climax
into
hush-a-by
lull-a-by
peaceful time is here /
off to bed / sleepyhead /
let emptiness come sneak into my solitude / & ravage all my
dreams / & bittersweet rememberings of yesterday / when all
my thoughts were young as innocence itself / & love &
understanding flowed from me like MAN-AH was completely in
control / & HAPPY DAYS / unsanitized for early primetime
viewing / meant more than suckin' lollipops out back behind
some diner / but no one really thought that we was fuckin'
up / TRADITION / cuz
no one saw
no decrease in
the surplus population
&
charcoal grey apologized /
discreetly / for the presence
of the colour pink / that
brightened up our wardrobes / then
someone read between the lines of jesus loves me /
this i know /
for the bible tells me so /
& found that it was not apPLICable / to faggots / according to
the christians / but not to dr. kinsey / who advised the church
& state that
OVER-ZEALOUS STRETCHING

OF THE BOUNDARIES OF CHOICE/
RESULTED IN LIBIDO
SCHIZOPHRENIA/
& Vindication toppled Vaseline/
& All my friends were normalized/statistically/
& Dr. kinsey opted for a sex change/& emerged as dr. ruth/
& I became a shadow in that s
o
l
o land
convention deems
FORBIDDENNNN/
where the semi-hemi-demi-folk/on one square mile of
anguish/ are doomed to dance the midnight mass to mad-
ness/as it boldly stalks & preys upon the hunted
& the hunters/
who give themselves like
sacrificial relics
to some unrequited passion ooooozing from the acid queen/
in neon never never land/where amyl nitrate castles kiss
the sky/& snowflakes mound
around
my tears
to form
an image... of a pumpkin... that can change into
a honda/or
a lincoln/or
an epic fairy tale of those men who wander
straight into some pansy paradise/
every evening/after sunset/where
they wrap their guilt in fantasies
of mounting virgin maidens/& everybody
knows that *GETTIN'* blown don't make
you queer/cuz
that's really just
benign
PARTICIPATION
that seduces *HOMOPHOBIA*
in all those eager washrooms
where the corporate heads
go
down
to meet
the public
made of frantic fathers fingering hipoCRAZY
& someone else's son/while looking for an
all-night store/via short-cuts through a
graveyard filled with
hearts that have no beat/

yet do not rest in peace
because
they're waiting/
like i am waiting/
for a gentle touch
which even desperate places
sometimes give/when i find
i am so very much

Singing.

All by myself; don't want to be
All by myself... etc.

*At the end of her song ETHIOPIA exits with great flourish
upstage right. There is much applause which will continue
until CHUCK enters from stage left.*

SCENE III

*CHUCK applauds mockingly. He lounges suggestively with a
beer in his hand, and slowly looks around the club.*

CHUCK   People, needin' people, are a fuck
                                    I said
                                    last night,
         as I stood up on the corner
         and watched this guy go walkin'
                                    round the block
                                    a dozen times,
         actin' like he couldn't find some street
         that he was lookin' for; dickhead didn't
         seem to know there weren't no street names
         printed on my cock!
But what the fuck;
There ain't a game that I ain't seen
         a thousand times or more,
         and most are just a fuckin' drag.
But – you got to pay the rent
         if you are lucky,
         so you deal with all the hazards of the job
                                    like the weather
                                    or no tricks
                                    or those eyes that say
                                    I want to come
                                    and love you
                                    for tonight!
         People, needin' people, are a fuck

I said
but
action's slow
so maybe I'll just give the guy a break
and he can give me head
and tell his problems to his pillow
while I get a little sleep.
Don't get me wrong – the name is Chuck, not free-lunch
chump
cuz
I don't fuck for I.O.U.'s
for Master Charge
or Visa
Just hard old cash... and services delivered
to the buyers
or to those I choose
to sleep with
cuz
I want to...
like the guy that was beside me
with his head against my shoulder
and his arm across my chest
cuz
his eyes had said
please let me come
and let me love you
for tonight...

And my mind was saying
People, needing people, are a fuck because
I know that need;
that need that gives your love its
definition;
then acts as your assassin
when your usefulness is over;
the need that made me tell someone
WHO LOOKS LIKE HIM:
You were older than the Sphinx, my love,
But younger than tomorrow's dawn;
When you looked into my eyes, my love,
And made me stop
And gaze upon the beauty of your mind.
You saw an empty soul, my love,
You knew the reason for my pain,
So you gently filled it up with love,
You gave me life again.

And to simply say: I love you,
Seems offensive;

It isn't sound enough,
Not quite profound enough a reason
Why you let me keep this all-intensive hold
On your emotions;
But it's that love that sees us through
When I hurt you like I do,
When without rhyme and without reason
I blindly carry out high treason
By the way I cast my doubts on your devotion;
But when everything seems wrong,
You touch my spirit with your song,
You are a mystery
And I guess I love the mystery that's you.

You softly touched my heart, my love,
And loneliness was put to flight;
We fuelled my inner glow, my love,
By letting me reflect the light
Of your eternal flame;
You reached and took my hand, my love,
When many others let me fall,
You taught me how to stand my love,
You heard a dying call.

And to simply say: I love you,
Seems so easy
It isn't quite enough,
Not quite precise enough
To truly tell you what I mean
When I reveal the depths of my devotion;
So, humbly, I would die for you,

And that's the best that I can do
Until I find some other way
To meet the price i have to pay
For being such a drain on your emotions;
You dismiss your pain in teardrops,
While you hold me till my fear stops,
You are a mystery
And I guess I love the mystery that's you.

Then you know what?
He put his arms around me
And he cried into my shoulder
And he told me I was the centre of his life–
Then we went and fucked with someone else!

And that, as they say,
Is the name of that tune!

So this guy that had the eyes
And who thought he'd found a mark...
I just pushed him out the way
    cuz
      I ain't got no time
      for all that shit;
But you know somethin' else?
I thought I heard him crying in his sleep...
But what the fuck!
I hated that dumb asshole
For makin' me think of that;

This mornin' when I told the guy to split,
He asked me what he did to make me mad.
I said: I'm not mad; I got some things to do;
I'll maybe see you round, sometime;

HUH! LIKE FUCK!

There he is, standin' over there;
Lookin'... always lookin'...
With those eyes.

People, needin' people, are a fuck!

    *CHUCK exits upstage right. There is a symphony of light. A
    sign with La Mirage flashes on and off. Music, Jacques Brel's
    "Carousel" begins softly.*

SCENE IV

    *The HOST enters from upstage left and speaks as he walks
    downstage centre to the HOST area.*

HOST   Behind the smile,
    The sparkling eye
    And easy laughter,
    There lurks a menace
    You cannot control;
    Once upon a possibility
                      perhaps
    But never now—

    And everything is rushing
    To a second when
        just before
        we strike,

We see the fear and shock
Distort your face,
And hear you
Try to reason
With the savage;
You shout unfair – unfair!
We did not know the rules
Of your game.

But we will grant you instant replay;
Of smiles that flashed so quickly
                    and so falsely;
Of eyes that twinkled
Only when the fire raged within;
You will recall the many times
You did not fail to add your insults
                    to some injury,
And made your jokes
                    you thought
At our expense;
You laughed–
We laughed–
And thinking that
We did not know
What you were laughing at,
You laughed some more–
And we laughed too...
And soon
You could not fathom
Why we laughed,
But in confusion
You laughed on...
LAUGH NOW!

Remember when,
Convinced you were our teacher,
You kept us at a distance;
You did not seem to realize
You gave us
Quite unwittingly,
The gift of objectivity...

We cannot see
            through eyes of blinded men;
We cannot hear
            through ears that have gone deaf;
We cannot understand
            your pleas for understanding;
Your cruelty has long since taught us

How to use
A new vocabulary;
Your vanity has always been our greatest weapon—
We knew it was the weakest link
That caused your chain to crumble;
So, we are sure
That you cannot appreciate
The irony
The profundity
The hilarity
Of the cataclysmic
Second!

Lights fade on the HOST. Music up softly, "Cotton Head Joe."

SCENE V

Lights fade up slowly on the OLD MAN who is watching the previous scene.

OLD MAN   How intricately you weave
Your foolish little webs of life;
More intent upon design than quality.
It's a lonely, troubled journey
From the cradle to the grave,
Tread softly;
Too many wait with baited breath
To snuff the tiny flame
That lights our way.
Scarcely recognizable,
Such action lurks behind the guise
Of many labels,
And I have heard it called concern
And guidance.

A thousand mothers kneel a thousand times
Beside a late-night bedside
And pray for sons like oaks,
And not like willows;
And frantic fathers armed with premature cigars
Envision football players who
If by chance and at some future time
Throw tainted ladies from a second story window,
Will be considered normal.
But each is quick to add
That if their pleas cannot be heard,
Second best still has a place,
So a daughter might be considered;

P.S.
Designate – professional virgin.

Fate provides the raw material,
We create the object,
And dream our dreams for others
And make them all come true:
And no one gives a damn about the consequence!

A thousand mothers cluck a thousand times
On morning phone-in shows,
And hope some neighbour's listening to
Their ten o'clock philosophy
Ably laced with coffee,
Laced with gin:
And if some voice is slightly edged,
Perhaps it's just because on yesterday,
A daughter stood in paralysing fear,
Thought that she would bleed to death
There in her bedroom,
Clutching a gift from mother,
A tiny pack of pills
And some instructions
To read directions carefully–
But that's called guidance;
And that quiet kid from down the street
Is always hanging around...
But he's Bobby's friend,
Bobby's friend...
How many nights has he stayed out lately?
Better keep an eye on that–
Thank God they're both so keen on sports
A thousand mothers whisper
In a thousand lonely kitchens,
Then draw themselves into themselves
And cry a thousand tears.
But that is called concern.

As many fathers rush into some office
And greet the boss on first name basis
And grieve that only salary denies
A deeper friendship;
And if some voice is slightly edged,
Perhaps it's just because last night,
When everything seemed right,
His wife had kept her pants up
And kept her nightie down;
And then besides, the kids next door
Might get the wrong impression–

So back to back they argued through the night;
Damn the kids – and damn them with their silence
Next morning at the breakfast table...
A thousand fathers down an extra double scotch,
Then try to prod a faint response
From the snoring mass of easy comfort, easy virtue,
Hulking near them in their sheets;
And wonder if the supper time has passed at home
Without them.

But you see
Children watch–
And children know–
Children hear–
And also listen;
And that is why at some unguarded moment,
A thousand mothers are made to ask a thousand fathers
Why their child went downstairs at two in the morning
And blew his brains out.

> *Lights fade on the OLD MAN. The song "There's A Man*
> *Goin' Round Takin' Names" is heard.*

SCENE VI

> *Lights rise on the MINISTER OF HEALTH AND WELFARE.*

MINISTER
OF HEALTH
AND
WELFARE   Seymore killed his wife today!
What you say, chile,
What you say?
Yes ma'am, shot her,
Just this mornin';
Killed hisself, too,
And the baby.
Lord have mercy, shot that infant?
No ma'am, beat him with a gun,
But Doctor said:
Nobody suffered much.

Seymore pressed his son against his shoulder,
Mindful that the slightest stir
Might tread upon some innocent preoccupation,
And camouflaged as gentle interruption,
Creep into the virgin world of baby thoughts
To feed on sweet contentment.

The floor groaned to the rocking chair,
A siren wailed to the night,
That they knew why the black man cried
In muffled silence;
Could it be tomorrow that some image
Might impress itself upon a tender mind
Not fortified against reality on the loose,
And deal a mortal blow to endless possibilities?
A faucet shed a midnight tear
And wondered why poor Seymore
Had to make like Abraham
With no replacement lurking in the bushes.

Black folks always seem to get those
Hand-me-down revisions!

But who's to say that Seymore was not right
Because he thought that there should be
No more tomorrows
Belching out their legacies of grief,
While sombre shadows inched along the precipice
Of his thinking,
And blotted out alternatives...
Blotted out the first and last command
That Seymore gave his son:
Let your blood call out to daddy,
Not to silent sidewalks
And dealers in indifference
Little son...
Daddy *UNDERSTANDS!*

Seymore knew that mass communication
Would slouch against his bedroom door
With cigarette and camera
And ever-ready pen
To serve a panting public;
Knew it as he fell across
His terror-stricken, coma-clad
About-to-be-emancipated woman;
Knew that she could never see
The purpose of the sacrifice;
Knew it as he saw the resignation in her eyes
Stop his breath–
Stop his heart–
But not his penetration;
Knew it as his senses reeled
And plunged into a sea of sweat
And baby blood;

Knew it as he wedged his head
Between her breasts
And blew his brains into her chest.

The T.V. cast an eerie glow
And hissed its disapproval.

Seymore killed his wife today!
What you say, chile,
What you say?
Yes ma'am, shot her,
Just this mornin';
Killed hisself, too,
And the baby.
Lord have mercy, shot that infant?
No ma'am, beat him with a gun,
But Doctor said:
Nobody suffered much.

Lights fade on the MINISTER OF HEALTH AND WELFARE.
The song "There's A Man Goin' Round Takin' Names" is heard.

SCENE VII

Lights rise on the MINISTER OF JUSTICE.

**MINISTER
OF JUSTICE** Don't no one need to die
                  like that
                  I'm thinkin',
On a cold and drizzly Monday afternoon,
Stretched out like discarded meat
On some got-no-time-to-give-a-fuck cement;
I'm lookin' at my boy
              down there,
And all that I can reason is
Don't no one need to die like that.

I'm tryin' to get this picture
                  out my mind,
And I can feel my hands
Against my face,
Against my eyes,
But I can't even cry a tear;
Jesus Christ, I'm hurtin' now,
I'm one big awful hurt;
But I can't even cry one tear.

That boy's my life;
That boy's my life
And someone up and blew him all away
Like he was fodder;
Now I know I should do something–
And I know I must do something–
But don't nobody see
I can't think right,
                              right now.

I feel the eyes
That's burnin' in my back,
And know that someone thinkin':
He ain't got no business here
Lookin' like he's lookin'–
Like I should have staggered on up home
And changed into my Sunday best
To watch my boy get killed...
They say they feelin' sorry
                              for his mama,
                              on her hands,
                              on her knees,

Crawlin' in his blood,
Beggin' for our boy to come alive–
Tryin' for to breathe that boy alive–
And I'd like to go and get beside her,
Hold her close and tell her
That everything's alright...
But I can't do that,
I don't know how,
Seems like...
Somehow I forget.

So someone please
Go up to her
And do my job for me
And say you looked behind my mask
And saw... that I was dyin'...
                              for my boy.

Forget you saw me take that drink
What old Joe handed me
Because he understood
I got to keep my mind froze up...
I ain't felt no real pain for years;
I just keep my mind froze up!

But I don't want to think no more;

I'm goin' in the house
To get a shave
And try to cry a little
Till the people come
                    to say
That they's so sorry–
And nod their heads and whisper that
As sure as there's a God above,
That lazy, useless, ugly drunk
Done went and killed his boy.

* * * * * * * * * * * *

She wrapped her arms
Around her ample bosom
And remembered
How a helpless bit of life
Had clung there
For protection:
She felt, somehow,
That simple act might ease the pain
Which, at that moment,
Threatened
To rip her chest wide open;
Then she gently swayed and moaned
While a dollar-forty-nine-day-Woolco Jesus,
From his designated spot
On the peeling-papered wall,
Kept calm blue eyes
Impassively preoccupied
With some distraction
Painted on the ceiling...
Divine insignificance.

The sweet and sickening fragrance
Of far too many flowers
Herded all together
In a cluttered shabby room,
Really didn't give a shit
About the figure
Which stood...
                alone...
And the omnipresent quiet
Was the solitary witness
As she went about the ritual
                        of grief.

Tears which had lain silent,
Manacled and caged,
Damned by endless days of self-restraint
And cast-off hope,
Slipped towards the floor
And pulled her to her knees–
She didn't feel the splinters;
What's a bit of pain,
                    more or less?
Jesus didn't seem to care!
He kept his concentration
                        on the ceiling–
Maybe he thinking
                of the cross
                of the nails
                or even Barbara Hutton
                and so on... and so on...
And so she turned away
To let her gaze
            fall
                    on her sleeping body...
Picked up one carnation
Which had fallen from the bunch
And even now prepared
                    to wilt
                        and die.

She smoothed the satin pillow
That was placed beneath his head
And thought about
The many times, seems like for years,
The last thing she had done each night
Was wonder if her boy was... comfortable...
But lately
He was never home
When exhaustion hypnotized determination...

Was it only yesterday
That he had grinned
And left the house
And said he'd be back soon?
You caught a glimpse of that thread-bare coat
And made a mental note
That sometime soon,
With several polished offices
Gleaming their approval,
He'd have a new one...
Only yesterday?

But now
She groped her way
                    into the kitchen,
And eased herself
                    into her rocking chair,
Folded her arms
                    across the faded housedress
                    that had played the losing game
                    with Oxydol;
She studied for an eternity
The figure that was slumped
                    upon a bench
                    across the room;
She said nothing–
He said nothing–
There was everything to say;
There was nothing to say;
So each one sat and tried to reason
                              how come
                              this:

How come a life
Weren't worth no more
Than a stupid little bullet?
How come that man had said
He wasn't takin' no abuse, no more...
And anyhow,
It looked as if that boy had had a knife
                              or pipe
                              or stick
                              or something.

How come
The people say that man was right?
'Cause you just can't be too careful!
But seems to me
That there are folks
Who'll never know the feeling of the desperate ones
Who go through life
Like tolerated guests
In a cold and foreign household;
Or ever understand how lucid rules
Ill-defined,
Let many glimpse the promised land
Through the ass-hole end of life's telescope.
But tomorrow night
                    on Wednesday,
He'll drop in to Joe's

And she will go to church,
And each will have some burdens
                              washed away;
Until it's time to go back home...

* * * * * * * * * * *

At eight o'clock on Tuesday,
A man went stumbling to the door
To greet the bearer of a gift–
Ten, hundred dollar bills,
And some words which said:
   It's just a little something
   To show you how I feel,
   And let you people understand
   That I fix up my mistakes.
And desperation made that man
Reach out his hand
And take it...

Later that same evening,
A tired and beaten mother
Slowly turned the pages
Of some book,
And looked at all the faces
Of those selected few
Thought worthy of being voted
As the Mother of the Year...
Worthy
Because of all her suffering...

And she gently took a pencil
And marked the letter X
Beside the picture of
Rose Kennedy!

It's really very sad,
Ain't it?

> *Lights out quickly on the MINISTER OF JUSTICE. One verse
> of "There's A Man Goin' Round Takin' Names."*

SCENE VIII

Lights rise on the PASTOR.

PASTOR It's sad, it's sad,
I heard them say,

That one so young
Should pass away
Unfulfilled,
And even yet
Unfulfilling.

Saltless tears – crocodile fashion;
Perfumed boredom,
Orchestrated passion, now;
Nothing then...
When even this charade
Might have somehow served to say
HOLD ON!

Only nature grieves
With sincerity.

And well she might;
For whose deft hands first fashioned
That bit of dust and ashes
Now commanded to return in peace
From whence it came?
Who sighed her latest breath
In eager nostrils
And feeling pleased,
She kilned that clay
A bit too long, for some,
And stands condemned
For mutilated handiwork
By those who cannot see the pleasure
Or the purpose
In that-birthmark...

For there are those who will not see
The method in your mystery,
And in frustration substitute
A madness,
All their own!

It's sad, it's sad,
I heard them say,
And watched the last car pull away–
And wink!

Lights fade on the PASTOR. Reprise of "Many Rains Ago."

SCENE IX

Lights rise on the HOST seated downstage centre. Music fades.

HOST   We have wandered, you and I, through some of the mansions of my mind, and I am only too aware that the journey has not always been an easy one. But there is one more stop which we must make together in a special place which I have come to call my quiet corner. I found it on some *FRY*day, at half past discontent when I was trying to remember some of the invaluable teachings that have helped me to chart a passage way through an oftimes turbulent and chaotic journey which I affectionately call my life.

And it was in that quiet corner where a cacophony of musings and teachings, as young as now, as old as antiquity, metamorphosed into a simple acknowledgement, valid and indisputable that:

pretentiousness will allow you
in the springtime of your twenties,
to think your life an epic
for a book;

but later, as the season
waxes lush into your thirties,
your saga will be captured
in a chapter;

with a sharpening of perspective
in the summer of your forties,
your story will be perceived
in just a paragraph;

you will humbly trace your journey
as you ponder through your fifties,
in the eloquent simplicity
of a sentence;

yet when you know
that all you know is nothing,
while cocooning in your sixties,
your who & what & where & when & how
becomes a word;

when wisdom comes to court you
in your waning autumn seventies,
the sum of you existance
will be measured in a look;

understanding renders counsel
in the winter of your eighties,
and will shape your life experience
into a smile;

and all at peace with silence
in the surity of your nineties,
your inner light will shine
upon the countless revelations
subtly etched in lines and creases
on your face:

and with a deference to acknowledgement,
you will merely
close your eyes.

So it was to my quiet corner I would go whenever I felt my
pot of human feeling bubbling low. And there I would allow
myself to drift a while and sift a while through many
moments long ago forgotten, but somehow hold within them
secrets telling us how we make tomorrows. And if I had
reached a point where I was so far down that any further
down was up, I could always hear the old ones softly whisper:

You must know that you are part of your creator,
And hold within you power to create.
Don't be afraid to fail
At attempting mankind's scale,
Perhaps you're not a singer–
You are a song!
You are a note of ringing splendour
In the universal anthem,
Know your sound–
Know your sound–
You have a life of many pages
To expand the book of ages,
Take a pen, take some ink,
And set it down.
Be a sentence, not a word,
Be of self, and not of herd,
It is your right,
You have the choice
To be your spokesman,
With your voice.

Now step outside your cage
And touch tomorrow.

Yet my most precious moments spent in my quiet corner are those during which I would hear Lorraine Hansberry say:

O, the things that we have learned in this unkind house that we have to tell the world about!

DESPAIR? Did someone say despair was a question in the world?

Well then, listen to the sons of those who have known little else if you wish to know the resiliency of this thing you would so quickly resign to mythhood, this thing called the human spirit...

LIFE? Ask those who have tasted of it in pieces rationed out by enemies.

LOVE? Ah! Ask the troubedors who come from those who have loved when all reason pointed to the uselessness and foolhardiness of love. Perhaps we shall be the teachers when it is done. Out of the depths of pain we have thought to be our sole heritage in this world o, we know about love!

And that is why I say to you that, though it be a thrilling and marvellous thing to be merely young and gifted in such times, it is doubly so, doubly dynamic — to be young, gifted and black.

And always, just as I was ready to step out from my quiet corner and reach for that nobility to which man alone can aspire, these words would flow from deep within my soul:

One thing about this naughty world in which we live, said a Mr. Green, *is that in whichever way you're goin', there's always a crowd of people to go along with you.*

If you're goin' up, well now, they say, we'll go along with you; and if you're goin' down, they will push you down. But I want to tell you wherever you may be, just keep a-goin'.

If you strike your finger on the thorn of a rose,
Keep a-goin',
If it hails or if it snows,
Keep a-goin',
There's no use to sit and whine,
When the fish ain't on your line,
Bait your hook and keep a'tryin',
But keep a-goin'.

Now suppose the weather kills your crop,
Well keep a-goin',
Though it's hard to reach the top,

Keep a-goin',
Suppose you're out of every dime,
Well gettin' broke just ain't no crime,
Tell the world you're feelin' fine
And keep a-goin'.

    Music begins softly, "Cotton Head Joe," as in Act I, Scene I.

Now when everything seems up,
Keep a-goin',
Drain the sweetness from your cup
And keep a-goin',
See the wild birds on their wing,
Hear the bells that sweetly ring,
And when you feel like singin', sing–

Keep your chin up–
And keep a-goin'.

    Music continues at full volume. Lights fade slowly on the
    HOST until a spot remains which in turn fades to black.

Harlem Duet

by Djanet Sears

Canada's 1998 Governor General's Literary Award winner for *Harlem Duet*, Djanet Sears is also an award-winning director and has several acting nominations to her credit for both stage and screen. She is the recipient of the Floyd S. Chalmers Canadian Play Award, a Harry Jerome Award, and Dora Mavor Moore Awards for both writing and directing. Djanet is a founding member of the Obsidian Theatre Company, and one of the driving forces behind the AfriCanadian Playwrights' Festival, a celebration and examination of African diasporic writing for the stage in Canada.

OTHELLO DECONSTRUCTED: DJANET SEARS' HARLEM DUET

by Leslie Sanders

The very name of *Harlem Duet* signals a concern with doubling. Two songs always resonate: Her and Him, She and He, Billie and Othello, Eurocentric and Afrocentric, the song of the West and an African Diasporic Blues. The play's focus is on Billie, whose experience of love and betrayal, the archetypal and classic provenance of the Blues, is its central story. Billie's betrayal is all the more painful and complex, however, because her lover abandons her for a white woman, a type of loss, it is important to note, that the Blues do not address. In the logic of this play, Billie's betrayal and loss is not only a Blues story, then; it is also a Western, canonical story, the story of Othello, in Shakespeare' s play by that name. Billie is Othello's first wife, his black wife, his black world. In love-making he turns her body into a country: "the heightening Alleghenies of Pennsylvania. The curvaceous slopes of California. The red hills of Georgia… I'm staking my claim." When he leaves her for the disembodied Mona, known to the audience only as a voice and the glimpse of an arm, he enters that other world, the white world in which he is truly "Othello" – a role we do not see played out, but whose contours and bitter end the audience knows from the beginning.

Othello is, without doubt, the best-known black character in Western theatre; in fact, it is Western canonical theatre's only significant role for a black character, although it has been far more often played by a white in black-face. Moreover, the character's fame extends well beyond the play. From a Eurocentric perspective, Othello came to signify the "noble" African in the West, a figure about whom the "West" has long been, at best ambivalent (Jordan). The phrase "unvarnished tale" appears frequently in the authenticating prefaces by white sponsors of African-American slave narratives. These words repeat those of another "dark-hued" character, Othello: "I will a round unvarnish'd tale deliver / Of my whole course of love" (I iii 90-91). The abolitionist William Lloyd Garrison doubly invokes Othello in his authentication of the 1845 *Narrative of the Life of Frederick Douglass* when he asserts that Douglass's "unvarnished tale" has "nothing… set down in malice, nothing exaggerated…," a phrase used by other authenticators as well (Olney). In another vein, and 150 years later, the press repeatedly identified O.J. Simpson with Othello, during Simpson's trial for the murder of his white wife, Nicole Brown Simpson and her friend Ronald Goldman, which transfixed the United States in 1995 (Crenshaw). These matters resonate in *Harlem Duet*.

Harlem Duet stays on the edges of Shakespeare's play, but it disturbs utterly how we will experience *Othello* forever after. Three aspects of this disturbance are particularly noteworthy. The first is that an effect of *Harlem Duet* is to give Othello a context: he comes from somewhere, has a country, a world, a world view. He is not the exotic Moor whose history we know only as the romance by which he courts Desdemona. He is a representative diasporic black man: over time, we see him as slave, we see him as performer, we see him as Harlem dweller and contemporary academic. In each era, he falls in love with whiteness, craving the gaze of the white woman as affirmation of his manhood. First she is the slave mistress who relies on him. Later, she is the stage director who gives him his big break, elevating him from minstrel to Shakespearean actor (albeit in *Pericles*, a play of uncertain authorship). Finally, she is an academic colleague, whose acceptance seems to cement his stature in the white world outside the Harlem apartment he had shared with Billie, that overlooks the Apollo Theatre, at the centre of the African diasporic world. Othello's Shakespeare, then, has not only come from somewhere, he has abandoned someone and somewhere else. His choice of whiteness is not singular, and is always dangerous.

The second impact of the *Othello* theme is that it forces the audience, regardless of who they are, into viewing the play from the perspective of black audiences. *Harlem Duet* makes obvious the particularity of the "stage reality"; the play exposes the assumed whiteness of all plays that emanate from white cultures. Thus it provides an experience of how those "other" in a culture might feel dislocated by the dominant culture, and wish themselves to dislocate and challenge its premises.

The play also invites the audience to view Shakespeare's Othello from the perspective of contemporary black communities. Few seeing *Othello* today will know that a year before its composition, Elizabeth I had banished all blacks from Britain (Fryer). For its early audiences in whose society racist views were beginning to solidify, the marriage of Othello and Desdemona was disquieting indeed. As white racism intensified, the spectacle that Othello provides became increasingly abhorrent, a matter until recently virtually unmentioned in Shakespeare criticism. The angle of vision, and consequently the disquiet in black audiences of *Othello* is quite different, although they, too, are discomforted the spectacle of Othello's interracial romance. *Harlem Duet* focuses attention on the experience in black communities when black men abandon black women for white women. Part of *Harlem Duet*'s response, its signifying on, *Othello* lies in its assumption the concerns of a black audience rather than of a white one. No matter who is in the audience, then, their view of *Othello* is disrupted, the significance of his blackness is changed. He no longer is seen as an alien in a white world, but rather as a member of the black community who is dazzled by whiteness and follows it away from the community's place and space. The Othello of *Harlem Duet* is far from heroic; as a result the canonical Othello is greatly diminished. Othello's relationship with Mona feeds his ambition, a fact noted, it is implied, by his colleague named Yago. His love for Mona is not quite comprehensible as other than an expression of ambition, but it is partly rendered understandable by its relationship with that other Othello. It is the effect of his betrayal on Billie, however, that forms the main focus of the play.

As heroine, Billie also disrupts dramatic expectations. She is not particularly strong or resilient, nor does she link her own sorrow and loss through the blues to the timeless repetition of love and pain. Instead, invoking other diasporic traditions, Billie turns to magic, studying alchemy, and importing Egyptian potions to poison a handkerchief Othello had once given her as sign of his love. Pretending acceptance of his marriage, she returns it to him as an apparent, but lethal, sign of good will. Having accidentally also splashed poison on herself, Billie retreats into madness, and is hospitalized. Yet, Billie's play veers away from the tragedy of that other play by drawing together what has been rent asunder by Othello's desertion. Although she has lost Othello, in the course of the play she reconciles with her father, Canada, who comes from Dartmouth, Nova Scotia to visit, and decides to stay. This reconciliation itself is critical to a variety of the play's concerns. Billie's Canadianness evokes the time in which Canada provided refuge to escaped slaves from the United States; it also brings the diaspora to Harlem. Her nationality is noted by other characters; her tastes in food cause remark even though other practices, particularly around hair, draw the community of women together. However, like Venice in *Othello*, Harlem is an international city. It is not "the United States,"; rather it is where the African diaspora gathers, where community is possible, where healing can occur.

Harlem Duet won the Floyd S. Chalmers Canadian Play Award and four Dora Mavor Moore Awards in 1997 and the Governor General's Award for Drama in 1998.

Works Cited:

Crenshaw, Kimberle Williams. (1997). "Color-blind Dreams and Racial Nightmares: Reconfiguring Racism in the Post-Civil Rights Era." In Birth of a Nation 'hood: Gaze, Script, and Spectacle in the O.J. Simpson Case. Toni Morrison and Claudia Brodsky Lacour, editors. New York: Pantheon Books.
Fryer, Peter. (1984). *Staying Power: Black People in Britain Since 1504*. Atlantic Highlands, N.J. : Humanities Press.
Jordan, Wintrop. (1969). White Over Black: American Attitudes Toward the Negro, 1550-1812. Baltimore, MD: Penguin.
Olney, James. (1985). "'I Was Born': Slave Narratives, Their Status as Autobiography and as Literature." In *The Slave's Narrative*. Charles T. Davis and Henry Louis Gates, Jr., editors. New York: Oxford University Press.

Leslie Sanders currently teaches at Atkinson College, York University.

Left to right:
Alison Sealy-Smith
Nigel Shawn Williams

photo by Cylla Von Tiedemann

Harlem Duet premiered on April 24, 1997, as a Nightwood Theatre production, at the Tarragon Extra Space, Toronto, Canada, with the following cast:

BILLIE	Alison Sealy-Smith
OTHELLO	Nigel Shawn Williams
MAGI	Barbara Barnes Hopkins
AMAH/MONA	Dawn Roach
CANADA	Jeff Jones

Double Bass	Lionel Williams
Cello	Doug Innes

Directed by Djanet Sears
Set and costume design by Teresa Przybylski
Lighting design by Lesley Wilkinson
Music composition and arrangement by Lionel Williams
Music and sound design by Allen Booth
Assistant Director: maxine bailey
Stage Manager: Cheryl Francis
Assistant Stage Manager: Andrea Ottley
Dramaturgy by Diane Roberts and Kate Lushington

<u>**CHARACTERS**</u>

BILLIE
OTHELLO
MAGI
AMAH
CANADA
MONA (an off-stage voice and an arm)

Note:
Live musicians are an integral component of this play.

ACT I

PROLOGUE

Harlem, 1928: late summer – night. As the lights fade to black, the cello and the bass call and respond to a heaving melancholic blues. Martin Luther King's voice accompanies them. He seems to sing his dream in a slow polyrhythmic improvisation, as he reaches the climax of that now famous speech given at the March on Washington. Lights up on a couple in a tiny dressing room. SHE is holding a large white silk handkerchief, spotted with ripe strawberries. SHE looks at HE as if searching for something. HE has lathered his face and is slowly erasing the day's stubble with a straight razor. SHE looks down at the handkerchief.

SHE   We keep doing this don't we?

HE   I love you... But–

SHE   Remember... remember when you gave this to me? Your mother's handkerchief. There's magic in the web of it. Little strawberries. It's so beautiful – delicate. You kissed my fingers... and with each kiss a new promise you made... swore yourself to me...for all eternity... remember?

HE   Yes. Yes... I remember.

Pause.

SHE   Harlem's the place to be now. Everyone who's anyone is coming here now. It's our time. In our place. It's what we've always dreamed of... isn't it?

HE   Yes.

SHE   You love her?

HE   I... I wish–

SHE   Have you sung to her at twilight?

HE   Yes.

SHE   Does your blood call out her name?

HE   Yes.

SHE	Do you finger-feed her berries dipped in dark and luscious sweets?
HE	Yes.
SHE	Have you built her a crystal palace to refract her image like a thousand mirrors in your veins?
HE	Yes.
SHE	Do you let her sip nectar kisses from a cup of jade studded bronze from your immortal parts?
HE	Yes.
SHE	Does she make your thoughts and dreams and sighs, wishes and tears, ache sweet as you can bear?
HE	Yes.
SHE	You love her.
HE	Yes. Yes. Yes.

He wipes his face with a towel. She stares at the handkerchief laying in her bare hand.

SHE   Is she White? (*silence*) Othello? (*silence*) She's White. (*silence*) Othello...

She holds the handkerchief out to him. He does not take it. She lets it fall at his feet. After a few moments, he picks it up.

SCENE I

*Harlem, present: late summer – morning. The strings thump
out an urban melody blues/jazz riff, accompanied by the voice of
Malcolm X, speaking about the nightmare of race in America
and the need to build strong Black communities.*

*MAGI is on the fire escape, leaning on the railing, reading a
magazine with a large picture of a blonde woman on the cover.
As the sound fades, she closes the magazine, surveying the
action on the street below.*

MAGI   Sun up in Harlem. (*she spots the postman*) Morning Mr. P.!
Don't bring me no bill now – I warned ya before, I'm having a
baby. Don't need to get myself all worked up, given my condition… I'm gonna have me a Virgo baby, makes me due
'bout this time next year… I can count. I just haven't chosen
the actual father/husband candidate as yet. Gotta find me a
man to play his part. I wanna conceive in the middle of
December, so I've booked the Convent Avenue Baptist church
for this Saturday. The wedding's at three. You sure look to be
the marrying kind. What you up to this weekend, yourself
sweetness? Oh well then, wish your wife well for me.
Package from where? California? Oohh. Yeh, yeh, yeh. I'll
be right – hey, hey, Amah girl… up here… let yourself in…
(*she throws a set of keys down to AMAH*) Mr. P., give that
young lady the package… yeh, she'll bring it up for me. (*beat*)
Thank you, sugar. (*beat*) You have yourself a nice day now.
Alright, sweetness. Mmn, mmn, mmn!

*AMAH unlocks the door, enters and makes her way to the fire
escape.*

AMAH   Magi, look at you, out on the terrace, watching the summer
blossoms on the corner of Malcolm X and Martin Luther King
Boulevards.

MAGI   Nothing but weeds growing in the Soweto of America, honey.
(*shouting out*) Billie!

AMAH   Where is she?

MAGI   I didn't want to wake her up 'till you got here. She didn't get
to sleep 'till early morning. I could hear her wailing all the
way downstairs.

AMAH   I can see a week. A couple of weeks at the most. But what is
this?

MAGI   Two months – it's not like she's certifiable though. (*shouting gently to BILLIE in the bedroom*) Billie! Billie, Amah's here!

AMAH   Well, least she sleeps now.

MAGI   She's stillness itself. Buried under that ocean of self help books, like it's a tomb. Like a pyramid over her. Over the bed. (*calling out once more*) Billie!

> *BILLIE's body moves slightly and an arm listlessly carves its way to the surface, shifting the tomb of books, several dropping to the floor.*
>
> *MAGI and AMAH make their way inside. On a large table is a vase filled with blossoming cotton branches. There is also a myriad of bottles and bags, and a Soxhlet extraction apparatus: flask, extractor and thimble, condenser, siphoning hoses, all held up by two metal stands. A Bunsen burner is placed under the flask.*

              I'm just making her some coffee, can I get you a cup?

AMAH   (*inspects the table and searches for a space to put the small package*) Thanks Magi. Where d'you want this? It looks like a science lab in here.

MAGI   Some healing concoction I've been helping her make – but she's way ahead of me these days. She's got a real talent for herbs, you know. She's been sending away for ingredients – I can't even figure out what most of them are – put the package down anywhere.

AMAH   If I can find a space.

MAGI   Right there. On top of that alchemy book – right in the middle. Yeh. Thanks for doing this Amah. For coming. It'll make her feel like a million dollars again.

AMAH   Please. Billie and me go so far back, way before Andrew. Besides, sister-in-laws are family too, you know. Jenny's been simply begging to come and see her, you know, for their once a week thing. They eat sausages, mashed potatoes, and corn. Some Canadian delicacy I guess–

MAGI   Aren't you guys vegetarians?

AMAH   Vegan.

MAGI   Vegan?

AMAH	We don't eat anything that has eyes. The sausages are tofu. You know they eat exactly the same thing every time. I was glad for the break. I guess I was kinda... well... it bugged me. Jenny's always full of Auntie Billie this, Auntie Billie that. Now I miss our one night a week without her. I mean – our time alone. And I see how it's a kind of security for her.
MAGI	Security for who?
AMAH	Oh, I can't rent your ground floor. They won't give me any insurance 'cause I don't have a licence. And I can't get a licence until I get a cosmetician's certificate. And I can't get a cosmetician's certificate until I finish this two-year course on how to do White people's hair and make-up. I told them ain't no White people in Harlem. I'd learn how to do work with chemical relaxers and Jheri curls. Now, I do dreadlocks. And do they teach that? Oh no. They're just cracking down on people who do hair in private homes – something about lost tax revenues. I don't know... I want my own salon so bad I can taste it. "The Lock Smiths".
MAGI	"The Lock Smiths".
AMAH	Billie's supposed to be helping me with the business plan. Besides we've started trying for kid number 2. I need the space.
MAGI	You're trying?
AMAH	I'm 10 days late.
MAGI	No!
AMAH	It's still early. Don't tell Billie... you know. I'll tell her.
MAGI	Good for you, girl! Did I tell you I was having a baby?
AMAH	Oh yeh. How was he, that new candidate you were telling me about... Warren, no Waldo–
MAGI	Wendel? Wedded Wendel as I've discovered.
AMAH	He didn't tell–
MAGI	Oh no. He believes that the nuclear family is the basis for a healthy society. That's why he's married. He keeps his own personal nuclear family at home in the event that he might someday want to spend time with it.

AMAH	Why'd you stop seeing George. I liked George.
MAGI	Well I liked him too.
AMAH	You two looked pretty serious there for a while.
MAGI	We'd been seeing each other the better part of... what... two years. I'm just not getting any younger. I mean, I kept dropping hints I was ready for him to pop the question. Seems like he don't know what question I'm referring to. So I decided to give him some encouragement. See, I've been collecting things for my trousseau, and I have this negligee... all white, long, beautiful lacy thing. Looks like a see-through wedding gown. So, I'm out on my balcony – you know, 'cause it's too hot inside, and I still ain't got around to putting in air conditioning. Anyway, I see him coming up the street. So I rush in and put on the wedding dress negligée, thinking, he'll see me in it, all beautiful like – want to pop the question, you know. So I open the door, me in the negligée, and he... he stands there. Mouth wide open. And he says, he guess he should go get a bottle of wine, seeing how this was gonna be some kind of special occasion an' all. Now I don't know whether he got lost... or drunk... but I ain't seen or heard from him since.
AMAH	Aahh nooo.
MAGI	I should have margarined his butt when I had the chance.
AMAH	Margarined his backside?
MAGI	If you want to bind a man–
AMAH·	You don't mean, what I think you mean?
MAGI	If you want to keep a man then, you rub his backside with margarine.
AMAH	And it works?
MAGI	I don't know. When I'd remember, I could never figure out how to get from the bed to the refrigerator.
AMAH	Margarine, huh?
MAGI	But you've got to be careful. He might be a fool. You don't want to be dragging no damn fool behind you the rest of your days.
AMAH	You're a regular charmer, girl.

MAGI Don't get me wrong. I don't cut the heads off chickens, or anything now.

AMAH You know, a Jamaican lady told me about one where you rinse your underwear and use the dirty water to cook the meal.

MAGI Nooo! Really?

AMAH Really.

MAGI Ooh, I like that. Boil down some greens in panty stock. Hmm!

AMAH Once I buried his socks under the blackberry bush by the front door. Sure enough, he always finds his way back home.

MAGI How is True Drew?

AMAH Oh, Andrew's real good. You know him. He was up here 'till late, night before last, even, playing broad-shouldered brother.

MAGI Yep, he's a good man. They're rare. And he went all the way down to D.C. for the Million Man March. Yeh, he's one in a million. If you ever think of trading him in…

AMAH Don't even think about it!

MAGI Can't blame a girl for trying. (*calling out again*) Billie! Billie you up yet?

MAGI gets no response. She goes into the bedroom.

Billie? Billie, sorry to wake you, but Amah's here. She waiting.

BILLIE emerges. We recognize her as the woman in the prologue. She slowly makes her way to the edge of the bed.

BILLIE If I could only stop dreaming, I might be able to get some rest.

MAGI You should jot them down. They're messages from other realms, you know.

BILLIE Jenny's in a large white room – the walls start pressing in all around her…

MAGI You OK?

BILLIE   Mm mm. Yeh. I'm fine. I'm good.

MAGI   (*gently*) Come on sweetheart, Amah's waiting.

BILLIE   Let me just wash my face, and my mouth.

> *MAGI leaves BILLIE to join AMAH, who is now on the fire escape.*

MAGI   She's coming... (*AMAH hands MAGI a cup of coffee*) Ooh... thanks.

AMAH   How is she?

MAGI   Better. Dreaming hard, though. Like she's on some archeological dig of the unconscious mind.

AMAH   His words hit her hard, huh.

MAGI   Like a baseball bat hits a mango. Like he was trying for a home run or something. The bat breaks through the skin, smashing the amber flesh, propelling her core out of the park, into the clouds. And she lays there, floating.

AMAH   Feeling sorry for herself.

MAGI   A discarded fruit sitting in a dish, surrounded by its own ripening mould.

AMAH   She feels so much.

MAGI   Yeh. Each of her emotions sprout new roots, long, tangled things, intersecting each other like strangle weed.

AMAH   She should go out though, get some fresh air once in a while.

MAGI   She does. Her trips out into the real world are brief, though. The grocers for tubs of things you add water to, she calls food; the pharmacy for the pills, and the bookstore. All her money goes up in smokes and writings that tell her she really ain't out of her mind. They'd make her feel better, more beautiful, more well, until she'd see some nice chocolate brown-skinned man, dangling his prize in front of her. 'Cause all the rot inside her would begin to boil, threaten to shoot out. So she comes home, takes some pills and sleeps again that fitful sleep 'till she wakes.

AMAH   So she knows?

MAGI	Ooh she knows. She knows she's still up there in the clouds.
AMAH	She never used to be like that, you know, about colour.
MAGI	Guess it ain't never been personal before.
AMAH	But it seems bigger than that...
MAGI	Girl, you've been married what... six years?
AMAH	Seven this February coming...
MAGI	How'd you feel if Drew just upped and left you?
AMAH	I can't even imagine...
MAGI	They've been together nine.
AMAH	She still moving?
MAGI	So she say... asked me to pick up some boxes.
AMAH	(*quietly*) Rumour has it he's getting married.
MAGI	So soon. He hasn't told her anything. He still hasn't even moved his stuff yet.
AMAH	And she sacrificed so much. Gave up her share of the trust from her mother's life insurance to send him through school.
MAGI	No!
AMAH	So when it's her turn to go... all those years.
MAGI	And those babies.
AMAH	Yeh, thank god they didn't have any babies.
MAGI	No, no... twice...
AMAH	No!
MAGI	First time, he told her he believed in a woman's right to choose, but he didn't think that the relationship was ready for–
AMAH	We didn't–
MAGI	Nobody did. Second time she miscarried.

AMAH   When? I don't–

MAGI   'Bout the same time he left – no, it was before that. She was by herself... set down in a pool of blood. She put it in a ziplock bag... in the freezer... all purple and blue...

AMAH   Oohh God... no... really?

MAGI   Yeh.

AMAH   Nooo... for real. I'm serious...

MAGI   Yeh!

AMAH   Show me.

MAGI turns toward the living area and heads for the kitchen; AMAH follows closely behind. They approach the fridge and MAGI is about to open the freezer door when BILLIE enters from the bedroom. AMAH and MAGI stop abruptly, as if caught in the act.

AMAH   Billie!

MAGI   (*overlapping*) Hey girl!

BILLIE waves to them as she exits into the bathroom. MAGI turns to AMAH.

Or maybe I lied. Gotcha!

AMAH   You... you... little heifer–

MAGI laughs. AMAH gets infected and joins her.

SCENE 2

Harlem, 1860: late summer – twilight. The instruments sing a blues from deep in the Mississippi delta, while a mature north- ern American voice reads from the Declaration of Independence. HIM steeps hot metal into cool water. He places the shackles on an anvil and hammers the metal into shape. HER is making repairs to a shawl with a needle.

HER   I pray Cleotis is in heaven.

HIM   Yeh... I... um... I...

HER	You think Cleotis went to heaven?
HIM	Well, I... I don't...
HER	You think he's in hell?
HIM	No. No.
HER	Probably somewhere in between, though. Not Hades. Not God's kingdom. He's probably right there in the hardware store. Probably right there watching every time that Mr. Howard proudly hoists the mason jar. Every time they pay their penny to see through the formaldehyde. Cleotis is probably right there watching them gawk at his shriveled, pickled penis... you seen it?
HIM	No.
HER	You know who did the cutting, though?
HIM	No... oh no...
HER	In France they got the vagina of a sister entombed for scientific research.
HIM	No!
HER	Venus, the Hottentot Venus. I read it in one of Miss Dessy's books. Saartjie – that's her real name, Saartjie Baartman. When Saartjie was alive they paraded her naked on a pay-per-view basis. Her derrière was amply endowed. People paid to see how big her butt was, and when she died, how big her pussy was.
HIM	Wooo!
HER	Human beings went and oohed and ahhed and paid money to see an endowment the creator bestowed on all of us.
HIM	That's... that's... so... so...
HER	They probably go to a special place though – Cleotis and Venus, Emmett. Purgatory. Venus and Cleotis fall in love, marry, but have no tools to consummate it. Must be a lot of us there walking around in purgatory without genitals.

     Beat.

HIM	I've been meaning to... I want... (*laughing to himself*) I would like to...
HER	Yes...?
HIM	Talk. We should talk.
HER	Talk-talk?
HIM	Talk-talk.
HER	About what...? What's wrong?
HIM	Why must something be wrong–
HER	I... I just figured... figure...

HIM takes HER's hand and kisses it, then places a white handkerchief into her palm.

HIM	My heart...

HIM closes HER's fingers around the handkerchief. He kisses her fingers. Opening her hand, she examines the cloth.

HER	Little strawberries on a sheet of white. Berries in a field of snow... (*sighing*) Ah silk. It's beautiful.
HIM	It was my mother's. Given her by my father... from his mother before that. When she died she gave it me, insisting that when I found... chose... chose a wife... that I give it to her... to you heart.
HER	Oh... it is so beautiful.
HIM	There's magic in the web of it.
HER	So delicate... so old.
HIM	A token... an antique token of our ancient love.
HER	My ancient love...
HIM	My wife. My wife before I even met you. Let's do it. There's a war already brewing in the south. Canada freedom come.
HER	Yes?
HIM	Yes.

HER   We're really gonna go?

HIM   People will come to me and pay me for my work.

HER   Yes sir, Mr. Blacksmith, sir.

HIM   Can we have us a heap of children?

HER   Four boys and four girls.

HIM   And a big white house.

HER   A big house on an emerald hill.

HIM   Yeh… a white house, on an emerald hill, in Canada. (*pause*) I want to be with you 'till I'm too old to know. You know that.

HER   Even when my breasts fall to my toes?

HIM   I'll pick them up and carry them around for you.

HER   And when I can't remember my own name?

HIM   I'll call it out a thousand times a day.

HER   Then I'll think you're me.

HIM   I am you.

HER   And when I get old, and wrinkled, and enormously fat, you'll–

HIM   Fat? Naw. If you get fat, I'll have to leave your ass.

     HIM kisses inside the crook of HER's arm.

HER   Oh-oh. You're prospecting again.

HIM   I'm exploring the heightening Alleghenies of Pennsylvania. (*he kisses HER*) The curvaceous slopes of California. (*he kisses HER*) The red hills of Georgia, the mighty mountains of New York. (*he kisses HER again*) I'm staking my claim.

HER   I don't come cheap, you know.

HIM   I know… I'm offering more than money can buy.

HER   How much more?

HIM	This much. (*he kisses HER*)
HER	I could buy that.
HIM	Could you buy this? (*he kisses HER deeply*)
HER	Beloved... (*she kisses HIM*)

SCENE III

Harlem, the present: late summer – morning. Strains of a melodious urban blues jazz keeps time with an oral address by Marcus Garvey on the need for African Americans to return to Africa.

MAGI	No, I hate it.
AMAH	Come on. No one hates it.
MAGI	I do.
AMAH	Bah humbug?
MAGI	What?
AMAH	Scrooge?
MAGI	Oh no, no, no. You know what I hate about Christmas? Seven days to New Year's Eve. And I hate New Year's Eve. And you know what I really hate about New Year's Eve? It's not the being alone at midnight. It's not the being a wallflower at some bash, because you fired your escort, who asked for time and a half, after 10:00 p.m. It's not even because you babysat your friend's kids the previous two. I really hate New Year's Eve, because it's six weeks to Valentines Day. And what I really really hate about Valentines Day – well, maybe that's too strong. No. I really hate it. What I really hate about Valentines Day is... it's my birthday. Don't get me wrong, now. I'm glad I was born. But I look at my life – I'm more than halfway through it, and I wonder, what do I have to show for it? Anyway...
AMAH	Well you come and spend Kwanzaa with us this year.
MAGI	I don't know about the seven days, girl? Look, I gotta go. I'm seeing a certain minister about a certain wedding.
AMAH	Whose wedding?

MAGI   Mine. And don't say a thing – you know, about him getting married, or anything.

MAGI indicates the refrigerator.

AMAH   Sealed.

MAGI   I'll drop by later.

AMAH   Alright.

MAGI   (*shouting*) Billie? I'm gonna drop by later with some boxes, OK?

BILLIE   (*off-stage*) Thanks, Magi.

MAGI exits. AMAH goes to the table and examines the small chemical factory.

AMAH   Saracen's Compound... Woad... Hart's tongue... Prunella vulgaris... (*she picks up a book lying among the small packages and vials*) "Egyptian Alchemy: A Chemical Encyclopedia"... (*she puts the book back in its place and picks up another vial*) Nux Vomica, warning: Extremely poisonous. Can be ingested on contact with skin...

AMAH quickly replaces the vial, wiping her hand on her clothes. She turns her attention to the kitchen. She cautiously approaches the refrigerator, and is about to open the freezer section when BILLIE comes out of the bathroom.

BILLIE   Hey Amah.

AMAH   Oh – hi girl, how you feeling?

BILLIE   Thanks for making the house call, Amah.

AMAH   Child, you look so thin.

BILLIE   Well, I'm trying to lose a little baby fat before I die.

AMAH   Coffee?

BILLIE   Oh... thanks. (*pours coffee*) You didn't have to come. I'm fine you know.

AMAH   You're very welcome. Come sit down. (*AMAH hands her the cup*)

BILLIE   I didn't mean... thank you.

AMAH   You washed your hair?

BILLIE   Yesterday.

AMAH   Good. A package came for you this morning.

BILLIE   Where?

AMAH   I put it beside the chemistry set. What is all that?

BILLIE   Don't touch anything!

AMAH   Alright – alright. I–

BILLIE   No. No. I – I mean, some of this stuff can be deadly unless mixed... or... or diluted. Some ancient Egyptian rejuvenation tonic. If it don't kill me, it'll make me brand new – or so it says. How's my baby?

AMAH   Jenny's fine. Andrew's taking her to her first African dance class today. You should see her in the little leotard...

BILLIE   I should be there.

AMAH   She's dying to come over for sausages and mashed potatoes.

BILLIE   Yeh, yes, soon. Real soon.

> *AMAH prepares to twist BILLIE's hair. She opens a jar of hair oil and takes a generous portion of the oil, rubs it onto her hands and gently works it into BILLIE's hair.*

AMAH   She was so cute, today – you know what she did? She over-heard me talking to Andrew about you, and I was saying I thought your breakdown was–

BILLIE   You told her I had a nervous breakdown?

AMAH   Oh – no. No. She overheard me–

BILLIE   I am not having a nervous breakdown.

AMAH   She didn't really understand. She thinks you've broken your legs and can't walk, you can't dance. She thinks you've bro-ken your throat, and that's why she can't talk to you on the phone, that's why you don't sing to her on the phone any-more.

BILLIE   Please don't tell her I'm crazy.

AMAH   I never said you were crazy.

BILLIE   I've just been... tired. Exhausted. I... I didn't want her to see this in me. She'd feel it in me. I never want her to feel this...

AMAH   I know.

BILLIE   But I'm fine now. Really, I'll be fine. I registered for school, I'm only taking one course this term, but that's cool. And first thing next week, I'm re-doing the business plan for the salon.

AMAH   You need to give me some of that tonic too, girl. That's the best kind of revenge, you know – living the good life.

BILLIE   I thought I was living that life.

AMAH   Maybe you were just dreaming.

> *AMAH takes a new lock of BILLIE's hair. Taking a large dab of oil, she applies it to the lock, rubbing the strand between her palms.*

BILLIE   Remember when we moved in? The day Nelson and Winnie came to Harlem, remember? Winnie and Nelson – our welcoming committee. They'd blocked off the whole of 125th – it took us 45 minutes to convince the cops to let us through. And me and you and Othe and Drew went down to hear them speak. And Drew went off in search of some grits from a street vendor. And you asked me to hold baby Jenny while you went to the restroom, when this man came up to us and took our picture. Asked to take our picture. Jenny in my arms. Othello beside me. "The perfect Black family". That's what he called us. "The perfect Black family".

> *The phone rings.*

AMAH   I'll get it.

BILLIE   No. Let it ring. I know who it is. I can still feel him – feel when he's thinking of me. We've spoken... must be three times, in the last two months. Something about $500 on my portion of his American Express card, which they'd cancel if I didn't pay the bill. Seems I did me some consumer therapy. Last time he called – mad – to announce that the card had been cancelled by AMEX, and that he hoped that I was pleased. (*beat*) And I was. Is that crazy?

AMAH   Don't sound crazy. Hold the hair oil for me.

BILLIE   I used to pray that he was calling to say he's sorry. To say how he'd discovered a deep confusion in himself. But now... (*the phone stops ringing*) I have nothing to say to him. What could I say? Othello, how is the fairer-sexed one you love to dangle from your arm the one you love for herself and preferred to the deeper sexed one is she softer does she smell of tea roses and baby powder does she sweat white musk from between her toes do her thighs touch I am not curious just want to know do her breasts fill the cup of your hand the lips of your tongue not too dark you like a little milk with your nipple don't you no I'm not curious just want to know.

AMAH   You tell Jenny colour's only skin deep.

BILLIE   The skin holds everything in. It's the largest organ in the human body. Slash the skin by my belly and my intestines fall out.

AMAH   Hold the hair oil up. (*she takes a dab of oil from the jar*)

BILLIE   I thought I saw them once, you know – on the subway. I had to renew my prescription. And I spot them – him and her. My chest is pounding. My legs can't move. From the back, I see the sharp barber's line, separating his tightly coiled hair from the nape of the skin at the back of his neck. His skin is soft there... and I have to kick away the memory nudging its way into my brain. My lips on his neck, gently... holding him. Here, before me – his woman – all blonde hair and blonde legs. Her weight against his chest. His arm around her shoulders, his thumb resting on the gold of her hair. He's proud. You can see he's proud. He isn't just any Negro. He's special. That's why she's with him. And she... she... she flaunts. Yes, she flaunts. They are before. I am behind, stuck there on the platform. My tongue is pushing hard against the roof of my mouth... trying to hold up my brain, or something. 'Cause my brain threatens to fall. Fall down through the roof of my mouth, and be swallowed up. Slowly, slowly, I press forward, toward them. I'm not aiming for them though. I'm aiming with them in mind. I'm aiming for beyond the yellow line, into the tracks. The tunnel all three of us will fall into can be no worse than the one I'm trapped in now. I walk – no, well hover really. I'm walking on air. I feel sure of myself for the first time in weeks. Only to be cut off by a tall grey man in a grey uniform, who isn't looking where he's going, or maybe I'm not – maybe he knew my aim. He looks at me. I think he looks at me. He brushes past. Then a sound emanating from... from... from my uterus, slips out of my mouth, shatters the spell. They turn their heads – the couple. They see me. It isn't even him.

The phone rings again.

AMAH   It could be your father, you know. He's been trying to get in touch with you. Says he doesn't know if you're dead or alive. He was calling Drew even up to this morning.

BILLIE   My father... I wouldn't have anything to say. It's been so long. What would I say?

The phone stops ringing.

AMAH   He's been in the hospital, you know. Something about his liver.

BILLIE   He hauled us all the way back to Nova Scotia from the Bronx, to be near Granma, when Mama died.

AMAH   I love that Nova Scotia was a haven for slaves way before the underground railroad. I love that...

BILLIE   He's a sot. That's academia speak for alcoholic. My Dad, the drunk of Dartmouth.

AMAH   You're still his children.

BILLIE   A detail I'm glad he's recalled.

AMAH   Better late than never.

BILLIE   Too little, too late.

AMAH   Forgiveness is a virtue.

BILLIE   What?

AMAH   Forgiveness is a virtue.

BILLIE   Girl, patience is a virtue.

AMAH   Well... forgiveness is up there...

BILLIE   Did Drew tell you about the time my father sang to me at my high school graduation dinner?

AMAH   Nooo. That's lovely. My father never sang to me at my graduation.

BILLIE   We were eating. He was standing on top of the banquet table.

AMAH	Nooo!
BILLIE	It's the truth!

Pause.

AMAH	Can I get a glass of water?
BILLIE	Yeh. Yeh, help yourself.

AMAH goes into the kitchen.

I've got O.J. in the fridge, if you want.

AMAH	Water will do, thanks. Do you have any… ice in your freezer?
BILLIE	I'll get it.
AMAH	I can get it.

BILLIE gets up quickly, and heads toward the kitchen.

BILLIE	It's OK. It's OK. I'll get it for you.

BILLIE opens the freezer and gets her the ice, closing the freezer door immediately behind her.

AMAH	Thanks. (*beat*) What's in there?
BILLIE	Frozen shit.

The phone begins to ring again. Both women look toward it.

SCENE IV

Same day: noontime. Accompanying the sound of rushing water and the polyrhythmic chorus of strings, Martin Luther King continues to assert his dream, its relationship to the American Constitution, and the Declaration of Independence.

OTHELLO	(*off-stage*) Billie! (*silence – he knocks again*) Billie?! (*to MONA*) I don't think she's there.

OTHELLO unlocks the door. He enters. We recognize him as the man in both 1860 and 1928.

Billie? Mona and I are here to pick up the rest of my things. Billie?

He hears the shower. He goes over to the bathroom door. He knocks.

Billie?… (*BILLIE screams – we hear something crash*) It's just me… I tried to call. You should get that machine fixed.

BILLIE   (*off-stage*) I'll be out in a minute.

> *OTHELLO returns to MONA at the entrance. We see nothing of her but brief glimpses of a bare arm and a waft of light brown hair.*

OTHELLO   It's OK Mona, she's in there. Why don't you wait in the car.

MONA   (*off-stage*) She'll have to get used to me sometime.

OTHELLO   I'll be down in a flash. It won't take me that long. (*MONA doesn't answer*) Hey, hey, hey!

MONA   (*off-stage*) Hey yourself. I do have other things to take care of, you know. (*OTHELLO kisses her*) OK… I still haven't found anything blue. I'll scour the stores. I'll be back in a couple of hours.

OTHELLO   Alright.

MONA   (*off-stage*) Alright.

> *OTHELLO brings in several large empty boxes. He closes the door and looks around. He sees a burning cigarette, picks it up, looks at it, then puts it out. He takes off his jacket. Then he takes several albums from a shelf and places them on the floor. He begins to form two piles. He picks up one of the albums and begins to laugh. BILLIE enters dressed in a robe.*

BILLIE   What are you doing here?

OTHELLO   I came over to pack my things. The movers are coming in the morning. I tried to call…

BILLIE   You took my pot.

OTHELLO   What…

BILLIE   My pot. The cast iron Dutch pot.

OTHELLO   Oh… well, you never use it.

BILLIE   I want it back.

OTHELLO   You never use it.

BILLIE   The one with the yellow handle.

OTHELLO   We need it to make gumbo.

BILLIE   She uses it?

OTHELLO   I need it to make gumbo.

BILLIE   She needs my pot? The one with the carrying rings.

OTHELLO   It was a gift to both of us.

BILLIE   From my father.

OTHELLO   I'll bring it back tomorrow.

BILLIE   If you don't have it here for me inside of 30 minutes, I will break every jazz recording on that shelf.

OTHELLO   You want me to go all the way back for something you don't even use.

BILLIE   Let me see…

OTHELLO   You never used it.

BILLIE   Abbey Lincoln…

> *She takes the album from the table. Takes the record from the jacket and breaks it in two. She reaches for another album. OTHELLO picks up the broken record.*

Aah. Max Roach. (*she takes the cover off the Max Roach album*)

OTHELLO   The Abbey Lincoln was yours. (*she breaks the Max Roach record too*) OK. OK, I'll go and get it. (*he picks up his jacket and proceeds to the door*)

BILLIE   Fine. It's fine.

OTHELLO   Excuse me?

BILLIE   It's fine. Tomorrow's fine.

> *Pause. He turns toward her.*

OTHELLO   OK.

Pause. He puts his jacket down again. Pause.

How are you? You look well.

BILLIE   I'm fine. And you?

OTHELLO   Great... good.

BILLIE   (*pause*) Well you know where your stuff is.

OTHELLO   Yep... yes.

BILLIE   (*pause*) Drink?

OTHELLO   What?

BILLIE   Would you like something to drink?

OTHELLO   Sure... yes. What do you–

BILLIE   Peppermint, fennel, chamomile... no... just peppermint and fennel. Coffee, wine, cognac, water.

OTHELLO   What are you having?

BILLIE   Cognac.

OTHELLO   Oh. Well... that'll do.

BILLIE goes to the kitchen.

Where's my suitcase?

BILLIE   Where you left it.

OTHELLO   (*pause*) So you're staying on then?

BILLIE   No.

OTHELLO   Where are you... you know... I mean, things are tight, money-wise, but I'll still put money in your account... when I can... I mean, I hope we can keep in touch. (*BILLIE hands him a glass of cognac*) Thank you.

BILLIE   You're welcome.

OTHELLO   (*pause*) You've lost weight. You look great. (*he takes a large gulp*) Aaahh! Yes!

> *OTHELLO looks at BILLIE for a moment. He then takes one of the boxes and places it at his feet. He approaches the bookshelf. He takes down a large book.*

"African Mythology"… is this mine or yours?

BILLIE   Mine… I think… I don't know.

OTHELLO   This is going to be interesting.

BILLIE   Take what you like. I don't care.

OTHELLO   (*he takes another book*) "The Great Chain of Being"?

BILLIE   From man to mollusk. The scientific foundation for why we're not human. An African can't really be a woman, you know. My department agreed to let me take only one course this year – I'm taking a reading course.

OTHELLO   Yours… yours… mine… "Black Psychology", you keeping this?

BILLIE   Yeh. (*she takes the books from him*) You'd think there was more information on Black people and mental health. You know… Christ, we've been here, what, 400 years. No money in it I guess…

OTHELLO   What's money got to do with it?

BILLIE   You know, grants… scholarships…

OTHELLO   Race is not an obscure idea.

> *He places several books into a box.*

BILLIE   In genetics, or the study of what's wrong with people of African descent – The Heritage Foundation will give you tons of dough to prove the innate inferiority of… the Shakespeare's mine, but you can have it.

OTHELLO   Sure, if you don't–

BILLIE   No. The Heritage Foundation – that's where that guy Murray, et al, got most of their money for Bell Curve – I think… there's just no-one out there willing to give you a scholarship to prove that we're all mad.

OTHELLO   We're all mad. This is the founding principle of your thesis?

BILLIE   Well, not mad… I mean… well… psychologically dysfunc-
tional, then. All cultural groups are to some degree ethnocen-
tric: we – they. But not all inter-cultural relations are of an
inferior/superior type.

OTHELLO   Thus we're not all mad. (*he returns to the bookshelf*)

BILLIE   No, no. In America, this race shit is classic behavioural disor-
der. Obsessions. Phobias. Delusions. Notions of persecu-
tion. Delusions of grandeur. Any one or combination of
these can produce behaviours which categorize oneself as
superior and another as inferior. You see, this kind of dys-
function is systemically supported by the larger society.
Psychology only sees clients who can no longer function in
society. We're all mad. We just appear to be functional.

OTHELLO   And your solution?

BILLIE   You'll have to buy my book. (*pause, then they continue packing*)
How's the teaching?

OTHELLO   Fine… great…

BILLIE   Good.

OTHELLO   (*pause*) I'll be heading the department's courses in Cyprus
next summer.

BILLIE   I thought you told me Christopher… what's his name?

OTHELLO   Chris Yago?

BILLIE   Yeh, Yago.

OTHELLO   Well everyone thought he would get it. I thought he'd get it.
So a whole bunch of them are challenging affirmative action.

BILLIE   Rednecks in academia.

OTHELLO   No, no… well… I think it's a good thing.

BILLIE   Pul-eese.

OTHELLO   Using discrimination to cure discrimination is not–

BILLIE   We're talking put asides of 5%. 5% of everything available to
Whites. They've still got 95.

OTHELLO   Billie… injustice against Blacks can't be cured by injustice against Whites… you know that.

BILLIE   And younger people won't have the same opportunities you had.

OTHELLO   Now look who's sounding White.

BILLIE   Who said you sounded White?

OTHELLO   It's implied… no-one at school tells me I don't know how to do my job… it's implied. I'll be at a faculty meeting, I'll make a suggestion and it'll be ignored. Not five minutes later, someone else will make the exact same suggestion and every-one will agree to it. Mona noticed it too. They think I'm only there because I'm Black. I've tested it.

BILLIE   So let me get this straight, you're against affirmative action in order for White people to respect you.

OTHELLO   For my peers… my peers to respect me. You know what it's like. Every day I have to prove to them that I can do my job. I feel that any error I make only goes to prove them right.

BILLIE   Well you must be perfect. Mona respects you.

OTHELLO   Well, she really sees me. She was the only other faculty to support me on the MLK Day assembly. When we played the video–

BILLIE   The "I have a dream" speech?

OTHELLO   They understood. For a moment I got them to understand.

He picks up several books and places them in a box.

BILLIE   "America has defaulted on this promissory note insofar as her…

OTHELLO & BILLIE   …citizens of colour are concerned.

OTHELLO   Instead of honouring this sacred obligation, America has given its coloured people a…

OTHELLO & BILLIE   …bad cheque…

BILLIE   …a cheque that has come back marked…

OTHELLO & BILLIE	…insufficient funds".
BILLIE	The man was a… a…
OTHELLO	Poet… visionary.
BILLIE	A prophet.
OTHELLO	After all he'd been through in his life, he could still see that at a deeper level we're all the same.
BILLIE	(*pause*) I'm not the same.
OTHELLO	In the eyes of God, Billie, we're all the same.
BILLIE	One day little Black boys and little White girls–
OTHELLO	You're delusional.
BILLIE	You're the one looking for White respect.
OTHELLO	Wrong again! White respect, Black respect, it's all the same to me.
BILLIE	Right on brother man!
OTHELLO	When I was growing up… in a time of Black pride – it was something to say you were Black. Before that, I'd say… my family would say we're Cuban… it takes a long time to work through some of those things. I am a member of the human race.
BILLIE	Oh, that's a switch. What happened to all that J. A. Rogers stuff you were pushing. Blacks created the world, Blacks are the progenitors of European civilization, gloriana… constantly trying to prove you're as good, no, better than White people. White people are always the line for you, aren't they? The rule… the margin… the variable of control. We are Black. Whatever we do is Black.
OTHELLO	I'm so tired of this race shit, Billie. There are alternatives–
BILLIE	Like what? Oh yes, White.
OTHELLO	Oh, don't be so–
BILLIE	Isn't that really what not acting Black, or feeling Black means?

OTHELLO   Liberation has no colour.

BILLIE   But progress is going to White schools... proving we're as good as Whites... like some holy grail... all that we're taught in those White schools. All that is in us. Our success is Whiteness. We religiously seek to have what they have. Access to the White man's world. The White man's job.

OTHELLO   That's economics.

BILLIE   White economics.

OTHELLO   God! Black women always–

BILLIE   No. Don't even go there...

OTHELLO   I... you... forget it!

BILLIE   (*quietly at first*) Yes, you can forget it, can't you. I don't have that... that luxury. When I go into a store, I always know when I'm being watched. I can feel it. They want to see if I'm gonna slip some of their stuff into my pockets. When someone doesn't serve me, I think it's because I'm Black. When a clerk won't put the change into my held-out hand, I think it's because I'm Black. When I hear about a crime, any crime, I pray to God the person who they think did it isn't Black. I'm even suspicious of the word Black. Who called us Black anyway? It's not a country, it's not a racial category, its not even the colour of my skin. And don't give me this content of one's character B.S. I'm sorry... I am sorry... I had a dream. A dream that one day a Black man and a Black woman might find... where jumping a broom was a solemn eternal vow that... I... let's... can we just get this over with?

She goes to the window. Silence. He moves toward her.

OTHELLO   I know... I know. I'm sorry...

BILLIE   Yeh...

OTHELLO   I care... you know that.

BILLIE   I know.

Silence.

OTHELLO   I never thought I'd miss Harlem.

BILLIE   (*pause*) You still think it's a reservation?

OTHELLO   Homeland / reservation.

BILLIE   A sea of Black faces.

OTHELLO   Africatown, USA.

BILLIE   (*pause*). When we lived in the Village, sometimes, I'd be on the subway and I'd miss my stop. And I'd just sit there, past midtown, past the upper west side, and somehow I'd end up here. And I'd just walk. I love seeing all these brown faces.

OTHELLO   Yeh…

BILLIE   Since they knocked down the old projects, I can see the Schomberg Museum from here. You still can't make out Harlem Hospital. I love that I can see the Apollo from our – from my balcony.

OTHELLO   Fire escape.

BILLIE   Patio.

OTHELLO   You never did find a pair of lawn chairs, and a table to fit in that space.

BILLIE   Terrace.

OTHELLO   I never saw the beauty in it.

BILLIE   Deck. My deck.

OTHELLO   I wish… (*he looks at her*)

BILLIE   That old building across the street? I didn't know this, but that used to be the Hotel Theresa. That's where Castro stayed when he came to New York… must have been the fifties. Ron Brown's father used to run that hotel.

OTHELLO   I… I… I miss you so much sometimes. Nine years… it's a long time.

BILLIE   I know.

OTHELLO   I'm really not trying to hurt you, Billie.

BILLIE   I know.

OTHELLO   I never meant to hurt you. (*he strokes her face*)

BILLIE   I know.

OTHELLO   God you're so beautiful.

> *He kisses her. She does not resist.*

BILLIE   I.... don't.... I feel... (*he kisses her again*) What are you doing?

OTHELLO   I... I'm... I'm exploring the heightening Alleghenies of Pennsylvania. (*he kisses her again*) The curvaceous slopes of California. (*he kisses her again*) The red hills of Georgia, the mighty mountains of New York. Such sad eyes. (*he kisses her again*) I'm an equal opportunity employer. (*pause*) I am an equal opportunity employer. (*pause*) I say, I'm an equal opportunity employer, then you say, I don't come...

BILLIE   I don't come cheap, you know.

OTHELLO   I'm offering more than money can buy.

BILLIE   How much more?

OTHELLO   This much. (*he kisses her*)

BILLIE   I could buy that.

OTHELLO   Could you buy this? (*he kisses her deeply*)

BILLIE   Be... Be... Beloved. (*she kisses him*)

SCENE V

> *Same day: early afternoon. The stringed duet croons gently as Malcolm X speaks about the need for Blacks to turn their gaze away from Whiteness so that they can see each other with new eyes. OTHELLO is lying in the bed. BILLIE is in the living room, smoking a cigarette.*

OTHELLO   I've missed you.

BILLIE   That's nice.

OTHELLO   By the looks of things, I miss you even now.

BILLIE   I'm coming.

OTHELLO   I noticed.

BILLIE   Sometimes... sometimes when we make love. Sometimes every moment lines up into one moment. And I'm holding you. And I can't tell where I end, or you begin. I see everything. All my ancestors lined up below me... like a Makonde statue, or something. It's like... I know. I know I'm supposed to be here. Everything is here.

OTHELLO   Sounds crowded to me.

BILLIE   It's actually quite empty.

OTHELLO   Not as empty as this bed is feeling right about now.

BILLIE   I'm coming. I'm coming.

> *She hurriedly stubs the cigarette out, and heads toward the bedroom. The apartment buzzer rings. BILLIE goes to the intercom.*

BILLIE   Hi Magi. I... er... I'm kinda busy right now.

MONA   (*through intercom*) It's Mona. Could I have a word with Othello.

OTHELLO   (*overlapping*) Shit!

BILLIE   One second please.

> *He rushes to the intercom, while attempting to put his clothes back on. BILLIE tries to hold back her laughter. Her laughter begins to infect OTHELLO. He puts a finger over his mouth indicating to BILLIE to be quiet.*

OTHELLO   Hey Mone... Mone, I'm not done yet. There's more here than I imagined. Why don't I call you when I'm done.

> *MONA does not respond. OTHELLO's demeanour changes.*

> Mone? Mona? I'm coming, OK? I'll be right... just wait there one second, OK? OK?

> *BILLIE is unable to hide her astonishment.*

MONA   (*through intercom*) OK.

OTHELLO   OK.

He steps away from the intercom to finish putting on his clothes. BILLIE stares at him.

I'll be back in… uh… I just have to go straighten… uh… she wants to help… help pack. You'll have to get used to her sometime. I mean… I…

BILLIE continues to stare steadily at OTHELLO as he struggles with the buttons on his shirt.

I'm sorry… well… I'll be right… I'll be back.

He exits. BILLIE does not move.

SCENE VI

Harlem, 1860: late summer – night. A whining delta blues slides and blurs while the deeply resonant voice of Paul Robeson talks of his forbears, whose blood is in the American soil. HIM is hammering a newly-forged horseshoe, HER rushes in holding a large carrying bag.

HER   Oh… let me catch – catch my breath… I thought I was seen… oh my… I… I've packed a change of clothes for both of us, some loaves… I liberated the leftover bacon from yesterday's meal, from out the pantry, seeing how it was staring me right in the face when I was cleaning. It won't be missed. I wish I could pack old Betsy in my bag. She'd be sure an' give us some good fresh milk each mornin'. Oh – and I packed a fleece blanket. I hear the nights get good and cold further north you go. And… did I forget… no… nothing forgotten. Oh yes, I borrowed the big carving knife – for the bacon, a' course. You still working on those shoes for Miss Dessy's stallion… let her send it to town, or get some other slave to do that… she's going to be mad as hell you took off in any event… may as well not finish the shoes, it won't placate her none…

HIM picks up the horseshoe with a pair of tongs. He inspects it carefully. He puts the shoe to one side and retrieves the shackles. He takes a chamois and begins to polish the metal. Pause.

O? O? Othello? The moon'll be rising. We've got to make any headway under cover of dark… Othello, why you trying to please her. I'm so tired of pleasing her. I'm so tired of pleasing White folks. Up in Canada, we won't have to please no White folks no how. I hear they got sailing ships leaving for Africa every day. Canada freedom come… O? Othello? Are you coming?

HIM	I can't.
HER	If we make it to the border there's people there'll help us wade that water – help us cross over.
HIM	I'm not going.
HER	A big white house on an emerald hill...
HIM	I know.
HER	You need more time, O? I can wait for you. Finish her shoes, I'll... I can wait–
HIM	No. No.
HER	(*pause*) You love her.
HIM	Her father going to war.
HER	You love her?
HIM	I love you. It's just... she needs me. She respects me. Looks up to me, even. I love you. It's just... when I'm with her I feel like... a man. I want... I need to do for her...
HER	Do you love her?
HIM	Yes.
HER	Fight with me... I would fight with you. Suffer with me, O... I would suffer with you...

Silence.

SCENE VII

Harlem, present: late summer – late afternoon. Dulcet blue tones barely swing as Louis Farrakhan waxes eloquent on African Americans being caught in the gravity of American society. Billie is carefully wrapping personal items in newspaper. She places them in a large pile on the floor. MAGI enters carrying several large cardboard boxes.

MAGI	And you know what he says, after turning on the baseball game, in the middle of my romantic dinner? Eyes glued to the screen, he says, I bet you've never made love to a man with 26-inch biceps!

BILLIE   (*smiles*) Oh... no...

MAGI   I'm telling you, girl. Macho Mack, spot him at any locale sell-
             ing six-packs. Easily recognizable, everything about him is
             permanently flexed. His favourite pastime? Weekend NFL
             football, Monday night football, USFL football – even
             Canadian foot... you look like you're feeling better. Amah
             did a great job with your hair.

BILLIE   What's her motto? We lock heads and minds.

MAGI   Hey, can I borrow that beautiful African boubou – I got me a
             date with an African prince. The brother has it going on!
             Oh... you already have boxes.

                 BILLIE begins placing some of the wrapped objects into a box.

BILLIE   They're his box–

MAGI   When... he came over?

BILLIE   I even spoke to her.

MAGI   You saw her?

BILLIE   No. Want this mask?

MAGI   You met her?

BILLIE   No. Want this mask?

MAGI   I'll keep it for you–

BILLIE   I... er... I don't know how long these things will have to stay
             in storage.

MAGI   You don't have to move, you know. It's not rented yet. I
             mean, I can always lower the–

BILLIE   No, no... I'm moving on.

MAGI   Good. Good. To where? Where are you going? You haven't
             given me a date or anything. I've got bills to pay too, you
             know. When d'you plan to leave? Where are you going?

BILLIE   I might go... stay with Jenny. I could go home.

MAGI   I'll keep it for you–

BILLIE	I don't want anything that's – that was ours. If you don't want it, that's OK, I'll just trash it.

> *BILLIE throws the mask onto the floor. It breaks into several pieces.*

MAGI	Something happened. What happened?
BILLIE	Nothing.
MAGI	Did he tell you about… what did he say to you?
BILLIE	I'm just tired. Tired of sleeping. Tired of night. It lays over me like a ton of white feathers. Swallows me up. The movers are coming in the morning to pick up his things. It's OK. I'm fine. You know… I've lived all my life believing in lies.
MAGI	Well, getting your Masters isn't a lie.
BILLIE	It's about proving, isn't it? Proving I'm as good as… I'm as intelligent as…
MAGI	Nothing wrong with that.
BILLIE	I don't want anything… believe in anything. Really. I've gotta get out of here. I don't even believe in Harlem any-more.
MAGI	Come on…
BILLIE	It's all an illusion. All some imagined idealistic… I dunno.
MAGI	When I go out my door, I see all the beauty of my Blackness reflected in the world around me.
BILLIE	Yeh, and all my wretchedness by the time I get to the end of the block.
MAGI	Billie, he's the one who wants to White wash his life.
BILLIE	Corporeal malediction.
MAGI	Corp-o-re-all mal-e… oooh that's good.
BILLIE	A Black man afflicted with Negrophobia.
MAGI	Girl, you on a roll now!
BILLIE	No, no. A crumbled racial epidermal schema…

MAGI	Who said school ain't doing you no good.
BILLIE	...causing predilections to coitus denegrification.
MAGI	Booker T. Uppermiddleclass III. He can be found in predominantly White neighbourhoods. He refers to other Blacks as "them". His greatest accomplishment was being invited to the White House by George Bush to discuss the "Negro problem."
BILLIE	Now, that is frightening.
MAGI	No, what's frightening is the fact that I dated him.
BILLIE	What does it say... about us?
MAGI	Who?
BILLIE	You and me.
MAGI	Girl, I don't know. I can't even want to go there.
BILLIE	Ohh... oh well... least he's happy though. What does he say? Now he won't have to worry that a White woman will emotionally mistake him for the father that abandoned her.
MAGI	Isn't he worried the White woman might mistake him for the butler?
BILLIE	He'd be oh so happy to oblige.
MAGI	I see them do things for White women they wouldn't dream of doing for me.
BILLIE	It is a disease. We get infected as children, and... and the bacteria... the virus slowly spreads, disabling the entire system.
MAGI	Are we infected too?

There is knocking at the apartment door.

Speaking of White minds parading around inside of Black bodies – you want me to stay?

BILLIE	Don't you have a date?
MAGI	Hakim. But I can cancel...

There is knocking at the door again.

BILLIE	I'm OK. I'm OK. I'm fine… truly.

BILLIE opens the door. OTHELLO enters.

OTHELLO	The pot! (*he hands the pot to BILLIE*) Magi!
MAGI	How's Harlumbia?
OTHELLO	Columbia?
MAGI	Harlumbia – those 10 square blocks of Whitedom, owned by Columbia University, set smack dab in the middle of Harlem.
OTHELLO	Harlumbia, as you call it, is dull without you.
MAGI	You could steal honey from a bee, couldn't you. Better watch you don't get stung. Well, I'm off to doll myself up. Billie…
BILLIE	Yeh, I'll get that boubou…

BILLIE goes into the bedroom. After a few moments of silence.

MAGI	Why haven't you told her yet?
OTHELLO	About? – Oh yes… yeh… I wanted to…

BILLIE returns with a beautiful multicoloured boubou.

BILLIE	He won't be able to resist you…
MAGI	Thank you, thank you. Later you two.
OTHELLO	I'll be in touch…
BILLIE	I'm keeping my fingers crossed for you.
MAGI	Good, I'm running out of time.

MAGI exits. OTHELLO enters. BILLIE closes the door. There is a long awkward silence. BILLIE continues placing wrapped objects into her boxes. OTHELLO steps on a piece of the broken mask. He picks it up, looks at it, then places it on the mantel. He goes over to the bookshelf and begins to pack more of his possessions into his boxes.

OTHELLO	They're coming at nine.
BILLIE	Oh… er… I'll be out of your way.
OTHELLO	You can be here…

BILLIE	No. No. No. I have an appointment... an early appointment.
OTHELLO	Either way... (*they continue packing*) Ah... I've been meaning to tell you... things are real... money's real tight right now, what with buying the apartment, and moving and every-thing... I won't be able to cover your tuition this semester. I'll try and put money in your account when I can. Maybe–
BILLIE	I told you, I'm only taking one course. If you cover that, I won't be taking a full load 'till next–
OTHELLO	I know, that's what I'm saying.... I can't... I just can't do it right now.
BILLIE	It's one course...
OTHELLO	It's $5000.
BILLIE	You promised...
OTHELLO	I'm mortgaged up the wazoo. I don't have it. I just don't have $5000, right now.
BILLIE	Ooh... okay.
OTHELLO	I would if I could, you know that. (*he continues to pack*) I think I brought the bookshelf with me when we first–
BILLIE	Take it all.
OTHELLO	I don't want all of it.
BILLIE	I'm keeping the bed.
OTHELLO	What about the rest...
BILLIE	If you don't want it... I'm giving it away...
OTHELLO	OK, if you're throwing it out...
BILLIE	I'm keeping the bed.

They continue packing in silence.

OTHELLO	We're getting married. (*pause*) Me and Mona. We're engaged... officially. (*very long pause*)
BILLIE	Congratulations.

OTHELLO I wanted to tell you... hear it from the horse's mouth... hear it from me first. You know...

BILLIE (*pause*) Yeh... yes. Yes. Congratulations.

OTHELLO Mona wanted me to tell you.

BILLIE Yes. Yes. Being a feminist and everything – a woman's right to know – since we're all in the struggle... I thought you hated feminists.

OTHELLO Well... I didn't mean that. I mean... the White women's movement is different.

BILLIE Just Black feminists.

OTHELLO No, no... White men have maintained a firm grasp of the pants. I mean, White men have economic and political pants that White women have been demanding to share.

BILLIE White wisdom from the mouth of the mythical Negro.

OTHELLO Don't you see! That's exactly my point! You... the Black feminist position as I experience it in this relationship, leaves me feeling unrecognized as a man. The message is, Black men are poor fathers, poor partners, or both. Black women wear the pants that Black men were prevented from wearing... I believe in tradition. You don't support me. Black women are more concerned with their careers than their husbands. There was a time when women felt satisfied, no, honoured being a balance to their spouse, at home, supporting the family, playing her role–

BILLIE Which women? I mean, which women are you referring to? Your mother worked all her life. My mother worked, her mother worked... most Black women have been working like mules since we arrived on this continent. Like mules. When White women were burning their bras, we were hired to hold their tits up. We looked after their homes, their children... I don't support you? My mother's death paid your tuition, not mine...

OTHELLO Can't we even pretend to be civil? Can't we? I know this isn't easy. It's not easy for me either. Do you ever consider that?

BILLIE You like it easy, don't you.

OTHELLO The truth is, this is too fucking difficult.

BILLIE   You wouldn't know the truth if it stood up and knocked you sideways.

OTHELLO   You don't want the truth. You want me to tell you what you want to hear. No, no, you want to know the truth? I'll tell you the truth. Yes, I prefer White women. They are easier – before and after sex. They wanted me and I wanted them. They weren't filled with hostility about the unequal treatment they were getting at their jobs. We'd make love and I'd fall asleep not having to beware being mistaken for someone's inattentive father. I'd explain that I wasn't interested in a committed relationship right now, and not be confused with every lousy lover, or husband that had ever left them lying in a gutter of unresolved emotions. It's the truth. To a Black woman, I represent every Black man she has ever been with and with whom there was still so much to work out. The White women I loved saw me – could see me. Look, I'm not a junkie. I don't need more than one lover to prove my manhood. I have no children. I did not leave you, your mother, or your aunt, with six babies and a whole lotta love. I am a very single, very intelligent, very employed Black man. And with White women it's good. It's nice. Anyhow, we're all equal in the eyes of God, aren't we? Aren't we?

          BILLIE stares at OTHELLO. He continues to pack.

SCENE VIII

Harlem, 1928: late summer – night. The cello and bass moan, almost dirge-like, in harmonic tension to the sound of Jesse Jackson's oratory. SHE holds a straight-edged razor in her bloodied palms. HE lies on the floor in front of her, motionless, the handkerchief in his hand.

SHE   Deadly deadly straw little strawberries it's so beautiful you kissed my fingers you pressed this cloth into my palm buried it there an antique token our ancient all these tiny red dots on a sheet of white my fingernails are white three hairs on my head are white the whites of my eyes are white too the palms of my hands and my feet are white you're all I'd ever and you my my I hate Sssshh. Shhhhh OK. OK. OK. I'm OK alright don't don't don't don't my eyes on the shadow sparrow my sense in my feet my hands my head shine the light there please scream no sing sing (*SHE tries to sing*) and if I get a notion to jump into the ocean, ain't nobody's business if I do do do do If I go to church on Sunday then shimmy down on Monday t'ain't nobody's business if I...

SCENE IX

*Harlem, present: late summer – early evening. The instruments
sound out a deep cerulean blues, while Malcolm X almost scats
the question, "What difference does colour make?" OTHELLO
continues to pack. BILLIE sits on the floor by the bed watching
him from the bedroom.*

OTHELLO   I didn't mean – what I said. You know that. I just... sometimes you make me so mad I... people change, Billie. That's
just human nature. Our experiences, our knowledge transforms us. That's why education is so powerful, so erotic. The
transmission of words from mouth to ear. Her mouth to my
ear. Knowledge. A desire for that distant thing I know nothing of, but yearn to hold for my very own. My Mama used to
say, you have to be three times as good as a White child to get
by, to do well. A piece of that pie is mine. I don't want to
change the recipe. I am not minor. I am not a minority. I
used to be a minority when I was a kid. I mean my culture is
not my mother's culture – the culture of my ancestors. My
culture is Wordsworth, Shaw, "Leave it to Beaver", "Dirty
Harry". I drink the same water, read the same books. You're
the problem if you don't see beyond my skin. If you don't
hear my educated English, if you don't understand that I am
a middle class educated man. I mean, what does Africa have
to do with me. We struttin' around professing some imaginary connection for a land we don't know. Never seen.
Never gonna see. We lie to ourselves saying, ah yeh, mother
Africa, middle passage, suffering, the Whites did it to me, it's
the White's fault. Strut around in African cloth pretending
we human now. We human now. Some of us are beyond that
now. Spiritually beyond this race shit bullshit now. I am an
American. The slaves were freed over 130 years ago. In 1967
it was illegal for a Black to marry a White in sixteen states.
That was less than thirty years ago... in my lifetime. Things
change, Billie. I am not my skin. My skin is not me.

SCENE X

*Harlem, same day: night. A rhapsody of sound keeps time with
Christopher Darden as he asks O. J. Simpson to approach the
jury and try on the bloody glove. The apartment is virtually
full of boxes. BILLIE is by the chemical factory at the table.
The book of Egyptian Alchemy sits open upon it. Something is
boiling in the flask and steam is coming out of the condenser.
With rubber-gloved hands she adds several drops of a violet liquid into the flask. She picks up a large white handkerchief with
pretty red strawberries embroidered on it.*

BILLIE   I have a plan, my love. My mate… throughout eternity. Feel
              what I feel. Break like I break. No more – no less. You'll
              judge me harsher. I know. While Susan Smith… she blamed
              some imaginary Black man for the murder of her two boys
              and that's why authorities didn't suspect her for nearly two
              weeks. Stopping every Black man with a burgundy sedan
              from Union, South Carolina, to the Oranges of New Jersey.
              And you're still wondering what made her do it. What was
              she going through to make her feel that this was her only way
              out. Yet I'll be discarded as some kind of unconscionable bit-
              ter shadow, or something. Ain't I a woman? This is my face
              you take for night – the biggest shadow in the world. I…
              I have nothing more to lose. Nothing. Othello? I am prepar-
              ing something special for you… Othe… Othello. A gift for
              you, and your new bride. Once you gave me a handkerchief.
              An heirloom. This handkerchief, your mother's… given by
              your father. From his mother before that. So far back… and
              now… then… to me. It is fixed in the emotions of all your
              ancestors. The one who laid the foundation for the road in
              Herndon, Virginia, and was lashed for laziness as he stopped
              to wipe the sweat from his brow with this kerchief. Or, your
              great great grandmother, who covered her face with it, and
              then covered it with her hands as she rocked and silently
              wailed, when told that her girl child, barely thirteen, would
              be sent 'cross the state for breeding purposes. Or the one who
              leapt for joy on hearing of the Emancipation Proclamation, fif-
              teen years late mind you, only to watch it fall in slow motion
              from his hand and onto the ground when told that the only
              job he could now get, was the same one he'd done for free all
              those years, and now he's forced to take it, for not enough
              money to buy the food to fill even one man's belly. And
              more… so much more. What I add to this already fully
              endowed cloth, will cause you such… such… wretchedness.
              Othe… Othello.

              *The contents of the flask have been transformed from violet to
              clear. BILLIE places the handkerchief onto a large tray. Then
              with tongs, she takes the hot flask and pours the contents over
              the handkerchief. She retrieves a vial from the table, opens it.*

              My sable warrior… fight with me. I would fight with you…
              suffer with me… I would suffer–

              *She starts to pour, but the vial is empty. The buzzer rings.
              BILLIE is surprised. The buzzer rings again. BILLIE turns off
              the Bunsen burner. She takes the flask into the kitchen and
              pours it into the sink. The buzzer rings once more. Going back
              to the table, she carefully takes the tray and heads toward the
              bathroom. There is a knock at her door.*

BILLIE (*from the bathroom*) You have a key, let yourself in... make yourself right at home, why don't you–

MAGI (*off-stage*) Billie? Billie, it's me. Magi.

BILLIE Magi?

MAGI (*off-stage*) Are you OK?

BILLIE Yes. Yes. I'm fine. Let me call you later, OK Magi?

We hear the sound of liquid being poured. The toilet flushes. MAGI off-stage mumbles something about BILLIE having a visitor.

BILLIE What?

MAGI mumbles something about a visitor again.

BILLIE What? Door's open!

MAGI enters and stands in the doorway. She is speaking quietly, as if not wanting someone to hear.

MAGI Sweetie, you have a visitor. Shall I–

BILLIE (*entering the living area*) Look I'm tired. He's been here practically all day already–

MAGI No, no, no. He said his name is Canada. (*BILLIE turns to MAGI*) He says he's your father. That's what he said. He said he was your father.

A man in his late sixties, brushes past MAGI. He wears a hat, and has a small suitcase in his hand.

CANADA Sybil? Sybil! There's my girl. Come and give your Daddy a big hug.

ACT II

SCENE I

Harlem, present: late summer – night. The cello and bass pluck and bow a funky rendition of Aretha Franklin's "Spanish Harlem" against the audio sound of Michael Jackson and Lisa Marie Presley's interview on ABC's "Dateline". CANADA is sitting on one of the chairs, amidst stacks of boxes.

CANADA   The first time I came to Harlem, I was scared. Must have been '68 or '69. Yeh... we we're living in the Bronx, and your mother was still alive. Everything I'd ever learned told me that I wasn't safe in this part of town. The newspapers. Television. My friends. My own family. But I'm curious, see. I says, Canada you can't be in New York City and not see Harlem. So I make my way to 125th. "A" train. I'm gonna walk past the Apollo, I'm gonna see this place. I'm gonna walk the ten city blocks to Lexington and catch the "6" train back, if it's the last thing I do. So out of the subway, I put on my "baddest mother in the city" glare. I walk – head straight. All the time trying to make my stride say, "I'm mean... I'm mean. Killed somebody mean." So I'm doing this for 'bout five, ten minutes, taking short furtive glances at this place I really want to see, when I begin to realize... no-one is taking any notice of me... not a soul. Then it dawns on me: I'm the same as them. I look just like them. I look like I live in Harlem. Sounds silly now. But I just had to catch myself and laugh out loud. Canada, where did you get these ideas about Harlem from?

The kettle whistles.

BILLIE   How do you like it? (*she heads to the kitchen to make tea*)

CANADA   Brown sugar. No milk.

BILLIE   I don't even know why I asked, I don't have any milk anyway.

CANADA   You can't take milk. Never could. When your mother stopped feeding you from her milk, that cow's milk just gave you colic. And those diapers... now that's an image I'll never forget.

BILLIE   So what brings you to these parts?

CANADA   Just passing through. Since I was in the neighbourhood, thought I'd stop on in.

BILLIE	Nova Scotia's nearly a thousand miles away.
CANADA	Well, I thought I should see my grandchild. Jenny's almost six and I've only talked to her on the phone. And Andrew and his wife, and you. Nothing wrong with seeing family is there?
BILLIE	Strong or weak?
CANADA	Like a bear's bottom.
BILLIE	Polar or Grizzly?
CANADA	Grizzly.

BILLIE returns with a tray.

Andrew told me what happened.

BILLIE	He did, did he?
CANADA	Said you were taking it kinda hard.
BILLIE	Oh, I'll be fine. I'm a survivor. But then again, you already know that.
CANADA	Tea should be ready. Shall I be mother?
BILLIE	Go ahead.

CANADA pours the tea.

BILLIE	I hear you were in the hospital.
CANADA	My liver ain't too good. Gave out on me. I guess you reap what you sow.
BILLIE	Still drinking?
CANADA	Been sober going on five years now.
BILLIE	Good. Good for you.
CANADA	Don't mean I don't feel like it sometimes though…
BILLIE	Well… how long do you plan to be in town?

CANADA   Just a few days. See Andrew and his family. See the sights.
             I'm staying there – at Andrew's. Went by there earlier... no
             one home. Must have given them the wrong time. Left a
             note though. Told them to find me at Sybil's.

BILLIE   Billie. I've always despised that name. Sybil.

CANADA   I gave you that name. It's a good name. It was your
             Grandmother's name. It means prophetess. Sorceress. Seer
             of the future. I like it. I don't see anything wrong with that
             name.

BILLIE   Sounds like some old woman living in a cave.

CANADA   (reaching for his suitcase) I brought something for you. (he
             takes out a small red box) Go on... open it. The box is a bit too
             big, but... (BILLIE opens the box) It's your mother's ring. I
             figured she'd want you to have it.

BILLIE   I hardly remember her anymore. I get glimpses of this ghost-
             ly figure creeping in and out of my dreams.

CANADA   When Beryl first passed on, I couldn't get her off my mind,
             like she'd gone and left us somehow. Left me... with two
             kids, one a young girl ripening to sprout into womanhood. I
             was sad, but I was good and mad too. One minute I'd be try-
             ing to etch her face into my mind, cause I didn't want to for-
             get. Next thing, I'd be downing another shot of rye... I could-
             n't carry the weight. I just couldn't do it by myself. That's
             when we moved to Dartmouth. What's that them old slaves
             used to say? "I can't take it no more, I moving to Nova
             Scotia."

BILLIE   I'm thinking of heading back there myself...

CANADA   (pause) 'Cause he left you, or 'cause she's White?

BILLIE   (pause) I remember that White woman... that hairdresser you
             used to go with... the one with the mini skirts... what was
             her name?

CANADA   That's going way back... you remember her?

BILLIE   She was boasting about knowing how to do our kind of hair.
             And she took that hot comb to my head... sounded like she
             was frying chicken... burnt my ears and half the hair on my
             head. I hated her stubby little beige legs and those false eye-
             lashes. She taught me how to put on false eyelashes.

CANADA   Deborah.

BILLIE   Debbie… yes… Debbie.

CANADA   (*pause*) I wish… I wish things between…

            The buzzer rings.

BILLIE   That must be Drew. (*she goes to the console by the door*) Drew?

AMAH   (*through intercom*) It's me. Amah. Is your–

BILLIE   He's here. Come on up.

CANADA   You know, an old African once told me the story of a man who was struck by an arrow. His attacker was unknown. Instead of tending to his wound, he refused to remove the arrow until the archer was found and punished. In the meantime, the wound festered, until finally the poison infected his entire body, eventually killing him… now, who is responsible for this man's death, the archer for letting go the arrow, or the man for his foolish holding on?

            There is a knock at the door. BILLIE gets up and heads toward it.

BILLIE   The drunk?

CANADA   A drunken man can get sober but a damn fool can't ever get wise.

            BILLIE opens the door. AMAH enters with some rolls of paper in her arms.

AMAH   (*kissing BILLIE's cheek*) Hi sweetie. And you must be Canada.

CANADA   Drew's wife…

AMAH   So very pleased to meet you at last.

CANADA   Delighted…

AMAH   We weren't expecting you until tomorrow. We ate out tonight. We would have come pick you up. Jenny's so excited.

CANADA   No, no… no need to fuss. I arrived safe and sound. And Sybil – Billie's been taking good care of me.

AMAH Drew would have come himself. Jenny insisted he give her a bath tonight. You know, it's a father-daughter thing. (*silence*) Anyway, we should get going. (*to CANADA*) You're probably starving. I can rustle something up for you in no time.

   CANADA reaches for his coat.

   (*to BILLIE*) Look, I'm gonna have to bring that child of mine over here. She's driving me crazy asking for you—

BILLIE No. No... not yet.

AMAH Well, if I go mad, you and Drew will have to take care of her. I want you to know that. Oh, Jenny asked me to give these to you. She made them specially for you. She wanted to give you some inspiration. You might not be able to tell, but one's of her dancing, and the other's of her singing.

BILLIE Tell her I miss her.

AMAH I will.

BILLIE Tell her I'll see her real soon.

AMAH I will.

BILLIE (*to AMAH*) I still have a bone to pick with you, though. (*indicating CANADA*)

AMAH No, no. You have a bone to pick with Drew.

CANADA I'll drop in again tomorrow, if that's OK with you.

BILLIE Tomorrow might not be so good. He's moving his stuff in the morning. We'd probably be in the way. I won't even be here until sometime in the afternoon.

CANADA Well then... we'll see how things go. (*he kisses BILLIE on the forehead*)

AMAH Come join us over something to eat—

BILLIE No. Thanks. I'm fine.

CANADA Good to see you, Sybil – Billie.

BILLIE Well it certainly was a surprise. Bye y'all.

   AMAH and CANADA exit. BILLIE closes the door, then leans against it as she studies the pictures Jenny drew.

SCENE II

Harlem, the present: the next day – late morning. Lyrical strains give way to an undulating rhythm while Malcolm X recounts the tale of how George Washington sold a slave for a gallon of molasses. The apartment looks empty of furniture, save for the bed, several piles of books, and boxes strewn around the living area. OTHELLO walks into the bedroom with a large green garbage bag. After a few moments, the door is unlocked and BILLIE peers through the doorway. She hears someone in the bedroom. She quietly closes the door behind her and places a small brown paper bag in her pocket. She makes her way into the kitchen area. She waits. OTHELLO exits the bedroom, green garbage bag in tow. He walks to the centre of the living room where he stands for a few moments taking it all in.

BILLIE   Got everything?

OTHELLO   (*startled*) Ahh! (*dropping the garbage bag, he turns around*) Christ...

BILLIE   Got everything?

OTHELLO   God, I didn't hear you come in.

BILLIE   My meeting ended earlier than I expected. I was able to get what I needed... I didn't see a van. I figured you'd be done by now.

OTHELLO   They just left. I was doing a final check. See if I'd forgotten anything.

BILLIE   So the move went well.

OTHELLO   Yes... yeh. It's amazing how much stuff there is.

BILLIE   Yeh. It's hard to throw things away.

OTHELLO   I know what you mean. We've got a huge place though.

BILLIE   Good. Good for you.

OTHELLO   (*pause*) This place looks pretty huge right now, though. Remember when we first came to look at this place?

BILLIE   Yes.

OTHELLO   (*pause*) Well... I guess that's it.

BILLIE　　I guess...

OTHELLO　(*pause*) Anyway... so when do you plan on leaving?

BILLIE　　Oh, I don't... I don't know.

OTHELLO　Ah.

BILLIE　　I haven't decided.

OTHELLO　I see... well...

BILLIE　　So when's the big day?

OTHELLO　Oh... well... er... three weeks.

BILLIE　　So soon?

OTHELLO　Just a small affair.

BILLIE　　Good. Good for you. Good for you both.

OTHELLO　Yeh...

BILLIE　　I... I've been meaning... well... I've been thinking.

OTHELLO　Hmn Hmn...

BILLIE　　I... er... I... um... I want to return something you gave me... centuries ago.

OTHELLO　Oh?

BILLIE　　The handkerchief?

OTHELLO　Oh! Really? Wow... no. No. It's not necessary. Really–

BILLIE　　No, no, let me finish. I've... been foolish. I understand that now. You can understand why. And... I'm sorry. That's what I wanted to tell you. And the handkerchief... it's yours. Held by me for safekeeping really. To be passed on to our children – if we had any. Since we don't, it should be returned to you, to your line...

OTHELLO　Why are you doing this?

BILLIE　　I just thought you might... I thought you would... after all... it's the only thing your mother left you...

OTHELLO   I don't know what to say.

BILLIE   I thought you'd be glad.

OTHELLO   Oh, I'm more than glad.

BILLIE   But I have to find it first.

OTHELLO   Are you sure about–

BILLIE   I'm sure. Give me a couple of days, to find it… clean it up a bit.

OTHELLO   I could come by.

BILLIE   Yes. You should have it before… you know… before your… big day.

OTHELLO   Thank you.

BILLIE   Just trying to play my part well.

OTHELLO   Thanks.

BILLIE   Forgive me…

OTHELLO   I know it's been hard.

BILLIE   Yeh..

OTHELLO   OK. Well…

He reaches to touch her face. She retreats.

BILLIE   I'll see you in a couple of days then.

OTHELLO   Alright.

BILLIE   Alright.

OTHELLO   Alright. And say Hello to Jenny for me. (*silence*) Alright.

OTHELLO exits. BILLIE takes the small package out of her pocket. She unwraps it, revealing a small vial of fluid. She goes into the kitchen, vial in hand, turns toward the fridge, opens the freezer door and stares into it.

BILLIE   Look this way and see… your death… Othe… Othe… (*she places the vial into the freezer*)

SCENE III

Harlem, 1862: late summer – night. Indigo blues groan as if through a delta, while echoes of a presidential voice reads from the Emancipation Proclamation. The sound fades. HER holds HIM in her arms like Mary holds Jesus in Michelangelo's "The Pieta". There is a rope around his neck. He does not move.

HER   (*caressing him*) Once upon a time, there was a man who wanted to find a magic spell in order to become White. After much research and investigation, he came across an ancient ritual from the caverns of knowledge of a psychic. "The only way to become White," the psychic said, "was to enter the Whiteness." And when he found his ice queen, his alabaster goddess, he fucked her. Her on his dick. He one with her, for a single shivering moment became... her. Her and her Whiteness.

SCENE IV

Harlem, present: late summer – night. A cacophony of strings grooves and collides as sound bites from the Anita Hill and Clarence Thomas hearings, the L.A. riots, the O. J. Simpson trial, Malcolm X, and Martin Luther King, loop and repeat the same distorted bits of sound over and over again. BILLIE is alone in the apartment. She goes into the freezer and removes the vial. Wearing rubber gloves, she places several drops of a liquid substance onto the handkerchief. She replaces the cap of the vial. BILLIE carefully folds the handkerchief, hesitates for a moment, looks around and spots the red box on the mantel. She puts the handkerchief back down on the tray and, with her hands in the air, like a surgeon scrubbing for surgery, she gets up and goes to the red box. With one hand she takes off one of the gloves. With the ungloved hand, she opens the red box and slips her mother's ring on her finger. She then takes the red box with her to the table. She very carefully replaces the one glove, picks up the handkerchief, and neatly places it in the small red box. She works slowly, and is mindful not to touch the sides of the box with the handkerchief itself.

She removes a single rubber glove once more, picks up the cover to the box, and places it on top of the other half. She is still for a few moments, staring at the box.

BILLIE gets up and crosses the room, as if looking for something, only to stop in her tracks and return to the box. She paces. Her pacing appears more methodical than hysterical. Suddenly she stops. She turns to look at the small red box.

She shakes her head and takes a seat on a large, full, cardboard box at her feet. Her breathing becomes more apparent as she begins to rock, almost imperceptibly at first. Finally she places her head in her hands.

After several moments, BILLIE's face slowly emerges from her hands.

She glares at the gloved hand incredulously, as she realizes that she has inadvertently transferred some of the potion onto her own skin. She quickly removes the second glove, and proceeds to wipe her face with her own clothes.

BILLIE   (*to herself*) Oh god! Oh my god! Shit! Shit! Shit! Shit!

BILLIE gets up and rushes to the kitchen sink, turns on the tap and frantically washes her hands and face in the water.

SCENE V

The following day: early evening. In counterpoint to the cello and bass, the distorted sound loop becomes a grating repetition. MAGI and CANADA are on either side of a large box, sitting on two smaller ones. The larger box is covered by a scarf to resemble a tablecloth, on top of which is a small feast. They are eating. MAGI gets up and goes to the door of the bedroom. She peeks in. After a few moments she closes the door and returns to her seat.

MAGI   She's in distant realms. I checked in on her when I got back from church. I thought she was speaking in tongues. I couldn't understand a thing she was saying. I don't think she slept a wink all night. Those pills work like a charm, though. (*beat*) How is it?

CANADA   Mmn! Those greens... she looks like an angel and cooks like one too.

MAGI   Can I get you some more?

CANADA   No, no, I don't want to appear too greedy now.

MAGI   Here... (*serving him another helping*) There you go. And I won't tell a soul. Promise.

CANADA   I haven't tasted cooking like this in a long time.

MAGI   My Mama would say, some food is good for the mind, some
            is good for the body, and some food is good for the soul.

CANADA   Your Mama taught you how to cook like this?

MAGI   Once she even taught me how to cook a soufflé. She used to
            have a restaurant downstairs from as far back as I can recall.
            And I guess the boys returning home from the war in Europe
            kept asking for the Parisian food, and it ended up on her
            menu. She'd say, now this Parisian food ain't good for noth-
            ing. Soufflé ain't nothing more than baked eggs. And eggs is
            for breakfast. Eggs don't do no one no good past noon.

CANADA   So you've lived here all your life?

MAGI   And my mother before me, and her mother before her. My
            great grandmother, worked for the family that lived here,
            most of her life. She never married, but she had two children
            by the man she worked for – seems his wife never knew they
            were his. One brown baby looks just like another to most
            White folks. And when the wife died, my great grandmother
            just stayed on. Everybody thinking she's just the maid, but
            she was living like the queen of the manor – him being her
            babies' father and everything. And his other children were all
            grown by then. So when he died, he left everything to his
            White children, 'cept this house. He left it in my great grand-
            mother's name, and it's been in my family ever since.

CANADA   So the White man's children ever find out? About their
            brown-skinned relatives.

MAGI   I don't know. The Van Dykes – they were Dutch. We used to
            watch the Dick Van Dyke show, and my Grandmother used to
            always say, "That there's your relative!" But we didn't pay
            her too much mind. More greens?

CANADA   If I eat another thing, I will truly burst. This was wonderful.
            Thank you. Thank you very much.

MAGI   You're more than welcome.

CANADA   When I was a boy, I used to love to sop the pot liquor.

MAGI   It's nearly the best part.

CANADA   You sure know the way to a man's heart.

MAGI   Haven't had any luck so far.

CANADA Yet.

> *There is an awkward silence between them, after which they both start speaking at once.*

MAGI (*overlapping*) Well I better get started with these dishes...

CANADA (*overlapping*) I should go in and check on Sybil... let me give you a hand.

MAGI No, no, it's quite alright. I can handle this.

> *BILLIE enters.*

CANADA Billie! Marjorie was kind enough to share her dinner with me.

MAGI Billie, come and have something to eat.

BILLIE I'm not hungry. I heard voices. I need to go back and lay down... get some reading done.

MAGI You can't have eaten anything for the day, girl.

BILLIE I'm fine.

CANADA What you need is a good meal inside you.

BILLIE I said I was fine.

MAGI I'll just take these things downstairs. (*she exits*)

CANADA I'll make you some tea, OK.

BILLIE I don't – don't need any tea. I don't want anything to eat. I'm fine. I'm sorry. I don't – don't – don't mean... to be like this... but I haven't seen you in God knows how long... and you just show up, and expect things to be all hunky dory.

CANADA (*pause*) Well, I'll be off then. (*he goes for his coat*)

BILLIE I'm sorry.

CANADA Me too. (*he heads for the door*)

BILLIE And I am glad you came... maybe this can be... you know... like a beginning of something... I don't know.

CANADA   I nearly came before... two or three times... you know, when I heard. I wished your mother was here. I really wished for her... her wisdom. I mean Beryl would know what to do. A girl needs her mother. And I know you didn't have her all those times... I mean, I couldn't tell you. What could I tell you? I kept seeing your face. It's your mother's face. You've got my nose. My mouth. But those eyes... the shape of your face... the way you're head tilts to one side when you're thinking, or just listening. It's all her. You've got her moods. I used to call them her moods. Once 'bout every three months, on a Friday, when she'd have the weekend off, she'd come home from that hospital, take off her clothes and lay down in her bed and stay there 'till Sunday afternoon. She'd say she'd done turned the other cheek so many times in the past little while, she didn't have no more smiles for anybody. She'd say, better she just face God and the pillow than shower me and the children with the evil she had bottled up inside her. See, if you spend too much time among White people, you start believing what they think of you. So I'd take you and Drew and we'd go visiting. We'd take the whole week-end and visit all the folks we knew, in a fifteen mile radius... when we'd get home, she'd have cleaned the house, washed the clothes and even made a Sunday dinner. And after I'd pluck the guitar... and she'd start to sing... and you'd dance... you remember? You'd dance. You'd stomp on that floor like you were beating out some secret code to God or something... I know you – we don't see eye to eye. I know you haven't wanted to see very much anything of me lately. But I've known you all your life. I carried you in my arms and on my back, kissed and spanked you when you needed, and I watched you start to talk, and learn to walk, and read and I just wanted to come... I just wanted to come. And I know I can't make everything alright. I know. But I was there when you arrived in this world. And I didn't think there was space for a child, I loved your mother so much. But there you were and I wondered where you'd been all my life, like something I'd been missing and didn't know I'd been missing. And I don't know if you've loved anybody that long. But behind your mother's face you're wearing, I still see the girl who shrieked with laughter, and danced to the heavens sometimes...

          CANADA slowly approaches BILLIE. She does not move. He takes her in his arms. He holds her in his arms for a long time.

SCENE VI

Harlem, 1928: late summer – night. The strident movement of the strings is joined by the rising tempo of the distorted sound loop. HE and SHE are both in a tiny dressing room, as in the prologue. On a counter is a shaving brush, a straight-edged razor, greasepaint and a top hat. HE wipes his face with a towel. SHE holds the handkerchief out to him. He does not take it. She lets it fall at his feet. After a few moments, he picks it up.

HE   (*referring to the handkerchief at first*) White, red, black, green, indigo… what difference does it make? That makes no sense… makes no difference. "If virtue no delighted beauty lack, Your son-in-law is far more fair than black." Far more fair than black. I want… I need to do this… for my soul. I am an actor. I–

SHE   (*kindly*) A minstrel. A Black minstrel…

He places the towel on the counter beside the toiletries.

HE   It's paid my way.

She caresses the towel.

SHE   Stay, my sable warrior… (*her hand stumbles upon the razor*)

HE   I'll not die in black-face to pay the rent. I am of Ira Aldrigde stock. I am a classical man. I long to play the Scottish king. The prince of Denmark. "The slings and arrows of outrageous…" or… or… "There's a divinity that shapes our ends, Rough-hew them how we will"… those words… I love those words. They give me life. Mona sees my gift. She's cast me as the prince of Tyre. She's breathed new life into a barren dream. She… she… she has a serene calmness about her. That smile… I bet they named her Mona because even at birth, she had that constant half smile, like the Mona Lisa. Skin as smooth as monumental alabaster… as warm as snow velvet.

SHE   (*exposing the blade*) My onyx prince…

HE   Ooohh…

SHE   (*approaching him from behind*) My tourmaline king… (*she leans her head on his back*)

HE   S'alright…

SHE   My raven knight...

             She wraps her arms around him. He turns his head toward her.

HE   Oh sweet...

SHE   My umber squire...

HE   I wish... I wish–

             Her hand rises, the razor is poised, nearly touching the skin of his neck, just below his ear, within his peripheral vision.

SHE   My Cimmerian lord...

             He turns around, as if to see what she's holding, and in that turn, his neck appears to devour the blade. The razor's shaft at once hidden by his flesh, swiftly withdraws, leaving a rushing river of red like a scarf billowing around his neck and her hands. He yields to gravity.

SCENE VII

             Harlem, the present: late summer night. The plucked strings and the distorted audio loop have become even more dissonant. BILLIE is clutching the small red box.

MAGI   ...you know, Hakim has seven children, and he's never been married. Brother Hakim. Spot him at any street rally where the subject is prefaced by the words "Third World". He's the one with the "Lumumba Lives" button prominently displayed on his authentic kente cloth dashi – Billie? Billie, what's up? You don't look so good. (*pause*) Billie?

BILLIE   Sybil. I'm Sybil.

MAGI   That's what your Daddy calls you.

BILLIE   Yes.

MAGI   Your Daddy sure is one good-looking gentleman.

BILLIE   Trapped in history. A history trapped in me.

MAGI   I'm serious. I mean... I wanna know if you mind? Really. You were still a little girl when your mama died.

BILLIE   I don't remember Beryl's funeral. I see my father dressed in black, sewing a white button, on to his white shirt, with an enormous needle. He attaches the button and knots the thread so many times it's like he's trying to hold onto more than just the button. Like he can't bear for anything else in his life to leave him.

MAGI   He's a nice man. Would you mind?

BILLIE   Am I nice?

MAGI   Billie, I bet you haven't eaten today.

BILLIE   Can you keep a secret?

MAGI   No, but that's never stopped you before.

BILLIE   Then sorry…

MAGI   OK, OK. I promise.

BILLIE   I am about to plunge into very dangerous waters. Give me your word.

MAGI   You're not going to do something stupid, now.

BILLIE   Your word?

MAGI   Yeh, OK.

BILLIE   I've drawn a line.

MAGI   A line? A line about what?

BILLIE   I'm returning the handkerchief – the one his mother gave him. The one he gave to me when we first agreed to be together…

MAGI   I don't understand.

BILLIE   I've concocted something… a potion… a plague of sorts… I've soaked the handkerchief… soaked it in certain tinctures… anyone who touches it – the handkerchief, will come to harm.

MAGI   Now that is not a line, Billie, that is a trench!

BILLIE   I'm supposed to…

MAGI   Billie, if this kind of stuff truly worked, Africans wouldn't be in the situation we're in now. Imagine all them slaves working magic on their masters – didn't make no difference. If it truly worked, I'd be married to a nice man, with three little ones by now. But if it makes you feel better–

BILLIE   He's going to marry her... officially...

MAGI   I know... I know. Remember, what goes around comes around. Karma is a strong and unforgiving force.

BILLIE   I haven't seen it affect White people too much.

MAGI   Is everything about White people with you? Is every living moment of your life eaten up with thinking about them? Do you know where you are? Do you know who you are anymore? What about right and wrong. Racism is a disease my friend, and your test just came back positive. You're so busy reacting, you don't even know yourself.

BILLIE   No, no, no... it's about Black. I love Black. I really do. And it's revolutionary... Black is beautiful... so beautiful. This Harlem sanctuary... here. This respite... like an ocean in the middle of a desert. And in my mirror, my womb, he has a fast growing infestation of roaches. White roaches.

MAGI   Billie?

BILLIE   Did you ever consider what hundreds of years of slavery did to the African American psyche?

MAGI   What? What are you...?

BILLIE   Every time someone mentions traditional values or the good old days – who exactly were those days good for?

               The phone rings. BILLIE goes over it. She sits on the bare floor but does not answer.

               Jenny... is that you Jenny? My beauty. My little girl. It's Sybil... Auntie Sybil... the woman who lives in the cave. (*she laughs*)

MAGI   I'll get it for you.

BILLIE   (*picks up the receiver*) Yes, yes, I'm here. Oh, Othe... Othello. I didn't recognize your voice. You sound... different. No. No, no, you can't pick it up. I mean – I've got it, yes. It's right here. No. No, I won't be in... no, no. I haven't changed my mind. But – I mean... I have to go... roaches. Yeh, blue roaches. Green roaches. So I have to go now. I – I just have to go. (*she replaces the receiver*)

MAGI   He's coming over?

BILLIE   I don't want a Mona Lisa smile...

MAGI   Oh Billie... Billie, you're all in bits and pieces.

BILLIE   I know. I know. A tumour. Suddenly apparent, but its been there, tiny, growing slowly for a long time. What kind of therapy to take? Chop it out? Radiate it? Let it eat me alive? I see roaches all around me. In me. Blue roaches. Green roaches. Aah! Get off! Get it off. I eat roaches. I pee roaches. Help! I'm losing... I don't don't... I'm falling...

MAGI   Billie? Billie?

BILLIE   I have a dream today.

MAGI   You had a dream?

BILLIE   I have a dream that one day every valley shall be engulfed, every hill shall be exalted and every mountain shall be made low... oh... oh... the rough places will be made plains and the crooked places will be made...

MAGI   (*overlapping*) It's gonna be alright, Billie. (*she goes to the phone and dials*)

BILLIE   (*overlapping*) ...straight and the glory of the Lord shall be revealed and all flesh shall see it together.

MAGI   (*overlapping*) It's Magi. You all better get over here, now. No, no, no. (*shouting*) Now. Alright. Alright.

   MAGI puts down the receiver and returns to BILLIE. She gently takes the red box from out of BILLIE's hands, and places it on the mantel.

BILLIE   (*overlapping*) ...this is our hope...

MAGI   (*overlapping*) It's gonna be alright. I know... I know...

BILLIE (*overlapping*) ...with this faith we will be able to hew out of the mountain of despair a stone of hope...

MAGI (*overlapping*) It's OK. It's OK. Let's start with a little step. Come on. Come with me. (*MAGI helps BILLIE up*) Come on... good. Let's get some soup into you. Warm up that frozen blood of yours. (*MAGI leads her to the door*) Warm up your insides. Come... come on... chase all the roaches out... (*BILLIE breaks loose of MAGI and rushes to the window*)

> MAGI is no longer in the room. OTHELLO appears wearing a brightly coloured dashiki. He is inspecting a broom, laying against the fridge. It is now Fall, seven years earlier. Save for the broom, and the fridge, the apartment is empty.

BILLIE Look... come, look... you can see the Apollo from the window. I love it.

OTHELLO Where?

BILLIE Over there. See.

OTHELLO Oh yeh – if I crane my neck.

BILLIE I could find some lawn chairs and table and we'd have a city terrace.

OTHELLO On the fire escape?

BILLIE We'd have our own little balcony.

OTHELLO Patio.

BILLIE Terrace...

OTHELLO We could buy a house up here.

BILLIE We can't afford to buy a house until I finish school. If I'm going to go to school full-time, this fall, like we agreed – you'd go to school, then I'd go to school – how can we afford a down payment on a house?

OTHELLO I know. I know.

BILLIE (*pause*) I love it. Don't you love it?

OTHELLO I love you.

BILLIE I love you and I love it.

OTHELLO   Think Chris Yago and Mona and the other faculty will feel uncomfortable coming up here… for meetings and the like…

BILLIE   It's on the subway line.

OTHELLO   And boy do they need to take the journey. I'll take them on a cultural field trip – blow their minds.

BILLIE   I've longed for this sanctuary.

OTHELLO   I know what you mean.

BILLIE   Black boutiques.

OTHELLO   Black bookstores.

BILLIE   Black groceries.

OTHELLO   Filled with Black doctors and dentists. Black banks.

BILLIE   Black streets teeming with loud Black people listening to loud Jazz and reggae and Aretha… (*singing*) "There is a rose in Spanish Harlem. (*he joins her*) A rose in Black and Spanish Harlem. Da da da, da da da…" maybe later we could buy a place on "strivers row", that's where all the rich Black folks live.

OTHELLO   Strivers row.

BILLIE   Owned by Blacks hued from the faintest gold to the bluest bronze. That's my dream.

OTHELLO   By then you'd have your Ph.D.

BILLIE   And a small lecturer's position at a prestigious Manhattan university. We might even have enough money to get a small house in the country too.

OTHELLO   A big house in the country too?

BILLIE   A big house with a white picket fence.

OTHELLO   On a rolling emerald hill.

BILLIE   I want 2.5 kids.

OTHELLO   (*he kisses her lightly*) You're mad, you know that.

BILLIE   That makes you some kinda fool for loving me, baby.

OTHELLO   Let's do it. There's an old broom right over there. Wanna jump it with me? (*he retrieves the broom*)

BILLIE   Are you asking me to m–

OTHELLO   Yes... yes, I am asking.

BILLIE   Yes... (*silence*) then yes.

> *OTHELLO kisses her. He places the broom in the middle of the floor. He takes BILLIE's hand. They stand in front of it.*

What will we use for rings?

OTHELLO   Think them old slaves had rings? Slave marriages were illegal, remember. This broom is more than rings. More than any gold. (*he whispers*) My ancient love.

BILLIE   (*she whispers*) My soul.

> *OTHELLO kisses her hand. The couple gaze at each other, preparing to jump over the broom. They jump. They hold each other. The landlady enters.*

MAGI   Oh – I'm sorry.

BILLIE   No, no. We were just... just–

> *OTHELLO picks up the broom and places it to one side.*

OTHELLO   I think we'll take it.

MAGI   I didn't mean to rush you. I can give you another few minutes if you need to make good and sure?

BILLIE   I think we're sure. (*to OTHELLO*) You sure? (*to MAGI*) We're sure.

> *MAGI looks gravely at BILLIE. They are the only ones in the room. We are back in the present. MAGI carefully approaches BILLIE. BILLIE stares at where OTHELLO stood, only moments ago.*

MAGI   Come on. Come with me. Come on... good. Let's get some soup into you. Warm up that frozen blood of yours. (*MAGI leads her to the door*) Warm up your insides. Come... come on... chase all the roaches out... one by one... one by one...

> *They exit.*

SCENE VIII

Harlem, present: late summer, afternoon. A lyrical rhapsody swings to the sound of a commentator describing the scene at the Million Man March. The apartment is virtually empty. CANADA is cleaning the kitchen, taking tubs and bags from out of the freezer. He gives them a brief once-over and then throws them into the trash. OTHELLO enters.

OTHELLO   Billie? Billie?

CANADA   Othello! Othello, good to see you son. (*they shake hands*) Good to see you.

OTHELLO   I didn't know... when did you get here?

CANADA   A few days.

OTHELLO   Billie didn't say a word.

CANADA   Well, Billie's in... she's... Billie's not here right now.

OTHELLO   (*scanning the apartment*) Did she leave anything for me. An envelope... a package – (*he sees the red box on the mantel*) Oh. Maybe... (*he goes over to it*)

CANADA   Oh, she said no one was to touch that... I'm supposed to throw it out.

OTHELLO   Great! (*he opens the red box and takes out the handkerchief*) It's OK, this is it. It's mine. This is what I was looking for.

CANADA   I was just about to throw it in with the trash from the fridge.

OTHELLO   Just in time, huh?

CANADA   Yeh, some of this stuff's about ready to crawl out by itself.

OTHELLO   I can imagine.

CANADA   I swear, one thing had actually grown little feet.

OTHELLO   Well, Billie wasn't one for cleaning... I guess neither of us was. (*there is an awkward silence between them*) Well... I should be off. (*he takes some keys from out of his pocket and places them where the red box was laying*)

CANADA   She tells me you're getting married.

OTHELLO   I do confess the vices of my blood.

CANADA   I'm real sorry it didn't work out... between you and Billie... I mean... I was hoping...

OTHELLO   Yes. I know.

CANADA   She's my child, so–

OTHELLO   I know, I know.

CANADA   You young'uns don't know the sweetness of molasses... rather have granulated sugar, 'stead of a deep clover honey, or cane sugar juice from way into the Demerara. Better watch out for that refined shit. It'll kill ya. A slow kinda killin'. 'Cause it kills your mind first. So you think you living the life, when you been dead a long time.

OTHELLO   (*silence*) Well sir... I should be somewhere.

CANADA   (*nodding*) Well, I hope we can catch up sometime...

> OTHELLO *goes to the door.*

OTHELLO   That would be great. Tell Billie I came by.

CANADA   I'll tell her that. She'll be glad to know.

OTHELLO   Good seeing you.

CANADA   You too... son... you too.

> OTHELLO *takes one last look at the apartment, takes out a tiny cellular phone, and exits. CANADA is still for a few moments. From the hallway we hear OTHELLO.*

OTHELLO   (*off-stage*) Chris Yago, please.

> CANADA *returns to the fridge, and continues to clean.*

SCENE IX

Harlem, 1928: late summer – night. The music softly under-scores the voice of Paul Robeson speaking about not being able to get decent acting roles in the U.S., and how fortunate he feels to be offered a contract to play OTHELLO in England. HE is alone. He proceeds to cover his face in black grease paint. He begins to speak, as if rehearsing, at first.

HE It is most true; true, I have married her.
It is most…
It is most true; true, I have married her.
For know, but that I love the gentle Desdemona,
(She) questioned me the story of my life
From year to year – the battles, sieges, fortunes,
That I have passed. These things to hear
Would Desdemona seriously incline;
But still the house affairs would draw her thence,
Which ever as she could with haste dispatch
she'd come again, and with a greedy ear
Devour up my discourse. Which I, observing,
Took once a pliant hour…
And often did beguile her of her tears,
When I did speak of some distressful stroke
That my youth suffered…

> *In the background we can hear a children's song. HE begins to add a white greasepaint to his lips, completing the mask of the minstrel.*

…My story being done,
She gave me for my pains a world of sighs.
She wished she had not heard it, yet she wished
That heaven had made her such a man. She thanked me,
She thanked me…
She thanked me…
She thanked me…

SCENE X

> *Harlem, the present: late summer – night. A beryline blues improvisation of "Mama's Little Baby" cascades alongside a reading of the Langston Hughes poem "Harlem". AMAH sits beside BILLIE in the visitors lounge of the psychiatric ward. AMAH is clearly saddened by BILLIE's state.*

BILLIE (*singing*) …Step back Sal-ly, all night long.
Strut-in' down the al-ley, al-ley, al-ley,
Strut-in' down the al-ley, all night long.

AMAH
& BILLIE I looked over there, and what did I see?
A big fat lady from Ten-nes-see.

> *BILLIE gets up and begins to dance.*

I bet you five dollars I can beat that man,
To the front, to the back, to the side, side, side.
To the front, to the back, to the side, side, side.

The two women laugh.

BILLIE   I haven't done that in... in years.

AMAH   I never knew that one – I just saw Jenny do it the other day.

BILLIE   I even remember the dance. (*singing under her breath*) ...Bet
you five dollars I can beat that man...

AMAH   It's not so bad here.

BILLIE   You'd think the doctors at Harlem hospital would be Black.
Especially in psychiatrics. Most of the nurses are Black.

AMAH   But they're nice to you – the doctors?

BILLIE   They help. I don't – don't want anymore pills. And that's
OK. They don't really understand, though. I had this dream.
Lucinda – she's my main doctor. Lucinda was sitting at the
edge of a couch and I asked her a question. But she couldn't
answer because her eyes kept flashing. Like neon lights.
Flash, flash, flash. That was it. That was the dream. I knew
it was important, but I didn't get it. And I told her. And she
didn't get it either. But it gnawed away at me... for days...
the flashing eyes. And that was it! The eyes were flashing
blue. Her eyes were flashing blue. She could only see my
questions through her blue eyes.

AMAH   Something in you really wants to heal.

BILLIE   Exorcism.

AMAH   Pardon?

BILLIE   Repossess.

AMAH   Self-possession?

BILLIE   I hate. I know I hate. And he loves. How he loves.

AMAH   Billie?

BILLIE   Why is that, you think?

AMAH   Some of us spend our entire lives making our own shackles.

BILLIE   Canada freedom come.

AMAH   And the experienced shackle-wearer knows the best polish for the gilt.

BILLIE   I wanna be free.

AMAH   It must be hard, though. I feel for him.

BILLIE   I'm not that evolved.

AMAH   Forgiveness.

BILLIE   Forgiveness…

AMAH   If I don't forgive my enemy, if I don't forgive him, he might just set up house, inside me.

BILLIE   I just… I – I despise – I know… I know… moment by moment. I forgive him now. I hate – I love him so – I forgive him now. And now. *(she moves as if to speak, but stops herself)* And I forgive him now.

AMAH   My time's up, sweetie.

BILLIE   I have a dream…

AMAH   Sorry?

BILLIE   I had a dream…

AMAH   Yes… I know.

BILLIE   Tell Jenny… tell her for me… tell her that you saw me dancing.

AMAH   I will tell her

BILLIE   And tell her… tell her that you heard me singing.

AMAH   I will.

BILLIE   And tell her… I'll see her real soon.

AMAH   I will tell her, Billie. I will tell her.

> *AMAH kisses BILLIE on the cheek and begins to exit.*
> *CANADA enters.*

BILLIE   (*in the background softly*)
Betcha five dollars I can beat that man.
To the front, to the back, to the side, side, side.
To the front, to the back, to the side, side, side.

CANADA   How's she doing?

AMAH   Mmm, so-so.

CANADA   Okay. Thanks.

AMAH   We'll really miss you when you go – back to Nova Scotia.

CANADA   Oh, I don't think I'm going anywhere just yet – least if I can help it. Way too much leaving gone on for more than one life-time already.

> *BILLIE stops singing for a moment, then segues into a version of Aretha Franklin's "Spanish Harlem", more hummed than sung.*
>
> *CANADA pats AMAH on the back. AMAH turns and exits. CANADA approaches BILLIE and sits down beside her.*
>
> *Shortly, he joins her in the song. He rests his hand on hers.*
>
> *After several moments: The lights fade to black.*